international
AIR POWER
REVIEW

AIRtime Publishing
United States of America • United Kingdom

international AIR POWER REVIEW

Published quarterly by AIRtime Publishing Inc.
120 East Avenue, Norwalk, CT 06851, USA
(Our UK office will be established shortly and the address will appear in IAPR Vol. 2)

© 2001 AIRtime Publishing Inc.
Breguet Br.1001-01 Taon cutaway copyright Mike Badrocke
Photos and other illustrations are the copyright
of their respective owners

Softbound Edition ISSN 1473-9917 / ISBN 1-880588-34-X
Hardcover Deluxe Casebound Edition ISBN 1-880588-35-8

Publisher
Mel Williams

Editor
David Donald
e-mail: editor@airtimepublishing.com

Assistant Editor
Daniel J. March

Sub Editor
Karen Leverington

US Desk
Tom Kaminski

Russia/CIS Desk
Piotr Butowski, Zaur Eylanbekov
e-mail: zaur@airtimepublishing.com

Europe and Rest of World Desk
John Fricker, Jon Lake

Correspondents
Argentina: Jorge Felix Nuñez Padin
Australia: Nigel Pittaway
Belgium: Dirk Lamarque
Canada: Jeff Rankin-Lowe
France: Henri-Pierre Grolleau
Israel: Shlomo Aloni
Italy: Luigino Caliaro
Japan: Yoshitomo Aoki
Netherlands: Tieme Festner
Spain: Salvador Mafé Huertas
USA: Rick Burgess, Robert F. Dorr, Brad Elward, Peter Mersky,
Bill Sweetman

Artists
Piotr Butowski, Chris Davey, Keith Fretwell, Grant Race,
John Weal, Vasiliy Zolotov

Designer
Zaur Eylanbekov

Controller
Linda DeAngelis

Origination by Chroma Graphics, Singapore
Printed in Singapore by KHL Printing

International Air Power Review is published quarterly in two editions (Softbound or Deluxe Casebound) and is available by subscription or as single volumes. Please see details opposite.

Acknowledgments
We wish to thank the following for their kind help with the preparation of this issue:

Gordon Bartley, BAE Systems
Paul E. Eden
Howard Gethin
Randy Harrison, Boeing Company
John Heathcott
Eric Hehs, LMTAS
Brenda Hogan, LMTAS
John Kent, LMTAS
Denny Lombard, Lockheed Martin Skunk Works
Peter R. March
Chick Ramey, Boeing Company
Nancy Tibeau, Boeing Company
Richard L. Ward
Simon Watson
David Willis

The editors welcome photographs for possible publication but can accept no responsibility for loss or damage to unsolicited material.

Subscriptions & Back Volumes
Readers in the USA, Canada, Central/South America and the rest of the world (except UK and Europe) please write to:
> AIRtime Publishing, P.O. Box 5074,
> Westport, CT 06881, USA
> Tel (203) 838-7979 • Fax (203) 838-7344
> **Toll free 1 800 359-3003**
> e-mail: airpower@airtimepublishing.com

Readers in the UK & Europe please write to:
> AIRtime Publishing, RAFBFE, P.O. Box 1940,
> RAF Fairford, Gloucestershire GL7 4BR, England

One-year subscription rates (4 quarterly volumes), via surface delivery:

> **Softbound Edition**
> USA $59.95, Canada Cdn $93, Mexico US $75,
> South America US $79, Middle East & Africa US $85,
> Asia and Australasia US $79, UK £48, Europe £55
> **Deluxe Casebound Edition**
> USA $79.95, Canada Cdn $122, Mexico US $95,
> South America US $99, Middle East & Africa US $105,
> Asia and Australasia US $99, UK £68, Europe £75

Single-volume/Back Volume Rates by Mail:

> **Softbound Edition**
> US $16, Cdn $25, UK £12 (plus ship. & hdlg for each)
> **Deluxe Casebound Edition**
> USA $20, Cdn $31, UK £17 (plus ship. & hdlg for each)

All prices are subject to change without notice. Canadian residents please add GST. Connecticut residents please add sales tax. For delivery rates by air please contact the publisher.

Volume Two
Autumn/Fall 2001

CONTENTS

By some margin the world's most powerful combat aircraft, the Tu-160 has been built in only small numbers due to the parlous state of the Russian economy in post-Cold War times. However, the type remains in service, and is the spearhead of the Russian airborne nuclear deterrent. It is also being modified to perform the conventional role.
Piotr Butowski

MAJOR FEATURES PLANNED FOR VOLUME THREE
Focus Aircraft: Northrop Grumman F-14 Tomcat, **Warplane Classic:** Focke-Wulf Fw 190, **Air Power Analysis:** Belgium,
Technical Briefing: IAR-93 Orao, **Variant File:** Super Puma/Cougar, **Special Feature:** Senior Bowl – the Lockheed D-21,
Pioneers and Prototypes: Myasishchev M-50 'Bounder'

PROGRAMME UPDATE

Joint Strike Fighter

On 29 March 2001 Boeing flew its X-32B STOVL JSF demonstrator for the first time. Final hover pit tests had been completed on 23 March, with high-speed taxi trials accomplished over the next couple of days. X-32B chief test pilot Dennis O'Donoghue was at the controls throughout, and he made the aircraft's maiden flight, a 50-minute trip from Palmdale to Edwards AFB. Initial handling trials in the conventional mode were undertaken during the sortie, also occupying the aircraft's second flight, which was flown by Major Jeff Karnes of the US Marine Corps.

During the X-32B's third flight on 16 April, on what O'Donoghue described as "the best day of my flying career", the Boeing test pilot achieved the first flow-switch between CTOL (wingborne) flight and jetborne (STOVL) flight, in which engine thrust is redirected from the main cruise nozzle to two lift nozzles in the lower fuselage. This first transition was made at 180 kt (207 mph; 333 km/h) and 9,500 ft (2896 m). The flight lasted 58 minutes.

Later that day, on the aircraft's fourth flight, O'Donoghue performed another seven flow-switches during the 52-minute sortie. These were made at 140 to 185 kt (161 mph; 259 km/h to 213 mph; 342 km/h) and as low as 6,000 ft (1829 m). Around 40 minutes of the flight were

conducted in STOVL mode, which included throttle transients, lift nozzle thrust vectoring and testing of semi-jetborne handling.

O'Donoghue reported that the transitions were extremely smooth and took approximately three seconds to accomplish. He highlighted the low pilot workload in switching between CTOL and STOVL modes, and the similarity between actual and simulated performance. Fourteen flights were made at Edwards for 14.1 hours, during which the aircraft was flown by five pilots. The X-32B then flew to NAS Patuxent River, Maryland, arriving on

On 16 April X-32B chief test pilot Dennis O'Donoghue performed the aircraft's first transition from wingborne to jetborne flight. As well as the obvious addition of the direct lift nozzles, the X-35B differs from the X-35A in having a redesigned wing of shorter span and lacks any leading-edge high-lift devices.

11 May with Karnes at the helm. The majority of STOVL testing will be performed at the Naval test centre, including further hover pit testing. The overall X-32B programme was scheduled to include 55 flights and around 40 hours.

Meanwhile, the Lockheed Martin team was

PROJECT DEVELOPMENT

International

Trouble for A400M?
The German Defence Ministry has announced that budget constraints will force it to cut a planned order for new Airbus A400M military transports to about 55 planes from the 75 that it had planned to buy. This move will reduce Germany's share of the work from 33 to 25%. Just days earlier, Turkey reduced its requirement for the turboprop airlifter from 26 to 20 aircraft and will suffer a reduction in the

amount of work allocated. Nine European countries have announced plans to equip their air arms with the A400M.

Eurofighter News
According to recent reports, the Eurofighter project is running behind schedule and the cost of developing the aircraft is set to rise to nearly $5.43 billion from a budgeted $4.09 billion. In a further blow, Greece has said it is postponing the purchase of 60 Eurofighter Typhoon fighter

aircraft until after 2004 in order to save money for social enhancement programs and the upcoming Olympic Games.

SOSTAR radar bid
Launched in 1993, NATO's long-term Alliance Ground Surveillance (AGS) programme is aimed at producing a NATO equivalent to the US Boeing 707-based Joint Surveillance Target Attack Radar System (J-STARS). NATO AGS requirements are for up to six J-STARS-interoperable aircraft and 24 ground stations costing an initial $US2 billion, for service from 2006.

Led by Northrop Grumman and Raytheon, with support from Belgium, Canada, Denmark and Norway, the NATO Transatlantic Advanced Radar (NATAR) consortium is now one of two major proposals for the AGS requirement. Its J-STARS' Radar Technology Insertion Program (RTIP) upgrade would be installed in a European aircraft platform such as the Airbus A321, and full J-STARS interoperability is claimed.

NATAR has been opposed since May 1999 by the European Stand-Off Surveillance & Target Acquisition Radar (SOSTAR)

group, comprising industrial members from France, Germany, Italy, Holland and, now, Spain, headquartered at the European Aeronautic Defence & Space's Dornier subsidiary in Friedrichshafen. Main shareholders in SOSTAR GmbH, formed in February 2001, are EADS and Thales (formerly Thomson-CSF), each with 28 per cent, plus Indra with 11 per cent and Fokker Space with 5 per cent. SOSTAR-X project costs will total about Euro85 million ($US78.6 million) for demonstrator definition, development and construction. The test installation core, fitted in a Fokker 100, will be a SOSTAR-X electronic-scanning radar, incorporating EADS and Thales gallium-arsenide active-array technology, in a ventral forward fairing. Mission avionics will include three console workstations, and datalinks for information transfers from aircraft to ground stations.

Ukraine

An-70 crash aftermath
On 27 January the prototype Antonov An-70 heavy-lift military transport was forced to make an

EADS's hopes of securing a 75-aircraft order from Germany for the A400M look increasingly bleak. With the purchase deemed 'uneconomic' by the German Federal Budget Court, other alternatives are being sought, including a re-investigation into acquiring the Antonov An-X, or a reduced A400M order of 40-55.

moving more cautiously to a mid-summer X-35B first take-off which, unlike the Boeing approach, will be made vertically. With BAE SYSTEMS' Simon Hargreaves, lead pilot for the STOVL demonstrations, at the controls, the X-35B underwent a series of mission rehearsal tests on the hover pit at Palmdale. By 23 March 2001 the aircraft had performed 26 lift-fan clutch engagements to test the transition from CTOL to STOVL mode, and had been run at full power in STOVL mode for over 90 seconds. During these trials the hover pit was reconfigured to represent a variety of ground effect conditions from full to none. At Pratt & Whitney's West Palm Beach facility, the X-35B propulsion team put a test engine/fan arrangement through 132 simulated missions, involving 171 dynamic clutch engagements. A flight-rated fan was fitted by 12 May, and the first hover pit operations in full first flight configuration began on 24 May.

Dassault Rafale

Development was announced by Dassault and its industry partners in January 2001 of a Rafale Mk 2 version of France's advanced combat aircraft, specifically for export markets. A prototype Mk 2 is planned to fly by late 2003, for deliveries starting from late 2005. Thales is supplying new electronically-scanned active radar and avionics, and SNECMA an uprated (to 19,842 lb/88.26 kN thrust) M88-3 turbofan. Dassault will develop the Rafale Mk 2 from a jointly-funded FFr9 billion ($US1.21 billion) industry programme. No state finance will be directly involved, but Dassault and its partners will be relieved of their former commitment to provide some 25 per cent of the $US1.9 billion costs of developing French navy and air force Rafales to F2 and F3 standards.

Initial deliveries have begun of 10 single-seat Rafale M versions to the Aéronavale, and

The colourfully-marked X-35B is seen on the hover pit at Lockheed's Palmdale plant in June undergoing engine trials prior to its first flight. To allow STOVL operations the aircraft is fitted with a counter-rotating lift fan, which works in conjunction with a thrust-vectoring rear engine nozzle and underwing lateral-control nozzles.

one Rafale C and two two-seat Rafale Bs are planned for delivery to the Armée de l'Air from 2004; all aircraft will be F1s, equipped and armed solely for air defence and superiority roles. From late 2004, production will switch and retrofit upgrades will be made to Rafale F2 limited multi-role versions, covering air-to-ground radar modes. Improvements will include Thales/SAGEM OSF (Optronique Secteur Frontal) sensors incorporating infra-red search and tracking (IRST), FLIR, SAGEM Armament Air-Sol Modulaire (AASM) IR-guidance targeting system, and laser-ranging, plus associated software, for compatibility with new weapons. These will include MBD MICA IR-guided short- and medium-range AAMs, and MBD APACHE dispenser and SCALP-EG cruise missiles.

Funding has been allocated for Dassault Rafale F3 production from about 2006, adding further weapons capabilities including EADS rocket/ramjet-powered supersonic ASMP-A nuclear cruise missiles, MBD ANF supersonic AShMs, and the Thales Topsight helmet-mounted sight/display system. These improvements will progressively be incorporated into the Aéronavale's remaining 50 Rafale Ms, which now include up to 40 two-seat BM combat versions, from 60 on order, and into the air force's requirement for 234 Rafales including 139 two-seaters. A Rafale F4 version is also in the pipeline, and will add Matra BAE Dynamics Meteor BVRAAM to its weapons capabilities by about 2010.

---

emergency wheels-up landing immediately after taking off from Omsk in Siberia. The cause has since been attributed to "cata-strophic failure" of a hydraulic line in the hub of the No. 3 ZMKB Progress/Zaporozhye D-27 prop-fan, causing the rear blades to go into reverse pitch; opening up the other propfans to compensate for the resultant loss of power led to the automatic shut-down of No. 1 engine from an overspeed indica-tion.

In late March, senior Antonov official Valery Panyech claimed that repairs to the An-70 at Omsk would be completed within 12 weeks, and the aircraft duly returned to the air in early June. While Russia had confirmed its requirements for 164 An-70s, and Ukraine for 65, negoti-ations were still continuing

between the two countries to launch production, pending Moscow payments of some $US50 million owed for the joint develop-ment programme. A contract for Ukraine's first five An-70s has been signed, and the aircraft will be built by the Aviant factory near Kiev and in Samara, Russia.

United Kingdom

Boeing/BAE FSTA bid

As one of three international contenders short-listed for the MoD's Future Strategic Tanker Aircraft (FSTA) project, BAE SYSTEMS has teamed with Boeing for the potential £5-7 billion Private Finance Initiative programme. This involves provision over 25 years of a complete air-to-air refuelling (AAR) service to the RAF, including

contractor ownership, management and maintenance of the aircraft, plus training facilities and some personnel.

In addition to the proposed BAE/Boeing FSTA consortium, on 7 March Boeing established a B767 Tanker Programmes Office within its Military Aerospace Sector, to market an air-refuelling version of this twin-turbofan transport.

Of the remaining two FSTA contenders, the recently-formed AirTanker group comprising the European Aeronautic, Defence & Space (EADS) company, Rolls-Royce, Cobham's FR Aviation, Brown & Root Services and Thales Defence is expected to base its AAR proposals on an Airbus. The final entrant, Serco-led SSM group, has not yet specified a preference for its AAR platform.

RAF partnership in pooled air transport and air refuelling exchange of services is now planned through the ATARES programme, following agreement reached with six other NATO members of the European Air

Group (EAG) in February. From its original mid-1995 establishment by Britain and France, the EAG has expanded to include Belgium, Italy and Spain, followed in February by Germany and the Netherlands.

ASRAAM performance

In April, UK Defence Procurement Minister Baroness Symons demanded that MATRA/BAe Dynamics (MBD) rectify deficien-cies in the UK's new Advanced Short-Range Air-to-Air Missile (ASRAAM), in order to achieve the capability needed by the RAF. The MoD maintains that the contrac-tors have not yet delivered the performance standards specified when ASRAAM was ordered in 1992, and has indicated that it will take delivery of the new missile only when it is evident that an acceptable standard can be met.

In addition to planned UK use by uprated RAF Harrier GR.Mk 9s and Tornado F.Mk 3s, RN Sea Harrier FA.Mk 2s and, eventually, Eurofighter, the ASRAAM has been ordered by the Australian govern-

After years of persistent rumours, Israel's Rafael finally unveiled its Derby air-to-air missiles by displaying four examples on this IDF/AF F-16D Barak. This new beyond visual range (BVR) missile has a range of some 37.5 miles (60 km) and employs an IAI MBT seeker head with programmable electronic counter-countermeasures (ECCM) capability. The missile can engage targets at both short range, using its lock-on before launch (LOBL) mode, and at medium range, in lock-on after launch (LOAL) mode. The missile can use the same launcher as the short-range Python 4 and, at 260 lb (118 kg), weighs some 25 per cent less than an AIM-120 AMRAAM.

RQ-4A Global Hawk

Northrop Grumman has completed the advanced concept technology demonstration phase of the Global Hawk high-altitude, long-endurance reconnaissance programme and the USAF has given contractor approval to begin the EMD phase. The move also authorises delivery of the first two production aircraft in fiscal year 2003 and means that the contractor and the air force will begin working toward Initial Operational Test and Evaluation and a Milestone III decision in fiscal year 2004. The UAV recently completed a flight across the equator that set world records for altitude and endurance by an autonomous, unmanned jet-powered aircraft during a 30-hour, 24-minute flight that reached an altitude of 65,191 ft (19870 m). The RQ-4A UAV took off from Edwards AFB, California, at approximately 6:52 pm local time on 19 March 2001, and flew along the Pacific Ocean coastlines of Mexico, Central America and portions of South America before returning to California. The air vehicle landed at Edwards at approximately 1:17 am local time on 21 March. The National Aeronautic Association (NAA) is currently evaluating the flight data to confirm the world records. Prior to the flight the air vehicle's environmental control system received modifications that allow the UAV to fly in extremely cold temperatures at high altitudes in equatorial latitudes. The flight served as a precursor for a deployment of the entire Global Hawk system to Australia. The deployment saw the UAV cross the Pacific Ocean for the first time, where it participated in the six-week, international joint-forces operation Tandem Thrust. During the maritime and littoral exercises Global Hawk demonstrated its military utility operating alongside other airborne, land-based, and ocean-going forces. As part of the deployment it flew 7,500 miles (12070 km) non-stop and unrefuelled and the 23-hour, 20-minute flight ended at Royal Australian Air Force Edinburgh in Adelaide on 23 April 2001.

Australia looks likely to proceed with the acquisition of the RQ-4A Global Hawk following the successful deployment of the fifth developmental aircraft, named Southern Cross II, to Australia in May (below). Some 11 missions were conducted over various regions of Austalia collecting images from its various sensors, including this electro-optical image of Broken Hill (right).

ment for the RAAF's upgraded F/A-18 Hornets. MBD has been actively working to improve the ASRAAM, as evidenced from further live launch tests of the weapon in the United States. Originally, the RAF was expecting deliveries of an estimated 1,000-1,500 ASRAAMs from December 1998, but the MoD has admitted that more time is needed to achieve their required performance. It insists that MBD must devise the necessary solutions for agreement on a new in-service date to be reached this summer.

Baroness Symons said that the MoD was determined to draw on the lessons from the ASRAAM programme when signing an imminent contract with MBD for the new Meteor beyond-visual-range AAM (BVRAAM). "The Meteor contract will include a series of key technological milestones which must be met," she stated, "ensuring that any performance shortfalls are identified and tackled during the development programme."

ASRAAM tests
The Naval Strike Aircraft Test Squadron at NAS at Patuxent River in Maryland recently began a series of firing tests validating the integration of the ASRAAM air-to-air missile with the F/A-18A. The unguided firing tests were part of a series carried out by the US Navy in support of the Royal Australian Air Force (RAAF), which will equip approximately 60 F/A-18 fighters with the advanced missile. Further live firing tests and the technical and operational evaluation tests will also be performed using RAAF aircraft at NAWS China Lake, California. Developed by Matra BAe Dynamics the 192-lb (87-kg) missile is capable of engaging any target within the visual acquisition range of the pilot and certain targets that are beyond visual range (BVR). It can be controlled by the aircraft's on-board radar, the sight on the pilot's helmet and by an autonomous infrared (IR) search and track mode.

Meanwhile, live tests of the new software version of the AMRAAM, claimed to remedy the concerns outlined in the UK MoD's criticism, has begun in the USA. The missile, fired from a USAF F-16C, destroyed a QF-4 target drone under a set of conditions that were the UK MoD's principal concern.

United States

Texan II at NAWCAD
The Raytheon T-6A Texan II trainer recently underwent a week of antenna pattern testing at the Naval Air Warfare Center Aircraft Division's antenna testing laboratory automated system (ATLAS) lab at NAS Patuxent River, Maryland. The tests of the ultra high frequency (UHF) radio system were designed to verify and diagnose problems discovered during operational testing (OT) at Randolph AFB, Texas and will assist engineers at Raytheon to find a more suitable place for the UHF antenna. During OT it was noted that crews had difficulty communicating with the control tower on the UHF radio when the airplane was descending toward the field and the suspected cause was a null or 'hole' in the UHF antenna pattern forward and above the aircraft. While operating from the air station, flight crews conducted five flights totaling 9.8 hours, that included flat turns and porpoise manoeuvres to define the null in the UHF antenna pattern. NAWCAD and Raytheon engineers agree that the problem is well identified and can easily be solved by selecting a new location for the UHF antenna. Once a new location has been identified the T-6A will likely return to Pax for follow-on tests.

Boeing tankers
Boeing has formed a new business unit that will market aerial refuelling or tanker aircraft to military customers. Eyeing potential sales of about 400 tankers over the next decade, the aircraft manufacturer plans to begin marketing a modified 767 jetliner later this year, and could begin making deliveries by 2003.

Fire Scout for production
Northrop Grumman's Ryan Aeronautical Center has received a $14.2 million modification to an existing contract exercising an option for one Fire Scout Vertical Take-off and landing Unmanned Aerial Vehicle (VTUAV) System, including associated support equipment, data, and initial training. The low-rate initial production (LRIP) VTUAV system includes three Model 379 air vehicles, two ground control stations, a data link suite, remote data terminals, and modular mission payloads. Designed to operate autonomously from any aircraft-carrying ship, the VTUAV will provide reconnaissance and precision targeting support for Navy and Marine Corps forces at sea and ashore. The air vehicle has an endurance greater than six hours and coverage of 110 nm (204 km) while carrying electro-optical/infrared sensors and a laser designator. The first of three planned LRIPs will be deployed with the USMC by April 2002.

AH-1Z begins Phase II

Zulu 1, the first Bell AH-1Z, arrived at NAS Patuxent River, Maryland recently aboard a C-5A operated by the Air Force Reserve Command's 439th Airlift Wing. Before leaving Bell Helicopter Textron's Flight Research and Test facility in Arlington, Texas, AH-1Z BuNo 162549 completed Phase I of its development testing and accumulated 59.9 flight hours. The attack helicopter also successfully completed harmonic vibration testing with 80 (72 Priority 1 and 8 Priority 2) different configurations of ordnance loaded on its weapon's stations. Phase II development testing will be carried out at Patuxent River, where three government and three company test pilots, all assigned to the H-1 Upgrade integrated flight test team (ITT), will continue expanding the Zulu's flight envelope. This ITT system offers a streamlined approach to testing but still captures the data required during

dedicated contractor, DT, and OT testing. It will also take advantage the 85 percent commonality shared between AH-1Z and UH-1Y mechanical and avionics components that will eliminate redundant test flights between the two types of aircraft and allow a reduction in test time. In addition to three AH-1Zs and two UH-1Ys being built for the flight test programme, two non-flying test articles (one AH-1Z and one UH-1Y) are being constructed. Zulu 2 and 3 and Yankee 1 and 2 are scheduled be delivered to Pax later this year. The engineering and manufacturing development (EMD) flight test programme will be complete by the summer of 2003 with operational evaluation (OPEVAL) following in the autumn of 2003.

Super Hornet helmet

The Naval Air Warfare Center Weapon Division at NAWS China Lake, California recently began flight testing an F/A-18F equipped with the Boeing-developed joint helmet-mounted cueing system (JHMCS). Once deployed, the system will allow aircrew to aim weapons and sensors simply by looking at targets. JHMCS allows users to track and attack targets by synchronising aircraft sensors with the user's head movements so they automatically point where the pilot

The RAF's Tornado F.Mk 3 Operational Evaluation Unit (F.3 OEU) is currently carrying out ASRAAM trials, as seen under the port wing of ZG731 in March 2001. On 22 May MBD successfully fired a new software-standard missile from a USAF F-16C, operating from Eglin AFB, Florida. The new software is claimed to meet the standards outlined in the public criticism by the UK government earlier in the year. So far the MoD has spent some £500 million of its £823 million procurement budget on development.

looks, and displaying flight information on the inside of the helmet visor. In addition to the Super Hornet, the system will equip the USAF's F-15, F-16 and F-22, and the system will fly aboard an F-16 later this year. The system also allows a crew to attack airborne targets at extreme angles using high off-boresight weapons like the AIM-9X missile, without the need to manoeuvre their aircraft into line with the target.

Production for WCMD

Lockheed Martin has received authorisation to begin full-rate production (FRP) of the wind corrected munitions dispenser (WCMD). WCMD enhances the accuracy of existing cluster munitions, including the CBU-87, CBU-98, and CBU-97, by providing corrections for launch transients, ballistic errors, and winds aloft and provides strike aircraft with an accurate pattern lay-down capability for cluster munitions. The $83 million contract covers 5,959 tail kits over the next 23 months. The USAF plans to order 40,000 WCMDs, and this contract increases existing orders for the weapon to

10,000. A separate contract covering field installation of the tail kits will be issued later in 2001.

JDAM approval

The joint direct attack munition (JDAM) has been approved for full production, clearing the way for nearly 90,000 guidance kits to be built by 2008. Boeing had previously received orders for 15,000 kits from the US Navy and Air Force and a $235.6 million contract covering a further 11,054 units. The tail kit is currently only used in conjunction with the 2,000-lb (907-kg) Mk 84 and BLU-109 warheads, however 1,000- and 500-lb (454- and 227-kg) versions are currently undergoing development testing. Those kits covered by the latest order include 2,110 BLU-109s and 8,272 Mk 84s for the USAF, along with 239 BLU-109s and 433 Mk 84s for the Navy. The weapon entered service in 1999 during the Kosovo campaign when B-2A bombers dropped 652 of the weapons in combat. JDAM's global positioning system/inertial navigation to guidance system provides the weapon with an accuracy of 26-46 ft (8-14 m).

Left: On 18 April the F-22 reached 1,000 hours of flight testing, the aircraft involved being Raptor 4003. Over 80 per cent of the development is now complete. The third of six avionics flight test aircraft, Raptor 4006, has begun its test programme at the F-22 Combined Test Force, Edwards AFB, California, with the remainder due to arrive before the end of the year.

Right: The first engineering and manufacturing development (EMD) Bell AH-1Z has begun its next phase of developmental testing at Naval Air Station Patuxent River, Maryland, following its arrival on 31 March 2001. The aircraft was transported from Forth Worth, Texas in the hold of a Air Force Reserve Command C-5A, the first time the aircraft had been loaded on a Galaxy. The AH-1Z was re-assembled on arrival, before delivery to the resident H-1 Uprades Program.

UPGRADES AND MODIFICATIONS

Australia

Hornet AMRAAM tests

A Royal Australian Air Force (RAAF) F/A-18 Hornet successfully fired two AIM-120 Advanced Medium Range Air to Air Missiles (AMRAAM) on the Woomera Instrumented Range during May 2001. The missile is being integrated into the Hornet weapons systems as part of an ongoing upgrade programme and will be formally introduced into service later this year.

Caribou life extension

The RAAF has announced plans to extend the life of the de Havilland Canada DHC-4 Caribou transport aircraft for another 10 years and will consider looking for a replacement Light Tactical Airlift Capability (LTAC) at the end of this decade. The RAAF currently has 14 piston-engined Caribou transports that are capable of operating from short airfields with rough or soft surfaces, allowing the supply of combat forces in locations where larger aircraft are unable to operate. The 35-year-old Caribous were originally to have been replaced by a new type acquisition in 2003.

Canada

Mods for Hercules

Canada's Department of National Defence (DND) has awarded Spar Aerospace a C$5 million contract to modify a CC-130 Hercules aircraft, incorporating reliability, maintainability and flight safety improvements to the aircraft's structure and electrical systems. The contractor will carry out the work at its Lockheed Martin-approved Hercules Service Center in Edmonton, Alberta and expects to complete the programme by June 2002.

France

Boeing to update E-3s

Boeing has received a US$25.5 million contract to equip the Armée de l'Air's (French air force's) fleet of four E-3F airborne warning and control system (AWACS) aircraft with a global positioning inertial navigation system (GINS) and update aircraft's altitude measurement system. Although system design, manufacturing, procurement, integration and acceptance testing will be carried out by Boeing, Air France Industries will modify the aircraft at its facility in Le Bourget, France under contract to Boeing. The upgrades will improve the aircraft's positioning accuracy and reliability allow the AWACS to meet near term requirements of the European Global Air Traffic Management (GATM) system for reduced vertical separation minimum (RVSM). The modifications will begin in July 2001 and be completed in October 2002.

Harrier GR.Mk 9a

United Kingdom

Recent MoD references to Harrier GR.Mk 9s for the RAF have indicated the existence of an unannounced upgrade programme being undertaken by BAE Systems for current GR.Mk 7 versions of these V/STOL ground-attack fighters. BAE prefers to describe the Harrier GR.Mk 9a upgrade as "a series of incremental improvements", starting with the installation of the uprated 23,800-lb

This modified Indian Air Force MiG-21bis (T-75) has been flying in support of the ADA's Light Combat Aircraft (LCA) programme. The LCA is currently undergoing envelope expansion flights, leading to the first supersonic flight later this year.

(105.85-kN) thrust Pegasus Mk 107 turbofan, for which Rolls-Royce received a £350 million contract for the first 40 engines in December 1999. The contract included options for another 86 Mk 107 powerplants, for the RAF's first-line inventory of 64 Harrier GR.Mk 7s, plus reserves.

Harrier GR.Mk 9a improvements are also planned to include advanced avionics, with requirements for active-matrix colour cockpit displays and INS/GPS (probably Honeywell's H-764G, installed in the Tornado GR.Mk 4). A new night/all-weather attack system, incorporating low-light sensors, digital tracker and Mil Std 1760 digital databus, mission computer and stores management system, would allow the use of advanced weapons. They are likely to include MBD's Storm Shadow long-range cruise missile and close-combat ASRAAM, plus Alenia Marconi Systems' Brimstone anti-tank and attack missile.

Following the late 2000 delivery from Rolls-Royce of the first Pegasus 107, with full-authority digital engine control (FADEC), service flight trials in a modified Harrier GR.Mk 7 are being supported by additional development engine deliveries. Full-scale production examples are to follow between 2002 and 2004.

United States

Hornet landing system

Naval Aviation entered a new era aboard USS *Theodore Roosevelt* (CVN 71) on 23 April 2001 when an F/A-18A, assigned to the Naval Strike Aircraft Test Squadron at NAS Patuxent River, Maryland, performed the first fully automated landing at sea using global positioning system (GPS) data. The equipment, known as joint precision approach and landing system (JPALS), uses GPS data supplied by satellites rather than radar to perform automated landings at sea. JPALS provides constant three-dimensional coverage for up to 100

The Israel Defence Force/Air Force has launched the Improved Baz (Buzzard) programme to enhance the multi-mission capability of its F-15A/B/C/D fleet. Major features include new computers, displays and guided-weapon compatibility. F-15A 678 is one of the first aircraft to have been converted. Note the two 'kill' markings and the new type of weapons pylon which can accommodate two Rafael Python 3 missiles.

Right: *The E-2C NP2000 Hawkeye testbed conducted its maiden flight, with new all-composite eight-bladed propellers, on 19 April 2001 from NAS Patuxent River, Maryland. The propellers are due to be integrated into the current E-2C and C-2 Greyhound fleets and aircraft-carrier suitability tests are due to commence in August 2001.*

Left: *The CFT (conformal fuel tank) F-16 underwent high-speed and heavy-load test flying at Eglin AFB, Florida in June, following successful low-speed lightweight trials at Edwards AFB in March. Forming part of the upper surface of the fuselage, the CFT allows the aircraft to carry an additional 3,000 lb (1361 kg) of fuel, eradicating the need for drop tanks and therefore freeing up underwing pylons for weapons.*

aircraft at ranges up to 200 nm (370 km). JPALS is scheduled to enter production in 2007 and fleet service by 2009. It will initially be installed in seven USMC AV-8Bs and on an LHA or LHD amphibious ship.

Blackhawk upgrade

The Defense Acquisition Board (DAB) has approved the development of an upgrade programme for the US Army's UH-60 utility helicopter fleet and issued a $219.7 contract to Sikorsky Aircraft covering research, development, test and evaluation (RDT&E). The programme is designed to extend the operating life of the Blackhawk fleet for a further 25-30 years and result in the remanufacture of existing UH-60A/Ls to a new configuration, known as the UH-60M. The new model will feature widechord composite spar main rotor blades, a digital avionics suite, an advanced flight control computer, a strengthened fuselage and advanced infrared suppression. The UH-60M will also standardise the fleet with the General Electric T700-GE-701C engine and the improved durability main gearbox currently installed in the UH-60L. As part of the RDT&E contract, Sikorsky will modify three existing Blackhawks to the UH-60M configuration and build one new UH-60M. The company expects to receive a low-rate initial production (LRIP) contract covering 12 UH-60Ms in 2004.

U-2S digital display

On 5 December 2000 Lockheed Martin began testing a U-2S equipped with new digital displays as part of the U-2 Reconnaissance Avionics Maintainability Program (RAMP). The cockpit modernisation replaces much of the U-2's 1960 vintage instrumentation with three 6 x 8-in (152 x 203-mm) multifunction displays, an up-front control and display unit, and an independent secondary flight display system. The system will offer improved reliability and improved

situational awareness, and the entire fleet of 31 U-2S and four U-2S(T) trainers will be modified by 2007.

USCG Falcon sensors

The US Coast Guard is upgrading the sensor equipment installed in its fleet of nine HU-25Cs and six of its HU-25As. The HU-25C air interceptor's AN/APG-66 radar will receive upgrades that will increase detection range, provide a sharper image and reductions in the systems size, weight and failure rates. It will also receive a new FLIR system with improved range and a sharper picture, and a new capability in the form of an electro optical (EO) device. The modifications will be rounded out with a new tactical work station (TWS) that will enable the surveillance sensor operator (SSO) to control, view and process the sensor data and view displays of land, targets, search patterns and the aircraft's location. The modified aircraft will subsequently be designated HU-25C+. Modifications to the

HU-25A will replace the aircraft's AN/APS-127 radar with the Telephonics AN/APS-143V(3) inverse synthetic aperture radar (ISAR). The aircraft will also be equipped with the Wescam 16D and the TWS. Once modified, these aircraft will be referred to as HU-25Ds.

DIRCM for Hercules

Air Force Special Operations Command has accepted the first MC-130H Combat Talon II, equipped with the AN/AAQ-24 directional infrared countermeasures (DIRCM) system, from Lockheed Martin at its Crestview, Florida facility. Developed by Northrop Grumman and BAE SYSTEMS, DIRCM transmits both missile threat location and direction to a turret assembly mounted on the aircraft. The turret contains a gimbaled four-axis target designator system that acquires and tracks the missile through post burnout, and maintains a focused beam of infrared (IR) energy on the target throughout its full range of

manoeuvring. AFSOC plans to install the system on 58 AC-130H/U and MC-130E/H aircraft and plans a laser-based follow-on version.

First updated P-3C

Lockheed Martin recently delivered the first P-3C Update II/II.5 aircraft equipped with Block Modification Upgrade Program (BMUP) components to the US Navy at its facility in Greenville, South Carolina. Developed as part of an ongoing P-3C modernisation effort, the BMUP converts older P-3C Update II/II.5 aircraft to an Update III functional mission system configuration and will mirror the capability of the Update III aircraft. The upgrade provides a significantly improved data processing system with colour high-resolution flat panel displays at each operator station, a new acoustic subsystem with improved acoustic receiver and data recorder, weapon system upgrades for the Mk 50 torpedo and AGM-84 Harpoon and a new electronic support measures (ESM) system.

USMC in Australia

US Marine Corps participation in the recent 'Tandem Thrust' exercise held during May 2001 included VMFA(AW)-533's F/A-18Ds, which deployed to Rockhampton, Qld. This colourfully-marked squadron commander's aircraft (below) is seen undergoing a 'hot refuel'. The Hornets were supported by KC-130F/Rs from VMGR-152 (right).

PROCUREMENT AND DELIVERIES

Angola

'Fencers' for FAPA?

Angola could be the third African country to receive Sukhoi Su-24 'Fencer' variable-geometry ground-attack aircraft, following earlier reports of the acquisition by Algeria of more of these advanced deep-penetration fighters from Russia, and earlier deliveries to Libya. Portuguese media reports quote Angolan air force (FAPA) Commander-in-Chief General Pedro Neto as confirming Su-24 deliveries from unspecified CIS sources, and operation from Catumbela air base.

In September 1999, Russian press reports claimed that Angolan UNITA rebel personnel were undergoing Su-24 training at Air Base 115 in Belarus. However, there have been no subsequent reports of Su-24 deliveries to UNITA, whose infrastructure support facilities seem unlikely to extend to combat aircraft as complex as the Su-24.

Australia

Chinooks delivered

Formal acceptance took place on 27 March of two new Boeing CH-47D Chinook medium-lift helicopters, delivered to C Squadron of Australian Army Aviation's 5th Regiment, based at Townsville, QLD. Officially delivered to Australia's Defence Materiel Organisation in February, the new Chinooks underwent final modifications in Australia before joining four CH-47Ds operated by the 5th Aviation Regiment since 1995.

Bangladesh

More MiG-29s planned?

Reports from Moscow in March, of a planned order from Bangladesh Chief of Air Staff Air Vice Marshal Jamal Uddin Ahmed for 16 MiG-29s, could treble the current 'Fulcrum' establishment of the air force (BAF). Eight MiG-29s were delivered to Bangladesh from late 1999 from a $US115 million

contract dated 28 June, which also included training 10 BAF pilots and 70 ground crew. A Russian Aircraft Building Corporation (RSK) MiG spokesman said that MiG-29 deliveries to Bangladesh could resume before the end of 2001, subject to contract finalisation.

Brazil

More C-130s and upgrades

Expansion of the current Brazilian air force (Força Aérea Brasileira) Hercules fleet of five C-130Es, five C-130Hs and two KC-130H tankers is planned by procurement from Lockheed Martin of 10 used C-130Hs, from an estimated $US76 million contract. Formerly operated by the Italian air force (AMI) from 1972, the C-130Hs and two others on option were traded back to Lockheed Martin as part of Italian procurement worth $US1.5 billion consisting of 12 new C-130J and 10 stretched C-130J-30 Hercules IIs, now being delivered.

Egypt

Egyptian Apache upgrades

The US Army has authorised Boeing to begin procuring long-lead items associated with an upgrade programme that will convert 35 Egyptian Army AH-64A Apaches to AH-64D Longbow configuration. The total value of the programme is anticipated to be approximately $400 million and deliveries are scheduled to begin in 2003.

France

France orders third Hawkeye

Northrop Grumman has been awarded a $50.2 million contract modification covering the delivery of one E-2C aircraft to the French Navy. The aircraft will be built to the Hawkeye 2000 configuration and be delivered in 2003.

Greece

Greek Hercs

The Elliniki Aeroporia (Greek Air

Seen demonstrating its famous 'wheelbarrow' manoeuvre is an Australian DHC-4 Caribou. The type has been reprieved as the programme to find a replacement has been postponed. The CN.235 and C-27J were lead contenders.

Force) will reportedly obtain two C-130Hs formerly operated by the Aeronautica Militare Italiana (Italian Air Force). The aircraft include MM61999 (c/n 4495) and MM62001 (c/n 4498).

India

Ka-31 order increased

Indian naval aviation acquisition of the Kamov Ka-31 'Helix-B' AEW helicopter will be more than doubled with a follow-on $US108 million contract signed in February with Rosoboronexport, for another five examples. Flight development was expected to start in March of the first of an initial batch of four Ka-31s ordered by the Indian Navy from a $US92 million contract in 1999, following its completion at the Kumertau Aircraft Plant in Russia, for delivery before the end of 2001.

Originally designated the Ka-252RLD or Ka-29RLD, the Ka-31 features an NNIIRT E-801 Oko 6 x 1-m (19-ft 8-in x 2-ft 3-in) rotating planar radar array, which folds flush below the fuselage for take-off and landing. It can detect surface vessels up to ranges of 250 km (135 nm), and track up to 20 air targets at ranges of 100 to 150 km (54 to 81 nm).

Further Hawk trainer delays

IAF hopes of finalising its long-awaited order from BAE SYSTEMS for 66 Hawk 115 advanced jet-trainers (AJTs), delayed late last

year because of India's requirement to replace components of US origin, were again frustrated in early March by the sudden resignation of Defence Minister George Fernandes, and other senior government and service officials.

Indonesia

Korean trainers

Indonesia's Air Force will purchase seven KT-1 turboprop trainers from Korea Aerospace Industries (KAI) at a cost of $60 million. In addition to serving as a basic trainer, the aircraft is equipped with four underwing hardpoints capable of carrying auxiliary fuel tanks, machine-guns, and rocket launchers. Besides operating as a trainer, the aircraft can be used in the forward air control role and in support of COIN missions.

Israel

Interest in Israeli AWACS

An AWACS version of the IAF's four-turbofan Ilyushin Il-76 transport, equipped with Elta's EL/M-2075 Phalcon phased-array radar, was reportedly among the main procurement interests of an Indian delegation, led by Vice Chief of Air Staff Air Marshal V. Patney, which visited Israel in early April. Possible air-refuelling tanker adaptations by Israel of the Il-76 were also on the agenda, in which prospects of expanded bilateral military co-operation were further

Recent IDF/AF acquisitions include a fifth Boeing 707 Re'em tanker conversion (left), which was delivered on 21 February 2001, and a second batch of Raytheon (Beech) 200CT/T King Airs (local name Zufit). The aircraft wears the badge of 'The Flying Camel Squadron'.

explored in discussions with Israeli defence and IDF/AF officials.

Ex-IDF/AF Skyhawks sold
The US Advanced Training Systems International company has bought ex-IDF/AF Skyhawks for its domestic operations. Ten Douglas A-4N Skyhawk fighter-bombers and three two-seat TA-4J combat trainer versions, withdrawn from long-term desert storage since their retirement from IDF/AF service, are being locally refurbished and fitted with Pratt & Whitney J52 engines by Air New Zealand's Safe Air Ltd MRO subsidiary, under a six-month $NZ1.5 million ($US590,690) contract.

Macedonia

Mi-8s supplied from Ukraine
Six Mil Mi-17 'Hip-H' military transport helicopters, operated by the Air Force of the Macedonian Army since its 1994 establishment, were supplemented in March by four armed Mi-8MTVs and the first two of four Mil Mi-24V 'Hind-E' attack helicopters. They were transferred from Ukraine, where the Ministry of Defence said that the Mi-8s would remain in Macedonia for possible sale or lease. The helicopters were supplied for counter-terrorist operations in the Tetovo region, although the Macedonian armed forces grounded their five remaining Mi-17s following a fatal crash of one on 19 March. Macedonia is also reported to have received two ex-Greek army Bell UH-1Hs.

Malaysia

Fennecs for Malaysia
Malaysia has approved the $24 million purchase of six Eurocopter AS555 Fennec helicopters for the Tentera Laut Diraja Malaysia (TLDM) (Royal Malaysian Navy) and hopes to have the aircraft in service by mid-2002. The aircraft will replace four elderly Westland Wasps that will be grounded in May 2001. Although designed as an anti-submarine helicopter, the Wasps, which were purchased from the UK just four years ago, have primarily served in surveillance and reconnaissance roles. Malaysia also has four Westland Super Lynx helicopters on order with delivery scheduled for 2003.

Mexico

US drug interdiction aircraft
Continued aircraft procurement by the Mexican government, with US assistance, in order to extend its drug traffic interdiction campaign is now planned to include an

On 23 May 2001 at Brize Norton the Royal Air Force received the first of four C-17s for service with the newly-formed No. 99 Squadron. The aircraft is seen touching down on British soil for the first time (above), and unloading after its flight from Charleston AFB, South Carolina (right).

Ericsson ERIEYE radar-equipped EMBRAER EMB-145 twin-turbofan airborne early-warning and control aircraft. Costing up to $US250 million, it will carry a Raytheon Sea Vue maritime surveillance radar and act as a key component in co-ordinating operations of other Mexican air, naval and ground elements.

These will include eight MD Helicopters 902 NOTAR Explorers ordered for the Mexican navy, to equip an Acapulco- and frigate-based coastal patrol squadron. Four MD 902s began operating early in 2001 in the Gulf of Mexico, while others were involved in six-day US weapons trials at Fort Bliss for qualification clearance of a 0.5-in GAU-19/A multi-barrelled machine-gun, an M2 gun pod of similar calibre, and a pod for launching seven 70-mm rockets.

Nigeria

Mil helicopters delivered
New procurement by the cash-strapped Nigerian armed forces has reportedly included deliveries of the first of six Mil Mi-35 'Hind' attack helicopters and three Mil Mi-34S light piston-engined helicopters, shipped into Port Harcourt from Russia in early April. Both types are new to Nigeria, which appears to have become the first military export customer for the Arseneyev-built Mi-34, in a reported $US100 million Nigerian Defence Ministry contract.

Oman

F-16 and Lynx procurement
Gulf Co-operation Council plans for enhanced mutual defence, agreed at a late December meet-

ing, were reflected in a 38 per cent military budget increase to OR926 million ($US2.4 billion) by Oman in January. This was followed in March by an Omani government announcement on recent plans to acquire Lockheed Martin F-16s and AgustaWestland Super Lynx ASW helicopters, for further implementation of these policies.

Additional Omani police requirements were reported for up to six AgustaWestland A 109 and AB 139 light helicopters.

Peru

More US aid sought
The Peruvian National Police has been seeking 15 upgraded Bell Huey IIs to replace a similar number of Bell UH-1Hs. This is in addition to recent orders for five Kaman K-Max single-seat heavy-lift utility helicopters, funded through a $US30 million American aid programme for drug interdiction roles. Eight Bell Textron 412EPs have also been requested by the Peruvian air force, together with additional sensors for its four twin-turboprop Fairchild/Swearingen C-26 electronic and optical surveillance aircraft.

Philippines

RAF Hercules transfer
Philippine air force Hercules strength is being reinforced from

procurement of four ex-RAF C-130Ks. This follows original procurement of one Lockheed C-130A, eight C-130Bs, five L-100-20s and three C-130H turboprop tactical transports, of which only about seven in all remain in service with the 222nd Heavy Airlift Squadron. A recent contract with Lockheed Martin for the RAF aircraft, taken in part-exchange for new RAF C-130Js, includes their refurbishment, plus provision of pallet-mounted surveillance and sensor systems for two aircraft to be used for maritime patrol and SAR roles.

Thailand

Thai Army orders S-70s
The Royal Thai Army has placed a $20 million order with Sikorsky Aircraft for two S-70 Blackhawk helicopters. Although the Royal Thai Navy already operates S-70Bs, these will be the first aircraft delivered to the army.

United Arab Emirates

Maritime patrol aircraft order
UAE interest in twin-turboprop tactical transport and maritime surveillance aircraft dates back to 1991, from Indonesian claims of an Abu Dhabi order for eight IPTN-built CN.235MPAs. A $US150 million contract was reportedly placed in the late 1990s for four of

these aircraft, to be fitted with the Thomson-CSF Airborne Maritime Situation Control System (AMAS-COS), but a UAE maritime patrol aircraft order was officially confirmed only in March this year.

UAE preference has now changed to the stretched C.295 with uprated Pratt & Whitney Canada turboprops, of which four EADS/CASA-built Persuader MPA versions are to be purchased in a $US114 million contract, for maritime patrol and surveillance.

United States

More Texan IIs ordered

Raytheon Aircraft recently received a contract covering the purchase of 59 T-6A Texan II trainers for the US Navy and Air Force. The contract, worth $148.3 million, includes 24 aircraft for the navy and 35 for the air force. To date the company has received orders for 167 production aircraft with 30 slated for the Navy and remainder for the USAF. Ultimately when production ends in 2017 the company expects to build 328 aircraft for the Navy and 454 for the USAF. The trainer will achieve initial operating capability (IOC) with 15 aircraft at Moody AFB, Georgia in June 2001 and the first T-6As destined for the 479th Flying Training Group (FTG) arrived on 7 May 2001. The Navy, is scheduled to begin training in 2003. Deliveries for this option will begin in May 2003.

VQ-7 to use 737 flight trainer

The Link Simulation and Training division of L-3 Communications has been awarded a $6.4 million contract for the lease and mainte-nance of a Boeing 737 aircraft that will serve as an in-flight trainer for US Navy E-6A/B flight crews with VQ-7 at Tinker AFB, Oklahoma.

AAR Aircraft Services will provide and support the 737 aircraft under a subcontract from Link. The contract covers an initial period from May to September 2001 but includes three annual options that run through September 2004.

Blackhawks ordered

Sikorsky Aircraft has been awarded a $47.6 million covering the conversion of five UH-60L aircraft into the HH-60L configuration on the production line.

Harrier updates

Boeing's McDonnell Douglas subsidiary will deliver two further remanufactured AV-8B+ aircraft under terms of a contract valued at $33.6 million. The aircraft will be delivered by September 2003.

Target drones ordered

Northrop Grumman received a $23.6 million contract to build 78 BQM-74E subsonic aerial target drones for the US Navy. The first drone will be delivered in February 2002 with the final delivery sched-uled for January 2003. The contract includes options for three subse-quent production lots.

Airborne Reconnaissance Low

Northrop Grumman's California Microwave unit has received a $10 million increment as part of $27.4 million US Army contract to begin work on a sixth RC-7B airborne reconnaissance low-multifunction (ARL-M) aircraft. The contract covers the purchase, conversion, integration and test of a de Havilland Canada DHC-7 aircraft and prime mission equipment. The aircraft will be modified at the company's facility at Washington County Airport in Hagerstown, Maryland and will to be completed within 24 months. The company

had previously delivered five ARL-M aircraft and the latest addi-tion was included in the FY00 defense appropriations and will replace a similar aircraft that crashed in Colombia during 1999. The RC-7B/ARL-M manned airborne collection platform is equipped with imagery, radar, communications intelligence, data links and communications systems that provide near real-time intelli-gence information to tactical commanders.

ATFLIR production

Northrop Grumman has received $69.4 million contract for the procurement of 15 low rate initial production (LRIP) Advanced Targeting FLIR (ATFLIR) units, four spare pods, and various weapons replaceable associated with the F/A-18E/F.

Strike Eagle contract

Boeing and the USAF have finalised the terms of a $571 million contract covering the production of ten F-15E Strike Eagles. The aircraft funded by the fiscal year 2000 and 2001 budgets will have several upgrades that will make them the most capable F-15Es delivered to date. The aircraft will be equipped with an

updated programmable armament control set (PACS) that will enable it to deliver the Joint Direct Attack Munition (JDAM), Joint Standoff Weapon (JSOW) and Wind Corrected Munition Dispenser (WCMD). In addition, three new active-matrix liquid crystal displays will replace the F-15E's current-cathode-ray tube displays and provide enhanced night-vision capability. The first aircraft will be delivered to the USAF in early 2002 and, when the final aircraft is deliv-ered in 2004, the service will have accepted 236 F-15Es.

Army trainers

Bell Helicopter has been awarded a $22.5 million contract for 17 TH-67 helicopters by the US Army. The aircraft will be built in Canada and the first aircraft will be deliv-ered in September 2001.

Tanker mods

Boeing has been awarded a $38.7 million contract covering the manufacture and installation of CFM-56/F108 re-engine kits. The contract includes the production of three kits associated with the RC-135 and the installation of three previously funded kits in RC-135s and two in KC-135s. By June two RC-135s were flying with F108s.

Left: Having been grounded since February 2000 due to a lack of serviceable engines, the Bulgarian air force's MiG-29 fleet resumed flying operations on 18 April 2001. Six MiG-29s have been relocated from Ravnetz to Graf Ignatievo, where they equip 2/3 IAE.

Below: Large numbers of Shenyang J-6 fighters remain in PLAAF service, most in the day-fighter version. This line-up, seen at Kunming, shows radar-equipped aircraft, most probably J-6As. Note the extended upper intake lip, which houses radar equipment.

AIR ARM REVIEW

Canada

CAF to be virtually halved

From a mid-2000 strength of some 500 aircraft, the Canadian air force is to lose almost half its inventory by late 2002, when only 282 aircraft are planned to remain in operation. Drastic inventory reductions are being implemented to release funding for the recently-launched $C872.35 billion Boeing CF-18 Hornet programme, $C1 billion Lockheed CP-140 (P-3) Aurora mission system upgrades, and the newly-approved $C2.8 billion Maritime Helicopter Project, under which the 30 (to become 28) Sikorsky CH-124A/B Sea Kings will be replaced on a one-for-one basis from late 2005.

In first-line units, only 80 of the current 122 CF-18s will be upgraded by Boeing, and disposal of the remaining 42 is now under consideration. Only 16 of 18 CP-140s will be modernised, and the three CP-140A Arcturus maritime surveillance/training versions will be withdrawn from service by 2004.

The air force is also disposing of almost its entire combat support and ECM training element, comprising 27 recently-upgraded Canadair CT/CE-133 (T-33A/N) Silver Stars that are due for retirement by March 2002, and eight similarly upgraded twin-turbofan Canadair CC/CE-144A Challengers that were sold (without their specialised electronics) for $US30 million in the US in January. Eight

CC-144B Challengers remain in service with 412 Squadron as VIP and personnel transports, but all seven DH Canada CC-115 Buffalo STOL transport are to be replaced by EH.101 CH-149 Cormorant helicopters from 2002. Twenty-four of 99 Bell CH-146 Griffon helicopters will also be withdrawn.

Colombia

US anti-narcotic aid continues

Further details have emerged of ongoing US counter-narcotic aid programmes. Plan Colombia comprises $US860 million, from a total of $US1.3 billion, and includes large-scale provision of military aircraft, mostly helicopters. They are operated by all three branches of the Colombian armed forces, as well as by the National Police air wing.

The main types involved in recent aid programmes have been upgraded Bell Huey IIs and Sikorsky UH-60 Black Hawks, although transfers have also been made through the State Department of 33 Bell UH-1Ns.

The police received the first eight of 25 Huey IIs from mid-1999. They followed initial receipt by the Colombian air force (Fuerza Aérea Colombiana) from 1997 of eight Bell UH-1H-II Huey IIs, with a 1,800-shp (1341-kW) Honeywell T53-L-703 turboshaft engine, transmission, gearbox, rotor blades and tailboom, to start upgrading its 73 returned UH-1Hs. A total of 42 more Huey IIs has been sought by

Colombia since late 1999, for delivery by 2002.

Original 1992 deliveries of 10 Sikorsky UH-60As and four UH-60Ls to the air force, seven to the army in 1998, and six UH-60Ls to the police from May 1999, were supplemented by deliveries by late 1999 of another three for the police and five army UH-60Ls originally built for Venezuela. FMS contracts totalling $US221 million had also been approved for seven armed UH-60Ls for the air force and seven for the army, plus funding provision for another 30.

Among fixed-wing aircraft in Colombia's US aid package, two FAC twin-turboprop Fairchild C-26 Merlins are being equipped with Northrop Grumman APG-66 air-to-air radar, FLIR systems and communications equipment to detect and track drug-smuggling aircraft. Surveillance will be assisted further by recent US transfers of special-mission Schweizer SA 2-37A aircraft. A Douglas C-47 FAC aircraft is being converted to AC-47 gunship standard with FLIR, night-vision and fire-control systems, plus armament.

Italy

Tornado unit disbanded

Italy's 21° Gruppo CIO, part of the 36° Stormo at Gioia del Colle Air Base, was deactivated on 1 March 2001. The move leaves only the 21° Gruppo CIO flying the Tornado F.3/Air Defence Variant.

The Koninklijke Luchtmacht (Royal Netherlands Air Force) revealed its 2001 display aircraft on 2 May. The MLU F-16AM is flown by 312 Squadron at Volkel Air Base.

New Zealand

Air Combat Force dropped

New Zealand's Prime Minister announced that as part of a wide-ranging $840 million defense plan it will disband the Royal New Zealand Air Force's Air Combat Force and withdraw its fleet of 17 A-4K/TA-4K Skyhawks and 17 MB.339 trainers saving $NZ840 million over the next 10 years.

Currently operated by No. 14 Squadron, the MB.339CBs, which entered service in 1991, will likely be maintained for sale in flying condition. The government will upgrade or replace the air force's fleet of six C-130H transports and provide the five P-3K maritime patrol aircraft with a limited upgrade. A squadron of 14 UH-1H helicopters will be upgraded or replaced.

United Kingdom

Merlin enters RAF inventory

The Westland Agusta EH.101 Merlin HC.Mk 3 entered service with the Royal Air Force's No. 28 Squadron at RAF Benson, Oxfordshire, when the first four aircraft were finally handed over during a small ceremony on 8 March 2001.

United States

Squadron activations

The 3rd Flying Training Squadron (FTS) was activated under the 479th Flying Training Group (FTG) at Moody AFB, Georgia on 3 April 2001. The squadron will eventually provide Specialized Undergraduate Pilot Training (SUPT) with the

Raytheon T-6A Texan II. On 1 April 2001 the Air Force Reserve activated the 39th FTS at Moody. The squadron will operate as an associate unit and provide instructors for both the T-3A and AT-38B/T-38C. The squadron is part of the 340th FTG at Randolph AFB, Texas. In other news from Moody, the first of four T-38Cs arrived at the base on 1 March 2001.

The 960th Airborne Air Control Squadron (AACS) was activated under the 552d Air Control Wing (ACW) at Tinker AFB, Oklahoma on 8 March 2001. The 'Viking Warriors' will provide the USAF with another unit to support its 10 aerospace expeditionary forces and allow each of Tinker's four AWACS squadrons to be assigned to two AEFs while the remaining two AEFs will be supported by crews from Pacific Air Forces (PACAF).

Squadron deactivations

Although it has already held an inactivation ceremony, the 31st Special Operations Squadron (SOS) at Osan Air Base, Republic of Korea will be inactivated on 30 June 2001. The squadron, which flies the MH-53J Pave Low III helicopter, is assigned to the 353d Special Operation Group at Kadena Air Base, Okinawa. The unit will however, be reactivated to fly the CV-22B variant of the Osprey tiltrotor once that aircraft enters service. Until the arrival of the Osprey however, the US Army will provide rotary-wing support for special operations and SAR missions in South Korea.

Argus retired

C-135E serial 60-0375, which served Detachment 2 of the 452nd Flight Test Squadron (FLTS) at Kirtland AFB, New Mexico as a flying laboratory, was retired to the Aerospace Maintenance and Regeneration on 18 April 2001. Known as 'Argus', the aircraft was the only C-135E capable of flying extended missions above 50,000 ft (15240 m) and had supported the Air Force Research Laboratory (AFRL).

New rescue wing

Following the inactivation of the 68th Fighter Squadron at Moody AFB, Georgia on 30 April 2001, the 347th Wing was redesignated the 347th Rescue Wing on 1 May.

Aircraft transitions

The New York Air National Guard's 174th Fighter Wing (FW) at Syracuse Hancock IAP will once again be equipped with Block 30 F-16C aircraft. The unit currently operates the Block 25 model but

Romanian anniversary

A celebration of 50 years of jet aviation within the Romanian air force took place at Ianca AB on 21 April 2001. Flight demonstations included MiG-21UM, MiG-21 Lancer, MiG-23UB, MiG-29, L-29 Delfin, L-39ZA Albatros, Harbin HJ-5 and IAR-99 with IAR-93MBs and a MiG-15 along with a C-130B and IAR-330L Puma SOCAT also present on static display. The Divizia 3 Aviatie Vânătoare Reactie (3rd Jet Fighter Division) had formed on 28 March 1951 at Ianca AB, near Braila.

Top: Contradicting reports that Romania's 'Floggers' were grounded, Grupul 93 Vânătoare (93rd Fighter Group) demonstrated this MiG-23UB.

Above: For several decades the Ianca airbase hosted various MiG-15 units. Although now retired from Romanian service, this MiG-15 has received a contemporary camouflage scheme.

Left: The Grupul 49 Vânătoare Bombardament (49th Fighter-Bomber Group) is based at Ianca operating the IAR-93B (left) and IAR-99 (right).

had previously operated the later aircraft until they were transferred to other units in 1999.

The Montana Air National Guard's 120th Fighter Wing has completed transition to (Block 30) F-16C aircraft. After receiving six aircraft from the 27th FW at Cannon AFB, New Mexico, a further 11 fighters were transferred from the 35th Fighter Squadron (FS) at Kunsan AB, Republic of Korea. The last of these departed Korea on 27 February 2001. Although the 120th transferred six Block 15 F-16A(ADF)s to the

Minnesota ANG's 148th FW, the majority of its aircraft were flown to Davis Monthan AFB, Arizona from storage.

The District of Columbia Air National Guard's 201st Airlift Squadron (AS) at Andrews AFB, Maryland will replace its aging C-22Bs (Boeing 727-100) with Boeing C-40A Clippers and the first of these is currently on order. The aircraft will be delivered in 2003.

The US Army Operational Support Airlift Command's (OSACOM) Puerto Rico Regional Flight Center at Isla Grande Airport

in San Juan has transitioned from the C-12D to the Cessna UC-35A Citation Ultra and now operates two of the aircraft in support of US Southern Command.

Clipper delivered

The first of four C-40A Clippers arrived at NAS Fort Worth Joint Reserve Base on 21 April 2001 where it was accepted by the 'Lone Star Express' of VR-59. The squadron had previously operated the C-9B Skytrain II but disposed of the last of those aircraft in October 2000.

HH-60Ls enter service

The US Army's 507th Medical Company (Air Ambulance) at Fort Hood, Texas has received the first of 15 advanced HH-60L medical helicopters. The aircraft based on the UH-60L airframe incorporates the systems developed for the Army National Guard's UH-60Q air ambulance. The UH-60Q is based on the UH-60A airframe.

On 2 May a Travis-based C-5, crewed by the 301st Airlift Squadron, made an emergency landing on Rogers Dry Lake at Edwards AFB after discovering that the nosewheel would not extend. A T-39 acted as chaseplane. The aircraft sustained little damage, and the eight crew members and nine passengers were unhurt.

OPERATIONS AND DEPLOYMENTS

USMC deployments

The 'Green Knights' of VMFA(AW)-121 concluded a six-month deployment to MCAS Iwakuni, Japan on 9 March 2001 when they returned to their home station at MCAS Miramar, near San Diego, California. The unit was replaced within Marine Air Group (MAG)-12 at Iwakuni by the 'Bats' of VMFA(AW)-242.

The 'Hawks' of VMFA(AW)-533 deployed to MCAS Iwakuni as part of MAG-12 during January, and most recently were forward deployed to Kadena Air Base, Okinawa where the squadron was certified to operate as a component of the 31st Marine Expeditionary Unit (Special Operations Capable). The squadron later travelled to Australia as the fixed-wing strike component of the 31st MEU(SOC) which is currently deployed aboard the ships of the USS *Essex* Amphibious Ready Group (ARG).

The 'Vikings' of VMFA(AW)-225 deployed 12 F/A-18D Hornets from Miramar to Al Jaber Air Base in Kuwait on 3 March 2001 and the remainder of the squadron followed via commercial transport on 5 March. The squadron will spend three months operating on Operation Southern Watch.

Updated Hornets in service

The 'Silver Eagles' of VMFA-115 at MCAS Beaufort, South Carolina have begun transitioning to the updated F/A-18A+ variant of the Hornet. Modified as part of the Reserve Upgrade programme the latest Hornet variant duplicates the avionics capabilities of the later F/A-18C. The initial four upgrades were carried out by the Naval Weapons Test Squadron at NAWS China Lake, California, but all subsequent modifications will be carried out by Boeing.

Inchon Deploys

The 'Black Hawks' of Helicopter Mine Countermeasures Squadron (HM)-15 deployed from their home station at NAS Corpus Christi, Texas for a four and a half month deployment to the Western Pacific Ocean aboard USS *Inchon* (MCS 12). Joining the seven-aircraft detachment of MH-53E Sea Dragons are two CH-46D Sea Knights operated by the 'Chargers' of Helicopter Combat Support Squadron (HC)-6 Detachment 3, at Naval Station Norfolk, Virginia. *Inchon*'s last deployed to the Mediterranean and Adriatic in 1999 and participated in Operation Shining Hope, by providing humanitarian assistance to Kosovar refugees.

Constellation and *Boxer* sail

The USS *Constellation* (CV 64) CVBG departed San Diego on 16 March 2001. CVW-2 is embarked aboard the carrier and the CVBG is composed of USS *Chosin* (CG 65), USS *Benfold* (DDG 65), USS *Kinkaid* (DD 965), USS *Thach* (FFG 43), the Canadian frigate HMCS *Winnipeg* (FFH 338), USS *Rainier* (AOE 7), and the attack submarines USS *Santa Fe* (SSN 763) and USS *Columbia* (SSN 771). 'Connie' subsequently relieved the USS *Harry S. Truman* (CVN 75) in the Persian Gulf on 30 April 2001.

The USS *Boxer* (LHD 4) Amphibious Ready Group (ARG), departed San Diego, California on 13 March 2001 for a six-month cruise to the Western Pacific and Persian Gulf. Besides *Boxer*, the ARG is composed of USS *Cleveland* (LPD 7), and USS *Harpers Ferry* (LSD 49) and the 11th Marine Expeditionary Unit (Special Operations Capable) is embarked aboard the ships. HMM-268 (Reinforced) is assigned as the aviation combat element (ACE).

PLANAF J-8II fighters approach close to a US Navy EP-3E days before the collision which caused an EP-3 to limp damaged to Hainan island, and a J-8 to crash into the sea with the loss of the pilot. The J-8s are carrying PL-8 (Python 3) missiles.

Big 'E' deploys

The USS *Enterprise* (CVN 65) CVBG and USS *Kearsarge* (LHD 3) amphibious Ready Group (ARG) with the 24th Marine Expeditionary Unit (MEU) embarked departed Norfolk, Virginia on 26 April 2001. Besides the *Kearsarge* the ARG is composed of the USS *Ponce* (LPD-15) and USS *Carter Hall* (LSD-50). In addition to CVN 65 the CVBG is comprised of Carrier Air Wing (CVW)-8, the guided missile cruisers USS *Philippine Sea* (CG 58) and USS *Gettysburg* (CG 64); guided missile destroyer USS *Stout* (DDG 55), and USS *Gonzalez* (DDG 66); destroyers and USS *Thorn* (DD 988); guided missile frigate USS *Nicholas* (FFG 47); logistics ship USS *Arctic* (AOE 8); and attack submarines USS *Providence* (SSN 719) and USS *Jacksonville* (SSN 699). Although they will not deploy until June, USS *McFaul* (DDG 74) and USS *Nicholson* (DD 982) are also assigned to the CVBG.

Chinese intercept Orion

After being intercepted by two Chinese People's Liberation Army fighters in international air space over the South China Sea, the crew of a US Navy EP-3E Aries II was forced to make an emergency landing at a military airfield in Lingshui on the island of Hainan on 1 April 2001. The aircraft, BuNo 156511/PR-32, was damaged by a mid-air collision with one of the Chinese Shenyang J-8 'Finback' fighters. The collision, which occurred at approximately 9:07 am local time some 70 nm (130 km)

southeast of Hainan, caused the J-8 to crash and the EP-3E to drop 5,000-8,000 ft (1524-2438 m) before the crew regained control. The crew of the ARIES II apparently destroyed much of the classified equipment and material aboard the aircraft before they were taken into custody by Chinese authorities and detained for 11 days. Although the crew was released on 12 April the Chinese refused to return the aircraft until 29 May 2001. A team of American technicians was allowed to inspect the aircraft and determined that it could be repaired and flown out of Hainan, however, China insisted that the aircraft be disassembled. Once taken apart, the Orion will flown back to the US aboard a leased Antonov An-124. Although China claims the US aircraft violated its air space and caused the J-8 to crash through aggressive maneuvering, the US Department of Defense charges that Chinese fighters have intercepted American reconnaissance flight on 44 occasions since mid-December 2000. On eight of these occasions the Chinese jets manoeuvred within 10-30 ft (3-9 m) of the EP-3Es. The EP-3E and its 24-man crew were assigned to VQ-1 at NAS Whidbey Island, Washington and had been detached, as part of a normal rotation, to Kadena Air Base on Okinawa. Following the incident the US suspended all surveillance missions around China however, the flights resumed on 7 May when a USAF RC-135 flew a mission that originated at Kadena.

In May 2000 the Cope Thunder exercise in Alaska drew participation from the Armée de l'Air, which sent Mirage F1CTs (above), Mirage 2000Ns, Transall C-160s, Mirage 2000-5Fs (right), and a single E-3F. The Dash 5s were given the opportunity to pit their RDY radars against the AESA radar-equipped F-15s of the resident 3rd Wing.

To mark the changing of the guard, the RAAF staged this formation of a Hawk Mk 127 with an MB.326H from No. 76 Squadron. Based at Williamtown, the unit performs the fighter lead-in training role, and also has a naval support role which it will assume from RNZAF Skyhawks when they cease operations from RANAS Nowra.

RAAF changeover

Farewell Macchi, Hello Hawk

On 26 March 2001, four CAC-built Macchi MB.326H aircraft of No. 79 Squadron, Royal Australian Air Force, took off from RAAF Williamtown for the relatively short journey to RAAF Wagga Wagga, and a significant chapter in the history of the RAAF quietly drew to a close. Apart from local news coverage, the event was largely ignored by both the RAAF and the aviation press, a great pity considering the length of time that the little Italian jet has been in service.

Now replaced by the BAE Systems Hawk Mk 127, the Macchi (affectionately known as a 'constant-speed/variable-noise' aircraft by its crews) first entered RAAF service in October 1967, initially as a trainer; later, it acted as a *de facto* lead-in fighter. The last two operational units to operate the aircraft, No. 76 Squadron at Williamtown, New South Wales and No. 79 Squadron at Pearce, Western Australia, have now completed conversion to the Hawk. The remaining Macchis will be used by either the RAAF

School of Technical Training (RSTT) at Wagga Wagga, or as display items.

In the last years of its Australian service career, the dwindling Macchi fleet was the subject of much shuffling in order to provide the two squadrons with sufficient airframes to complete their lead-in fighter training and fleet support tasks. This shuffling was the result of the high fatigue index of all RAAF Macchis, despite a Life Of Type Extension (LOTE) programme carried out between 1978 and 1984, and a further rewinging undertaken in the 1990s. Aircraft that previously had been retired to the RSTT were overhauled and returned to service as the fleet index surpassed them.

A great deal of part-swapping (particularly of wings) was performed by No. 76 Squadron at RAAF Williamtown and by the prime civilian contractor, Hawker Pacific in Perth, in an attempt to provide the lowest fatigue-indexed 'package' for the squadrons. Fortunately, this situation was eased somewhat by the fact that No. 79 Squadron did not require aircraft with the lowest fatigue index, as their tasks were more of the straight-and-level nature than those of their counterparts at Williamtown. Nevertheless, delays in the introduction of the Hawk into service resulted in

these exchanges becoming increasingly difficult to juggle, and it is to the credit of all involved with the Macchi that sufficient aircraft numbers could be generated to the end.

The first Hawk aircraft were handed over at Williamtown in October 2000, allowing No. 76 Squadron to pass all of its serviceable Macchis to No. 79 Squadron for the final three months of operations. The re-equipment timetable was so tight (No. 79 Squadron received its first four Hawks in December of the same year) that no attempt was made to apply No. 79's markings to the newcomers, and at a ceremony to mark the 'official' retirement at Pearce in March 2001, more aircraft wore No. 76 Squadron colours than No. 79.

Twenty-two of the surviving Macchis are enjoying a further (ground) career with the RSTT, four have been passed back to the Royal Australian Navy (the RAN operated 10 in its own right before the aircraft were transferred to the RAAF upon the demise of the FAA fixed-wing fleet in 1984) and another seven will be retained for display purposes by the RAAF. The remainder will either be gifted or tendered for sale, subject to the approval of the Equipment Disposal Committee (EDC).

No. 79 Squadron is based at RAAF Pearce, and was the last operator of the Macchi (below). With the arrival of the Hawk (left), No. 79's primary tasks will be initial conversion training, instructor training and fast-jet navigator training for the F-111 force. The squadron will also undertake fleet co-operation missions – just as it did with the MB.326 – as will No. 76 Squadron.

The RAAF has adopted a low-viz, two-tone grey scheme for its Hawks. The aircraft often operate over water in the secondary fleet support role, in which they mimic anti-ship aircraft and missiles.

The Lead In Fighter (LIF) project, or Project Air 5367, was drawn up once it became clear that the Macchi was fast approaching the end of its useful life, and involved two phases. Phase One was essentially an Invitation to Register Interest, and the companies (and products) invited to do so were Aero Vodochody (L-59F Albatross), Alenia/Aermacchi/EMBRAER (AMX-T), Aermacchi (MB-339FD), British Aerospace (Hawk Mk 100), Dassault (Alpha Jet ATS) and McDonnell Douglas (T-45A Goshawk). After due consideration, Aermacchi, BAe and McDonnell Douglas were issued with a Request For Tender (RFT) as Phase Two of the project.

The selection of BAe as the preferred supplier was announced in 1996, and a contract was signed on 24 June 1997. The $AU850 million contract was unique in that it combined the acquisition of 34 airframes (33 operational aircraft and a static test specimen) with maintenance support throughout the projected 25-year life of the aircraft. Twelve of the operational aircraft, and the test article, were assembled at Warton, UK, with the remainder undergoing assembly in Australia.

The Australian assembly effort is a partnership between companies including BAE Systems, Hunter Aerospace and Qantas. A $AU15 million production line facility was constructed at Newcastle airport, across the runway from Williamtown, and opened by Prime Minister John Howard on 15 April 1999. BAE Systems is assembling the aircraft in partnership with Hunter Aerospace, and Qantas is building the Adour turbofans at its Mascot Jet Base. Training aids and simulators are the responsibility of BAE Systems in Adelaide.

The RAAF Hawk Mk 127, though structurally similar to the baseline Hawk 100, differs substantially in its avionics fit. The aim is to provide functional characteristics similar to those of the F/A-18A Hornet fleet, and the systems, integrated by MIL-STD-1553 databus, include three multi-function displays, F/A-18A-compatible HUD and HOTAS, FLIR, and radar simulation and RWR systems.

In order to meet the strict in-service entry date, an incremental capability was negotiated between the Defence Acquisition Organisation (DAO) and BAe to ensure that the first Hawks would be on line to assume the initial pilot training duties of the Macchi. Even so, systems integration problems have meant that this target has slipped by five to six months, resulting in frenetic activity to keep the Macchis flying past their initial retirement date.

To support development, BAe's test aircraft, ZJ100, underwent a lay-up to incorporate the LIF avionics architecture and began test flying the Mk 127 cockpit in mid-1999. The Warton-assembled production aircraft were allocated UK MoD serials for their trials work, and the first, ZJ632 (DT001/A27-01), made its maiden flight on 16 December 1999. Officially rolled out at a ceremony at Warton on 24 January 2000, the aircraft was also the first to appear in RAAF camouflage, albeit with red and blue RAF roundels and fin flash temporarily applied.

The first flight of an Australian-assembled Hawk took place on 12 May 2000, when BAE Systems' Gordon McClymont and Garth Gardener took aircraft DT010 aloft, with RAAF serial A27-10 temporarily applied, from Newcastle (NSW) for a 70-minute sortie. The successful flight explored the general handling characteristics, aircraft systems and avionics, and followed on from the first public showing of DT013 at Williamtown on 7 April of that year.

Deliveries to Australia began with the departure from Warton of DT003 (ZJ634/A27-03) and DT004 (ZJ636/A27-04) on 24 August 2000.

Flown by BAE Systems' Phil Dye and John Turner, the pair routed through Europe, the Middle East, India and Southeast Asia before eventually arriving at the LIF facility at Williamtown. The remainder of the ferry flights have been carried out in the same manner, with only two aircraft (in April 2001) yet to leave the UK. One of these aircraft, DT027 (ZJ644/A27-26), is specially instrumented to support testing, and initially will see service with the Aircraft Research and Development Unit (ARDU) on development and weapons clearance trials before delivery to a squadron.

While the aircraft were undergoing construction, the initial group of RAAF pilots, including No. 76 Squadron CO Wg Cdr Dave Willcox, and a number of aircraft technicians, travelled in the opposite direction to begin training at Warton. Initial ground crew training had commenced at Williamtown in January 2000, and aircrew conversions for instructors followed shortly after the return of the group from the UK.

The RAAF accepted the first aircraft during a ceremony at Williamtown on 22 November 2000, and deliveries to Nos 76 and 79 Squadrons

Above: The RAAF's Hawk Mk 127 is a potent emergency fighter/attacker in its own right, with wingtip launch rails for Sidewinder missiles and a variety of air-to-ground weapon options. The nose contains a forward-looking infra-red, and the cockpit is among the most modern fitted to a trainer. The Hawk is designed to provide valid lead-in training not only for today's Hornet force, but also for whatever fighter the RAAF may choose to fill its outstanding Hornet replacement requirement.

Left: Like most RAAF aircraft, Hawks operate from underneath simple shelters, necessary to protect crews from the strong sun and occasional sub-tropical rainfall which affects the east coast in particular.

Debrief

Not only has the Hawk introduced a much more capable training aircraft to the RAAF, it is also more reliable and more economic to operate. This trio is led by an aircraft with No. 76 Squadron marks.

have followed in quick order. By April 2001 26 aircraft had been accepted by the RAAF, with the delivery of the 33rd and last expected in October.

As delivered, the aircraft are to a basic Operational Capability One (OC-1) standard as part of the incremental approach to the aircraft entering full operational service. This initial capability allowed pilot training and conversion to begin, with the first LIF student course commencing at Williamtown on 2 April. The fleet is to be brought progressively to OC-2 standard, which will encompass such things as clearance of weapons management and mission planning systems, integration of the inertial navigation system, and dry carriage trials of a bolt-on inflight-refuelling probe. The move to OC-2 is due to be completed by the end of 2001, and will be followed immediately by an upgrade to the definitive OC-3 status. This final step will begin in 2003/04, and will see all systems integrated and operational, weapons trials finalised, and the wet transfer of fuel from the RAAF's 707 fleet. OC-3 is currently due to be completed by the end of 2004.

As the LIF tag suggests, the Hawks' primary role will be to provide a stepping stone for fast-jet crews who are coming off the PC-9/A and are destined for F-111s or Hornets. Pilots initially will spend three months learning to fly the

aircraft with No. 79 Sqn at Pearce, before moving across the country to No. 76 Sqn at Williamtown to undertake the Introductory Fighter Course. Following graduation, they will then be posted either to No. 6 Sqn at Amberley if they are destined for F-111s, or No. 2 OCU at Williamtown to begin Hornet conversion.

As components of the recently formed No. 78 Wing, Nos 76 and 79 Squadrons are organised along similar lines. No. 79 is divided into two flights: 'A' Flight is primarily concerned with the conduct of the LIF Conversion Course, refresher flying and QFI courses; 'B' Flight provides the Introductory Strike Navigators Course, and is also responsible for operational fleet support tasks. The main focus of 'A' Flight, No. 76 Squadron is the conduct of the Introductory Fighter Course, while 'B' Flight will operate the Hawk on operational missions, such as Army or naval fleet support.

The secondary role for the Hawk is one of support for the army and navy, so these requirements were taken into account during the initial project definition studies. Naval support tasks

are currently undertaken by the A-4 Skyhawks of No. 2 Sqn RNZAF, and the successful LIF candidate was required to have sufficient performance to assume these duties.

Some weapons trials have been carried out in the UK, but the bulk will be performed in Australia by ARDU. The first weapons to be cleared for use will be the standard ADEN 30-mm cannon, AIM-9M Sidewinders (on wingtip-mounted LAU-7 rails), BDU-33 10-kg (22-lb) practice bomb dispensers, and the Mk 82 and GBU-12 bombs. All of these weapons offer a large increase over the capability of the Macchi, which could only carry gun pods and 5-kg (11-lb) practice bombs.

Crews who have completed conversion to the aircraft are very impressed by its performance – again, particularly in comparison to the Macchi – and look forward to the completion of the final incremental capability phase. Once this is complete, the Hawk Mk 127 will not only be the ideal interim step between PC-9 and Hornet, but will be a potent weapons platform its own right.

Nigel Pittaway

Inside the ARIES II

Lockheed EP-3E

The collision between a Chinese Navy Shenyang J-8II interceptor and a US Navy reconnaissance aircraft 'on a routine surveillance mission over the South China Sea', about 70 miles (113 km) off the island of Hainan, focused international media attention on what had hitherto been a little-known type, the Lockheed EP-3E Aries II Sigint aircraft.

ARIES II deployment

The ARIES II Orion entered service during 1991, VQ-1 receiving the first conversion (156507) during the spring, and VQ-2 receiving the second, 157320, on 29 June 1991. Replacement of the original ARIES was a relatively slow process. VQ-1 retired the oldest remaining EP-3E Aries I (and actually the oldest US Navy Orion), 148887, in July 1994, this also marking the completion of the squadron's transition to the ARIES II. VQ-2 followed suit, upgrading to an all ARIES II fleet by April 1997.

Delivery of the last of the original batch of EP-3E ARIES II aircraft was delayed by a Congressional investigation into US Sigint capabilities. This had been prompted by concerns that the EP-3E and USAF RC-135 might represent unnecessary duplication, and led to a freeze in the conversion programme. A study was launched which aimed to select one type for retention and further development, with the 'loser' being phased out. In the event, the study showed that the two types were complementary, and that there was no over-capacity, and the decision was taken to retain both types.

The loss of one VQ-2 ARIES II in an accident led to a 13th machine, and this aircraft, now undergoing the P-3C to EP-3E conversion process, will be delivered in 2002.

ARIES IIs are split between two units, one serving the needs of the Pacific Fleet and one serving the Atlantic Fleet. VQ-1 (Fleet Air Reconnaissance Squadron One, or FAIRECONRON ONE) is home-based at NAS Whidbey Island, Washington, following the 1994 closure of its home since 1971 – NAS Agana, Guam. VQ-1 provides electronic reconnaissance from the east coast of Africa to the west coast of the United States, and operates a permanent

detachment in Japan. Until 1991 this was at Atsugi, but since then it has been at Misawa. VQ-1 has also maintained a continuous presence in the Arabian Gulf since July 1992.

The Atlantic unit has been based in the Mediterranean since its inception, long before the Orion era. VQ-2 (Fleet Air Reconnaissance Squadron Two, or FAIRECONRON TWO) has been based at Naval Station Rota, Spain, since 1960. Today the squadron flies four EP-3E ARIES IIs and two standard P-3C Orions from its home-base at Rota, and parents a two-aircraft detachment at Naval Support Activity Souda Bay, Crete.

The intense nature of EP-3E operations can be gauged by the fact that VQ-1 and VQ-2 tend to fly more operations, with fewer aircraft, than any other naval squadron, and this is illustrated by VQ-2's recent record. In the summer of 1990, the squadron provided Elint support during Operation Sharp Edge (the evacuation of 2,000 personnel from war-torn Liberia). From August 1990 to April 1991, VQ-2 provided combat reconnaissance during Operations Desert Shield, Desert Storm, Proven Force, and Provide Comfort. Since July 1992, VQ-2 has flown more than 10,000 hours in support of NATO and United Nations forces in the former Yugoslavia, participating in Operations Deny Flight, Provide Promise, Sharp Guard, Joint Endeavour, Decisive Endeavour, and Deliberate Guard, sometimes maintaining a detachment at Sigonella in Italy.

BuNo. PR-32 was the aircraft which survived the collision with a PLANAF J-8 over the South China Sea, and is seen here on Hainan airfield shortly after landing. Apart from the obvious damage to the nosecone, the aircraft was also hit in the no. 1 propeller, under the wings and the port aileron.

Lockheed EP-3E ARIES II

EP-3Es are the only US Navy Orions to retain the white/grey scheme, but only some of the fleet (those converted by Lockheed) are thus painted. Those aircraft converted by NADEPs Jacksonville and Alameda are in the standard all-over grey TPS scheme.

Antenna configuration

Externally, the Aries II retains the distinctive ventral 'M&M' radome and dorsal and ventral 'canoe' antenna fairings which characterised the earlier EP-3B and original ARIES aircraft. The ventral radome still houses the system's OE-319 Big Look antenna, while the OE-320 group of direction-finding antennas is housed in the upper and lower canoes.

The OE-319 surveillance antenna is associated with the AN/ALQ-110 Big Look radar analysis system, and reportedly consists of a 5-ft 11-in x 12-ft 2-in (1.8 m x 3.7 m) mechanically scanned antenna which receives signals in the 0.3 to 18 GHz frequency range (and which may be able to transmit between 0.3-10 GHz). The antenna may be derived from that of the AN/APS-20 search/AEW radar, and is believed to be able to accurately localise emitters when operating in its active mode. The antenna is believed to be capable of operating in a full 360° scan pattern, or to operate in narrower 'cake-slice' sector scans, and can be 'aimed' in elevation. The array may also host the antenna for the AN/ALQ-108 IFF jammer.

The OE-320 antenna group in the long dorsal canoe and the shorter ventral canoe is believed to consist of single fore-and-aft rows of 2-ft (60-cm) diameter circular DF antennas that can scan at speeds of up to 200 rpm and which cover the 0.5-2 GHz and 2-18 GHz frequency bands. The description of the spinners as being of equal size is perhaps surprising, groups of antennas of different sizes being more usual for wide-band DF. The system can be directed to cover 15°, 30°, 60° or 120° sectors relative to the host aircraft's centreline, and antennas can be automatically or manually directed onto a signal of interest.

The ARIES II has slender, low-profile antenna pods for the AN/ALR-76 Elint system on both wingtips. AN/ALR-76 is designed to detect, identify, classify, locate and track radar emitters and to provide any necessary audio threat warnings and automatically actuate onboard countermeasures systems. Each wingtip pod contains a single reception assembly, and these in turn house four cavity-backed planar spiral antennas. AN/ALR-76 output can be fused with other acquired data to create a fused situational awareness display.

The EP-3E also carries an AN/ALR-81(V) microwave ELINT receiver system, believed to cover the 0.5-40 GHz frequency range. Other Elint equipment carried includes the AN/ULQ-16(V)2 pulse analyser, which can

VQ-1 supports the Pacific Fleet's activities from its home base at Whidbey Island. Most operational sorties, however, are launched from Misawa in Japan where a permanent detachment is maintained. The aircraft are also highly active in the Persian Gulf, flying mostly from Bahrain.

provide pulse repetition frequency and interval, pulse width, pulse amplitude, scan time and rate, illumination time and bandwidth information of hostile emitters.

Details of the EP-3E's Comint systems are less widely known, though it is believed that they include an AN/ALD-9(V) communications band direction-finder system. This is a dual-channel, interferometric communications band direction-finder, which utilises bit slice processing and is served by the array of blade antennas under the outer wing panels and rear fuselage. The ARIES II is believed to be capable of 'listening in' to military and civilian radio traffic in all wavebands (intercepting, analysing, locating and recording signals) and can also do the same to other forms of electronic communications, including faxes and telephone conversations. Speculation that the EP-3E can read e-mails, and 'break into' enemy computer networks is believed to be incorrect. This capability is said to exist, but only on one (USAF) platform.

The EP-3E has a vital Link 11 High/Ultra High Frequency (HF/UHF) datalink system to allow it to download data in near real time. This is also known as TADIL-A (TActical Digital Intelligence Link) and is a NATO-standard encrypted, digital datalink that is fitted to a variety of other ships and aircraft. Its antenna may be contained in the unusual 'flower pot' radome below the rear fuselage.

Aircrew and their stations

Aircrew for the two EP-3E squadrons come from a variety of sources. Pilot and Flight Engineer training is provided by Patrol Squadron Thirty (VP-30), while Naval Flight Officers receive Inter-Service Navigation training at Randolph Air Force Base, Texas. Basic and Advanced Electronic Warfare Officer training and ARIES II-specific aircraft operator training is undertaken by the Fleet Aviation Specialized Operational Training Group Detachment (FASOTRAGRU DET) at Whidbey Island, Washington.

The normal crew complement of the ARIES II is 24, and there are 24 numbered seating posi-

tions, of which 15 are mission crew stations, five are flight crew and four are described as 'ditching stations', but which are believed to accommodate extra, supernumerary or relief crew members during take-off and landing. By comparison, the basic P-3 ASW aircraft has a crew of only 11, with four flight crew. The crew usually includes seven officers and 17 enlisted aircrew (or eight officers and 16 enlisted aircrew personnel according to some sources). The flight crew usually consists of a pilot, a co-pilot, a single flight engineer and one or two navigators (all officers except for the flight engineer). The navigator sits just outside the flight deck, facing to starboard, occupying crew station 6, next to what may now be a relief crew station, but which was hitherto the navigator/communicator station. On the port side (in station 4) is the secure communications operator, who sends near real-time information to Fleet or theatre commanders, and even to defence officials at the Pentagon and the national command authorities. The data is inevitably transmitted in encrypted form.

The mission crew consists of equipment operators, some of whom are Aviation Electronics Technicians (ATs) who serve dual roles, as both Operators and Maintenance Technicians. Three of the mission crew are usually officers, these being (from front to rear) the occupants of stations 12-14 in the centre of the cabin: the ESM supervisor (or 'evaluator' in official parlance), the EW Combat Co-ordinator and the Special Systems (Comint) evaluator. The Electronic Warfare (EW) co-ordinator is the Mission Crew commander, and is responsible for targeting the sensors, and for the integration of acquired Elint and Comint data and for its dissemination to offboard users. He sits between the Elint and Comint supervisors, placing him quite literally at the centre of all mission activity.

Not all members of the crew are intelligence specialists. To confuse things further, it is known that VQ-2 uses alternative terms for some of its crew-members, including: Electronic Warfare Mission Commander (EWMC); Electronic Warfare Aircraft Commander (EWAC); Senior Electronic Warfare Tactical Evaluator (SEVAL); and Electronic Warfare Operator (EWOP).

Working aft from the bulkhead which separates the main part of the cabin from the flight deck and nav/comms area, the first position

(on the starboard side) is station 7, described as the record operator/flight technician. Stations 8-14 are behind this, on the port side, and from front to back accommodate the Manual ESM (or Manual Elint) operator at station 8, the Brigand operator at station 9, the Lab operator at station 10, and the Radar/ESM (Big Look) operator at station 11. The duties of the commissioned personnel at stations 12-14 have already been described.

The manual ESM operator is tasked with signals analysis and with fine-tuning Elint receivers. The exact responsibilities of the Brigand and Lab operators is unknown, although stations 9 and 10 have previously been described as the low-band and high-band signal collection stations, respectively responsible for long-range early warning, height-finding and meteorological radars and for high-band radars such as those carried by enemy fighters. The Big Look operator at station 11 manages the EP-3E's long-range Elint receivers, and is thought to be responsible for the evaluation of newly acquired signals, and operation of the nose-mounted AN/APS-134 search radar.

The rearmost of the three stations crewed by commissioned officers is station 14, the Comint special task supervisor/collection director station. It was once believed that, prior to the Deepwell programme, EP-3Bs and EP-3Es were effectively 'empty' aft of the Elint-related stations on the port side. This is now in doubt, since official crew position drawings show crew stations 15 through 19 on the starboard side on all EP-3Es. On aircraft 148888, 149668 and 150494, these are marked as special stations, whereas the other EP-3Es are shown as having Deepwell (Comint) stations in this location. On ARIES II, these positions all accomodate Special Systems (eg Comint) operators. They are primarily linguists who listen to and record radio transmissions, and may include civilian experts, or linguists from other branches of the US Forces. Finally, at crew station 20, facing aft on the port side, just behind the entrance door and its powered, folding ladder, is the S&T (Scientific/Tech)

operator, sometimes described as a 'sixth Comint operator', and sometimes as the maintenance station. The station is in the same position as the 'in-flight tech' on standard maritime P-3Cs.

SSIP upgrade

Even before the EP-3E ARIES II conversion programme was complete, a follow on upgrade was launched. Known as the Sensor System Improvement Program (SSIP), this aimed to increase frequency and direction-finding coverage, and to improve interoperability and data exchange with other platforms and assets. The programme was split into two phases, with the priority systems being addressed under the first.

The first aircraft to receive the SSIP were the last two ARIES II conversions, which received the upgrade while still on the ARIES II modification line at NADEP Jacksonville.

The new SSIP subsystems were not intended to counter any specific threat, but aimed to improve the aircraft's ability to cope with the complex signal environment in which the EP-3E now routinely operates. The SSIP also enhances 'connectivity' between the EP-3E and other allied systems, using a broad range of command-and-control, communications and intelligence (C³I) links, and, as such, forms part of the Joint SIGINT Avionics Architecture Family. In addition, software improvements allow the EP-3E to create an integrated, fused tactical picture by linking inputs from on- and off-board (organic and non-organic) sensors.

The SSIP modification was achieved through a 'Story-series' of system improvements. The Story Teller, Story Book and Story Classic subsystems, as well as a new modification of the AN/ULQ-16 system, were networked on an Ethernet Local Area Network (LAN), also interfacing with the existing Electronic Support Measures (ESM) Mission Avionics System.

Story Teller consists of three ruggedised TAC-3 work stations with high-resolution colour monitors, together with various interface units and RT-1273AG Satellite Communication-

capable radios. The Story Teller operators use the system to manage and manipulate selected organic and non-organic data and to view a composite tactical situation display, correlating multiple inputs from onboard sensors and from selected external datalinks. The operator can then transmit 'value-added' information over various communications nets and datalinks. Story Teller is installed at crew stations 12, 13, and 14.

The Naval Aviation Officer at station 14, was no longer 'I' branch capable, becoming simply a Story Teller Operator. To compensate for this, the Scientific and Technology Operator, at station 20, became 'I' branch capable, taking over the Comint supervisor function.

Story Book is installed at station 9 and is an integrated special signal acquisition, data processing, and data fusion system, built around a single ruggedised TAC-3 work station with its associated high-resolution monitor. The Story Book operator can assess the tactical picture and quickly add SIGINT data to communications datalinks. Story Book includes hardware and software interfaces to the aircraft's GPS and INS systems.

The Story Classic system is installed at stations 15 through 20 and provides an upgraded search and acquisition system for low-band signals. Three of the stations have ruggedised TAC-3 work stations, while two have x-terminal work stations, all with ruggedised high-resolution colour monitors. Story Classic includes a signal acquisition, distribution, and exploitation system which incorporates general search and directed search capabilities through a pool of 24 WJ 8607 receivers, and a set of SP-202 Spectrum Processors, together with a WJ-8700 Dual High Frequency (HF) receiver.

The AN/ULQ-16 Signal Data Processor was already installed at stations 8, 10, 11, 12, and 20 but has been modified with upgraded electromagnetic pulse processing capabilities, using dual channel real-time video inputs and new displays and processor software.

The EP-3E ARIES II SSIP also incorporated an advanced System Maintenance Diagnostics (SMD) system, which carries out extensive functional, troubleshooting and status checks preflight, in-flight and post-flight. The system makes maximum use of existing ARIES II diagnostic software, integrating it into the SSIP subsystem software.

It was originally planned that the first phase of the SSIP would be completed by early FY 2001, and four aircraft had been modified by early 2000. Software and hardware problems delayed the completion of SSIP operational testing, however, slowing the modification schedule, and delaying SSIP's operational employment. Under the EP-3E ARIES II SSIP Test and Evaluation Master Plan, Developmental Testing was completed in December 1999 with 10 major discrepancies, and Operational Test

This EP-3E is in standard configuration. One VQ-1 aircraft has been seen with a large antenna pod, with flat-sided outward-facing panels, under the outer wing

and Evaluation (OT&E), was conducted in July 2000. The EP-3E ARIES II SSIP then underwent a 'Verification of Correction of Discrepancies' process, completing this during FY01. Because the installation of SSIP and follow-on upgrades continued to take invaluable aircraft out of the front line, placing great pressure on the remaining assets, the Navy established a requirement to procure four additional EP-3E 'pipeline' aircraft to allow the front-line fleet to be maintained at a viable level.

The second phase of the SSIP will include further upgrades, including an Elint upgrade called Story Finder, an emitter location system called Story Seeker, an onboard sensor fusion upgrade called Story Maker, and an optical collection and processing upgrade called Story Scanner. These latter systems are reportedly still undergoing R&D.

JMOD upgrade

A further major modernisation effort for the EP-3 is now underway. This is known as the Joint Signals Intelligence Avionics Family (JSAF) Block Modernization Program (JMOD). The JMOD programme builds on the enhanced connectivity provided by the SSIP upgrade to provide the EP-3E with a fully state-of-the-art open-architecture Sigint collection and dissemination system, meeting the Joint Airborne Signal Intelligence Architecture (JASA) requirement levied on all airborne reconnaissance

platforms. The open architecture will expedite the incorporation of new and improved sensors as they become available, and has made it easier to include commercial-off-the-shelf (COTS) hardware and software. This is expected to enable the EP-3E to remain viable beyond the year 2020.

The JMOD upgrade is divided into three block modifications. JMOD Block 1 provides improved on-board data handling and processing. JMOD Block 2 will add a new low band subsystem and the new Common Data Link, which provides crucial connectivity for network-centric warfare, and which improves data fusion capabilities. JMOD Block 3 will add a precision targeting system. JMOD is fully funded, and limited production began in FY 2001. One aircraft will be produced per year through FY 2002, and thereafter the rate will increase to two aircraft per year until the programme is completed during FY 2007.

It now seems likely that the EP-3E ARIES II (156511) which had to force land at Lingshui on Hainan Island following its collision with a J-8II fighter, will be returned to the USA, and will probably be restored to flying status. As one of only four or five EP-3Es so far fitted with Story Teller, its return will doubtless be eagerly anticipated in a community already over-stretched and working hard in a vital front-line role.

Jon Lake

Cabin arrangement key

Crew stations (red)
1 Pilot
2 Co-pilot
3 Flight Engineer
4 Secure Comms Operator
5 Communicator/relief crew member
6 Nav/Comms Operator
7 Record Operator
8 Manual ESM Operator
9 Brigand Operator
10 Lab Operator
11 Radar/ESM Operator
12 ESM Supervisor
13 EW Combat Co-ordinator
14 Special System Evaluator
15 Special Operations Supervisor
16 Special Systems Operator
17 Special Systems Operator
18 Special Systems Operator
19 Special Systems Operator
20 S&T Operator
21/22 Ditching stations
23/24 Ditching stations

Electronics racks A-K (yellow)

Additional electronics (green)
FELC   Forward Electrical Load Center
MELC   Main Electrical Load Center
Record Recording equipment

Crew facilities (blue)

Left: Crew station 6 is occupied by the nav/comms operator.

Below: Stations 15-19 are the 'special systems' consoles, mainly for communications intelligence.

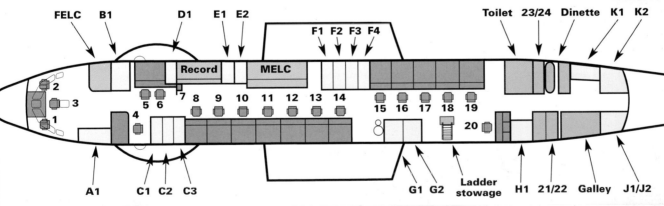

Left: Secure communications are handled from this console (crew station 4).

Right: Stations 8 to 14 accommodate the main Elint operators, and also the Elint Supervisor, Comint supervisor and overall mission co-ordinator.

Right: In the rear of the mission compartment is crew station 20 for the Scientific/Technical Operator. In Story Teller-equipped aircraft the occupant of this station acts as the Comint ('special systems') supervisor.

Aviación Naval Uruguaya

Air arm review

The Uruguay navy's Servicio de Aeronautica (Aeronautical Service) was created on 7 February 1925. Five years later its first Italian-built CANT 18 seaplane trainer and CANT 21 reconnaissance flying-boat arrived, based at Libertad island in the bay of Montevideo. This site was chosen as the service's first base. Known as Base Aéronaval No. 1, it was formally commissioned in 1934.

In exchange for the use of Uruguayan bases, the United States granted credits under the Lend-Lease Act of 1941, and six Vought OS2U-3 Kingfishers and three Fairchild PT-23A trainers were purchased, followed by a single Grumman J4F-2 Widgeon. The navy understood the limitations of having just one base, so on 10 September 1947 the service accepted what was to become its principal airfield. Base Aéronaval No. 2 Capitan de Corbeta Carlos Curbelo was established near the town of Laguna del Sauce. As BA1 was only suitable for waterborne aircraft, it was closed in 1950.

At the end of the 1940s a rapid expansion took place with the delivery of 16 Grumman TBM-1C Avengers and three North American SNJ-4 Texan trainers. They were followed in April 1952 by 12 Grumman F6F-5 Hellcats to form the navy's first combat unit. By this time

Two T-34Cs are the backbone of the training effort, having served in the role for 20 years. Additional aircraft are required if funds can be found. Until recently, the Turbo-Mentors were partnered by T-34Bs.

the service had adopted the name of Aviación Naval Uruguaya and the first helicopters entered service with the delivery of two Bell 47Gs in February 1955. In 1956/57 three Martin PBM-5 Mariners took over SAR duties from the Kingfishers, and two Piper PA-18A Super Cubs were taken on charge on 22 May 1956. Transport assets were boosted by three Beech TC-45J Expediters in May 1961 with a secondary task of multi-engine training.

A new US military agreement resulted in the supply of three Grumman S-2A Trackers in March 1965 and these aircraft took over the patrol and ASW missions from the Mariners, which were retired.

In 1971, two ex-US Navy Sikorsky UH-34J

Seabats were delivered by US transport aircraft to Montevideo's Carrasco Airport. However, on 14 November of the same year both helicopters collided during an aerial demonstration. The next Sikorskys delivered were four ex-US Army CH-34J Choctaws, which arrived in 1972. Two went into service and operated until 1988, while the other two were used for spares. The deal was made possible because the ANU had sold its last Kingfisher to a museum in the United States.

The A-model Trackers were in turn replaced by three ex-MASDC S-2G Trackers after reconditioning at Grumman's St Augustine plant in the early 1980s.

Ground attack capability came in 1979 with the delivery of nine French-built ex-Argentine Navy Sud T-28F Fennecs. Four were solely for spares and the last two were withdrawn from use in 1994. Also, on 25 July 1979, from Argentina came three Beech C-45 Expediters for transport work. All the C-45s were struck off charge in the early 1980s.

Training

Training has always been undertaken in-house. A single Beech T-34B Mentor was received on 15 October 1966, and was supplemented by two ex-Argentine navy SNJs in August 1970. To expand and modernise the fleet three Beech T-34C Turbo-Mentors arrived in April 1981, though unfortunately one

The EAE has three aircraft assigned, two Jetstream T.Mk 2s (below) which were formerly used for observer training by the Royal Navy, and a single patrol-configured King Air 200T (left). The King Air has an underfuselage search radar, necessitating the fitment of ventral fins to restore directional stability.

crashed on 22 March 1982. In 1985 the service traded an SNJ for a T-34B of the Fuerza Aérea Uruguaya, and all of the surviving (of 10 delivered) SNJs were disposed of in the mid-1980s. Since the early 1990s advanced training has been conducted using two Piper PA-34-200T Senecas. The Senecas were also used for liaison duties, as were the three Cessna 182s delivered in early 1990. Budgetary cuts led to the sale of the Senecas and C.182s, while the Beech T-34B Mentors were withdrawn from use and put into storage in the late 1990s.

The Escuela de Aviación Naval, responsible for training, was thus left with only two T-34C Turbo-Mentors and a new training programme had to be devised. Total training for each student is approximately 150 hours, consisting of 30 hours solo, 16 hours aerobatic, 12 hours visual navigation, 13 hours basic instrument, 25 hours radio instrument, 14 hours of night flying, 15 hours of gunnery practice and 25 hours of formation flying. Once this phase has been successfully passed there follows 50 hours advanced training on the twin-engined aircraft or Wessex helicopter.

ASW/SAR

After retirement of the S-2G Tracker, the sole ASW capability of the Escuadrón Antisubmarino y Exploración was provided by a single Beech 200T Super King Air, which was handed over to the ANU on 15 November 1980. For

The EdH received a total of eight Wessexes, of which one has been lost and two withdrawn. Four of the operational aircraft are HC.Mk 2s (right), which retain their RAF camouflage and serials, while the last surviving radar-equipped Wessex Mk 60 (ex-Bristows) is painted in high-visibility colours (below).

Veteran of the ANU's helicopter fleet is the Bell 47G, which was not retired until 2000 after a 45-year career. The ANU's helicopter operations have been dominated by the Sikorsky S-58 and its derivatives.

SAR tasks this aircraft is capable of dropping sea survival equipment and is fitted with an APS-128 search radar. ASW capacity was augmented on 14 January 1999 with the delivery of two ex-Royal Navy British Aerospace Jetstream T.Mk 2s. All year around there is one aircraft and helicopter on stand-by for SAR duties.

Helicopters

The longest serving helicopter with the Escuadrón de Helicopteros was the Bell 47. A total of seven aircraft was in service from February 1955 until early 2000, when the last was withdrawn from use due to corrosion in the rotor head. An unusual type was the Bell

222, which was used from 31 October 1980 until 1992, when it was sold in Argentina as part of cost-cutting measures. Replacement came in the form of two (ex-Ghana, via Bristows) Westland Wessex Mk 60 logistic support helicopters in August 1991, followed by one more in April 1994. With the delivery of five ex-Royal Air Force Wessex HC.Mk 2s in February 1998, one of the Mk 60s (serial 063) was put on display near the gate of Base Aéronaval No. 2, next to one of the Grumman S-2A Trackers, while another (serial 064) was put into storage. Unfortunately one of the Wessex HC.Mk 2s (serial 083) was lost in an accident while on a rescue mission on 2 March 2001.

Future plans

In order to make some money, the ANU has hatched an ambitious plan to acquire ex-US Navy Rockwell T-2 Buckeyes to establish a training unit in which Argentinian and Brazilian naval pilots will be trained. At the time of writing, negotiations are under way to purchase these aircraft. Another item on the shopping list is two more Beech T-34C Turbo-Mentors, some light aircraft for shore patrol and another Jetstream.

Dick Lobuis

ORDER OF BATTLE

Comando de la Aviación Naval
BA2 Capitan Curbelo, Laguna del Sauce
Grupo de Escadrones

Escuadrón Antisubmarino y Exploración	Bc 200, Jetstream T.2
Escuadrón de Helicopteros	Wessex HC.2/Mk 60
Escuela de Aviación Naval	T-34C

Eurofighter Typhoon
Programme round-up

With production of the first batch of Eurofighters well under way, and the first flight of a production aircraft due before the end of 2001, the four-nation Eurofighter programme is moving rapidly towards service entry in 2002 and NATO declaration in 2006, while major enhancements to the basic aircraft are under active discussion between the four core nations and prospective buyers.

Although the idea of a multinational fourth-generation European fighter dates back to the late 1970s, the programme, in its current form, began with a European Staff Requirement issued in 1985, shortly after France left the consortium to develop the Rafale. In 1995 a Revised European Staff Requirement was issued, by which time the first three prototypes were already flying. Work-share arguments were finally resolved in 1996.

On 22 December 1997 the Defence Ministers of the four nations signed the Memorandum of Understanding which covered Production Investment, Production and Support, and a month later contracts were signed between Eurofighter GmbH, the umbrella company for the four manufacturers, and NETMA (NATO Eurofighter and Tornado Management Agency), which represents the customers. These contracts confirmed production for the Aeronautica Militare Italiana, Ejército del Aire, Luftwaffe and Royal Air Force at 620 aircraft.

In September 1998, shortly after the name

Typhoon had been adopted for export aircraft, the Supplement 2 production order was signed, covering the initial fixed-price batch of 148 Batch 1 aircraft (and 363 EJ200 engines), these to be completed in the basic configuration optimised for air defence with only limited air-to-surface capability. Construction of major assemblies had already begun at the various plants. Two further batches, each of 236 aircraft (Batch 2 with 519 engines and Batch 3 with 500 engines), will include expanded air-to-surface capabilities, although these have yet to be fully

defined. Batch 3 will represent the full multi-role capability, and will incorporate several additional planned technologies. On top of the 620 production aircraft (and 1,382 engines) committed to by the four partner nations, an optional batch of 90 aircraft has been signed for under the overall deal.

Of the first batch, 52 are two-seaters, to enable training to begin in earnest in the four customer air forces. A total of 100 two-seaters is included in the overall purchase, with 25 in Batch 2 and 23 in Batch 3.

Development Aircraft batch

Aircraft	company	seats	first flight	test role
DA1	DASA	single	27 Mar 1994	handling, engine trials (originally with RB.199)
DA2	BAe	single	6 Apr 1994	envelope expansion and carefree handling (originally with RB.199)
DA3	Alenia	single	4 Jun 1995	EJ200 integration, stores release, gun firing
DA4	BAe	two	14 Mar 1997	two-seat handling, radar integration
DA5	DASA	single	24 Feb 1997	avionics and weapons integration
DA6	CASA	two	31 Aug 1996	two-seat avionics and systems
DA7	Alenia	single	27 Jan 1997	weapons integration

Left: Visually the most stunning of the Development Aircraft is DA2, which is painted black to cover up the black patches liberally applied to the aircraft (mainly on the starboard side) for air pressure trials.

Above: The Italian DA3 leads the two German aircraft (DA1 and DA5) in a formation of three Eurofighters while on trials at Decimomannu. By 2001 DA2 had been the busiest in the fleet, with over 300 flights.

DA7 is the lead weapons trials aircraft and has conducted all the AIM-9 and AIM-120 firings so far. The clearance of these missiles is of utmost importance, as they are the baseline air defence weapons for IOC.

DA3 was the first to fly with EJ200 engines, and has been used for various stores trials. In 1999 it undertook pit drop tests of free-fall weapons, and is due to undertake gunnery trials. Amid great controversy, the Royal Air Force deleted the 27-mm Mauser BK 27 cannon from its Eurofighters.

Initial deliveries and IPAs

Batch 1 deliveries comprise 55 for the RAF, 44 for the Luftwaffe, 29 for the AMI and 20 for the EdA. One of the airframes will be used for static testing. The first five aircraft from the production line will be designated Instrumented Production Aircraft (IPA) and they will join the seven-aircraft DA trials fleet. IPAs represent the Interim Operating Capability (IOC) configuration, and are being built on the production lines, unlike the largely hand-built Development Aircraft. However, they also include additional test equipment. The first of the IPAs were, at the time of writing, expected to have flown by the end of 2001. The IPA batch breaks down as follows:

No.	Company	configuration
IPA1	BAE SYSTEMS	two-seat
IPA2	Alenia	two-seat
IPA3	EADS-Deutschland	two-seat
IPA4	EADS-CASA	single-seat
IPA5	BAE SYSTEMS	single-seat

Five of the DA batch (DA3 to 7) are being progressively modified to IOC standard, so that the initial production configuration can be tested by 10 aircraft.

Smart production

Eurofighters are manufactured as a number of single-source major components, but are assembled at four different lines (to satisfy the needs of the local customer) at Warton (BAE Systems), Manching (EADS-Deutschland), Caselle (Alenia) and Getafe (EADS-CASA). The production effort has been designed for maximum flexibility and efficiency. The highly flexible CAD/CAM (Computer-Aided Design/Manufacture) allows other assembly lines to be easily established, should export customers require this.

To provide enormous economy and streamlining of the production process, a complex delivery schedule has been formulated to provide maximum efficiency in transporting components between sources and assembly lines. The 'Just in Time' concept has been applied, whereby components arrive at the assembly lines as they are needed. The special trucks which ferry components will rarely travel empty: for instance, a truck delivering a forward fuselage from BAE Samlesbury to EADS-D Manching will return from Germany with a centre fuselage for Warton. In late 2000 the first production components began arriving at the assembly lines.

Each assembly line is a state-of-the-art facility. Warton's Hangar 302 (former Tornado assembly line), for example, has a sophisticated automated laser alignment facility (as does EADS-CASA's assembly line). The three main fuselage sections are mounted on three computer-controlled jacks each. A laser tracks optical marks on each component and supplies inputs to a computer, which then moves the jacks to manoeuvre the components into the perfect marry-up position for attachment.

Following marry-up of the major components, the aircraft moves to a second team which installs systems and equipment. A third team handles customer acceptance, painting and attending to any problems which surface during the three-flight (average) acceptance tests.

Warton's facility can handle 15 aircraft at a time and, while the first aircraft through (IPA1, also known as BT001) will spend around 12 months in final assembly while working practices are established, by aircraft 20 the line hopes to be turning an aircraft from components into finished product in 16 weeks. Output from Warton is expected to peak at 4.5 a month, with some excess capability built in to handle any export work.

While production gears up, over 90 per cent of the Interim Operating Capability flight trials have been completed, and much of the production-standard equipment has been cleared. Trials continue, and will ramp up when the five IPAs join the test fleet. By 4 June 2001 the DA

Left: Spain's single prototype, DA6, has been involved in two-seat handling trials, including 'carefree' handling. It has also been used for hot climate tests (at Morón) and trials of the environmental control system (for which EADS-CASA is the lead company).

Below: Arranged on the Manching flightline is a Eurofighter (DA1) and the three aircraft types it is replacing in Luftwaffe service (MiG-29, Tornado IDS and F-4). The Phantom here is actually one of the Greek aircraft being upgraded by EADS-Deutschland.

Above: DA1 streams its brake chute while the nose is kept high for aerodynamic braking. Eurofighter's FCS has evolved through a number of iterations, the latest of which is Phase 3 (IOC). Phase 4 will allow the use of air-to-ground stores. The aircraft is inherently stable in yaw, neutral in roll and unstable in pitch.

Right: DA4 (foreground) and DA7 climb out on a test sortie in Italy. DA7 has a forward-facing camera mounted in a fairing at the top of the fin.

fleet had accumulated 1,298 hours in 1,586 flights. The total development programme is scheduled to encompass 4,000 hours in the air.

DASS

At the time of writing the two-seater DA4 was in lay-up prior to rejoining the test programme for ground-based DASS (Defensive Aids Sub-System) trials. DASS is a fully automated (with optional pilot override) system encompassing missile warning and laser warning receivers, ECM/ESM (in the port wingtip pod), Towed Radar Decoys (two in the starboard wingtip pod), chaff (in the rear of the permanently fixed outer wing pylons) and flares (in the flap tracks). Germany and Spain initially stayed out of the EuroDASS consortium which has developed the suite, although both have subsequently joined. There are some differences between the customers: Germany and Italy have not specified the laser warning receivers, while Italy is studying an alternative to the TRD in the form of the Cross Eye electronic countermeasures system.

Cockpit

One of the most impressive features of the Eurofighter is its cockpit. No first-generation data is presented to the pilot: all has been processed and fused by the system to present an overall 'big picture' based on input from various sensors, including those offboard (via the MIDS system). The system can be controlled with minimum pilot workload thanks to the VTAS (Voice Throttle And Stick) system, which combines HOTAS (Hands On Throttle And Stick) inputs with DVI/O (Direct Voice Input/Output). The DVI/O system can theoretically handle 600 words, but initial capa-

bility has been capped at 80 to avoid any potential phonetic difficulties. When combined with the MIDS (Multiple Information Distribution System) datalink, DVI/O allows pilots to sort targets and allocate them to other members of the formation by voice alone. For obvious reasons, safety-critical actions, such as weapons firing or undercarriage deployment, remain as manual actions. As well as providing aural warnings, the aircraft's system can also be interrogated by voice, and provide voice answers. Fuel state and "how far to X?" are obvious questions which can be responded to by the system, without the pilot having to change the display set-up.

Weapons progress

Weapons testing has been primarily undertaken by Italy's DA7, which undertook the first live firing of an AIM-9 Sidewinder on 15 December 1997. Two days later an AIM-120 AMRAAM was jettisoned to begin the trials of the primary BVR weapon of the Eurofighter in its initial configuration. Sidewinder and AMRAAM trials have continued to clear the weapons for IOC. Due to the longer lead times associated with guided weapons, trials have focused on these two weapons, with several

subsequent launchings. Testing of air-to-ground weaponry has, by mid-2001, been restricted to pit drops, but will involve air tests as IOC approaches. For the IOC aircraft only free-fall weapons such as iron, cluster and laser-guided bombs will be cleared.

On 16 May 2000 UK Defence Minister Geoffrey Hoon announced the UK's decision to purchase the European consortium Meteor beyond-visual-range air-to-air missile, ending a long and hotly fought contest with Raytheon. The Meteor uses ramjet power to achieve long range, yet retains maximum end-game manoeuvring energy. The seeker head and guidance system builds on work performed for the MBD MICA missile used by the Mirage 2000-5 and Rafale. Following the decision to release an RAF Eurofighter for test and integration work, the six-nation Meteor BVRAAM group hopes to bring forward the missile's in-service date to 2007/08. The UK is leading the team, which also includes France, Germany, Italy, Spain and Sweden. As well as being adopted as the primary Beyond Visual Range armament for the Eurofighter, Meteor is also planned for Gripen and Rafale. Development of Meteor continues, using a BAe 125 aircraft equipped to represent the missile, and a BAC One-Eleven fitted with

The Eurofighter can carry a maximum of three fuel tanks, carried on the centreline (1000-litre only) and two wing tanks (1000- or 1500-litre). The 1500-litre tanks are restricted to subsonic flight. Both tanks have been tested by the Italian aircraft, DA3 and DA7. The latter is shown above carrying a three-tank fit. The starboard tank is covered with photo-calibration marks, and is seen left during the first jettison trial on 17 June 1998. In the view below DA3 is seen carrying two of the larger tanks, which were first tested in February 1999. Two-seaters have less internal fuel, although the loss of the forward transfer tank is offset by the addition of a small tank in the extended spine.

Production-standard EJ200-03Z engines began flight tests in October 1999, fitted to Italy's DA3 prototype at Caselle. By that time development EJ200 engines had already accumulated more than 3,600 hours in the seven prototypes, of which 1,170 had been in the air. In December the first inflight relight was accomplished. In late March 2001 NETMA awarded the Eurojet consortium a technical certificate for the production-standard EJ200-03Z engine, signifying the end of long-running flight trials and bench tests of the engine. BAE SYSTEMS' DA2 returned to flight test in June 2001 fitted with 03Z engines in place of the final development engine – the 03Y.

Captor radar

In February 2001 the first two production-standard Captor (previously ECR90) radars were delivered to Eurofighter – one to BAE SYSTEMS and one to Alenia. Eurofighter had received 16 pre-production radars, dubbed the 'C' model, which were tested in DA4, DA5 and DA6. Another CAPTOR radar is flying in a test BAC One-Eleven, which by mid-2001 had amassed some 400 hours of inflight testing in the course of over 200 flights. The 'C' model radar first flew in the One-Eleven in 1996, and in the Eurofighter on 25 February 1997 (DA5).

From the outset the radar has shown excellent air-to-air performance, while retaining plenty of scope for incremental modification to keep the radar abreast of projected air threats for at least the first 25 years of the Eurofighter's operational career. In March 2001 Captor underwent a seven-sortie evaluation, including a mission flown by Germany's DA5 on 28 March during which it flew against 16 F-4Fs and four MiG-29s from JG 73 at Laage. A series of head-on and tail-chase engagements were undertaken, in a clutter-rich environment. Operating mostly in TWS (track-while-scan) mode, the radar performed excellently. A total of 147 Captors is currently on order to equip the 148 aircraft in Tranche 1 production (one is a static test airframe). The radars are completed at BAE SYSTEMS' Crewe Toll facility, which has the capacity to produce up to 10 sets a month.

Like the Batch 1 aircraft, the initial Captor production sets are optimised for air-to-air work, although they possess considerable air-to-surface capability, including moving target and sea search modes. This capability is expected to be enhanced with a series of upgrades planned for the first two years of Eurofighter operations.

Simulator

On 1 May 2001 Eurofighter GmbH announced that it had been awarded a $949 million contract to supply the combat simulators for the four nations developing the aircraft. Under the overall programme name ASTA (Aircrew Synthetic Training Aid), Eurofighter will produce 18 FMS (Full Mission Simulators) and nine CT/IPS-E (Cockpit Trainer/Interactive Pilot Stations – Enhanced) systems. The principal contractors on ASTA are BAE SYSTEMS and Thales. The FMS offers a full mission simulation, including dogfighting, weapons and electronic warfare.

Enhanced Eurofighter Programme

As air defence is the priority for all four core nations, the first Eurofighters are being deliv-

Captor radar. To cover the gap between Eurofighter and Meteor service entry, the MoD is procuring up to 400 AIM-120B AMRAAMs commercially, which will form the initial missile equipment of the RAF's aircraft alongside MBD ASRAAMs. Germany will employ the IRIS-T short-range weapon, but will initially use AIM-9L Sidewinders, as will the other nations.

In late December 2000 MATRA BAe Dynamics conducted the first full flight test of the Storm Shadow/SCALP EG long-range stand-off missile, from a Mirage 2000. Two of these weapons are to be carried by Eurofighter in the stand-off precision strike role. Both the RAF and Italy have specified the missile for their aircraft, while Greece has ordered the weapon for its Mirage 2000-5 Mk 2 fighters, and would probably fit it on Eurofighter if the Greek buy ever comes to fruition. Germany has opted for the KEPD-350 Taurus stand-off missile.

While reconnaissance is a stated role of the Eurofighter, none of the partner nations has outlined a formal requirement for this capability as yet. However, pod-mounted sensors will be integrated later in the programme when such requirements materialise.

Fuel and powerplant trials

Eurofighter is designed to operate with 1000-litre (220-Imp gal) and 1500-litre (330-Imp gal) drop tanks. The small tanks were first carried by DA3 in December 1997, and in June 1998 DA7 successfully jettisoned a tank. In February 1999 DA3 (primary external stores trials airframe) flew with the big tanks, fully fuelled, and in March it exceeded Mach 1 with the 1000-litre tanks. By the end of the month it had taken two of them to Mach 1.6. The same speed was reached in December 1999 with three tanks installed.

ered to IOC standard, with AIM-9L and AIM-120B missiles, and a limited air-to-ground capability. Full Operating Capability is slated for March 2005, followed by a declaration to NATO intended for January 2006. Beyond that, the Batch 2 production configuration has yet to be defined, but will be essentially similar to FOC with additional software/avionics changes.

More radical are the improvements which are being studied for the Tranche 3 production aircraft under the Eurofighter Enhancement Programme, driven currently by the UK and Germany, although Italy and Spain may join the programme later.

As well as integration of new 'smart' weapons, and the adoption of Storm Shadow, Taurus and Meteor, Tranche 3 Typhoons may also feature CFTs (Conformal Fuel Tanks) and TRN (Terrain-Referenced Navigation). It is planned that advances in helmet displays can allow the removal of the HUD (head-up display). ITP, the Spanish engine partner, has studied thrust-vectoring for the EJ200 engine, and the engine itself has a 30 per cent thrust growth potential in its current form. Already under review (but not yet funded) are staged thrust increases to 103 kN (23,155 lb) thrust (as the EJ230), and 117 kN (26,300 lb).

By around 2010, Tranche 3 Typhoons could be equipped with electronically-scanned ('e-scan') active array radars. The AMSAR (Airborne Multi-role multi-function Solid-state Active-array Radar) programme is a technology demonstration being conducted by BAE SYSTEMS (UK), Thales (France) and EADS (Germany) to produce a radar with a fixed, electronically-steered antenna array, using similar technology to the AESA radar being fielded on USAF F-15s and planned for F/A-18E/F, F-22 and JSF. An AMSAR prototype scanner is expected to fly in the BAC One-Eleven in around 2003, but its first application is expected to be the Dassault Rafale, primarily to enhance the French fighter's exportability. AMSAR is not expected to be integrated into the Captor until the Tranche 3 Eurofighters in 2010. However, that schedule could be brought forward.

Further technologies, such as those forming part of the FOAS (Future Offensive Aircraft System) study, may be injected into Eurofighter as they become available. The Eurofighter is itself a central part of the FOAS studies, and could potentially form the basis of the new aircraft. However, FOAS has a wide-ranging brief, which includes UCAVs (Uninhabited Combat Air Vehicles) and other aircraft types, present or planned. BAE SYSTEMS also conducted a 'Sea Typhoon' study for a carrier-borne version. This was mooted as a potential aircraft to be carried by the UK's two planned aircraft-carriers, although the MoD is now

Advanced weapons such as the Storm Shadow and Meteor, shown here on DA7, will not be available until much later in the decade. The ASRAAM forms part of the FOC armament fit.

Above: The Captor (originally ECR90) radar first flew in 'A' model form in this BAC One-Eleven in January 1993. In July 1996 the 'C' model was installed, which first flew in DA5 in February 1997. DA4 (illustrated) flew with ECR90 from the outset. The One-Eleven has played an important part in the radar development programme, and will be fitted in the future with the AMSAR 'e-scan' antenna, which may be fitted to Tranche 3 aircraft.

Right: Mounted on the port forward fuselage is the Eurofirst (consortium led by FIAR) PIRATE (Passive Infra-Red Airborne Tracking Equipment), which functions as a FLIR for low-level flight and target acquisition, and as an IRST in the air-to-air role.

committed to the Joint Strike Fighter (if the programme survives) to be its FJCA (Future Joint Combat Aircraft).

Deployment plans

■ **UK:** The Royal Air Force will receive 232 Eurofighters in total (plus 65 options), of which 55 are included in the first production batch (37 single-seat, 18 two-seat). Single-seaters will number 195 and two-seaters 37, most of which will serve in a training function. An option exists for a further 65 aircraft. Priority has been given to replace the 80 or so Tornado F.Mk 3s which currently undertake the air defence mission. Although training should begin at Warton in March 2002, first deliveries to the RAF are expected in June, but these aircraft will remain at BAE SYSTEMS' Warton facility where an Operational Evaluation Unit (OEU) will be established. This is to be No. 17 Squadron, which was the unlucky unit when a decision was made to reduce the number of Tornado GR.Mk 1 squadrons in 1995. Up to 12 aircraft will be based at Warton.

An Operational Conversion Unit (OCU), scheduled to be No. 29 Squadron, will be formed at Coningsby in 2004, and the OEU will move in to the Lincolnshire base. The first front-line unit will form there in January 2005. The Tornado F.3 OCU, currently at Coningsby, will move to Leuchars to make room for the incoming OCU. Leeming is scheduled to receive Eurofighters from 2005/6, and Leuchars from 2008, at which point the Tornado F.Mk 3 is expected to retire. Further Eurofighters, with expanded multi-role capabilities, will replace

the Jaguar force at Coltishall, although no base has yet been specified.

■ **Germany:** The Luftwaffe currently has a requirement for 180 Eurofighters, with no options, split between 147 single-seaters and 33 two-seaters. The type will enter service first with JG 73 'Steinhoff' at Laage in January 2003, which currently operates one squadron of F-4Fs and one squadron of MiG-29s. Displaced F-4F ICE aircraft will be distributed to the other Phantom wings, as they await conversion to the Eurofighter in the order JG 74 (late 2005 at Neuberg), JG 71 (early 2007 at Wittmund) and JG 72 (mid-2010 at Wittmund). Deliveries of the 140 air defence-optimised aircraft should be complete around 2010. The remaining 40 will be from the third production batch, with full multi-role capability, to replace the oldest of the Luftwaffe's Tornados.

■ **Italy:** The AMI is receiving 121 aircraft (105 single-seat and 16 two-seat), of which the first (a two-seater) should be delivered in July 2002. Options are held on a further nine. The AMI plans to equip five fighter groups and an operational conversion unit, within three wings. Each of the six Gruppi is expected to be allo-

DA7 is seen firing an AIM-9L on 15 December 1997 (above), and during the first AIM-120 jettison trial on 17 December (left). Missile trials are conducted over the Decimomannu range in Sardinia.

cated 15 aircraft, with the remainder being held in reserve. At the time of writing the AMI had yet to release official confirmation of the units which will operate the type, but it was widely tipped that the first unit to form (from February 2004) will be a squadron (Gruppo) in the 4° Stormo at Grosseto. The other two wings expected to gain Eurofighters are the 36° Stormo at Gioia del Colle and the 37° Stormo at Trapani.

■ **Spain:** The Ejército del Aire, in whose service the aircraft will be designated C.16 Tifón (CE.16 for the two-seaters), is receiving 87 aircraft. Sixteen further aircraft are held on option. EADS-CASA's prototype, DA6, is designated XCE.16 and operates from the air force's CLAEX (Centro Logístico de Armamento y Experiment-ación) test centre at Torrejón. In late 2002 the first series production aircraft will be delivered to begin the formation of a training unit at Getafe, the EADS-CASA factory airfield near Madrid, which will provide a cadre of six instructors for the OCU. First-batch deliveries will be made in 2002 (two), 2003 (four), 2004 (eight) and 2005 (six), for a total of 20. From the second production batch Spain will receive seven aircraft per year from 2006 to 2009, and five in 2010 (33). The third batch will be delivered from 2010 to 2015 and will make up the Spanish total to 87, which includes 16 two-seaters.

First Spanish unit to form will be the OCU at Morón – nominated as 113 Escuadrón of Ala 11 – which forms in January 2004. This unit will have a strength of seven two-seaters and eight single-seaters. The first front-line unit will be Ala 11's 111 Escuadrón, which is expected to be declared operational in 2007 with 18 aircraft. In 2010 Ala 11's third squadron, 112 Escuadrón, will be declared operational, also with 18 aircraft. Ala 11 (until recently a Mirage F1 oper-

ator) will thus have 51 C.16/CE.16s assigned. The remaining 36 aircraft will be divided equally between 141 and 142 Escuadrones of Ala 14 (currently flying the Mirage F1 at Los Llanos), which start forming in 2008/9 and complete their re-equipment process in 2015.

Overseas marketing

Although the Eurofighter has been developed with the interests of Germany, Italy, Spain and the UK uppermost, the type has obvious export potential to other air arms seeking to acquire a highly capable fighter, although it faces stiff competition from Rafale and advanced variants of the F-15, F-16, F-18 and Su-35. For nations seeking to acquire new fighters after 2010 the JSF, if the programme survives, becomes a major rival, as could export versions of the Lockheed Martin F-22.

Initial marketing arrangements between the four partner nations reflect traditional ties and previous sales campaigns. BAE SYSTEMS is pursuing Australia, Singapore and the Middle East, while EADS-Deutschland leads the sales effort in Europe to Greece, Netherlands and Norway. EADS-CASA's main responsibilities lie in South Korea, South America and Turkey, while Alenia works in Brazil.

In November 1999 Eurofighter International (EFI) was formed to undertake all Typhoon sales, the four partners holding similar stakes in the new company to their overall shares in the programme (UK 37.5 per cent, Germany 30 per cent, Italy 19.5 per cent, Spain 13 per cent). While the individual partners pursue sales interest to Request For Information level, Eurofighter International takes over for the Request For Proposal and subsequent transactions. EFI provides a channel for contractual purposes. In effect, the original EPC (Eurofighter Partner Company) sales team would continue the deal under secondment to EFI. Some potential competitions have already gone the way of other aircraft, notably the sale of 80 F-16s to the United Arab Emirates. Following is a brief run-down of the principal Eurofighter sales efforts.

■ **Australia:** Faced with a considerable rise in the technological capabilities of nations to the north, Australia has outlined plans for a new fighter to replace the F/A-18 Hornets currently in service (and currently being upgraded with ASRAAM and AMRAAM missiles). A Request For Information was issued in 1998, and in December 2000 Project Air 6000 was outlined. This foresees up to 75 new fighters for the RAAF (from 2012) with which to defend the nation and its northern approaches, plus another 25 strike aircraft to replace the F-111 fleet from 2020. A single type would be procured for both requirements. The Typhoon is one of the leading contenders.

■ **Brazil:** Alenia, due to its connection with EMBRAER through the AMX programme, leads a sales attempt in Brazil as the Força Aérea Brasileira searches for a new fighter.

All information is presented on the HUD, helmet and three MHDDs (Multi-function Head-Down Displays), although the current Eurofighter cockpit retains hidden standby instruments. In Batch 3 Eurofighters the HUD is expected to disappear in favour of a full helmet visor display, as also envisaged for the JSF.

Eurofighter weapon options

In its initial guise, the Eurofighter will be equipped for air defence only, with a traditional AIM-9L Sidewinder/AIM-120B AMRAAM combination. Alternatives to AIM-9L, to be fielded by FOC aircraft, will be the ASRAAM and IRIS-T. AMRAAM will give way to the Meteor in the late 2000s. Air-to-surface stores are initially restricted to free-fall weapons, but the repertoire will grow to include the Brimstone anti-armour weapon (RAF), ALARM, Storm Shadow and Taurus. Anti-ship missiles such as the Kongsberg Penguin may also be integrated.

Above: This configuration represents the RAF's intended air dominance loadaout, with four Meteors, two ASRAAMs and three 1000-litre supersonic tanks.

Left: The Meteor consortium pools the missile expertise of France, Germany, Italy, Spain, Sweden and the UK. The ramjet-powered weapon has a very fast flyout to extreme range. It is designed to fit the AMRAAM recesses.

Right: A free-fall option for the Eurofighter is the BL755 cluster bomb, of which six can be carried (including twin racks on the inboard pylons). This aircraft also carries 1500-litre fuel tanks.

Above: Brimstone is an anti-armour weapon based on the AGM-114 Hellfire. Up to 18 can be carried on triple launchers, although this aircraft is loaded with 12. It has a maximum-range tank configuration of one 1000-litre and two 1500-litre tanks.

Below: This aircraft has all 13 hardpoints occupied by a mixed loadout of two Storm Shadows, two ALARMs, four Meteors, two Paveway LGBs, two ASRAAMs and a single 1000-litre tank.

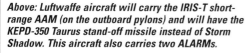

Above: Luftwaffe aircraft will carry the IRIS-T short-range AAM (on the outboard pylons) and will have the KEPD-350 Taurus stand-off missile instead of Storm Shadow. This aircraft also carries two ALARMs.

Below: Paveway laser-guided bombs will be included in the initial batch of air-to-ground weapons. Note the AMRAAM carriage on the wing.

The intensity of the flight trials programme has meant that the DA aircraft have not been able to stray too far from their test centres. DA5 was spared to visit Norway as part of EADS-Deutschland's concerted effort to secure a purchase from the Luftforsvaret. Here it is seen over Oslo, the capital, in 1998.

■ **Chile:** EADS-CASA led Eurofighter's bid to provide a new fighter to the Fuerza Aérea de Chile. This effort foundered when the FACh selected the Lockheed Martin F-16.

■ **Czech Republic:** In June 1999 the Czech Republic issued a Request For Information to Eurofighter, along with other manufacturers, for a notional 36-aircraft fighter force. EADS-Deutschland led the Czech proposal initiative. Due to the Czech government insisting that any proposals be made in Czech currency, US manufacturers, Dassault and EADS-Deutschland withdrew from the competition in May 2001, leaving the SAAB/BAE SYSTEMS Gripen as the only effective competitor. In the light of this, it is likely that the requirement will be restructured and reissued.

■ **Greece:** Representing Eurofighter's first sales success, the Greek government announced in February 1999 that it would purchase at least 60 Typhoons in a deal worth a reported $10.2 billion, with options for another 30. Under the initial deal, Greece would have made annual payments from 2001 to ensure a delivery timescale of 2006-2010. The acquisition was confirmed on 8 March 2000 but, in January 2001, Greece began negotiations with EADS, which headed the Eurofighter sales effort, to postpone payments, and the original timescale of the deal looked increasingly shaky. On 29 March the Prime Minister Costas Simitis announced that the deal would be postponed until after 2004, to allow the funding of various social programmes, including the hosting of the Olympic games in 2004. Greece is also due to stage a general election that year. Despite the postponement of the Greek deal, at the time of writing the nation remained committed to an eventual Typhoon purchase.

■ **Republic of Korea:** In June 2000 South Korea sent out Requests For Proposal for its F-X next-generation fighter requirement. Contenders invited to bid were Eurofighter (via EADS-CASA), Dassault, Boeing (for the F-15K) and Sukhoi (Su-35). F-X identified an immediate need for 40 'heavy fighters' for delivery in 2004-05, with as many as 80 more required. In April 2001 NETMA extended an invitation to South Korea to join the Eurofighter programme, including final assembly of some aircraft and around 30 per cent manufacture of compo-

nents. If South Korea chose this option, it would have a say in the final Tranche 2 specification, allowing it to integrate anti-ship weapons which are a key part of the F-X requirement. Furthermore, NETMA would agree to the early delivery of two Eurofighters to allow time to fully integrate Korean requirements. However, a slippage in the F-X programme was expected because of a downturn in the Korean economy.

■ **Netherlands:** The Koninklijke Luchtmacht has identified a 100+-aircraft requirement to replace its F-16AM/BM fighter force at around the end of the decade. A Request For Information was sent to Eurofighter in June 1999, and in April 2000 the KLu Chief of Staff was treated to a flight in DA4. In early 2001 NETMA (NATO Eurofighter and Tornado Management Agency) sent an invitation to the Dutch to become a participant in the Eurofighter programme in an attempt to woo them away from the JSF. The Dutch parliament is reviewing the possibility of joining the JSF programme with a decision expected in late 2001/early 2002. Dutch participation in the Typhoon programme would involve the Tranche 3 Enhanced Eurofighter production machines expected to enter service in around 2010. Even if the KLu did not purchase Typhoons, Dutch companies such as Philips, Signaal and Stork could become part of the Eurofighter production team.

■ **Norway:** Norway was one of the nations being actively courted by Eurofighter, led by EADS-Deutschland. Faced with the need to replace its F-5 and F-16A/B fleet, the Royal Norwegian Air Force looked at the Typhoon, Rafale and an updated version of the F-16 (Block 50N), with service entry planned for "no

later than 2006". Rafale was later dropped from the competition. The initial plan was to acquire 20 aircraft to replace Northrop F-5s, with another 10 as a follow-on option. Norwegian evaluation of the Typhoon included a visit by DA5 to Rygge air base in June 1998, during which compatibility with local hardened shelters was validated, assignment of a liaison officer to NETMA in October, and flights by a Norwegian pilot in December 1998 and August 1999. In May 2000 a decision was imminent, but the incoming Labour government then announced that the competition would be shelved because the money earmarked for fighter acquisition "was missing".

In February 2001 a major round of cuts was announced, reducing the air force's combat force to 48 F-16s, against protests from the air force that a minimum of 62 fighters was required. At the same time, Defence Minister Bjørn Tore Godal said that the fighter replacement programme would be reinstated, but it would not provide aircraft in time for the 2006 deadline set by the air force. By March 2001 the choice appeared to be between industrial participation (in either the JSF or Typhoon Tranche 2/3 programmes), or an off-the-shelf approach which would allow F-16, Rafale, Gripen and others to be re-evaluated, as well as JSF and Typhoon. The revised requirement is for 48 aircraft for delivery from 2008. To spread costs, this could possibly be divided between two 24-aircraft batches, one in 2008-2010 and the second in 2015-18. A further batch of 12, which would bring the overall buy much closer to the air force's requirement, is being discussed, providing that funding can be made available. If Eurofighter is selected, Norwegian

Having been laid up from December 2000 to June 2001, DA2 has resumed envelope expansion work with production-standard EJ200-03Z engines. The aircraft achieved Mach 2 on 23 December 1997, and in April 1999 topped 50,000 ft (15240 m).

industry can expect to participate strongly as a member of the manufacturing team. Kongsberg Defence and Aerospace (KDA) already builds composite rudders and flaperons for the Eurofighter, under contract to BAE SYSTEMS.

■ **Poland:** Poland issued an RFI for a long-term 60-fighter purchase in June 1999, responded to by EADS-Deutschland. The competition was still active in mid-2001, with the less expensive Gripen, Mirage 2000-5 and F-16 seen as principal contenders.

■ **Saudi Arabia:** BAE SYSTEMS leads Eurofighter's efforts in the Kingdom of Saudi Arabia. No specific requirement or timescale regarding a new air superiority fighter has been officially stated, but the Saudis are being kept informed as part of an 'awareness campaign'.

■ **Singapore:** Eurofighter was one of a number of companies which responded to a Request For Information issued by the Republic of Singapore Air Force in late 1999, covering 20-40 air superiority fighters. BAE SYSTEMS leads the sales effort. Detailed evaluations of the competing types was expected by RSAF personnel in the summer of 2001 with a view to proceeding to a Request For Proposal.

David Donald

Seen here on DA2, the starboard wing pylon houses two TRDs (towed radar decoys) for the DASS. Each is trailed on a cable to lure radar-guided missiles away from the aircraft. Another key element of the DASS – the chaff dispenser – can be seen in the rear of the outboard pylon. Flares are housed in the undersides of the flap tracks.

Alaskan Air Power
Part 2: National Guard, US Army and USCG

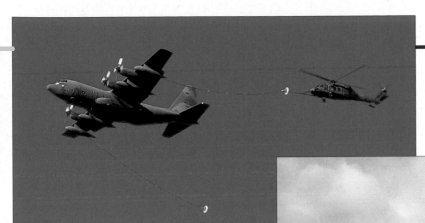

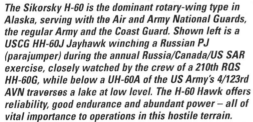

All locally-based tanker assets are operated by the Air National Guard, and consist of the Lockheed HC-130H(N) tankers of the 210th RQS (left), which refuel the squadron's rescue helicopters, and the Boeing KC-135Rs of the 168th ARS (below). The Stratotanker is seen being sprayed with de-icing fluid, a common sight at its Eielson base which, being situated in the heart of Alaska, endures some of the coldest weather of any USAF location.

The Sikorsky H-60 is the dominant rotary-wing type in Alaska, serving with the Air and Army National Guards, the regular Army and the Coast Guard. Shown left is a USCG HH-60J Jayhawk winching a Russian PJ (parajumper) during the annual Russia/Canada/US SAR exercise, closely watched by the crew of a 210th RQS HH-60G, while below a UH-60A of the US Army's 4/123rd AVN traverses a lake at low level. The H-60 Hawk offers reliability, good endurance and abundant power – all of vital importance to operations in this hostile terrain.

While the USAF is the dominant US military force in the 49th state, it by no means eclipses the importance or roles of the aviation-related forces assigned to US Army Alaska (USARAK), Coast Guard District 17 or the Alaska Air and Army National Guards. Many Alaskans, both urban and rural, along with numerous fishermen and outdoor enthusiasts, rely on the robust SAR and airlift capabilities of Alaska's smaller services to help when times are tough.

Having an inherent joint forces perspective is a prerequisite to assuming the helm of Alaskan Command (ALCOM), which also has command responsibilities extending to the Army, Coast Guard and National Guard forces within the state. ALCOM CO USAF Lieutenant General Norty Schwartz, formerly the Deputy Commander US Special Forces Command, certainly sees his role not only in dichromatic hues of silver and blue but also in the wider political and military spectra that extend from army ground-pounder green to the shadowy black of special ops and even to the deep purple of combined service efforts.

In an interview during Northern Edge 2001, a high-visibility joint force exercise focusing mainly on peace enforcement operations, Schwartz reflected on both his SOF background and its influence on his ALCOM leadership philosophy. "At the operational level of war, the art is bringing together all of the assets that one has at one's disposal and arraying them in a way that maximises their strengths and minimises their vulnerabilities. I hope that very few of us [major command commanders] are deliberately parochial – but sometimes you only know what you know. I think that one of the beauties of the community that I grew up in for most of my career is there is an irreverence – I mean not a lack of discipline, but an openness, a willingness to look at all manner of options for getting the job done. From kinetic to non-kinetic. From close to distant. That is what a joint force commander must do. He must look at all the possibilities and look at the forces he has available to decide what is the art of the possible."

Air and Army National Guards

The Alaska Air and Army National Guards are commanded by Major General Phil Oates from his headquarters in Anchorage. The Alaska Air National Guard has two main units. The 176th Wing is stationed at Kulis Air National Guard Base, co-located at the Anchorage International Airport, and comprises the 144th AS with nine Lockheed C-130Hs and the 210th RQS with six Sikorsky HH-60G Pavehawks and four HC-130Ns. The 210th RQS maintains Det 1 with one Pavehawk at Eielson to cover interior Alaskan SAR and Cope Thunder/Northern Edge-related CSAR operations. The Guard operates a Rescue Command Center at Camp Denali near Anchorage. In an average year, the RCC handles about 400 missions a year, of which about 25 per cent are covered by the 210th RQS, 25 per cent by AK ARNG Blackhawk detachments, 25 per cent by

Kulis ANGB, located across the runway from the civil terminal of Anchorage International Airport, is home to the 144th AS and 210th RQS of the 176th Wing. The Hercules from both squadrons share the main ramp, while the 210th's HH-60Gs operate from a small apron in front of the main hangar.

the Civil Air Patrol and the rest by State Troopers and local police and fire departments.

The other main AK ANG unit, the 168th ARW, is stationed at Eielson AFB and has nine Boeing KC-135R Stratotankers, one of which is kept on alert status to support air defence 12/19 FS F-15Cs. Other 168th customers include visiting US and allied aircraft deployed to Alaska for exercises, and transpolar/transpacific

transport aircraft. During last year's Eielson runway repaving, the 168th operated from Wainwright Army Airfield and the Fairbanks International Airport. The 168th offloaded 1,376,492.5 US gal (5210574.7 litres) of fuel during FY 2000 in the course of 525 sorties. This number is lower than normal because its KC-135s were undergoing the Pacer Crag conversion for four months (the upgrade programme is now completed).

The Alaska Army Guard has at its disposal 24 UH-60L Blackhawks flown by A/B/C companies of the 207th AVN (GS). Several of the Blackhawks are stationed at detachments in Bethel, Juneau and Nome. Fixed-wing assets include eight C-23B+ Sherpas, and one Beechcraft C-12F Huron (King Air 200). The Sherpas replaced the much-loved Twin Otter and, while they are well liked for their docile flying characteristics and ability to carry bulky but lightweight cargo, they have poor short-field handling, high approach speeds and 'sketchy' roll-out and braking on icy runways. Privately, many crews have expressed their desire to transfer the aircraft 'down south' where it would be better suited, and replace it with the Lockheed Martin C-27J or a Bell/Boeing V-22 variant (especially after a recent C-23B+ crash in Georgia that killed 24).

The Army Guard Operational Support Airlift Command has a small detachment at Elmendorf that flies three Beechcraft C-12Fs and two Cessna UC-35As. The ARNG is currently accept-

The 168th Air Refueling Squadron at Eielson AFB previously operated a mix of KC-135Ds and Es (the Ds were unusual in being demodified reconnaissance aircraft), but now fly Pacer Crag-updated KC-135Rs. One aircraft is kept on alert to support the air defence alert tasking of the 3rd Wing's AESA radar-equipped F-15Cs.

Left: White-out! An HH-60G Pavehawk from the 210th Rescue Squadron performs a landing on a snowfield on Mount Spurr at 11,000 ft (3350 m) altitude. At high altitude landings are made with almost no flare and with considerable forward velocity. The HH-60Gs are equipped with Bendix-King RDR-1400C colour radar.

Right: As well as providing inflight refuelling for the Pavehawks, the 210th's HC-130H(N)s also provide 'top cover' during SAR operations, and are used for long-endurance searches. They carry air-droppable survival kits, and have launcher tubes mounted on the rear ramp for dropping marker flares. The aircraft were newly-built for the 210th and incorporate several improvements compared to other HC-130 models.

Left: A Pavehawk crew delicately approaches the drogue of a 210th RQS HC-130. The squadron is nicknamed the 'Second Tenth', reflecting the traditions and reincarnation of a dedicated Alaskan rescue unit (the original unit, the 10th Air-Sea Rescue Squadron, was activated at Elmendorf in 1946).

ing the delivery of new-build HH-60L Rescuehawks fitted with a FLIR turret – making them well suited for inland Alaskan rescues, which often take place at night and in poor weather.

Major General Phil Oates is the Adjutant General of the Alaska Guard, reporting directly to the state's governor. Prior to his current job and while an active-duty Army colonel, he served as ALCOM's executive officer under Lieutenant General David McCloud who died in 1998 in the crash of his Yak-52. Oates is in a

great position to know the intimate working of Alaskan military policy and is never at a lack of words concerning his command, the military in Alaska in general, and the AK Guard in particular.

The Adjutant General is proud of the men and women under his command and rarely misses an opportunity to discuss in depth where he sees the Guard currently and where he sees it going under his command. "Alaska has some of the most challenging and diverse training areas on the planet. The environment –

mountains, seas, high desert, ice and snow, and temperatures that range from as little as -40º F [-40º C] to over 90º F [32º C] in the summer, above the Arctic Circle – adds to the beauty, drama and mystery that is Alaska. Soldiers and airmen have to be on their top form. They must face the dangers of everyday living while also meeting the challenges of their assignments. In the world of aviation – whether it is fixed wing or helicopters – the extremes of climate and conditions test metal and man. Fortunately, we have solid maintenance teams, good facilities, and a very positive attitude toward safety.

"Alaskans, by nature, tend to be gregarious, and, for the most part, they live to be outdoors. They like doing things that are worthwhile and that bring a sense of accomplishment. Aviation

As fitted to this HH-60G, ski pads are routinely added to helicopters for operations from snow as they spread the aircraft's 'footprint' when operating from soft surfaces. They are often used in summer for operations from swampy muskeg and tundra landing zones.

Right: CH-47s undertake an assault exercise on 'Simpsonville', the urban fighting exercise area located near Fort Greely. The CH-47D is used as both a troop transport and as a heavylift assault helicopter, as well as being a player in covert SOF and CSAR operations.

Left: Since the retirement of the CH-54B Tarhe from the Alaska National Guard, the CH-47s fly all heavylift tasks. Here an aircraft from the 'Sugarbears' positions a 'Hummer' alongside SUSVs (Small Unit Support Vehicles) at 'Simpsonville'.

Below: The 4/123rd AVN is unusual in being qualified for operations from US Navy ships. Here a UH-60A and CH-47D practise deck work on the USS Juneau (LPD-10). The Blackhawk is fitted with the ESSS (External Stores Support System) with fuel tanks.

is central to us. We can only get to six of our 76 units by road. We rely upon it [aviation] to get us where we need to go.

"Part of what I do includes ensuring that we have the right assets and support to meet our mission assignments. We have to work equipment acquisition or add-on issues well in advance, through the Congress and the National Guard Bureau. And we have to ensure our aircrews are trained and mission-ready to meet their federal responsibilities. I believe we have some of the very best aviators in world right here in Alaska. We're lucky that some of them are flying our Army Guard, Air Guard planes and helicopters.

"We're very fortunate that aviation is at the core of our existence in Alaska. By that I mean, you simply cannot hop on an interstate highway to go visit your folks. You're just about forced to fly to wherever family or friends are. Certainly, our business takes us aloft.

"We have some of the very highest numbers of women in our Air and Army Guard units, here in Alaska, compared to the rest of the nation's military forces, and even with a number of other countries. With over 2,000 members, more than 24 per cent of our Alaska Air Guard flying units are women. The active Air Force runs at between 13 per cent and 16 per cent. I actually believe the numbers will grow over a period of time. We're certainly seeing more women taking leadership roles, more women in the cockpit, more women in aviation support units. It is a positive trend that we clearly advocate and believe in.

"When we look at the art of the possible in our future, we know that there are some emerging roles in space operations. As an example, the Alaska Air Guard is presently working with the 11th Air Force and the North American Air Defense Command in developing a concept of operations whereby the Air Guard would assume operational responsibilities for the Battle Control Center at Elmendorf AFB and the Space Surveillance at Clear Air Force Station over the next several years. The Alaska Army

Guard, as has been widely reported, is working with the National Missile Defense Program, and as we presently believe (if approved by the President and Congress) will field and operate the initial systems here in Alaska possibly in the next four to five years."

Next-generation airlift

Under the patronage of the state's senior US senator, Ted Stevens, the AK ANG is likely to start flying the Boeing C-17A Globemaster III in the next four to five years. The aircraft would be stationed at Kulis ANGB, taking over from the C-130s of the 144th AS. In the recent past, the Guard showed interest in assuming an AC-130H Spectre role but is now likely to focus on C-17 acquisition.

Throughout the winter and spring of 2001, AK ANG/ARNG aircrews and their C-130s, C-23B+s and UH-60Ls deployed to the Central American countries of Honduras and

Guatemala to assist in humanitarian relief and logistic missions.

When questioned about the C-23B+, Oates acknowledged the type's shortcoming but stuck by the pugnacious utility aircraft. "The C-23B+ Sherpa is expected to remain as a primary support aircraft for the Alaska National Guard. It is a relatively 'stock' aircraft within the US Army inventory and thus has value in other places besides Alaska. There are some limitations for the Sherpa that are inherent in the Alaskan environment – unimproved runways and icing are the main restrictors for employment – though that is where the UH-60Ls shine. The C-27J has some aspects that could lend itself to operational value (in light of the Sherpa's shortcomings) in Alaska and other remote parts of the world. However, unless or until the Army takes some action to acquire them, the Sherpa will remain as our fixed-wing asset."

The 4/123rd's B Company flies the CH-47D from Fort Wainwright. In this inhospitable land the Chinook is of inestimable value, and is called upon to perform a myriad of tasks, including many on behalf of the civilian authorities. It is also used for rescue work in the highest of the mountains.

US Army

US Army Alaska (USARAK) is commanded by Major General James. J. Lovelace, Jr from his headquarters at Ft Richardson, which is co-located with Elmendorf AFB on the outskirts of Anchorage. The Ft Wainwright garrison is the 172nd Separate Infantry Brigade (Light) 'Snowhawks', one of three US Army Pacific early entry forces that take turns as the American '911' force in the Pacific. Army aviation units in Alaska perform many roles including assault, transport, medevac, high-altitude SAR, special forces ops and support of the AK ARNG. During NE 2001, the Fort Richardson-based 1st Battalion of the 501st Infantry conducted a mass night drop (under 4 per cent illumination) of nearly 400 infantrymen in sub-zero temperatures with not a single major injury.

All active-duty Army rotary-wing aviation units are stationed at Ft Wainwright, namely the 4/123 AVN (TAB) B Company 'Sugarbears' flying 16 Boeing Vertol CH-47D Chinooks and D Company 'Renegades' flying 15 Sikorsky UH-60A Blackhawks. Det 68 Medical Air Ambulance Company 'Dustoff' flies six UH-60A medevac Blackhawks. Although the Blackhawks are early models, excellent maintenance efforts mean the helicopters are capable of flying at rates equal to or exceeding 'lower 48' UH-60 units. The 4/123 is one a handful of Army units that maintains current deck landing

Dustoff! USARAK has six dedicated medevac UH-60As at its command, assigned to the 68 MedCo. Examples are seen here deck landing on Juneau (right) and involved in a Northern Edge combined arms exercise (below). Until recently, the ArNG unit at Fort Richardson had a MedCo attached, equipped with UH-1Hs.

qualifications for operation with Navy surface units. The unit makes every effort to perform DLQs (deck landing qualification) whenever a Navy amphibious warfare ship is in Alaskan waters. Chinooks from the unit provide high-altitude rescue and logistics on Mt Denali up to a height of 17,000 ft (5180 m) – on several occasions, overflights of the summit at altitudes approaching 21,000 ft (6400 m) have occurred.

Army aircrews wear standard issue flight suits and survival vests, but most fliers carry extra survival gear on their persons (such as hand-held GPS units) and few are seen boarding aircraft without a stuffed B-3 bag or rucksack of extra clothes, food and sleeping bag. Crews wear the new issue HGU-56P helmet, use AN/PVS-6 NVGs, and carry standard 9-mm Beretta semi-automatic pistols. (Due to the numbers and sizes of polar, grizzly, brown and black bears, a standard joke among Alaskan aircrews is to tell newcomers that they should file off the front sight of the pistol. When asked why, the reply is inevitably, "So it won't hurt so much when the bear shoves it up your ass.")

Alaska plays host to the massive Northern Edge exercise, which draws in units from other areas of the world to take advantage of the huge unrestricted exercise and live-fire facilities. Here a pair of Apaches 'unmasks' to fire live AGM-114 missiles. The plume is normally undetectable, but not so in Alaska's cold.

The Chinooks are equipped with door guns (designations), as are the Blackhawks – many of which fly with the External Stores System and extra fuel tanks as a standard configuration.

Ft Wainwright's field, known as Wainwright Army Airfield or Ladd Army Airfield, has one 8,500-ft (2590-m) runway oriented 06/24. In addition to Army aircraft, firebombers use the base and NASA's Lockheed ER-2 flies from the field when conducting polar missions. Due to the resurfacing of the Eielson runway during most of 2000, the 354th FW flew both its F-16CG/DGs and A/OA-10As from Ladd Field. The move necessitated the cancellation of all but one Cope Thunder in 2000.

Although Ft Greely is due to be closed in 2001, it may become the home of the US's NMD interceptors at some point in the near future.

Currently, the base is minimally manned but is a player in Cope Thunder/Northern Edge exercises due to its proximity to the restricted ranges and impact areas. Greely has three runways: one 7,500 ft (2286 m) oriented 18/36, one 6,100 ft (1860 m) heading 06/27, and an ancillary runway oriented 24/09 which is 4,600 ft (1400 m) long.

Bryant Army Airfield at Ft Richardson is home to AK ARNG Sikorsky UH-60L Blackhawks and Shorts C-23B+s. The compacted gravel strip is just long enough for Sherpa operations, at 2,900 ft (884 m), and is oriented 16/34. Although not garnering much high-profile media coverage, USARAK continues to pursue its daily training for any contingency that could occur in the Pacific Basin, while maintaining a readily apparent level of professionalism and *esprit de corps*.

In that light, it comes as no surprise that Major General Lovelace takes every opportunity to spotlight his force's capabilities and

achievements. "The Army aviation forces here in Alaska are among the best in the world, and their physical location here provides four tangible benefits: they train with the forces they will deploy with; they are acquainted with the Pacific Theatre; they have formed relationships with our allies in the region; and they gain valuable, unique skills from the Alaskan environment. We have among the best aviation units in the world here. I am extremely proud of these fine aviators' versatility and dedication to mission accomplishment no matter what the challenge. Great aviators is what makes a great aviation unit. What I would like to see is upgraded equipment and facilities, but that is not a unique desire; that is what all commanders ask for."

US Coast Guard

Coast Guard District 17, headquartered in Juneau, is commanded by Rear Admiral Thomas Barrett. Barrett is also the Commander

Naval Forces Alaska and, in that capacity, reports directly to CO ALCOM. The USAF and Army have more personnel, larger bases and higher visibility, but it is the Coast Guard that has the greatest direct effect on most Alaskans. This is not surprising, considering the state's enormous coastal area and the high number of commercial fishermen and small boat users. CCGD 17's AOR encompasses 3,853,500 sq miles (10 million km²) extending from 40º North latitude to the North Pole, and spans the Pacific from 3 miles (5 km) off the eastern Russian Coast to Canada's western coast. Due to the 200-mile (320-km) Exclusive Economic Zone and the state's unique geography, CCGD 17's law enforcement coverage exceeds 950,000 sq miles (2.5 million km²).

There are two air stations in Alaska. CGAS Kodiak is equipped with six Lockheed HC-130H Hercules used for SAR, long-range maritime and law enforcement patrol and logistics. Most Hercules law and treaty enforcement

OSACOM's (Operational Support Airlift Command) Alaska Regional Flight Center at Elmendorf AFB operates two Cessna UC-35As for fast staff transport. The UC-35A is based on the Citation Ultra executive jet.

Replacing the much-missed UV-18A Twin Otters with the ArNG's 207th AVN is the Shorts C-23B+ Sherpa. This is a reworked Shorts 360 with twin fins instead of the original single fin. The main role is supplying the outlying garrisons at Bethel, Juneau and Nome.

Alaskan Air Power: Part 2

Workhorse of the USCG's long-range patrol effort in Alaska is the now-elderly and overstretched HC-130H Hercules fleet. As well as SAR searches, the aircraft undertake maritime surveillance, law enforcement and environmental protection patrols. The HC-130s are fitted with the APS-137 inverse SAR radar (as used in the P-3 and S-3) for maritime searches. Another task is the transport of fuel and equipment to remote sites to extend the operational reach of the HH-60J helicopters. The 17th District's six Hercules are based at Kodiak (right), but are regular visitors to Sitka (below).

patrols occur at mid to low level – further stressing the ageing airframes. CGAS Kodiak's rotary-wing assets include four Sikorsky HH-60J Jayhawks that are the workhorse of the Alaskan SAR fleet. Considering the vastness of Alaska, the Jayhawks' lack of flight-refuelling capability, coupled with a 300-mile (480-km) action radius, makes some long-range rescues exceedingly difficult. In order to accomplish the missions, HC-130Hs carry fuel in bladders to a remote site, or the helicopter crew will utilise civilian fuel supplies or pre-positioned fuel stores. The Jayhawks' other roles include patrol, law enforcement, surveillance and naval CSAR. Five Eurocopter (Aérospatiale) HH-65A Dolphins are assigned to CGAS Kodiak and, on average, two are deployed on 'Hamilton'-class 378-ft (115-m) high-endurance cutters for ALPAT (Alaska Patrol) duties. During the summer fishing season, one HH-60J from either Kodiak or Sitka is deployed to a small Aviation Facility in the eastern Gulf of Alaska hamlet of Cordova. CGAS Kodiak and the associated support facility for the four cutters based there is the largest facility in the entire Coast Guard.

Air Station Sitka is located on the Pacific coast in the southeast panhandle and normally has three HH-60Js on call. Long-range icebreakers working in Alaskan waters on polar opera-

Swimmer away! One of Sitka's Jayhawks drops a rescue swimmer during a training exercise. The HH-60J is the USCG's standard MRR (medium-range recovery) platform, having replaced the Sikorsky HH-3F Pelican.

tions carry two HH-65As from USCG Polar Aviation Detachment 143 in Mobile, Alabama and can always be tasked by district headquarters to perform SAR and LE flights as needed. District 17 has the closest direct communication ties between the US and the Russian Federation of any unit in the US armed forces. Due to the mutual SAR and fisheries enforcement needs of both counties, and the shared boundaries in the Bering Sea, a direct line is available from the Rescue Coordination Center in Juneau to Russian Federal Border Guard units in the Russian far east (Vladivostok and Petropavlovsk). The line is commercial and the RCC watch-standers use ATT voice translation services or e-mail to bridge language problems (watch-standers prefer e-mail in English, as it is less ambiguous). The shortcomings of Russian forces and their inability to perform certain tasks when called upon mean that this link has resulted in several rescues being conducted after case data and permission was transmitted to Alaskan USCG units, who performed the recoveries.

Due to the seasonal lighting conditions, esoteric commercial fish harvesting schedules and harrowing weather and sea conditions, Alaskan USCG helicopter and C-130 crews often have to brave seas exceeding 50 ft (15 m) and winds so strong they break wind meters. Numerous awards and medals, both military and civilian, have been bestowed upon Alaskan CG helicopter flight crews, and a common

sentiment among them is that if you can handle Alaskan maritime SAR operations, flying anywhere else is a cakewalk.

Pilots and aircrew are required to attend and complete USCG seashore and adverse training. Hercules crews wear the standard CG blue Nomex flight suit and carry additional survival suits and gear in B-4 bags. Helicopter crews wear the tight-fitting, flame-resistant and waterproof aircrew dry coverall (ADC) made by Switlick that has rubber gaskets on the wrists, ankles and neck. The ADC is currently being replaced by a new model manufactured by Multifab. They also wear the standard GC helicopter helmet to which the AN/PVS-6 NVG can be fitted, along with the LPU-26/PE survival vest and the HEEDS three-minute emergency oxygen supply device (also used by Army crew). Rescue swimmers wear dry suits and use standard off-the-shelf US diver masks and flippers, and carry a waterproof Uniden HH-940 radio in a small dry bag. Alaskan CG aircrews do not carry small arms but boarding party officers may carry Beretta 9-mm pistols under their Mustang full-body insulated work suits.

The Juneau RCC handled 1,114 cases in FY 1998, 911 in FY 1999 and, as of August, 1,140 in 2000. In addition to high-seas rescues, the USCG provides medevac services for rural villages, fish camps, hunters and cruise ship passengers, and is credited with saving 367 lives in FY 1999. In FY 2000, District 17 conducted 816 SAR cases and is credited with 220 lives saved and 234 lives assisted.

Hercules upgrades

Alaskan USCG forces are stretched thin in many instances and are routinely over-tasked. Some aircraft – particularly the HC-130Hs – wear out, suffer high breakdown rates and require intensive maintenance (though the Hercules are slated to be upgraded with a pallet-mounted electro-optical and FLIR system in the next couple of years, and an engine upgrade has been discussed but not funded). According to RADM Barrett, the only reason that missions are not cancelled is, "The amazing efforts of our maintainers. Some of these people are 20 years old and responsible for an aircraft worth millions of dollars and the lives of the people who fly them ... and it is because of their tireless efforts that we are able to do the job day in and day out. Sure, we could use new airplanes and systems, but in this current budget environment we have to do with what we have. We need another aircraft (HH-60J) in Sitka and the 130s need help or replacement. Unfortunately, like all the other services, we are facing the need to replace equipment and the problem of retaining people – though Coast Guardsmen and women in Alaska love it here and are always asking to stay longer. Retention and aircraft condition is a problem but we overcome it with hard work and the commitment to

our mission, which is to save lives. Despite those problems we are able to accomplish the missions in the extreme environment that is Alaska. Our people shine and I am amazed and proud at what they achieve."

US Navy

With the early 1990s closure of Adak NAS, located mid-way along the Aleutian Island arc, no US naval aircraft are stationed in Alaska. When the Adak-based P-3C Orions departed, the last nuclear weapons in Alaska (approximately 50 B57 depth bombs) were transferred as well. EP-3 variants flew clandestine missions from Eareckson AFS on Shemya Island into the mid-1990s. Although no USN aircraft currently call Alaska home, EA-6B Prowlers, E-2C Hawkeyes, SH-60F Seahawks, USN and USMC F/A-18s (serving as DACT aggressors) and USMC KC-130Ts are frequent participants in Cope Thunder and Northern Edge exercises. Navy/US STRATCOM Boeing E-6B Mercury TACAMO aircraft make periodic calls at Elmendorf AFB – not surprising, considering the Gulf of Alaska is a main Trident SSBN bastion. Due to PACOM commander Admiral Dennis Blair's impressions of the training and growth possibilities of Alaska, and in particular of Northern Edge during NE 2000, there is a possibility of an increased naval aviation presence, and a carrier battle group may join the exercise in the 2002-2005 time range. The 3rd Fleet has been designated the lead organisation in the Pacific for developing new joint command and control capabilities, and is to function as a JTF commander during future Northern Edges.

Mark Farmer

Above: An HH-60J hovers close to the USCG cutter Sedge *during a SAREX. The HH-60J is based on the Navy's HH-60H Rescue Hawk but lacks combat equipment. Jayhawks are fitted with Bendix/ King RDR-1300 weather radar in the nose 'thimble', and routinely carry three 120-US gal (454-litre) fuel tanks (two to port, one to starboard). The asymmetric load is dictated by the need for clearance for the winch mounted above the starboard cabin door. An alternative load on the starboard pylon is the Spectrolab Nitesun searchlight. The cockpit lighting is NVG-compatible for nocturnal operations.*

Right: The standard USCG shipborne helicopter is the HH-65A Dolphin, also used for short-range SAR from its shore base at Kodiak. In Alaskan waters Dolphins can be found flying from the locally-based cutters, detached from CGAS Kodiak, or from icebreakers. In the latter case they are deployed from CGAS Mobile's AvDet 143 'Arctic Wolfpack', to which this aircraft is attached.

Tu-160 'Blackjack'
Russia's 'Big Stick'

The vast bulk of Tu-160 no. 05 Ilya Muromets settles on to the Engels runway. In the background is a row of around 30 Tu-22 'Blinders' which await the scrapman's torch. In the bleak economic reality of the 1990s, the 'Blackjack' seemed to be doomed to be just another footnote in the history of the Soviet/ Russian military machine, despite its awesome capabilities. Yet at the end of the decade a hardening of Russian foreign policy and a strengthening of the resolve to maintain capable military forces has breathed new life into the programme, although the required funds have yet to filter through to the operational fleet in any significant amount.

Following the end of World War II, a bipolar political system was established in the world in which the US and the USSR represented opposite ideologies. The military priority for both countries was the possession of intercontinental weapons capable of hitting the other on its own territory, which became even more urgent when arsenals were supplied with nuclear bombs having devastating effect yet comparatively light weight. The 1950s was a time of particularly hectic activity into means of intercontinental delivery for nuclear bombs, and over the next dozen or so years many options for achieving this task were proposed. The Soviets began work on an intercontinental supersonic bomber in 1952.

In a task assigned to aircraft designers on 19 July 1955, the range of the future aircraft was stipulated as 11000 to 12000 km (5,940 to 6,480 nm) at a supersonic cruising speed of 1700 to 1800 km/h (918 to 972 kt), or 14000 to 15000 km (7,560 to 8,100 nm) with inflight refuelling. Myasishchev's design bureau built a prototype of the M-50 'Bounder' supersonic bomber, but it could hardly be considered a success. The M-50A, first tested in flight on 27 October 1959, made only 23 flights, and its maximum performance figures were a speed of 1050 km/h (567 kt) and a range of 3150 km (1,700 nm). Further tests were cancelled.

The contemporary stage in the history of Soviet strategic bombers began in 1967. Two years before this date, Nikita

Khrushchev, who did not think highly of air forces and who stopped many developing aviation programmes, left active political life. Also, in 1965, the US formulated a specification for a new AMSA (Advanced Manned Strategic Aircraft), the future B-1. With consideration to the existing XB-70 Valkyrie bomber, as well as the new AMSA, the Soviet government announced on 28 November 1967 a competition for a strategic bomber with very high technical parameters. The aircraft was to reach 11000 to 13000 km (5,940 to 7,020 nm) and have a supersonic cruising speed of 3200 to 3500 km/h (1,728 to 1,890 kt) at an altitude of 18000 m (54,864 ft). The maximum range at subsonic speed was to be 16000 to 18000 km (8,640 to 9,720 nm) at high altitude or 11000 to 13000 km (5,940 to 7,020 nm) at sea level. The basic armament of the aircraft was to be nuclear missiles, including heavy Kh-45s and small Kh-2000s. New types of conventional and nuclear bombs were options for alternative armament.

Sukhoi's proposal

The design bureaux of Pavel Sukhoi and Vladimir Myasishchev contested the first stage of the competition. Sukhoi's design bureau in Moscow, formally named at the time as Moscow Engineering Plant 'Kulon' (Coulomb) (and before 1966 known as OKB-52, Opytno-Konstruktorskoye Byuro, Test-Design Bureau), specialised in tactical aircraft, and this work on heavy bombers was a one-off. The first

A true son of the free-spending Cold War era and the latest in a long and distinguished line of heavy bombers from the Tupolev design bureau, the Tu-160 'Blackjack' remains in limited service and sporadic production. The tiny operational fleet is crippled by a lack of money, and rarely flies. Yet only a fool would discount the 'Blackjack' from their military plans: the Tu-160 is the heaviest and most powerful combat aircraft in the world by a considerable margin. It has true global reach, and can release its deadly cargo of nuclear cruise missiles with great precision. Following the lead of its smaller counterparts in the US Air Force, the 'Blackjack' is belatedly adopting conventional capabilities to occupy a more versatile position in the post-Cold War Russian air force.

Sukhoi design made maximum utilisation of components already prepared for the T-4 (*izdeliye* 100) Mach 3 medium bomber. Recognising the necessity of a variable-geometry wing in the optimum design of a heavy multi-purpose aircraft, Sukhoi's designers simply replaced the delta-shaped wing of the T-4 aircraft with a variable-geometry one. In this form, and named T-4M, the project was ready in 1968.

The T-4M (M standing for modification) had a length of 50 m (164 ft), wingspan ranging from 22.5 m (73 ft 10 in) (at sweep of 72°) to 43.4 m (142 ft 5 in) (sweep of 15°); the take-off weight was from 131000 kg (288,800 lb) (normal) to 149000 kg (328,483 lb) (maximum), including an armament weight of 4000 kg (8,818 lb) for a single Kh-45 missile to 18000 kg (39,682 lb) for bombs. With four Kolesov/Rybinsk RD36-41 turbojet engines, the aircraft's maximum speed was 3200 km/h (1,728 kt), whereas the cruising speed would be 3000 to 3200 km/h (1,619 to 1,728 kt) at an altitude of 20000 to 23000 m (65,620 to 75,460 ft). The designed supersonic range was 7000 km (3,780 nm); subsonic range was 10000 km (5,400 nm) at high altitude and 3500 km (1,890 nm) at low altitude. The maximum range of 16000 km (8,640 nm) required by the armed forces was possible at subsonic speed only with two inflight refuellings.

Drawbacks of the T-4M's design were soon disclosed. The whole armament had to be carried outside the airframe because the packet arrangement of the engines meant that the internal armament chamber could not be installed without increasing the aircraft's size. The necessary rigidity of the long outer parts of the wings could not be attained. The T-4M project was subjected to design corrections up to the end of 1969, but eventually Sukhoi gave it up in favour of the next aircraft.

Although the new project was named T-4MS (S for strategic), or *izdeliye* 200, it had nothing in common with the original T-4. As the result of research work, a variable-

'Blackjack' crews are the elite of the Russian long-range air force, but they receive very little flying due to lack of funds. The cockpits of early production aircraft were only partially pressurised, requiring the use of pressure suits for high-altitude operations.

geometry flying wing was conceived, with high lift-to-drag ratio and great airframe capacity that could be used for fuel and equipment. The airframe of the T-4MS consisted of a middle wing and small movable wing ends. The mid-wing aspect ratio was 0.5 and the relative thickness was 6 per cent. The aerodynamic torsion, equal to -3.5 per cent at the mid-wing ends, was selected for minimum balancing drag at a speed of 3200 km/h (1,728 kt). The relative thickness of movable parts of the wings varied from 11 per cent near mid-wing to 7 per cent at the ends. The sweep could be adjusted from 30º to 72º. Model tests of the aircraft in the TsAGI (Central Aero- and Hydrodynamics Institute) wind tunnel revealed a very high lift-to-drag ratio: 17.5 at Mach 0.8 and 7.3 at Mach 3.0. The propulsion system of the T-4MS was to consist initially of four RD36-41 turbojet engines rated at 156.9 kN (35,280 lb thrust) each, which later were to be replaced by K-101 engines of Nikolai Kuznetsov design, each 196.1 kN (44,094 lb thrust). The crew, consisting of two pilots and a navigator/system operator, was located in a common cockpit in the aircraft nose.

The dimensions of the T-4MS were as follows: length 41.2 m (135 ft 2 in), maximum wingspan 40.8 m (133 ft 1 in) (at sweep angle of 30°), minimum wingspan 25 m (82 ft) (at sweep angle of 72°), height 8.0 m (26 ft 3 in), lifting surface area 482.3 to 506.5 m² (5,191.6 to 5,452.1 ft), undercarriage track 6.0 m (19 ft 8 in) and undercarriage base 12.0 m (39 ft 4 in). The 170000-kg (374,780-lb) design take-off weight of the aircraft included 63000 kg (138,890 lb) for the airframe, 97000 kg (213,845 lb) of fuel and 9000 kg (19,841 lb) of armament. Maximum design speed

was 3200 km/h (1,728 kt), cruising speed at high altitude was 3000 to 3200 km/h (1,620 to 1,728 kt), maximum speed at low altitude was 1100 km/h (594 kt), and cruising speed at low altitude was 850 km/h (459 kt). The aircraft's practical ceiling was 24000 m (78,740 ft). Its range at 3000 km/h (1,620 kt) and an altitude of 20000 to 24000 m (65,618 to 78,740 ft) was 9000 km (4,860 nm) (or 7500 km/4,050 nm with temporary RD36-41 engines), range at subsonic speed and an altitude of 11000 m (36,090 ft) was 14000 km (7,560 nm) (or 11000 km/5,940 nm with RD-36-41s), its take-off run was 1100 m (3,609 ft) and landing run was 950 m (3,117 ft).

On strategic missions, typically two Kh-45 missiles were to be carried inside the bomb bay (total weight 9000 kg/ 19,840 lb). Two other missiles of the same type could be carried externally, between the engine nacelles. An alternative variant of the aircraft was to carry 24 short-range Kh-2000 missiles externally. Total maximum warload was to be 45 tonnes (99,180 lb) (at the cost of the fuel, since the maximum take-off weight was limited to 170 tonnes/ 374,680 lb).

Myasishchev's proposal

Myasishchev's design bureau, which disbanded in 1960 at the same time as it stopped work on the M-50 'Bounder', was reinstated in October 1966 under the new name EMZ (Experimentalnyi Mashinostroitelnyi Zavod, Experimental Engineering Plant). In 1967-68 Myasishchev worked under the designation M-20 on four different projects for supersonic strategic bombers. He started with variable-geometry winged aircraft in a classical configuration, with engines installed in the rear part of fuselage and air intakes at the sides or under the fuselage. This configuration was similar to prototypes of the F-111 or MiG-23 flying at the time (but much larger) and covered projects M20-1, M20-2, M20-5 and M20-6, all known by the common name of M-20 variant I.

The next configuration – M-20 variant II – was a canard with a considerable mid-wing sweep and less-swept wing panels. A characteristic feature of this project was wingtips that deflected down when flying at high speed. The variants of this project featured different engine arrangements (e.g., a packet at the rear part of the fuselage or in separate nacelles under the mid-wing), as well as different tailfins (single or double). Such variants as M20-7, M20-10, M20-11, M20-12, M20-14 and M20-15 fell within this project. The next series of projects included the M20-16, M20-17, M20-18, M20-19 and M20-21 (known collectively as M-20 variant III), which were canards with variable-geometry

Sukhoi Mach 3 bomber projects

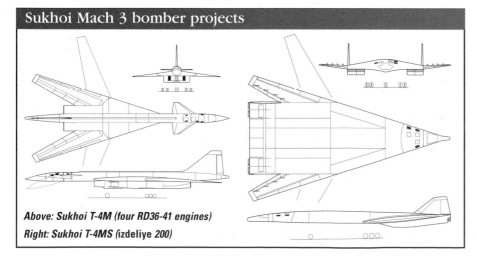

Above: Sukhoi T-4M (four RD36-41 engines)
Right: Sukhoi T-4MS (izdeliye 200)

Myasishchev M-20 studies

M20-2 (M-20 variant I)

M20-14 (M-20 variant II)

M20-18 (M-20 variant III)

M20-23 (M-20 variant IV)

Above and below: M20-21 (M-20 variant III)

wings and four to six engines under the rear part of fuselage or inside it. The differences between these variants were insignificant. The fourth configuration, M-20 variant IV (variants M20-22 and M20-23), was an aircraft with a variable-geometry wing in conventional configuration and with four engines located in separate nacelles under the mid-wing, very similar to both the American AMSA design and to later Tu-160s .

The idea of wing flow laminarisation via blown air on the wing surface appeared in two Myasishchev project variants: M20-9 with a triangular wing, and M20-4 with a swept wing. All the M-20 variants had a take-off weight of 300 to 325 tonnes (661,200 to 705,280 lb) (or up to 345 tonnes/760,380 lb with additional fuel tanks).

Tupolev's Mach 2.3 bomber

Tupolev (formally the Moscow Engineering Plant 'Opyt', meaning experience or test) had been known as OKB-156 before 1966. In 1970 the design bureau joined Sukhoi and Myasishchev in the quest for a supersonic strategic bomber. His design team stood the best chance of building the

aircraft, given the bureau's familiarity with such types dating to the 1930s. Tupolev began designing his aircraft in quite a different way – less concerned about the requirements of the air forces, and demanding that the specifications be adjusted to feasible limits. The essential change concerned the aircraft speed. According to Tupolev, the increase in combat potential of an aircraft at Mach 3.0 to

Aircraft '29', one of the 'Blackjack' prototypes, blasts off in front of a packed house at the MosaeroShow at Zhukovskiy. With a light fuel load and no weapons the Tu-160 has power in abundance. At a typical light take-off weight (150 tonnes) the Tu-160 has a very healthy thrust:weight ratio of 0.66:1. This combines with the battery of high-lift devices on the wing to produce astonishing climb performance at low speeds, making for an impressive airshow spectacle. More importantly, from an operational point of view, it allows the Tu-160 to fly heavyweight missions from relatively short airfields, although the amount of specialist ground equipment required hinders the aircraft's mobility considerably.

Tupolev 160M (*izdeliye* L) designs

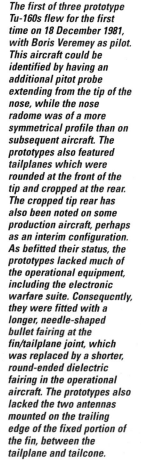

Above and left: An early 160M configuration had packaged engines and rounded wingtips.

Above: An interim 160M design with folding wingtips and split engine pairs.

The final 160M design iteration (above and below left) had cropped wingtips and split engine pairs. It showed a close resemblance to the Tu-244 advanced SST design (below).

---

airliner, developed in parallel, were very similar; they shared the requirement for as great a range as possible when flying at supersonic speed at high altitude. Both aircraft took the form of a triangular flying wing with a smooth blending between the wing and fuselage, which ensured, according to calculations, a lift:drag ratio of 7 to 9 at supersonic speed and up to 15 for subsonic speed. In August 1972, Tupolev ordered the Rybinsk RD36-51 (*izdeliye* 61) non-afterburning turbojet engine for both the Tu-160 bomber and the passenger-carrying Tu-144D. The engine's thrust was 225.6 to 235.4 kN (50,727 to 52,931 lb), its weight was 4200 kg (9,260 lb) and fuel consumption was 1.23 to 1.24 lb/lbfh (pound of fuel burned per pound aircraft weight per flying hour) (when flying at Mach 2.2 at an altitude of 18000 m/59,055 ft). The engine was ready in 1978; it passed ground tests but was never used for flying because, in the meantime, other engines were chosen for the Tu-160 and the Tu-144 programme was cancelled.

In 1972 the air forces assessed Sukhoi's T-4MS and Myasishchev's M-20 projects, and decided that Sukhoi was the winner. Nevertheless, none of the projects met the air forces' requirements (and it may be supposed that the actual performances would have been even worse than those calculated in the designs). It was obvious that aircraft able to meet the required characteristics could not be made. The second stage of the competition began in the same year, when the air forces approved a reduction of the maximum speed to Mach 2.3. Tupolev's projects were compatible with this speed, enabling his flying-wing project 160M to take part in the second stage of the competition. Myasishchev proposed an M-18 bomber with a variable-geometry wing, apparently identical to the last, fourth variant of the M-20 project but made of aluminium instead of titanium, and capable of a maximum speed of Mach 2.3. Sukhoi decided to concentrate on fighter aircraft, giving up the competition for the strategic bomber.

Project gains form

The air forces chose Myasishchev's M-18 project with its variable-geometry wing, a project also supported by TsAGI and the Technological-Scientific Council of the Ministry of Air Industry. Tupolev's proposal lost because a flying wing is a single-mode aircraft, optimised for a specific speed and altitude (in this case, 2500 km/h; 1,350 kt at an altitude of 18000m/59,055 ft). The air forces approved the reduction of the maximum speed, but the requirement for a maximum range of 14000 to 16000 km (7,559 to 8,639 nm) was, for them, beyond discussion. Moreover, the aircraft was to

---

3.2 (3200 to 3500 km/h; 1,728 to 1,890 kt), compared with an aircraft at Mach 2.3 (2500 km/h; 1,350 kt), did not offset the cost of its construction and the associated technological risk. Therefore, his project – named Aircraft 160 (but initially known as Aircraft 156) – was designed for the maximum speed of Mach 2.3 (2500 km/h).

In 1970-72 Tupolev prepared a series of designs for the 160M (*izdeliye* L) bomber, designated L-1, L-2, etc., configured as a delta-shaped flying wing. At the same time, he continued tests of the Tu-144 supersonic airliner and began preliminary work on a second-generation supersonic transport known as Tu-244. The 160M bomber and the 244

The first of three prototype Tu-160s flew for the first time on 18 December 1981, with Boris Veremey as pilot. This aircraft could be identified by having an additional pitot probe extending from the tip of the nose, while the nose radome was of a more symmetrical profile than on subsequent aircraft. The prototypes also featured tailplanes which were rounded at the front of the tip and cropped at the rear. The cropped tip rear has also been noted on some production aircraft, perhaps as an interim configuration. As befitted their status, the prototypes lacked much of the operational equipment, including the electronic warfare suite. Consequently, they were fitted with a longer, needle-shaped bullet fairing at the fin/tailplane joint, which was replaced by a shorter, round-ended dielectric fairing in the operational aircraft. The prototypes also lacked the two antennas mounted on the trailing edge of the fixed portion of the fin, between the tailplane and tailcone.

be capable of getting to the target following a compound flight profile: most of the route was to be flown at subsonic speed at high altitude, but the 2000-km (1,080-nm) zone of anti-aircraft defence was to be circumvented by flying at 2500 km/h (1,350 kt) at high altitude or at 1000 km/h (540 kt) near the ground. The aircraft could not be too particular about airfields and had to be capable of deployment to more than the longest airstrips in the Soviet Union.

All these demands could only be met by an aircraft with a variable-geometry wing. Its medium position ensured long range at subsonic cruise speed, full sweep enabled high supersonic speed, and full spread during take-off allowed an increase in the weight of fuel and armament. Calculations indicated that, at supersonic speed, the range of an aircraft with a variable-geometry wing was similar to that of an aircraft with a fixed delta wing – but at subsonic speeds, range was 35-35 per cent greater. The aerodynamic configuration, which eventually was accepted for the Tu-160, has a lift:drag ratio of 18.5 to 19 when flying at subsonic speed and 6.0 at supersonic speed.

The use of a variable-geometry wing, particularly in such a heavy aircraft, led to a more sophisticated structure and increased weight due to structural nodes and pivoting gear. A new quality of technology was necessary for the application of variable geometry in the Tu-160, and a special state programme co-ordinated directly by Piotr Dementyev, Minister of Air Industry, was launched to create a new metallurgic technology. Production of large, very strong components was prepared, as was unique tooling to produce structural details, including vacuum welding of titanium alloys.

Myasishchev's winning design was completed by Tupolev because the former's team was just too small to bring it to fruition. In 1973 Tupolev prepared the first design of the Tu-160 (*izdeliye* K) with a variable-geometry wing using the general layout of Myasishchev's M-18. In successive projects, the design was gradually improved and began to resemble more closely the present Tu-160. After selection of the general layout and basic parameters of the new bomber, the Tupolev bureau, plus the scientific institutes of the air forces and Ministry of Air Industry, began selecting aircraft systems and structural elements.

The engine parameters specified according to the expected profile of flight were to be afterburning turbofans with a bypass ratio between 1 and 2. At first, NK-25 engines from the Tu-22M3 'Backfire-C' bomber were tried for the new bomber (the flight tests of this engine began in 1974).

The NK-25's thrust (245.18 kN/55,130 lb with afterburning) was sufficient, but its great consumption of fuel gave no expectation that it would attain the required range. Therefore, in 1977, the design team of Nikolai Kuznetsov of Samara (then Kuibyshev) began work on the NK-32 three-shaft turbofan engine that made use of many elements of the NK-25; it would have the same thrust, but fuel consumption rates of 0.72 to 0.73 lb/lbfh in subsonic cruise flight and 1.7 lb/lbfh at supersonic speed. The first flying tests of NK-32 engines were carried out in 1980 under the fuselage of a Tu-142 testbed, and series production began in 1983. Plans to install the modern and economical Kuznetsov NK-74 engines in the Tu-160 did not extend beyond the design stage.

Powerplant configuration

Tupolev considered 14 different variants of engine arrangement, including four engines arranged in pairs one above the other, four engines in a common nacelle under the fuselage, and three separate engines with round air intakes. Eventually, four engines were arranged in pairs and installed under the mid-wing (with a free space between them for armament bays) with two-dimensional vertical-wedge inlets.

The formal documents ordering construction of the Tu-160 by Tupolev's design team comprised two resolutions of the USSR Council of Ministers, dated 26 June 1974 and 19 December 1975. According to these documents, the Tu-160 was to be a multi-mode strategic missile carrier powered by four NK-32 engines. Its practical range with two Kh-45 missiles (a weight of 9000 kg/19,840 lb) at subsonic speed was set at 14000 to 16000 km (7,560 to

Bort 29, a 'sting'-tailed prototype, turns sharply as the gear cleans up after take-off. Despite its size the Tu-160 is surprisingly agile at low speeds. In this regime roll control is effected by outboard ailerons (which also droop for extra lift) and overwing spoiler sections. At medium/high speeds, when the flaps are retracted and the wings are swept back to the intermediate or full-swept position, roll control is handled by the differentially moving tailplanes. This view emphasises how far back the engines are mounted, necessary for centre of gravity requirements, and also shows the unusual wing fence surface in its low-speed, flat position. Hinging this surface solves the problem of where to 'park' the trailing-edge section of the outer panel when it is swept back: in the Boeing B-1B the same portion fits into a slot fitted with an inflatable rubber seal and a hinging cover.

Myasishchev M-18 design

 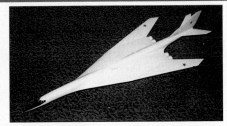

The M-18 was the eventual winner of the advanced bomber competition, although its development was subsequently entrusted to Tupolev. The M-18 was very similar to the final M-20 configuration, but was designed for Mach 2.3 flight rather than for the Mach 3 demanded of the earlier series.

Above: The first prototype Tu-160 is seen how it appears today at Zhukovskiy, derelict and missing its tailplanes, among other components.

Right: The original weapon envisaged for the Tu-160 was the massive Raduga Kh-45 missile, of which two were to be carried internally, as shown in this model. Two more were planned to be carried on wing pylons on short-range missions. The Kh-45, of which a handful were built and tested, was a supersonic weapon which employed inertial mid-course guidance and active radar over the final 90 km (56 miles) or so of its flight. The 'Blackjack' was again considered for carrying two giant missiles in the Tu-160M project of the early 1980s, which involved a lengthened fuselage to house a pair of 5000-km (3,107-mile) 3M25 Meteorit-As. Both missile projects were cancelled.

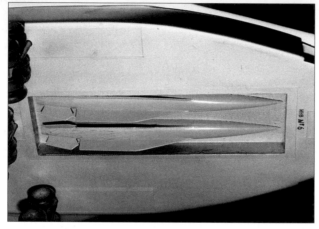

During the drawn-out process which resulted in today's Tu-160, the design underwent many changes. One of the main areas of contention was the engine configuration. This model, while resembling the final form in many areas, has large wedge-shaped variable-area ramp intakes at the wing roots. The wedge shape was retained for the final iteration, but was turned on its side so that the intakes could be positioned beneath the wings.

8,640 nm), and range in variable-profile flight (including 2000 km/1,080 nm at supersonic speed or at high subsonic speed at an altitude of 50 to 200 m/164 to 656 ft) was to be 12000 to 13000 km (6,480 to 7,020 nm). Maximum speed was specified in the resolution at 2300 to 2500 km/h (1,242 to 1,350 kt) and speed at low altitude was 1000 km/h (540 kt), ceiling was 18000 to 20000 m (59,055 to 65,617 ft), and maximum weight of the armament was 40000 kg (88,183 lb).

Aleksei Tupolev (son of Andrei Tupolev, founder of the design bureau) was in charge of the work on the Tu-160 during its early period. At the initial design phase, in 1975, Valentin Bliznyuk was appointed as chief designer (and is still in charge of this programme); his closest assistant was Lev Bazenkov. During work on the Tu-160, Georgiy Cheryomukhin was in charge of the aerodynamic department, Vyacheslav Sulimenkov – structural strength department, Vadim Razumikhin – control system department, and Semyon Vigdorchik – engineering department. Construction of the mid-wing and wing pivoting node was under the direction of Daniil Gapeyev, construction of landing gear – Yakov Livshits, construction of airframe structure – Iosiph Nezval. Valentin Klimov was the head of the Tupolev branch office at Zhukovskiy near Moscow, Anatoliy Yashukov was the prototype test engineer, Andrei Misheykov was the chief engineer at Tupolev's experimental workshop in Moscow, and Vitaliy Kopylov managed the

Kazan factory. All these men contributed considerably to the development of the Tu-160.

In January 1975 Tupolev's team began the next stage: preparation of preliminary design and construction of a full-size mock-up, for which the Tu-160 had been given the name *izdeliye* 70. In 1977 the preliminary design and mock-up bomber were submitted for state committee acceptance. In this form, the weight of the Tu-160 with a normal warload of 9 tonnes (19,840 lb), comprising two Kh-45 missiles, was to amount to 260 tonnes (573,040 lb), the empty weight was 103 tonnes (227,012 lb) and fuel weight was 148 tonnes (326,192 lb). As can be seen from later data, the Tu-160 gained weight in the process of design and construction so that eventually its empty operating weight became 117 tonnes (237,868 lb) and its take-off weight, 275 tonnes (606,100 lb).

The name 'Tu-160' appeared in the press several years before the aircraft came into being – probably the one such event in the history of Soviet combat aircraft. During the Strategic Arms Limitation Treaty 2 talks in the late 1970s, Leonid Brezhnyev, or someone on his team, informed the Americans of preparations for a new heavy bomber. No details were given other than the name of Tu-160 and that it would be manufactured in a Kazan factory extended for that purpose. This leaked information subsequently appeared in *Air Force Magazine* in November 1978 in an article about 'Backfire' aircraft.

Weapon controversy

For a long time, there were no doubts concerning the bomber's weaponry. Former Soviet long-range bombers were armed with one or two heavy missiles, initially the subsonic KS (AS-1 'Kennel'), then the supersonic K-10S (AS-2 'Kipper'), Kh-20 (AS-3 'Kangaroo'), and finally the excellent Kh-22 (AS-4 'Kitchen'), which is still in use. In a continuation of this line for the strategic bomber, the Soviets prepared new Kh-45 missiles. The normal variant of the Tu-160 was to carry two such weapons inside the bomb bay and, if necessary, two more missiles suspended externally, at the cost of performance.

The Raduga (Rainbow) design bureau in Dubna near Moscow, which until the mid-1960s had been branch office OKB-2-155 of the Mikoyan design bureau, began work under Alexander Bereznyak's direction on the Kh-45 missile in July 1965, at the same time as the programme for Sukhoi's T-4 medium strike aircraft was launched. Over the next 10 years, Raduga built a dozen or so Kh-45 missiles (or *izdeliye* D-4) for testing. The missile was made of titanium alloys, had a length of 10.8 m (35 ft 5 in), weighed 4500 kg (9,920 lb) and reached a range of 500 to 600 km (270 to 324 nm). It was guided to the target by an inertial navigation system and in the final part of the flight by an active radar seeker known as Garpun (Harpoon), with a search range of 150 km (81 nm) and a lock-on distance of 90 km (49 nm). Short-range Kh-15 strike missiles, developed within the Kh-2000 programme that also launched in 1965, were an alternative armament for the new bomber.

Other missile variants were proposed. In 1968, soon after the first competition for the strategic bomber was announced, a new research and development programme – Echo – was launched to develop a low-altitude strategic stand-off missile. There were many ideas for supersonic missiles, but the contractors of this programme, GosNIIAS (Gosudarstvennyi Nauchno-Issledovatelskiy Institut Aviatsionnykh Sistem, State Scientific-Research Institute of Aviation Systems) and the Raduga design bureau suggested the then-unfashionable, small subsonic Kh-55 with an absolutely new terrain-following navigational system. This idea was rejected as pure fantasy by the committees of the air forces and Air Industry, which held that two Kh-45 supersonic missiles were the only armament for the Tu-160. Work on the Kh-55 missile went ahead only on the medium-range version with a traditional homing system, i.e., inertial navigation during its path to the target and active radar seeker in the terminal phase.

As such, the armament provided for in the preliminary design of the Tu-160 of 1976 constituted two Kh-45 missiles for the basic variant, and alternative variants carrying 24 Kh-15s, or 10 to 12 Kh-15Ms (these missiles remained in the design stage), or 10 to 15 of the new Kh-55s.

These plans were turned upside-down in 1976-77 when the Soviets learned about American work on the AGM-86 (ALCM-B) strategic cruise missile. The Kh-45 was deleted from the Tu-160's armament list and Raduga resumed work on a strategic version of the Kh-55. The basic armament of the Tu-160 was fixed as six to 12 subsonic strategic Kh-55 missiles in revolving MKU6-5U launchers, with 12 to 24 Kh-15s being the alternative. Consideration was also given to other types of medium- and short-range missiles, guided and unguided bombs but, as yet, they have not been realised.

Raduga's cruise missile

The Raduga Kh-55 (*izdeliye* 120) was launched for the first time in 1978 and series production began in 1981; the missile was officially commissioned in 1983, together with the Tu-95MS 'Bear-H'. Several years later, in 1986, series production began of the strategic version, Kh-55SM (*izdeliye* 125), intended for Tu-160s and later versions of the Tu-95MS bomber. More than 3,000 Kh-55 missiles were built in two production plants, in Smolensk and Kharkiv (Ukraine). The Kh-55SM strategic cruise missile (AS-15B 'Kent' to NATO), also designated RKV-500B (given officially by the Soviets during the SALT-2 negotiations), can be used for attacking targets with known co-ordinates and is equipped with a homing system comprising an accurate INS updated by a terrain-reference system that compares the terrain below to a map stored in the missile's memory. Its BSU-55 flight control system uses the terrain-following feature when flying at low altitude, and during anti-intercept manoeuvres in a horizontal plane. The Kh-55SM has a 200-kT nuclear warhead. It weighs 1500 kg (3,309 lb) (including an additional conformal fuel tank), its length is 6.04 m (19 ft 10 in) and its wingspan is 3.1 m (10 ft 2 in). Cruising speed is between Mach 0.48 and 0.77. Official maximum range of the Kh-55SM is 3000 km (1,620 nm), or 2500 km (1,350 nm) without the additional tank. The missile has straight wings which unfold and control fins, and is propelled by an R95-300 turbofan engine lowered after launch from the bottom rear part of the fuselage.

When Kh-15s are the armament, 24 of these nuclear short-range attack missiles can be installed in four short revolving MKU6-1U drums (six missiles per drum). The drums are located in a line inside the armament bays. The Tu-160 has been adapted to carry such weapons (there are suitable fasteners and connectors in the bay) but, according to reliable sources, this type of armament was not implemented in service aircraft.

The Kh-15 (*izdeliye* 115, NATO AS-16 'Kickback'), developed by the same Raduga design team as the Kh-55, is an analogue to the US AGM-69 SRAM commissioned in 1980.

It has an inertial navigation system (although without correction) and carries a 350-kT nuclear warhead. In the first phase of flight the missile climbs to about 40000 m (131,230 ft) and then dives, accelerating to Mach 5. The Kh-15 has a launch weight of 1200 kg (2,646 lb), a length of 4.78 m (15 ft 8 in) and a diameter of 0.455 m (1 ft 6 in); its maximum range is claimed to be between 150 and 300 km (81 and 162 nm).

An anti-radar version of the missile, designated Kh-15P, was commissioned in 1988. This missile has a passive final homing system and a conventional 150-kg (330-lb) high-explosive warhead. It is very probable that Kh-15Ps are used by Tu-160s to destroy enemy radar sites, thereby breaking through the air defence system.

No other weapons are mentioned in official materials or publications, but the actual set of missiles carried by the Tu-160 remains a mystery. The length of the armament bay – 11.28 m (37 ft) – remained the same as that designed to accommodate Kh-45 missiles (which are 10.8 m/35 ft 5 in long), much longer than necessary for Kh-55s, which are 6.04 m (19 ft 10 in) in length. Kh-45s were dispensed with in 1976/77, so there has been enough time to redesign the bomber. That this has not been done suggests that, apart from the Kh-55, other large missiles were considered for the Tu-160, perhaps Meteorit-A missiles, although these did not pass their tests.

A traditional self-defence system proposed initially for the Tu-160 included a tail turret with a six-barrelled, 30-mm GSh-6-30 cannon (GSh, Gryazev Shipunov). However, the designers later replaced the gun with a Baykal self-defence system, most of the components for which – some 80 per cent – are located in the aircraft's tail, in a so-called 'carrot'. A Mak (Poppy) infra-red missile launch and approach sensor is installed at the very end of the tail, as are a radar warning device, electronic jammer and a battery of 24

The vast size of the blended wing/fuselage body can best be appreciated from above, as can the width of the rear fuselage section, which is appreciably fatter and flatter than in the B-1B. This volume, combined with that in the outer wing panels, is put to good use in carrying an extraordinary 148000 kg (326,279 lb) of internal fuel, compared to 87728 kg (193,403 lb) in the B-1B. Subsonic range differences between the two types are of a similar magnitude.

Bort 29 taxis past the Tu-142LL engine testbed at Zhukovskiy. This unpainted prototoype provides detail of the aircraft's construction, notably the blending of the wing body into the forward fuselage. On the nosewheel the Tu-160 has a prominent mudguard. As well as side protectors, there is a bar guard stretching across behind the wheels. This prevents debris being thrown up into the intakes.

Above: The Tu-160's undercarriage retracts rearwards. The mainwheel bogies are angled nose-down so that the forward wheel touches first. The main strut is slightly angled to absorb the full impact at the Tu-160's normal landing incidence.

Right: At the heart of the Tu-160's attack capability is the Obzor-K nav/bombing radar in the nose. Mapping fixes from the radar are used to update the inertial navigation system. There is also a terrain-following radar fitted under the large radome. The forward-looking optical sight is visible behind the window of the undernose fairing.

Although the 'Blackjack' began life as a Myasishchev design, Valentin Bliznyuk of the Tupolev OKB can rightly be regarded as the aircraft's father. As head of the large design team, Bliznyuk turned a paper and tunnel model study into the world's largest combat aircraft.

APP-50 three-round 50-mm chaff/flare dispensers. Initially, the system's failure rate was very high due to extreme vibration in this region of the airframe, and it often generated false indications, e.g., the radar of an F-16 fighter could be interpreted as a ground-based anti-aircraft radar. In the course of production, the fairing projecting aft at the intersection of the tailplane and tailfin was shortened, thereby reducing tail vibration.

Not all plans for the self-defence system have been executed. For instance, the implementation of R-77 medium-range missiles proposed for self-defence was not pursued.

Prototypes under test

After acceptance of the project in 1977, the experimental workshop of Tupolev's design bureau in Moscow began construction of three prototypes from sub-assemblies mostly supplied from other production plants, such as Kazan (fuselage), Novosibirsk (outer wings and tailplanes), Voronezh (bomb chamber doors) and Gorkiy (landing gear). The first Tu-160 prototype, designated 70-01 and intended for testing the basic flight characteristics, had incomplete equipment. Prototype 70-02 was used for static tests, and 70-03 was practically an equivalent of serial aircraft. Prototype 70-01 was eventually assembled in

Zhukovskiy in January 1981. After many months of testing the aircraft's systems and equipment, on 14 November a Tu-160 taxied for the first time to the airstrip and made the first high-speed taxi.

On 25 November 1981 the aircraft, being prepared for its next test taxi, was parked near two Tu-144 airliners. This was the image of the Tu-160 that appeared in the first photo published in the world's press. It caused quite a sensation. The media speculated that the aircraft had been revealed for purposes of propaganda, in order to be photographed by American satellites (according to general opinion, the photograph was taken by a reconnaissance satellite). The truth is more prosaic: a passenger on an airliner landing at nearby Bykovo airport took the picture and passed it to the West. The aircraft was then temporarily named 'Ram-P' (from Ramenskoye, which was a common name used in the West for the Zhukovskiy test airfield) and then 'Blackjack' by NATO. In this way, the world became acquainted with the heaviest combat aircraft of all time.

The maiden flight of prototype 70-01 was made with Boris Veremey at the controls on Friday 18 December 1981, the eve of the 75th birthday of Leonid Brezhnyev, General Secretary of Communist Party of the Soviet Union. Today, the designers argue about the connection between these two dates, saying their convergence was incidental. It may be true: in the history of Soviet aviation, many aircraft were first tested in flight in December in order to satisfy the year's schedules. In this case, the flight's date was probably changed by a few days to match the official anniversary. The duration of the first flight was 27 minutes; the aircraft climbed to 2000 m (7,217 ft) and – according to Veremey's memoirs – flew 150-220 km (81-119 nm) from the airfield (which is doubtful in such a short flight). With Veremey in the cockpit were co-pilot Sergey Agapov and navigators Mikhail Kozel and Anatoliy Yeremenko.

Three months after the maiden flight, in February 1982, Boris Veremey first exceeded the speed of sound with the Tu-160. During one of the experimental flights he also achieved the top speed of 2200 km/h (1,188 kt). Some critical situations arose during test flights, for example when Veremey landed with the front leg of the landing gear still retracted; after his masterful landing and a small repair, the tests continued. One of the most interesting tests was the flight by Nail Sattarov in which the upper covers of the cockpit were removed in order to test the effect on the crew of a broken cockpit canopy.

Prototype 70-01, partly dismantled, stands at Zhukovskiy. Externally, it differs very little from later aircraft, the most conspicuous change being a long probe at the nose tip. The internal differences are greater: not only are some parts of equipment absent, but some structural elements are makeshift, e.g., made of substitute materials. Prolonged work on the new materials and engineering of their treatment was the main reason for delay in the construction of the second flying prototype, 70-03, which did not take off until 6 October 1984. The first stage of Tu-160 testing was carried out at Zhukovskiy, then, after investigations into systems and armament began, trials were gradually moved to Akhtubinsk to the NII VVS (Nauchno-Issledovatelskiy Institut Voenno-Vozdushnikh Sil, Scientific-Research Institute of the Air Force; today it is known as 929th GLITs VVS, Gosudarstvennyi Lyotno-Ispytatelnyi Tsentr, State Flight-Test Centre of the Air Force). During Tu-160 armament tests, the launched missile was followed by an Il-76SKIP (Samolyotnyi Komandno-Izmeritelnyi Punkt, Airborne Command-Measuring Post) gathering telemetry information.

Serial production starts

Under the personal patronage of Dmitriy Ustinov, Soviet Minister of Defence, construction began in 1976 at Ulyanovsk on the Volga River of a new production plant intended for series production of the Tu-160. However, several years later, the plans were changed (reportedly under the influence of then-Prime Minister Aleksei Kosygin) and Ulyanovsk was re-roled for production of the world's heaviest transport aircraft, the An-124. The Tu-160 prototypes were made in co-operation with the Kazan factory, a traditional manufacturer of Tupolev bombers. Eventually, series production was also located in Kazan, which was extended for this purpose and which implemented new production tooling.

Construction of Kazan aircraft factory No. 124 began in 1932 and its first aircraft left the production line in 1938. In October 1941, soon after the German invasion of the USSR, the factory – located 700 km (435 miles) east of Moscow – was evacuated to Moscow factory No. 22, which specialised in the production of bombers (e.g., Tupolev's TB-3 and SB) and was one of the biggest factories of the Air Industry. Both factories were merged to become factory No. 22. During the war it undertook mass production of Pe-2 light bombers, as well as small numbers of heavy TB-7s (Pe-8). Still heavier Tu-4 'Bulls' (copies of the B-29 Superfortress) were manufactured after the war. In the jet age, the factory made Tupolev's medium bombers – Tu-16 'Badger', Tu-22 'Blinder' and Tu-22M 'Backfire' – as well as such passenger aircraft as the Tu-104 and Il-62. Now the factory bears the name Kazanskoye Aviatsionnoye

Proizvodstvennoye Obyedineniye (KAPO, Kazan Aviation Production Association) named after S.P. Gorbunov and, apart from Tu-160s, builds Tu-214 airliners.

The first series Tu-160 took off from Kazan on 10 October 1984 (only four days after the first flight of prototype 70-03), but it was two and a half years before the first aircraft was handed over to the air forces. The fourth aircraft built in Kazan (number 2-03, i.e., the third aircraft of the second production batch) took off for the first time on 15 August 1986 and became the first aircraft commissioned into service (together with number 3-01).

In Pryluky

At mid-day on 23 April 1987 (or, according to some sources, on 17 April), the first two Tu-160 aircraft, numbers 2-03 and 3-01, landed at Pryluky airfield, 130 km (81 miles) east of Kiev. One of these aircraft was piloted by Major General Lev Kozlov, deputy commanding officer of 37th Air Army (Long Range Aviation), and the other by a factory pilot from Kazan. A few weeks later, on 12 May, Lev Kozlov

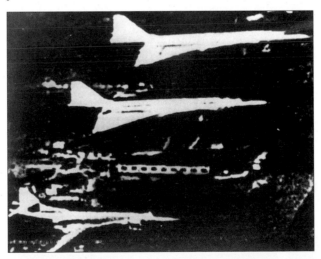

Bort 87 is one of the test aircraft. Early trials, which were primarily concerned with aerodynamics, performance and systems, were conducted from Zhukovskiy. As the trials programme moved towards testing the aircraft from an operational standpoint, the focus shifted to Akhtubinsk. In 2001 four Tu-160s remained in airworthy trials status at Zhukovskiy – two assigned to the air force and two with the Tupolev OKB, although they fly only sporadically.

Left: The first picture revealed in the West was this 1981 image showing a Tu-160 parked at Zhukovskiy next to two Tu-144 airliners. At the time, the airfield was thought to be named Ramenskoye, and new new types were assigned 'Ram-' designations. The Tu-160 became 'Ram-P'.

Below: In August 1988 US Secretary of Defense Frank Carlucci was shown the 'Blackjack', along with other Soviet hardware, at Kubinka. This was one of two aircraft which flew past during the demonstration.

took off for the first time from Pryluky in a Tu-160, marking the start of training of the regiment's pilots. On 1 June a then-commanding officer of the regiment, Colonel Vladimir Grebennikov, and commander of the Tu-160 squadron, Major Alexander Medvedyev, made their first independent flights.

Originally, Tu-160s were to serve with the Myasishchev 3M 'Bison' bomber-equipped 1096th Heavy Bomber Regiment stationed in Engels on the Volga estuary, the greatest base of the Soviet strategic air forces. However, these plans were changed, and the first Tu-160s were assigned to the 184th GvTBAP (Heavy Bomber Regiment of Guards) at Pryluky. Preparation of Pryluky and this regiment to operate the Tu-160s had started a few years earlier: the airstrip was strengthened and extended to 3000 m (9,843 ft), and in 1984 the regiment had obtained Tu-22M3 'Backfire-Cs' to accustom the crews to heavy supersonic aircraft with variable-geometry wings. One squadron remained equipped with Tu-16P 'Badger' electronic warfare aircraft. The future Tu-160 pilots undertook theoretical training in Kazan and Kuibyshev (now Samara).

The 184 Gvardeyskiy Ordena Lenina Boyevogo Krasnogo Znameni Poltavsko-Berlinskiy Tyazholo-bombardirovochnyi Aviatsyonnyi Polk (Poltava-Berlin Heavy Bomber Regiment of Guards awarded with Lenin's Order and Combat Red Banner) was one of the oldest Soviet bomber units. Its first combat mission – as the 9th Long Range Heavy Bomber Regiment of Guards – was made on the first night of the Soviet-German war, 22/23 June 1941; a month later the regiment made the first Soviet air raid on Berlin. During World War II, the regiment was equipped with Il-4 and Yer-2 aircraft. After the war it

briefly used 'Lend-Lease' B-25 bombers, and then was the first Soviet regiment to be equipped with the Tu-4 'Bull', a copy of the B-29 Superfortress. From the 1950s to the 1980s, the regiment flew several versions of the Tu-16 'Badger'.

Intensive Kh-55SM cruise missile-firing exercises began soon after the 184th received the Tu-160, at the end of July 1987 (the first aircraft to launch the missile was crewed by pilot Vladimir Grebennikov with navigator Igor Aninkin). By November 1991, one of the aircraft had launched seven missiles, and others had three or four launchings each. The first firing exercises were made on the NII VVS firing ground in Kazakhstan (later, other firing grounds were also used). Telemetry-monitoring Il-76SKIP aircraft always followed the launching aircraft and the missile.

At the end of 1987 there were three Tu-160s at Pryluky, and before the end of 1988 the first squadron of 10 aircraft was complete, with Alexander Medvedyev as the commanding officer. At the end of 1991 – also the time of the disintegration of the USSR – the regiment had two squadrons of Tu-160s, totalling 19 aircraft, as well as one squadron of Tu-134UBL training aircraft. As new 'Blackjacks' arrived, older Tu-16s were transferred to other units, or retired. The Tu-22M3s were also withdrawn, since they were expensive to operate as training aircraft, and at the beginning of 1991 the 'Backfires' were replaced by Tu-134UBL training aircraft (the last Tu-22M3 left Pryluky in March 1991).

Typical routes for Tu-160s flying from Pryluky air base were over Soviet territory to Baikal and back again, or across the North Pole. During the longest flight made by Colonel Valeriy Gorgol, who was commanding officer of the regiment from 1989 to 1993, his Tu-160 flew for 12 hours and 50 minutes over the North Pole, to within 450 km (243 nm) of the Canadian coast, and back. In May 1991, during one such flight, the first contact between 'Blackjacks' and Western aircraft occurred: over the Barents Sea, two Tu-160s deviated from their usual westerly route along the Norwegian coast near Tromsø, and were escorted by F-16A fighters from the 331st Squadron of the Royal Norwegian Air Force.

Presentations

On 2 August 1988, Frank C. Carlucci, then-US Defense Secretary, became the first foreigner to go inside a Tu-160, at Kubinka air base near Moscow. The Soviets had prepared the aircraft wearing tactical number 12, onboard which Carlucci spent 15 minutes examining the cockpit. When he stood up from the left pilot seat, he hit his head hard against the upper console (it is now called 'shchitok Karluchi', Carlucci's console). At Kubinka, Carlucci was also shown two other 'Blackjacks', which flew above the airfield at low altitude (one piloted by V. Grebennikov and the other by A. Medvedyev), each with one engine off (see below). Carlucci was given basic data on the aircraft, and was told its maximum range without refuelling was 14000

'Blackjack' cockpit

Below: The central console has the thrust levers offset to starboard for primary operation by the co-pilot. The console also has fuel transfer controls and flap selection levers.

Below: This is the electronic warfare console, dominated by the circular threat warning display. The pilot has a similar, but simpler, display on the far left of the instrument panel.

The most notable feature of the Tu-160's flight deck is the stick control column, which gives the aircraft a 'fighter' feel while obscuring the instrument panel less than a conventional yoke. Otherwise, the Tu-160's flight deck is entirely conventional with a mixture of dial and strip instruments. The centre of each pilot's display has an attitude reference display, compass display, vertical speed indicator and airspeed indicator. Between the two pilot displays is a variety of nav/comms data entry panels and auxiliary displays such as wing sweep and undercarriage indicators. The dashboard is painted in the blue colour favoured by Russian psychologists for cockpits, with the vital flight instruments framed in white.

km (7,560 nm). Next year, the aircraft was shown to then-Chairman of the Joint Chiefs of Staff, Admiral William Crowe. This presentation also took place at Kubinka, on 13 June 1989, and the aircraft had the side number 21.

The Tu-160 was shown to the public for the first time on 20 August 1989, flying over Tushino airfield in Moscow. The first public ground presentation was at MosaeroShow '92 held in August 1992 at Zhukovskiy. The first international presentation of the Tu-160 was in June 1995, at the Paris air show, where it was presented with a wooden mock-up of the Burlak space missile suspended under its fuselage.

Records

In 1989-90 the Tu-160 set a series of 44 world air records. The first were set by a military crew under the command of Lev Kozlov in the aircraft with side number 14, and two other series were set by the crew of the Tupolev design bureau under Boris Veremey in prototype 70-03. On 31 October 1989, L. Kozlov achieved 1731.4 km/h (934.88 kt) on a 1000-km (540-nm) closed circuit with a load of 30000 kg (66,138 lb) in class C-1-r (aircraft weighing 240 tonnes/528,960 lb). It was also the record for loads of 25, 20, 15, 10, 5, 2 and 1 tonnes, and without a load. In the same flight, Kozlov set the altitude record in level flight, 12150 m (39,862 ft); the load record – 30471 kg (67,176 lb) – raised to an altitude of 2000 m (6,562 ft); and reached 13894 m (45,584 ft) altitude with a 30-tonne (66,120-lb) load. On 3 November 1989, B. Veremey flying with a take-off weight of 275 tonnes (606,100 lb) (class C-1-s) achieved 1678 km/h (906 kt) on a closed 2000-km (1,080-nm) circuit with a load of 25 tonnes (55,100 lb). On 15 May 1990, B. Veremey reached 1720 km/h (929 kt) on a 1000-km (540-nm) circuit with a load of 30 tonnes (66,120 lb) (as well as 25, 20, 15, 10, 5, 2 and 1 tonnes, and without load). This time the aircraft weight was 251 tonnes (553,204 lb) and the performances were recorded in class C-1-s.

Service problems

Under a decision by the Soviet Minister of Defence, the aircraft was handed over to the combat unit in Pryluky before completion of state acceptance tests (which were

The wing joint fences aid directional stability when the wings are swept to their 65° supersonic position. The fences actually consist of three separate surfaces. When the wing is fully forward the three sections are: the leading, independently raising, section lies flat to cover most of the gap between wing and engine nacelle; the central section forms part of the outer wing section, maintaining the wing's aerofoil shape, and has a simple hinge set at 45° to the direction of flight (45° + 20° minimum wing sweep = 65° maximum sweep); the rearmost section forms part of the drooping main flap.

Bort 24 lands at Pryluky on a murky day. The aircraft has a full ILS system installed. The navigation system is based on an inertial unit, which provides a continuous plotted position on a moving map. The system's accuracy is refined using radar fixes against known points or automatic celestial sightings. The system interfaces with the inertial system of the Kh-55SM missile, so that the missile 'knows' its exact position and attitude at the point of launch. The aircraft's system also prepares the digital terrain map for the missile.

All weapons are carried in two similar-sized bays located either side of the wing carry-through structure. Each bay is covered by four doors, the forward pair of which are longer – corresponding to the length of the MKU6-5U launcher – allowing Kh-55SM weapons to be launched by opening just one set of doors.

completed in 1989) and before official commissioning of the aircraft into service. In a situation known as 'trial service', each take-off and landing was recorded on film from a special stand near the airstrip, and changes were constantly introduced into the aircraft's construction and equipment. This trial service was supervised by a group of experts, sometimes as many as 300, from the Tupolev design bureau and the Kazan factory. With the regiment, the aircraft was equipped with an INS featuring astro correction, which improved accuracy when overflying oceans and other terrain devoid of pinpoints. Due to problems with starting the engines, the number of additional inlets at the sides of the air intakes was increased from five to six, and at the same time their control was simplified to improve air inlet conditions and reduce noise. The tailplanes were changed: metal honeycomb filling in some structural parts was replaced by composite filling.

Three serious breakdowns happened during the aircraft's service in Pryluky, fortunately all with happy endings. In the first case, a 1.5-m (4-ft 11-in) tailplane section was torn off in the air due to excessive stress, but the aircraft was landed successfully by pilot A. Medvedyev. After this accident, Tu-160 flights were halted for some time and the tail units were improved on all aircraft: the tailplane structure was strengthened and made 50 cm (19.69 in) shorter. The new tailplanes were delivered from Kazan to Pryluky as 'oversize' load in the fuselage of Il-76 cargo aircraft. In the second mishap, the wheel brakes were blocked on take-off, tearing open the tyres. In the third instance, in May 1993, the undercarriage bogie rotating gear failed, but Valeriy Gorgol managed to land successfully. All the disclosed defects were addressed in successive production series, and retroactively in existing aircraft.

Pilots are satisfied with the Tu-160 and with its impres-

sive combat potential. It is the most powerful combat aircraft built in the USSR (several years ago, the commanding officer of a Tu-160 regiment, Valeriy Gorgol, told the author that "my regiment of Tu-160s outweighs the remaining armed forces of Ukraine"). The aircraft is very pleasant to handle, much simpler than its Tu-22M3 forerunner, and the earlier control wheel has been replaced by a control stick. This stick was at first strongly criticised and was not accepted, until it was realised that the aircraft could be controlled without physical effort; it is much more convenient, does not obscure the instrument panel and allows simultaneous control of the throttle. Thanks to its excellent thrust-to-weight ratio, the aircraft climbs easily (once it even took off with accidentally-open wing spoilers). The thrust margin allows take-off even with one engine stopped (not, of course, at maximum take-off weight) and the flight can be continued with two engines only. This feature proved to be very useful when the Tu-160s were displayed in flight for Frank Carlucci. One engine in each of the two selected aircraft refused to start and, after brief consideration, the pilots took off with only three engines running. The aircraft's landing characteristics are excellent, 'holding onto the air' until it reaches the landing speed of 260 km/h (140 kt). The failure rate of the Tu-160 – which, for obvious reasons, was high during the first phase of service – is no greater than for other aircraft, including the American B-1B Lancer.

Seat problems

The assessment of the crew comfort, unfortunately, is not so favourable. Tu-160 crews, when questioned at Pryluky about the conditions of their work in the air, had reservations about the equipment that related directly to their personal comfort and safety. In the first aircraft delivered to the regiment, crews criticised the emergency ejection system. The pilots' seats are movable for easier ingress and for better comfort during the flight, but can be ejected only in the extreme forward position. In the first aircraft, if the seat was in another position, the navigator had to push it forward manually. Now, the aircraft are equipped with a pneumatic cylinder that pushes the seat automatically prior to ejection. The seats, designed for fighter aircraft, were not suitable for bomber pilots spending 10-plus hours in a seated position. Only after some time were the seats equipped with pneumatic pulsating cushions that provide massage during long flights. In the first aircraft, cockpit pressure was equivalent to the ambient pressure at an altitude of 5000 m (16,404 ft), meaning that oxygen masks had to be used all the time; this inconvenience has been remedied. The noise level in the cockpit is so high that crew seated side-by-side can hear each other only via intercom. On a more positive note, a small corridor leads to a galley and toilet, equipment that had not previously been installed in a Soviet bomber.

There were also reservations concerning the cockpit ergonomics of the first 'Blackjacks'. For instance, the indicators for main and stand-by instruments were of different types, so the pilots had to switch between two 'mind-sets'; they are now uniform. The cockpit equipment is of conventional type, the result of a conscious decision to use the equipment of other aircraft to ease crew training and to allow alternate flying in different aircraft types. This decision limited the aircraft's abilities – which could be justified in the initial period of aircraft service – and will probably be changed in the course of a planned modernisation if it is deemed economically viable.

The most critical remarks came from ground personnel. Preparing a Tu-160 for flight requires 15-20 special vehicles with running generator units, resulting in smoke and noise levels that far exceed acceptable standards (the noise level is 130 dB). This problem was analysed and an easy solu-

tion was offered by the design bureau, which suggested adopting the American solution applied to the B-1B, i.e., organising special maintenance areas with underground installations and power supply units. However, the armed forces rejected this solution, maintaining that the whole system is required to be mobile.

The complexity of ground service practically ties an aircraft to its airfield. Several times, aircraft from Pryluky air base were forced by bad weather to land at stand-by Uzin airfield (170 km/106 miles southeast of Pryluky), home of the 182nd Heavy Bomber Regiment with Tu-95MS and the 409th Air Tanker Regiment with Il-78s. In each case, a long column of vehicles had to be brought from Pryluky to Uzin, including tank trucks with liquid nitrogen and equipment for nitration of the fuel with hydraulic oil. Similar situations happened during shows for VIPs at Kubinka, Ryazan, Machulische and other places.

Where the Tu-160 mainly differs from the B-1B is in its Mach 2+ performance. This is largely due to the complex variable-area intakes, which were deleted when the B-1 design was resurrected. Downstream of the main intake is a set of six (five in early aircraft) large auxiliary louvre intakes which admit extra air at low air speeds. The mass flow of the NK-32 engine is reported as 365 kg (805 lb) per second, and its dry power is more than the full afterburning power of the B-1B's F101.

Tu-134UBL pilot trainer

The Tu-134UBL (Uchebno-Boyevoi dlya Lyotchikov, combat trainer for pilots) is a special version of the Tu-134 'Crusty' airliner designed for training pilots and navigators of Soviet Long Range Aviation. It features special equipment and its most conspicuous external detail is the long, sharp front fuselage containing the radar antenna. Tu-134s were transformed into training versions by the factory in Kharkiv. The Tu-134 is very similar to the Tu-160 in its flying characteristics, particularly the thrust load, take-off and landing path. The cost of one hour of flying a Tu-134 is one-quarter that of a Tu-160 flight.

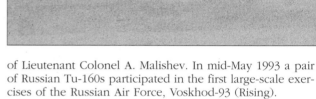

Tu-160s served at Pryluky with the 184 GvTBAP for five years, forming the spearhead of the Soviet Union's strategic deterrent. Although the greater 'muscle' of that deterrent lay under the oceans in submarines, or in ICBM silos, the bomber fleet offered far greater flexibility, chiefly on account of its ability to deploy swiftly, to re-target rapidly and to be recalled in flight after launch.

With their red stars crudely obliterated, four Tu-160s await their fate at Pryluky. Transferred by default to the Ukraine in 1992, the 184 GvTBAP fleet effectively lost its combat capability, as many pilots returned to Russia and technical support was withdrawn. The 'Blackjacks' made only a few flights under the Ukrainian flag, and were held in open storage throughout the 1990s. Their greatest value was as a bargaining chip with Russia, although the initial round of talks concerning their sale broke down. Subsequently, eight were returned to Russia and the remainder scrapped.

Tu-160 operations impose very strict requirements for runway cleanliness. After rejecting five engines damaged by impurities sucked from the ground, the regiment had to form a so-called 'fourth squadron' for cleaning, in addition to the three normal ones. This additional squadron, equipped with vehicles with old jet engines installed on them, was responsible for blowing all dirt from the concrete surface.

In Engels

Prior to the disintegration of the USSR, 19 'Blackjacks' entered service with the air forces, all stationed at Pryluky. On 24 August 1991 the Ukrainian parliament decreed it was taking under its control all military units stationed on Ukrainian territory; the Ukrainian Ministry of Defence was created on the same day. For several months, these events had no effect on the life of the 184th Heavy Bomber Regiment in Pryluky. Air military units did not begin to swear allegiance to Ukraine until spring 1992. The day for this for the Pryluky regiment was 8 May 1992, and it caused a split among members. About 25 per cent of the pilots and most of the ground personnel swore the oath for Ukraine, the first being the regiment's commanding officer, Colonel Valeriy Gorgol.

A group of about 30 pilots went to Engels air base in Russia, where the first Russian Tu-160 unit was forming, the 121st Sevastopol Heavy Bomber Regiment of Guards. At that time, Russia had just three Tu-160s at the Kazan factory, and several others used for tests at Zhukovskiy. On 16 February 1992 the first of the Kazan aircraft arrived at Engels airfield, the remaining two being ferried before May, but they spent several months on the ground because there were no pilots. On 29 July 1992, Alexander Medvedyev took off for the first time in a Russian Tu-160 from Engels. On 22 October 1992 the crew of the regiment's commander, Lieutenant Colonel Anatoliy Zhikharyev (currently the commanding officer of the 22nd Division of Strategic Bombers), made the first Russian test launch of a Kh-55SM from a service Tu-160, followed the next day by the crew

of Lieutenant Colonel A. Malishev. In mid-May 1993 a pair of Russian Tu-160s participated in the first large-scale exercises of the Russian Air Force, Voskhod-93 (Rising).

Engels, the greatest air base of the Russian strategic air forces, had previously housed Myasishchev 3M 'Bison' aircraft, originally used as bombers and subsequently as air tankers. The last flight of a 3MS-2 'Bison' from Engels occurred on 23 March 1994. Afterwards, these aircraft were stored, and their destruction began in August 1997.

The production of Tu-160s at Kazan continued for some time, but the air force soon ran out of money and in June 1994, the sixth – and, for a long time, the last – aircraft destined for the Engels regiment left the factory. At Kazan, four unfinished airframes remained in various states of completion.

Meanwhile, the Pryluky regiment, in a very brief time, virtually lost its combat value. Nineteen Tu-160s from the 184th Heavy Bomber Regiment were grounded because of lack of technical support from the design bureau and manufacturer, lack of spare parts and lack of appropriate fuel. Flights, made sporadically, lacked a combat element for many reasons, not least of which was the lack of areas suitable for exercises with strategic missiles. From the very beginning, Ukraine considered the Tu-160 bombers to be a

Above: An Engels-based aircraft cruises at high altitude. With wings in the intermediate 35° position, the aircraft is optimised to cruise at Mach 0.77. It can theoretically fly for nearly 14000 km (7,560 nm) in this configuration without refuelling, with an endurance of about 15 hours. When launched from bases in the Russian Arctic, it has the range to cover all of the United States on a two-way over-the-Pole trip.

Left: The 121 GvTBAP was the unit chosen to operate the Russian Tu-160s, although it was scheduled to adopt the historic 184 GvTBAP number. The Tu-160s are currently operated by a single squadron, although this should increase to two when the eight ex-Ukrainian aircraft are cleared for service (they are currently going through an overhaul programme at the Kazan factory). At present the 121 GvTBAP also operates the Tu-95MS 'Bear-H' which, like the Tu-160, employs the Kh-55 cruise missile as its primary weapon.

'trump card' in talks with Russia. Economically, the aircraft were unsustainable for Ukraine, and militarily, they were completely unnecessary to its armed forces. From 1991, Russia and Ukraine held talks about transferring the strategic aircraft to Russia, the main bone of contention being money. Russian experts, who examined the aircraft in Pryluky and Uzin (home to Tu-95MS 'Bear-Hs') in 1993 and 1996, assessed the aircraft's technical condition as good, but the price of US$3 billion initially demanded by Ukraine was not acceptable to Russia. In April 1998, when it became apparent that negotiations would yield no results, the Ukrainian Council of National Security and Defence decided to scrap the aircraft, with the exception of several destined for civil research programmes and for museums. In November 1998 at Pryluky, the first Tu-160 was ostentatiously cut up.

Bombers for gas

In April 1999, immediately after the commencement of NATO air attacks against Yugoslavia, Russia resumed talks with Ukraine about the strategic bombers. This time, Russia proposed buying back eight Tu-160s and three Tu-95MS 'Bears' manufactured in 1991, in the best technical condition, as well as 575 Kh-55 and Kh-55SM missiles (in total,

1,068 examples of various Kh-55 missiles remained in the Ukraine following the break-up of the USSR), documentation and ground equipment. Finally, at Yalta on 6 October 1999, Russia and Ukraine signed an agreement to sell the aircraft, according to Russian conditions. The contract's value of US$285 million was deducted from Ukraine's outstanding payments to Russia for the supply of natural gas.

On 20 October a group of Russian military experts went to the Ukraine to take possession of the aircraft, and on 5 November 1999 the first two ex-Ukrainian bombers – a Tu-160 and a Tu-95MS – landed at Engels. In a solemn welcoming ceremony, the pilots received gifts from the commander of Russian Long Range Aviation, Lieutenant General Mikhail Oparin, and the aircraft were dressed with Russian flags. During successive months, all eight 'Blackjacks' in the purchase agreement arrived at Engels, the last two on 21 February 2000. The Russians are pleased with the technical condition of the aircraft, although in 2001 all the Tu-160s will be overhauled at the Kazan factory.

Along with buying back the aircraft from Ukraine, the Russian Ministry of Defence signed a contract with the Kazan factory at the end of June 1999 to transfer to the

Above: Accompanied by Su-27 'Flankers' from the 'Russian Knights' aerobatic display team, Tu-160 Bort 01 thunders past the gallery at the Zhukovskiy air show. Such flypasts have become one of the highlights of the MAKS show, which has become the main occasion that a 'Blackjack' can be seen in public. The type has only ventured once to the West – to Paris in 1995 – perhaps indicative of the air of security that still surrounds this bomber or, more prosaically, a reflection of the huge logistic effort required to move the specialised ground equipment.

Above right: Bort 01 was the first aircraft delivered to the 121 GvTBAP at Engels, arriving in February 1992 to initiate Russian air force service with the type (at the time the other operational aircraft were all in the Ukraine). Visible in the background is a line of Myasishchev 3M 'Bisons' which had previously equipped the regiment. After a period in open storage, the 3Ms were sectioned in situ from 1997, and slowly carted away for scrap.

Right: When the wings are fully swept, the curving planform of the fixed wing portion combines with the straight-edged swivelling portion to highlight the prominent 'knuckle' which marks the wing pivot point. The two pivots form the tips of an immensely strong wing box section which lies at the heart of the aircraft's structure. All available portions of the aircraft, including inside the wing box, are used for fuel carriage.

armed forces a nearly-complete Tu-160 bomber that had been languishing at the factory for some time. This aircraft, number 8-02, took off from Kazan on 10 September 1999 and on 5 May 2000 it was commissioned into service with the Engels regiment as '07'.

Current organisation

Russian Long Range Aviation is now organised in the 37th Air Army of the Supreme High Command (with headquarters in Moscow), itself consisting of five divisions: the 22nd and 73rd Divisions with Tu-160 'Blackjack' and Tu-95MS 'Bear-H' bombers, and the 31st, 55th and 326th Divisions with medium-range Tu-22M 'Backfire' bombers. The 22nd Donbass Red-Banner Heavy Bomber Air Division at Engels consists of three air regiments: the 121st

Sevastopol Heavy Bomber Regiment of Guards (Engels) with Tu-160 and Tu-95 bombers, the 182nd Heavy Bomber Regiment (Engels) with Tu-95s, and the 203rd Air Tanker Regiment of Guards (Ryazan) with Il-78 ' Midas' air tankers. After the incorporation of the eight aircraft from the Ukraine, Russian Tu-160s will be organised in a new regiment, which will probably be given the historical number of '184' (the former 184th Regiment of Ukrainian Air Forces at Pryluky was disbanded on 1 December 2000).

Russian long-range aircraft – in common with the nation's other military aircraft – fly very little. In 2000, the average annual flying time of a 37th Army pilot was merely 10 hours (down from 20 to 25 hours in previous years). Nevertheless, Russian strategic aircraft, for the first time in many years, have begun to venture on long-distance flights. On 25-26 June 1999, during Exercise Zapad-99 (West), a pair of Tu-160 bombers (one piloted by Igor Sitsky, the other by Vladimir Popov) made a 12-hour flight from Engels, along the Norwegian coast, reaching almost to Iceland. On the way back, one of the aircraft launched a Kh-55SM missile over the exercise ground in the Caspian Lowland. Exercises in April 2000 were restricted to Russian territory, but in February 2001 a pair of Tu-160s from Engels again travelled along the Norwegian coast and over the North Sea, approaching to within 150 km (81 nm) of Great Britain. On the way, they were intercepted by Norwegian F-16s and British Tornados.

The current number of Tu-160 bombers in the Russian Air Force – 15 – may increase over the next few years. According to basic directives of technological policy for 2001-2010, approved by the Russian Air Force in December 2000, Tu-160 production at Kazan will be continued –

although it is unclear if this means only that the three aircraft started before 1994 will be completed, or if new aircraft will be ordered. The transfer of at least two 'Blackjacks' from Zhukovskiy to the air forces is also under consideration. Little publicised talks about buying back three more bombers from Pryluky were undertaken, although the Ukraine eventually scrapped all of its remaining aircraft.

The total number of Tu-160 aircraft built to the end of 2000 was 35, comprising three prototypes built in Moscow and 32 series aircraft built in Kazan; another three (unfinished) aircraft are at the Kazan factory. Presently, 15 aircraft are at Engels and 11 have been scrapped by the Ukrainians: one was on display at Poltava museum in Ukraine since April 2000 (under international treaty, Ukraine was required to dispose of its strategic bombers by October 2001). Six aircraft are at the test centre at Zhukovskiy

Top: A Tu-160 nudges into the drogue trailed by an Il-78 'Midas' tanker. Il-78s form part of the same heavy bomber division as the Tu-160s, and their primary role is to extend the range of the Tu-160 and Tu-95MS 'Bear-H' strategic bombers.

Above: Ilya Muromets takes part in an air show flypast with the MiG-29s of the 'Swifts' aerobatic team.

Left: Bort 07 is the most recent aircraft to be delivered to the 121 GvTBAP, entering service with the Engels-based 'Blackjack' regiment in May 2000.

Ilya Muromets demonstrates the intermediate wing sweep position. While Western observers have dismissed the Tu-160's low observable characteristics, Russian authorities claim that they are better than those of the B-1B, citing the blended wing/fuselage as being of low-RCS design. The large intakes would appear to be an obvious source of radar returns, but it has been suggested that there is some sort of radar blocker in front of the engine compressor face. In the Cold War scenario, low RCS was always of lesser concern to the Soviet Union, as the US did not have the same scale of multi-layered air defence system as employed by the USSR.

(including four airworthy ones: two belonging to Tupolev and two to the air force). Another two airframes were intended for static and fatigue tests. One Tu-160 (the second series aircraft) crashed in March 1987 after suffering an engine fire soon after take-off from Zhukovskiy; the crew, commanded by Valeriy Pavlov, ejected and survived.

Non-nuclear 'Blackjack'

Modernisation of the aircraft, which was pointless when Russia had only six Tu-160s, may be justified for 15-plus examples. The upgrade would consist of extending service life, upgrading equipment and introducing new missiles. Tu-160 bombers are relatively young; the oldest of them were made just 10 years ago. Their service life was originally designed to be 20 years, but under this programme it would be doubled, allowing the aircraft to remain in service until at least 2030. Navigation, communication, self-defence and other systems would certainly be the subject of upgrades, too. The Kh-55SM missiles would be repaired and their service life prolonged.

The task formerly assigned to Tu-160s was nuclear attack in a global conflict, or nuclear deterrence (these aircraft are armed only with nuclear 200-kT Kh-55SM cruise missiles).

Aviation is the most effective means of power projection: a nuclear missile carried by a bomber can be launched to hit its target, or return to base in the bomb bay. Neither intercontinental ballistic missiles nor strategic nuclear submarines can achieve this.

Now that the Cold War is over, though, one vital potential application of Russian Long Range Aviation is participation in non-nuclear regional conflicts. For this purpose, the Tu-160s are to be armed with several new types of conventional weapons currently under test. Although new conventional missiles are being commissioned only now, work on them began much earlier, in the late 1980s. Added impetus came from the experience of Desert Storm operations in 1991 and from later operations of the US Air Force, which proved spectacularly the effectiveness of long-range aviation coupled with smart conventional weapons. All information about new missiles for the Tu-160 is vague, but it seems likely that at the end of October 1999 a decision was made to start series production of new Kh-101 and modernised Kh-555 missiles. Anatoliy Kornukov, commander in chief of the Russian Air Force, announced at a press conference on 11 January 2001 that a "modernised version of the Kh-55 missile with non-nuclear warhead" (i.e.,

'Blackjack' names

Some time ago, the Russians began to give names to their strategic aircraft. The first, at the beginning of 1995, were the aircraft with side numbers 05 and 06, named after mythical Russian popular hero *Ilya Muromets* (these aircraft were prepared for an air parade over Moscow on the occasion of the 50th anniversary of victory over Germany on 9 May 1945; aircraft No. 05 took part in the parade piloted by then-Commander In Chief of the Russian Air Force, Colonel General Piotr Deynekin, while 06 was a reserve aircraft). Subsequently, other aircraft received names: 01 (*Mikhail Gromov*), 02 (*Vasiliy Reshetnikov*) and 04 (*Ivan Yarigin*). Bort 05 was subsequently renamed *Alexander Golovanov*. 07 was named *Alexander Molodchiy*. At the time of writing, the aircraft from Ukraine had not been incorporated into service, so had not received names.

Above: Alexander Molodchiy (07).
Below: Vasiliy Reshetnikov (02) at Engels.

Above: Ivan Yarigin (04) at Engels.
Left: Mikhail Gromov (01) with Kh-55SM cruise missile.

Kh-555) would be launched for the first time in the same month.

Long-range stealthy cruise missile

The most important new weapon for the Tu-160 – the non-nuclear Kh-101 cruise missile developed by the Raduga design bureau – is now being tested and is scheduled to begin series production in 2003. The missile has a 400-kg (882-lb) high-explosive/penetrating warhead, and a total weight of 2200 to 2400 kg (4,850 to 5,290 lb). It is equipped with an electro-optical terrain-reference navigation system similar to that of the Kh-55 missile, as well as a TV seeker for terminal homing to ensure impact accuracy within 12 to 20 m (39 to 66 ft) (or, according to other sources, within 6 to 9 m/20 to 29 ft). Russians boast of the missile having an unusually small radar cross-section of about 0.01 m² (0.108 sq ft). Its flight profile varies from a minimum altitude of 30 to 70 m (98 to 230 ft) to a maximum of 6000 m (19,685 ft). Cruising speed is 190 to 200 m (623 to 656 ft) per second (Mach 0.57-0.60); maximum speed is 250 to 260 m (820 to 853 ft) per second (Mach 0.75-0.78). According to Russian sources, the range of the Kh-101 is 5000 to 5500 km (2,670 to 2,970 nm). A modernised Tu-160 could carry 12 Kh-101 missiles inside its weapon bays.

Successive new types of armament are coming into being, such as the Kh-555 missile, a variant of the Kh-55SM with a conventional warhead and a homing system borrowed from the Kh-101. Under development is a subsonic, low-altitude medium-range Kh-SD missile that also borrows the navigation and homing systems and onboard software of the Kh-101. The Kh-SD (Sredney Dalnosti, medium range) will have a launch weight of 1600 kg (5,250 lb) and will carry a conventional penetrating or cassette warhead. Work on this missile is much less advanced than that of the Kh-101 or Kh-555, and it will be developed only upon completion of the Kh-101 and will rely on Kh-101 elements. The Tu-160 will be able to carry up to 12 Kh-SD missiles (its size is similar to that of the current Kh-55).

Tu-160 versus B-1

The question of similarities between the Tu-160 'Blackjack' and the earlier American B-1B Lancer arises with the first glance at a Tu-160. The B-1A took off for the first time on 23 December 1974, but on 30 June 1977 then-US President Jimmy Carter decided to stop work on the aircraft and focus on the development of cruise missiles. When it became apparent that both types of weapon could be used jointly, in November 1979 the Americans began

If the conventional upgrade reaches fruition, the Tu-160 fleet can expect more flying as it trains for new roles.

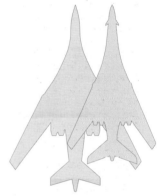

Above: Size comparison of the Tu-160 (red) and B-1B.

Below: Overwing spoilers dump lift on landing. Lightly laden, the Tu-160 can stop in about 1200 m (3,940 ft).

Hypersonic successors

Even at the beginning of the 1980s, as the Tu-160 was starting flight tests, work on its successor began. It was expected to be a hypersonic strike aircraft. Two successors to the Tu-160 were designed, named Tu-260 and Tu-360. Design work on the Tu-260 (or Aircraft 230) began in 1983 against an order for a Mach 4 bomber. According to the preliminary design completed in 1985, the Tu-260 was to be a tailless aircraft with delta-shaped wing. Design take-off weight was 180 tonnes (396,720 lb), including 106 tonnes (233,624 lb) of fuel for the four Soloviev D-80 turbojet engines. Flying at Mach 4 at an altitude of 25000 to 27000 m (82,020 to 88,580 ft), the Tu-260 was to cover a distance of 8000 to 10000 km (4,320 to 5,400 nm).

Unlike the Tu-260, which was designed for Mach 4, the Tu-360 (or Aircraft 360) was to reach Mach 6 and cover a distance of 15000 km (8,100 nm) carrying 10 tonnes (22,040 lb) of armament. The general layout of the Tu-360 was similar to that of the Tu-260, but its size was much greater, and it required a brand new propulsion arrangement. The maximum speed available from kerosene-fuelled engines is 4500 km/h (2,430 kt), above which cryogenic fuel is the optimum solution. As such, six variable-cycle turbojet/ramjet engines fuelled with liquid hydrogen were provided for the Tu-360. Design take-off weight of the aircraft was 350 tonnes (771,400 lb), empty weight was 200 tonnes (440,800 lb), length was 100 m (328 ft), wingspan was 40.7 m (133.53 ft) and lifting surface area was 1250 m² (13,455 sq ft). The required range could not be guaranteed: according to its design, the Tu-360 could manage only 9000 to 10000 km (4,860 to 5,400 nm) at Mach 6. Armament

Tupolev Tu-360 Mach 6 bomber

was to be carried inside two weapon bays located in the wingroots. Crew consisted of two pilots.

In the first stage of development a small (70 to 90-tonne/154,280 to 198,360-lb) model of the Tu-360 was to be built, but work was stopped in the aftermath of the USSR's collapse and the prolonged economic crisis in Russia. Before financing ceased in 1992, a nickel-alloy wing torque box measuring 10 x 4 x 0.8 m (32.8 x 12.1 x 2.6 ft) was built, as were some elements of the fuselage, tanks for the liquid hydrogen and fuel pipes made of unique composite material.

redesigning the B-1A into the cruise missile-carrying B-1B. The first B-1B prototype (converted from the second B-1A prototype) took off on 23 March 1983 and the first series aircraft flew on 18 October 1984. Production of the B-1B came to an end in 1988 after the construction of 100 aircraft.

There are many similarities between the B-1B and Tu-160: both have blended fuselage/wing centre-section airframes and variable-geometry wings. The interior arrangement of the fuselage is similar, with two armament chambers, as is the arrangement of engines in two double underwing nacelles near the fuselage, and the cruciform empennage.

There are also some significant differences. The Tu-160 is 27 per cent heavier than the B-1B and the thrust of its engines is 79 per cent greater. The B-1B is practically a subsonic aircraft (it can fly Mach 1.2 at high altitude, but this feature is not very useful). To reach its required maximum speed of 2200 km/h, the Tu-160 has adjustable air intakes (the non-adjustable intakes of the B-1B are simpler in design and have a smaller radar cross-section), its transverse section was made as small as possible, and the crew cockpit extends forward in front of the landing gear (the B-1B's cockpit is located above the landing gear bay and its fuselage is considerably thicker at this point). The 'Blackjack' has relatively small aerodynamic drag and radar cross-section, both believed to be much smaller than those of the B-1B. The Americans adapted their aircraft to carry armament on external pylons, whereas the Soviets located all the armament inside the airframe.

Moreover, the aircraft are optimised for different roles. The B-1A was designed as a specialised long-range penetration aircraft, attacking targets from low altitude with SRAMs carried in three small bays inside the fuselage. Later, with the advent of ALCMs, two front armament bays of the B-1B were interconnected to accommodate eight cruise missiles. The type's emphasis was changed again, to conventional mission enhancement, in August 1993 when Rockwell/Boeing initiated the Conventional Mission Upgrade Program (CMUP). In contrast, the 30-year-old Tu-160 has remained a nuclear strategic stand-off platform all its life, and only now is a Russian programme similar to the CMUP being implemented.

	Tu-160 'Blackjack'	B-1B Lancer
Wingspan, fully swept	116 ft 9.5 in (35.6 m)	78 ft 3 in (23.85 m)
Wingspan, fully spread	182 ft 9 in (55.7 m)	136 ft 8 in (41.66 m)
Length	177 ft 6 in (54.1 m)	145 ft 9 in (44.42 m)
Empty operating weight	257,941 lb (117000 kg)	192,000 lb (87090 kg)
Max. take-off weight	606,270 lb (275000 kg)	477,000 lb (216367 kg)
Thrust-to-weight ratio	36 per cent	26 per cent
Maximum Mach number	2.05	1.2
Maximum speed at s/l	556 kt (1030 km/h)	520 kt (963 km/h)
Maximum range	7,532 nm (13950 km)	about 6,500 nm (12040 km)

The Tu-160 and B-1B met face-to-face on 23-25 September 1994 in Poltava, Ukraine, during celebrations marking the 50th anniversary of Operation Frantic, the shuttle flights of American bombers between western Europe and the USSR (bombing Germany on the way).

'Blackjack' projects

Only the standard Tu-160 (Aircraft K, *izdeliye* 70) has so far been built, but a number of proposals have been made.

■ **Tu-160M:** this was to have been armed with two large supersonic missiles, one in each weapon bay, dating from the beginning of the 1980s. It is very probable that the Tu-160M was to be armed with two 3M25 Meteorit-A missiles (also known as Grom (Thunder), or as AS-X-19 'Koala' by NATO) developed by the NPO Mashinostroyeniya design bureau of Vladimir Chelomey. Work on Meteorit in ground-based (-N), submarine (-M) and airborne (-A) versions followed from a government resolution dated 9 December 1976, when the Tu-160 armament system was being formed and the dimensions of the weapon bays were known. Nevertheless, for unknown reasons, the missile was too long (12.8 m/41.99 ft), so the Tu-160M's bays had to be lengthened by the insertion of additional segments into the fuselage. The Meteorit-A missile, weighing 6300 kg (13,889 lb), was to fly up to 5000 km (2,670 nm) at 3000 km/h (1,620 kt) at an altitude of 22000 to 24000 m (72,180 to 78,740 ft). The homing system was similar to the Kh-55's, i.e., inertial with terrain-reference correction. The first test launching of a Meteorit missile from the ground took place on 20 May 1980, and from the air (a Tu-95MA test aircraft) on 11 January 1984. Unfortunately, the tests were unsuccessful from the beginning and work on Meteorit was soon stopped.

■ **Tu-160PP:** When designing the Tu-160, consideration was given to the problem of bomber survivability in a long, lonely flight across a zone of enemy fighter activity and air defence. Therefore, in 1979 the Tu-160PP (Postanovshchik Pomekh, jammer) was proposed, an escort aircraft designed to protect a group of bombers beyond the range of friendly fighters. In addition to a powerful set of elec-

The Tu-160's first outing to the West was in 1995, when a 'Blackjack' appeared at the Paris air show (below) masquerading as a Tu-160SK with wooden mock-up Burlak space vehicle. The concept was to provide a low-cost method of placing small satellites into orbit. The Burlak dummy was carried to the show in sections, stowed in the aircraft's weapons bays (above). The 'Tu-160SK' was subsequently displayed at Zhukovskiy (below right).

The primary weapon of the Tu-160 is the Raduga Kh-55SM cruise missile (AS-15B 'Kent'), of which up to 12 can be carried on two six-round MKU6-5U rotary launchers. The missiles are carried with their wings folded back and their tailfins folded. The missile is powered by an R95-300 turbofan which is lowered from the rear fuselage after launch. The warhead has a yield of 200 kT. Test and training launches are nearly always tracked by an Il-76SKIP aircraft. Five of these 'airborne measuring and control station' aircraft are in use, fitted with Shmel radar in a 'toadstool' rotodome and superficially resembling the A-50 'Mainstay'. In line with the Tu-160's projected conventional roles, Raduga has developed the Kh-555, a version with a conventional warhead. Whether production missiles would be newly built or converted from Kh-55SMs is unknown. Large numbers of the latter are held by Russia, which purchased the entire stock held by the Ukraine.

This is the standard Kh-55SM, shown in flight configuration with its turbofan, wings and control fins deployed. Note the conformal fuel tank which can be scabbed on to the side.

The Kh-65SE is a proposed version of the Kh-55 associated with the Su-34/35, but has 'Blackjack' potential. This version is an anti-ship weapon with active radar seeker and conventional warhead.

The Tu-160 can carry 24 Kh-15s on four MKU6-1U launchers. This weapon is available in either standard form with a 350-kT nuclear warhead, or Kh-15P conventional anti-radiation configuration.

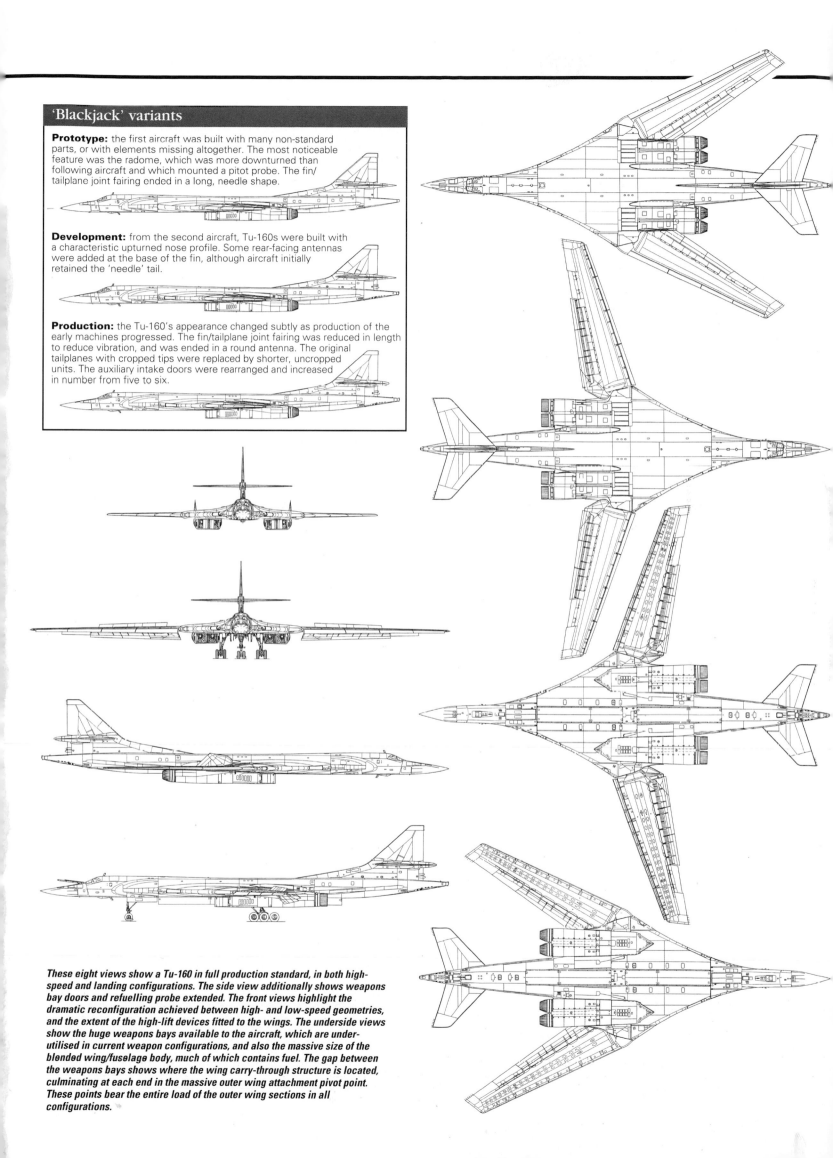

'Blackjack' variants

Prototype: the first aircraft was built with many non-standard parts, or with elements missing altogether. The most noticeable feature was the radome, which was more downturned than following aircraft and which mounted a pitot probe. The fin/tailplane joint fairing ended in a long, needle shape.

Development: from the second aircraft, Tu-160s were built with a characteristic upturned nose profile. Some rear-facing antennas were added at the base of the fin, although aircraft initially retained the 'needle' tail.

Production: the Tu-160's appearance changed subtly as production of the early machines progressed. The fin/tailplane joint fairing was reduced in length to reduce vibration, and was ended in a round antenna. The original tailplanes with cropped tips were replaced by shorter, uncropped units. The auxiliary intake doors were rearranged and increased in number from five to six.

These eight views show a Tu-160 in full production standard, in both high-speed and landing configurations. The side view additionally shows weapons bay doors and refuelling probe extended. The front views highlight the dramatic reconfiguration achieved between high- and low-speed geometries, and the extent of the high-lift devices fitted to the wings. The underside views show the huge weapons bays available to the aircraft, which are under-utilised in current weapon configurations, and also the massive size of the blended wing/fuselage body, much of which contains fuel. The gap between the weapons bays shows where the wing carry-through structure is located, culminating at each end in the massive outer wing attachment pivot point. These points bear the entire load of the outer wing sections in all configurations.

tronic countermeasures, the aircraft was also to carry medium- and long-range AAMs. Work on the Tu-160PP did not proceed beyond the mock-up stage.

■ **Tu-160R:** projected strategic reconnaissance aircraft.

■ **Tu-160 Voron carrier:** In the wake of the capture in Vietnam of an American D-21 unpiloted reconnaissance vehicle, and its shipment to the USSR, in 1971 Tupolev's design team was ordered to build a Russian equivalent. The project's codename was Voron (Raven) and work on it continued for many years, with varying degrees of intensity. The Voron and its Tu-160 carrier (or maritime Tu-142) were to form a strategic reconnaissance system. After being launched from the carrier aircraft, the Voron was to accelerate to a cruising speed of 3500 to 3800 km/h (1,890 to 2,052 kt) at an altitude of 23000 to 24000 m (75,460 to 78,740 ft) by means of a powerful rocket engine suspended under its fuselage. Then, after dropping the empty accelerating engine, the vehicle was to cover a distance of 4600 km (2,484 nm) powered by an RD-012 ramjet engine. After completion of its task, the Voron was to parachute a capsule with reconnaissance material. The Voron vehicle was to be 13.06 m (42.85 ft) long, its design wingspan was 5.8 m (19.03), wing area was 37 m² (398 sq ft) and launch weight was 6300 kg (13,889 lb) (or 14120 kg/31,129 lb with the rocket booster).

Work continues on a strategic reconnaissance project incorporating a Tu-160 aircraft and a Voron unpiloted vehicle, but the vehicle is very different to its 1970s counterpart.

■ **Tu-160V:** The Tu-160V (Vodorod, hydrogen) of the 1980s was a project with a liquid hydrogen powerplant. Since cryogenic fuel needs much more space than kerosene, the Tu-160V's fuselage had to be enlarged to accommodate hydrogen tanks.

■ **Tu-161:** A long-range intercepting fighter was designed as a development of the Tu-160PP escort aircraft. It was intended to hunt transport aircraft carrying supplies from the United States to Europe, and was to patrol the Atlantic, receiving initial indications of targets from reconnaissance satellites. The Tu-161 was to be equipped with a powerful radar and 12 long-range air-to-air missiles.

■ **Tu-170:** In the late 1980s, the Soviets were designing a Tu-160 variant adapted for carrying only conventional weapons. The objective of this conversion was to circumvent the SALT-2 limitations. Material for the Tu-170 project is now being used for the current modernisation programme of Tu-160s.

Space launch

A possible civil application of the Tu-160 was presented at the Le Bourget air show in 1995. A Tu-160SK (the original designation was Tu-160SC, for space carrier, but it was somehow changed to SK) could act as the launch platform

Next-generation strategic bomber project

In addition to hypersonic aircraft, a new subsonic bomber similar to the American B-2 was designed. Preliminary work began in the mid-1980s on the B-90 (bomber for the 1990s), a subsonic flying wing with an aspect ratio of about 7, made of composite materials. High-bypass ratio (about 5-6:1) turbofans and the size of the airframe are intended to achieve a record range.

Keeping in mind the considerable parallelism between Tupolev's airliners and its bombers (e.g., the Tu-16 and Tu-104 of the 1950s, and the first designs of the Tu-160 and Tu-244), an examination of one of the developments of the new Tu-404 airliner could shed light on the new bomber. Tupolev presented the model at the Paris air show of 1993, showing a giant 700/850-seat airliner with a flying wing layout, having wide fuselage/wing centre-sections, moderately swept outer wings and a twin tailfin. The essential difference between the layouts of bomber and airliner is the arrangement of the engines. In the airliner they are located outside, above the rear part of fuselage, whereas in the bomber they will be installed inside and have air intakes arranged in the wing's leading edge. For shorter take-off and landing (or for increasing the take-off weight by 10-15 per cent), the engine nozzles will be flat with thrust vectoring. Analytic work on this bomber continues and its commissioning is expected after 2015.

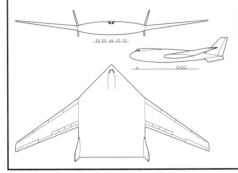

A model and drawing show the Tu-404 airliner study. A stealthy subsonic bomber project is thought to be based on a similar design.

for the Burlak space vehicle developed by the Raduga missile design bureau, analogous to the American Pegasus system. The Burlak was designed as an inexpensive low-Earth orbital vehicle able to carry a load of 825-1100 kg (1,819-2,425 lb), depending on the orbital altitude. The Burlak-M, with an additional hypersonic ramjet engine, was to carry 50 per cent more payload. Weighing 32000 kg (70,546 lb), the Burlak is suspended beneath the Tu-160's fuselage, between the engine nacelles. According to the design, the Tu-160SK is capable of carrying the Burlak 5500 km (2,970 nm) from the airfield. The space vehicle is launched at an altitude of 13500 m (44,291 ft) at a speed of 1800 km/h (972 kt). Work on this system continued for some time in co-operation with Germany (the vehicle was called Burlak-Diana), but this joint effort later ended.

In 1999 the project returned in another form. Three Ukrainian Tu-160s were to be sold to Platforms International Corporation of Mojave, in the US, to be used as a launch platform for a two-stage '2001' spacecraft developed from the Burlak. Other, heavier rockets were later suggested for the Tu-160, but eventually the whole project was abandoned. Tupolev still presents the Burlak at expositions, but practically no work on it is ongoing.

Piotr Butowski

Six Tu-160s are at Zhukovskiy, including four theoretically airworthy aircraft, of which two are earmarked for upgrade to operational status. These two remain derelict outside the Tupolev complex. The aircraft with its wings missing has the pointed tailplane fairing of early test aircraft. In President Putin's more hawkish Russia, the chances for further 'Blackjack' production, or at least the completion of three unfinished airframes still at Kazan, are high.

Tu-160 'Blackjack' technical details

Only one standard version of the Tu-160 has been manufactured, the other versions being no more than projects. The Tu-160 is a four-engined, all-metal, low-winged monoplane with variable-geometry wings. The **fuselage** and central wing section form a common shape with appended empennage and movable wing panels. The long, narrow fuselage/wing centre-section (LERX type), blended for maximum radar deflection, is subdivided into four compartments: nose (radar unit, crew cockpit and nosewheel undercarriage unit), front (fuel tanks and front weapon bay), centre (main undercarriage units, engine nacelles and rear weapon bay) and rear (fuel tanks and equipment).

The aircraft can carry 148000 kg (326,279 lb) of **fuel** in the 13 tanks installed inside the fuselage/wing centre-section and in the movable wing panels. The fuel transfer system is used to balance the aircraft when accelerating to supersonic speed. The retractable probe of the inflight-refuelling system is mounted in the upper part of the aircraft's nose.

Located inside the nose is the Obzor-K (Survey) **radar**, used for ground observation as well as detection of air targets. Another radar – Sopka (Hill) – used for terrain following when flying at low altitude is installed below the same fairing. Under the front fuselage is a forward-looking OPB-15T optical sight and video. The aircraft is equipped with the K-042K astro-inertial long-range navigation system that plots the current position on the map.

Weapons are carried inside the fuselage in two tandem **weapon bays**, each 11.28 m (37.00 ft) long and 1.92 m (6.29 ft) wide. Basic armament comprises six (maximum 12) Raduga Kh-55SM (AS-15B 'Kent') cruise missiles installed on six-round MKU6-5U revolving launchers (MKU stands for Mnogozaryadnaya Katapultnaya Ustanovka, multi-round catapulting device). Each missile is dropped by pneumatic-hydraulic catapult from the lowest point of the revolving drum, and then fired. The drum is then revolved by 60° into position for the next launch. An alternative weapon is the Raduga Kh-15 (AS-16 'Kickback') short-range attack missile, but reportedly it has not been implemented on service aircraft. Twenty-four Kh-15 missiles can be carried in four short MKU6-1U revolving drums (in tandem pairs). The Tu-160 is theoretically capable of carrying 40000 kg (88,183 lb) of free-falling nuclear or conventional bombs.

A new airborne **navigation/attack** system – Sprut-SM (Octopus) – had to be developed for the strategic Kh-55SM. Sprut-SM includes the computerised SURO-70 (Sistema Upravleniya Raketnym Oruzhem, missile weapon control system) sub-system that exactly aligns the co-ordination axes of the inertial navigation systems of both aircraft and missile. It also generates a digital map of the terrain along the planned itinerary of the missile, which is transmitted from the aircraft to the missile prior to launching.

For the first time, Russian aircraft were equipped with the Sigma pre-flight data management system. About 100 **computers** are used to control various onboard systems (including 12 computers for the fire control system). A single central computer concept was considered and abandoned during the course of aircraft design, the designers opting instead for a multi-computer system which was considered to be "more reliable".

From the front the blending of the fuselage and wing is apparent, providing the Tu-160 with an enormous internal fuel volume despite its slender lines. Like the B-1B, the shape is optimised for low radar cross section.

Tu-160 'Blackjack' specification

Dimensions
Wingspan: 35.6 m (116 ft 9.5 in) at 65° sweep, 50.7 m (166 ft 4 in) at 35° sweep, and 55.7 m (182 ft 9 in) at 20° sweep
Maximum length: 54.1 m (177 ft 6 in)
Maximum height: 13.1 m (42 ft 11 in)
Length of engine nacelle: 13.28 m (43 ft 7 in)
Tailplane span: 13.25 m (43 ft 6 in)
Wing area: 293.15 m² (3,155.4 sq ft) fully spread, 232 m² (2,497.2 sq ft) fully swept
Aspect ratio: 10.58 fully spread, 5.46 fully swept
Sweepback: fixed at 20°, 35° or 65°

Weights
Empty operational: 117000 kg (257,937 lb)
Maximum take-off: 275000 kg (606,261 lb)
Maximum landing: 155000 kg (341,710 lb)

Performance
Maximum operating Mach number: Mach 2.05
Maximum speed: 2200 km/h (1,188 kt)
Maximum speed at sea level: 1030 km/h (556 kt)
Cruise Mach number: Mach 0.77
Minimum speed at 140000 kg (308,642 lb): 260 km/h (140 kt)
Take-off distance: 900 and 2200 m (2,953 and 7,218 ft) at 150 and 275 tonnes (330,600 and 606,100 lb) weight, respectively
Landing distance: 1200 and 1600 m (3,937 and 5,250 ft) at 140 and 155 tonnes (308,560 and 341,620 lb) weight, respectively
Maximum climb rate: 4200 m (13,780 ft) per minute
Practical ceiling: 15600 m (51,181 ft)
G limit: 2
Practical range without inflight refuelling, at Mach 0.77, carrying six Kh-55SM missiles dropped mid-range: 12300 km (6,641 nm), with 5 per cent fuel reserve
Maximum theoretical range: 13950 km (7,533 nm)
Maximum duration without inflight refuelling: 15 hours
Combat radius at Mach 1.5: 2000 km (1,080 nm)

Above and right: The tail section houses a considerable array of rear-facing antennas for the passive warning system and active jamming system. The small dark panels are three-round APP-50 chaff/flare dispensers. Scabbed on to the side of the rear fuselage is a fairing which may be a side-facing antenna, or a waveguide/conduit serving the tail-mounted jammers and antennas. In the underside of the tailcone is the housing for the brake chutes, seen with doors open above. There is no rudder, directional control being provided by an all-moving fin which pivots above the tailplane.

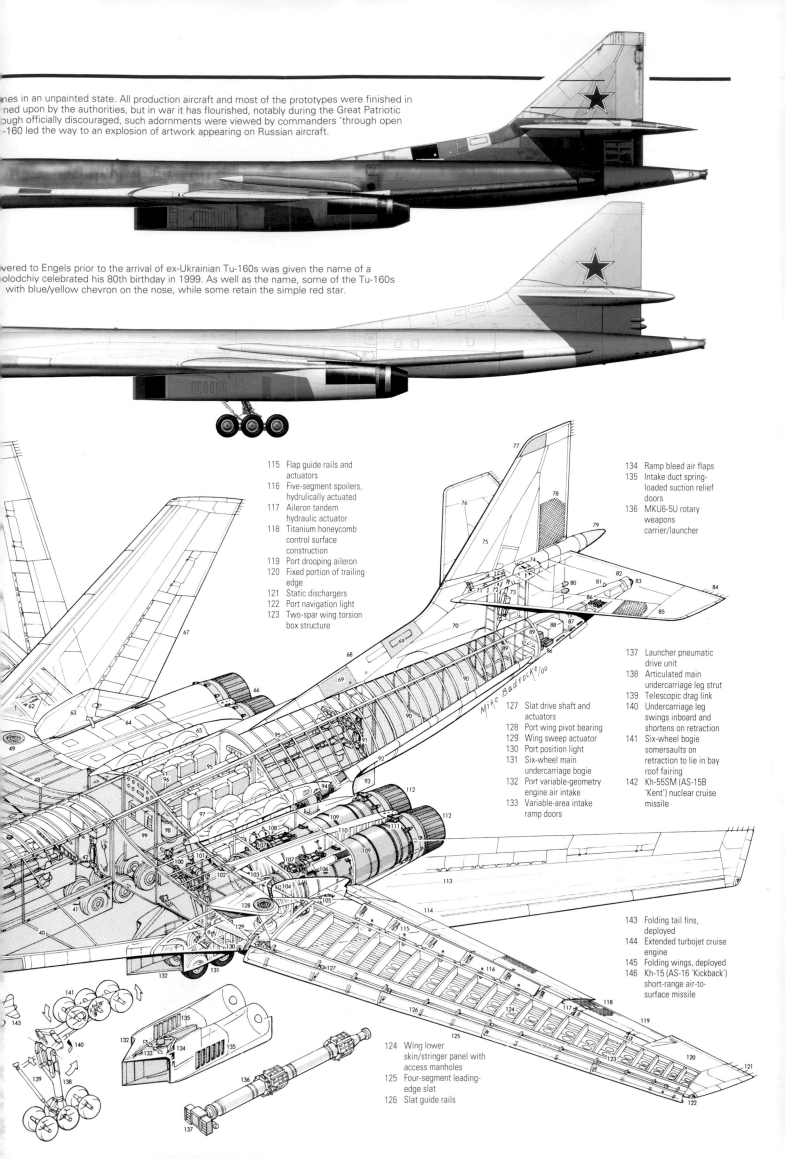

nes in an unpainted state. All production aircraft and most of the prototypes were finished in
ned upon by the authorities, but in war it has flourished, notably during the Great Patriotic
ugh officially discouraged, such adornments were viewed by commanders 'through open
-160 led the way to an explosion of artwork appearing on Russian aircraft.

vered to Engels prior to the arrival of ex-Ukrainian Tu-160s was given the name of a
olodchiy celebrated his 80th birthday in 1999. As well as the name, some of the Tu-160s
with blue/yellow chevron on the nose, while some retain the simple red star.

115 Flap guide rails and actuators
116 Five-segment spoilers, hydrulically actuated
117 Aileron tandem hydraulic actuator
118 Titanium honeycomb control surface construction
119 Port drooping aileron
120 Fixed portion of trailing edge
121 Static dischargers
122 Port navigation light
123 Two-spar wing torsion box structure

127 Slat drive shaft and actuators
128 Port wing pivot bearing
129 Wing sweep actuator
130 Port position light
131 Six-wheel main undercarriage bogie
132 Port variable-geometry engine air intake
133 Variable-area intake ramp doors

134 Ramp bleed air flaps
135 Intake duct spring-loaded suction relief doors
136 MKU6-5U rotary weapons carrier/launcher

137 Launcher pneumatic drive unit
138 Articulated main undercarriage leg strut
139 Telescopic drag link
140 Undercarriage leg swings inboard and shortens on retraction
141 Six-wheel bogie somersaults on retraction to lie in bay roof fairing
142 Kh-55SM (AS-15B 'Kent') nuclear cruise missile

143 Folding tail fins, deployed
144 Extended turbojet cruise engine
145 Folding wings, deployed
146 Kh-15 (AS-16 'Kickback') short-range air-to-surface missile

124 Wing lower skin/stringer panel with access manholes
125 Four-segment leading-edge slat
126 Slat guide rails

Mike Badrocke/00

Bort 01/ Mikhail Gromov Gromov, after whom the LII is also named, was a famous pilot and Hero of the Soviet Union. The Tu-160 was named on the day of his 100th birthday in 1999.

Bort 02/ Vasiliy Reshetnikov Bort 02 is named for Reshetnikov, who was an influential commander of Long-Range Aviation.

Bort 04/ Ivan Yarygin Yarigin was a wrestler who took Olympic Gold in 1972 and 1976, and many other titles. He was proclaimed by the Soviets as the strongest man in the world.

Bort 05/ Aleksandr Golovanov Bort 05 was renamed after Golovanov, who was commander of Long-Range Aviation during 1942-1944, and 1946-48.

Borts 05-06/ Ilya Muromets The name of the hero of Russian folklore – who protected the nation from all kinds of enemies – adorned two Tu-160s, although 05 was later renamed.

Bort 29 This prototype aircraft has appeared several ti all-over white. During peacetime nose art has been frov War of 1941-45 and, more recently, in Afghanistan. Alth fingers', as the Russian expression goes. In 1995 the T

Bort 07/ Aleksandr Molodchiy The last aircraft de legendary bomber pilot and Hero of the Soviet Union. M sport a Russian flag and double eagle insignia on the fin

Tu-160 'Blackjack' cutaway

1 Glass-fibre radome
2 Flight refuelling probe, extended
3 Probe housing
4 Navigation/attack radar scanner
5 Scanner tracking mechanism
6 Sopka terrain-following radar scanner
7 Radar mounting bulkhead
8 Obzor-K radar equipment
9 Windscreen panels
10 Instrument panel shroud
11 Conventional control column and rudder pedals actuating quadruplex digital fly-by-wire flight control system
12 Cockpit sloping front pressure bulkhead
13 OPB-15 optical bombsight in ventral fairing
14 First pilot's Zvezda K-36DM ejection seat
15 Pilot's jettisonable roof hatches
16 Co-pilot's ejection seat
17 Upper VHF antenna
18 Rear crew member's seat jettisonable hatches with rear-view periscopes
19 Electronic warfare officer's ejection seat
20 Crew galley unit
21 Navigator/bombardier's ejection seat
22 Instrument consoles, port and starboard
23 Nosewheel leg-mounted taxiing lights
24 Lower VHF antenna

25 Nose undercarriage leg struts with hydraulic steering jacks
26 Twin nosewheels, aft retracting
27 Nosewheel spray/debris deflectors
28 Rear breaker strut
29 Hydraulic retraction jack
30 Avionics equipment racks, port and starboard, foldaway supernumerary seat and crew rest bunk between
31 Flush antennas
32 Cockpit rear pressure bulkhead
33 Crew entry hatch via nosewheel bay, open
34 Toilet
35 Nose undercarriage wheel bay
36 Weapons bay retractable spoilers
37 Forward weapons bay doors
38 Forward fuselage chine fairing
39 Port forward/oblique EW antenna
40 Port forward fuselage integral fuel tank
41 Starboard undercarriage six-wheel bogie
42 Weapons bay door actuator
43 Forward weapons bay, six Kh-55SM on rotary launcher
44 GPS antenna
45 Starboard forward oblique EW antenna

46 Starboard forward fuselage integral fuel tank
47 Starboard engine air intakes
48 Centre-section wing pivot box carry-through structure
49 Wing pivot bearing
50 Wing sweep actuator
51 Variable-sweep wing sealing fairing
52 Starboard position light
53 Starboard wing integral fuel tank
54 Four-segment leading-edge slat
55 Slat guide rails
56 Starboard navigation light
57 Wing fully forward, 20° sweep position
58 Starboard wing in cruise position, 30° sweep
59 Starboard drooping aileron
60 Three-segment double-slotted flap
61 Spoiler panels (five)
62 Slat guide rails and screw jacks
63 Wing root segment folded to vertical fence position
64 Starboard engine nacelles
65 Main undercarriage stowage fairing
66 Starboard engine exhaust nozzles
67 Starboard wing in maximum sweep position, 65°
68 Fin root fairing
69 Flush antenna panels
70 Lower fin segment
71 Rudder hydraulic actuators
72 Rudder pivot mounting
73 Tailplane hydraulic actuators

74 Tailplane bearing and sealing plate
75 All-moving upper fin segment/rudder
76 Starboard all-moving taileron
77 Fin tip antenna fairing
78 Titanium honeycomb core control surface construction
79 Rear EW antenna
80 Navigational antennas
81 IFF antenna
82 Tail navigation light
83 RWR antenna
84 Static dischargers
85 Port all-moving taileron
86 Chaff/flare launchers
87 Brake parachute housing and doors
88 Aft equipment bay
89 Fin/tailplane mounting main bulkheads
90 Aft fuselage integral fuel tanks
91 Rear weapons bay door actuator
92 External cable duct
93 Rear weapons bay doors
94 Auxiliary power unit (APU)
95 Rear weapons bay with 12 Kh-15 missiles on dual tandem rotary launchers

96 Electrical systems equipment
97 Main undercarriage stowed position
98 Port hydraulic reservoir
99 Wing pivot box integral fuel tank
100 Main undercarriage pivot mounting
101 Hydraulic retraction jack
102 Flap and slat drive unit
103 Telescopic flap and slat drive shaft
104 Port wing root seal/vertical fence, retracted position
105 Engine fuel control equipment
106 Bleed air system pre-cooler
107 Engine accessory equipment gearboxes
108 Fire suppression bottles
109 Trud/Samara NK-32 afterburning turbofan engines
110 Engine bay centre keel
111 Exhaust nozzle actuators
112 Variable-area exhaust nozzles
113 Port wing fully swept position
114 Three-segment double-slotted trailing-edge flap

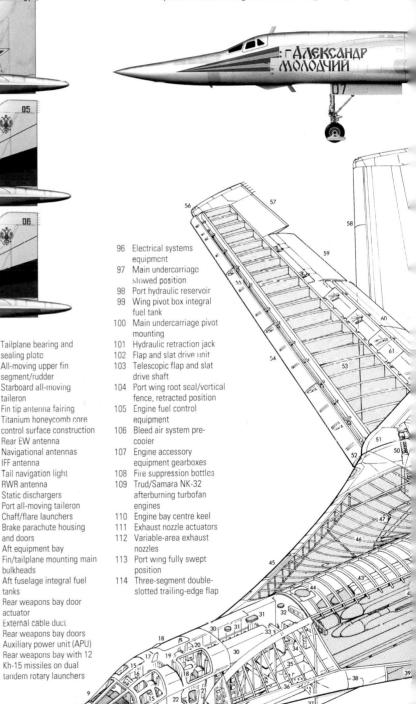

Wing structure and control surfaces

The main structural strength element of the aircraft is the central wing stringer, 12.4 m (40.68 ft) long and 2.1 m (6.89 ft) wide, that connects both wing-pivoting nodes. The stringer is made of two halves, upper and lower, milled of titanium alloy and welded together in a vacuum chamber according to a unique engineering process. Outer, movable wing panels are set for three manually-selected positions: 20° for take-off and landing, 35° for Mach 0.77 cruising speed, and 65° for supersonic flight. Each movable wing panel has four-section leading-edge slats, a three-section double-slotted trailing-edge flap, and an aileron. Five-section spoilers are installed ahead of the flaps.

With the wings fully swept, the inner section of each three-section trailing-edge flap is raised to become a large aerodynamic fence between the wing and the fixed glove to improve directional stability. A mid-mounted slab (taileron) tailplane may be deflected symmetrically or differentially. The all-moving upper section of the tailfin, above the tailplane, forms the rudder. The flight control system is quadruple fly-by-wire, and has a stand-by mechanical mode. The usefulness of a mechanical control system is considerably limited, since the aircraft is statically unstable.

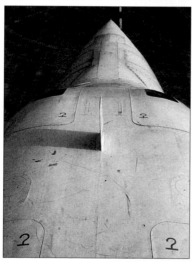

This Tu-160 (above) is seen with all its wing surfaces fully deployed. The four-sections of leading-edge slats (right) extend across nearly the full span of the pivoting wing section. The three sections of double-slotted flaps (left) are augmented by drooping ailerons (further outboard) and five sections of spoilers immediately ahead of the flaps. The ailerons are only used for roll control at low speeds: at high speed differential tailplane movement is employed.

Unique to the 'Blackjack' is the unusual folding inner portion of the pivoting wing section trailing edge (above left). With the wing fully forward the section lies flat to fill in the 'missing' segment of the trailing edge, but with the wing swept back it is raised to the vertical to provide additional directional stability (above right).

Crew accommodation

The crew of four is seated in the aircraft's nose in a common pressurised cockpit. The commander-pilot occupies the front left seat, with the co-pilot to his right. The rear seats are occupied by the navigator/offensive weapons operator and the navigator/EW and communications operator. All the crew have Zvezda/Tomilino K-36LM 'zero-zero' ejection seats. Access to the cockpit is via the nosewheel undercarriage bay.

The K-36LM ejection seats can be removed through the upper escape hatches (right), using a hoist (below). Note the doors covering the retractable refuelling probe, centrally mounted forward of the windscreens.

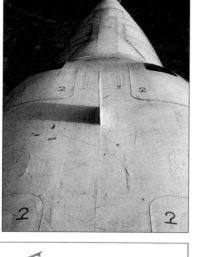

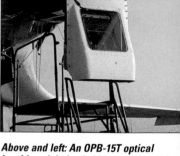

Above and left: An OPB-15T optical bombing sight iand video are mounted under the forward fuselage, covered by a drop-down window fairing.

Right: The Tu-160 crew accesses the aircraft by climbing a ladder to a hatch in the nosewheel bay. A narrow corridor leads forward to the flight postions

Powerplant

The propulsion system consists of four NK-32 (or *izdeliye* R) engines designed by Nikolay Kuznetsov's design team at Kuibyshev (now Samara), in widely separated pairs under the wing centre-section, with the nacelles protruding far beyond the wing trailing edge. The NK-32 is a turbofan with a bypass ratio 1.36:1, compression of 28.2 and temperature at the turbine entry of 1630° K (1357° C/2,473° F). Maximum thrust is 137.3 kN (30,872 lb) dry or 245.18 kN (55,140 lb) with full afterburning. The engine weighs 3650 kg (8,047 lb), its inlet diameter is 1.455 m (4.77 ft), and its overall length is 7.453 m (24.45 ft). The engine has three shafts, with a three-stage low-pressure compressor at the front, aft of which is a five-stage medium-pressure compressor followed by a seven-stage high-pressure compressor. The low- and medium-pressure turbines are single-stage, whereas the high-pressure turbine has two stages. The engine has automatically adjustable nozzles.

Above: The nozzles of each NK-32 engine are enormous to handle the huge mass flow. The area is automatically controlled for optimum thrust at all settings and conditions.

Left: Access to the engines for in situ maintenance is easy thanks to hinged cowling panels. These also facilitate removal of the engines.

Along with the Tu-22M3's NK-25, the NK-32 is the most powerful engine to have been installed in a combat aircraft. The nacelles project far behind the wing trailing edge to maintain the centre of gravity. Electric controls are fitted, with hydromechanical back-up, although a FADEC (full authority digital engine control) system is under review.

This cutaway exhibit shows the inner workings of the NK-32. The combustion chamber and afterburner are optimised to produce maximum thrust, but at minimum temperature to reduce IR signature, and to produce no smoke. It has been reported that the first compressor stage is designed for minimum radar reflectivity to reduce frontal RCS.

Undercarriage

The tricycle landing gear is retracted and lowered hydraulically. The front double-wheel leg (far left) retracts aft; its wheels measure 1080 x 400 mm (42.5 x 15.7 in). The main landing gear (below and left) consists of two six-wheel bogies (three tandem pairs), retracted into the mid-wing, between the fuselage and engine nacelles. The main wheels measure 1260 x 425 mm (48.4 x 16.7 in), and the track is relatively narrow, only 5.4 m (17.72 ft); the wheelbase is 17.88 m (58.66 ft). Three braking parachutes with a total surface area of 105 m² (1,130 sq ft) are located in the tail.

1917
БЪЛГАРСКА ВОЕННОМОРСКА АВИАЦИЯ

Bulgarska Voenno-Morska Aviatzia

Bulgaria's naval air arm photographed by Senior Lieutenant Valentin Georgiev

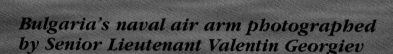

Above: OPLEV/OMEV originally took delivery of six factory-fresh Mi-14PL 'Haze-As', serialled 801-806 in 1979/80. 'Bord 806' was lost in January 1986, thankfully without casualties. They were to Soviet navy standards, and were capable of employing the 1-kT Spetzbomba Skat nuclear depth charge. Conventional weapons include the deep-water AT-1 torpedo, PLAB-250 depth charges (up to eight) or cluster-packed PLAB-50-64 and PLAB-MK depth bombs. Four second-hand 'Haze-As', serialled 806-809, were acquired in 1990 free of charge. The serial '806' was reassigned to one of the new aircraft.

Above: Bulgarian naval aviation has been closely associated with the Black Sea city of Varna since its inception. Here one of OMEV's Mi-14PLs crosses the city square at around 60 ft (20 m) and 110 kt (200 km/h).

Right: The Mi-14PL's most capable ASW sensor is the Oka-2 dipping sonar. It can be submerged to 100 m (328 ft) and can operate both passively and actively. The standard procedure is to begin with a 360° passive search. If a contact is suspected, the operator switches to active mode.

During the last decade of the Cold War, the Bulgarian navy created a small but potent air arm. The OPLEV (Otdelna Protivolodachna Eskadrila Vertoleti – Independent ASW Helicopter Squadron) was based near the city of Varna at Tchaika Naval Air Station, the oldest active air base in Bulgaria. As the name suggests, the main task of the squadron was ASW: the principal 'trade' was expected to be the Turkish submarine fleet operating in the Black Sea.

Post-Cold War realities caused a significant shift in the squadron's roles. New tasks were assigned, such as sea/land civilian search and rescue, medevac and casevac for the civilian population in the event of large-scale natural or industrial disasters, anti-smuggling patrols and fishery protection. To reflect the changes the unit was redesignated in September 1990 as the OMEV (Otdelna Morska Eskadrila Vertoletyi – Independent Naval Helicopter Squadron).

Despite current funding shortages, the Bulgarian navy continues to rely on its own air arm. Four of the 10 Mil Mi-14 'Haze' helicopters were considered serviceable and these have taken part in several NATO Partnership for Peace exercises in the Black Sea, as well as in 'real-world' SAR, security and anti-drug operations. The well-proven Mi-14s are set to serve for some years yet, as the current budgetary situation will delay their replacement beyond at least 2005.

Alexander Mladenov

Right: The OMEV 'Haze' fleet is outwardly kept in superb condition, although severe budgetary cuts have resulted in low serviceability. In 2000 funds were provided to overhaul two PLs (808 and 809) and the sole BT (811), allowing them to serve until 2007/8.

Below: A 'Haze-A' is brought to the hover during ASW operations, ready to deploy the Oka-2 sonar. The SAU-14 autohover system provides artificial stabilisation in roll, pitch and yaw in the hover, and keeps the helicopter motionless in relationship to the dipped sonar transducer. Once a contact has been established, the Landaish mission computer guides the helicopter to weapon release point in auto or semi-auto mode.

Above: Night training is routinely practised, in both ASW and SAR roles. Night-vision goggles have been in use since 1997. As well as the radar and sonar, the Mi-14PL is equipped with Baku sonobuoy equipment and a towed APM-60 MAD 'bird', the latter normally stowed behind the cabin when not in use.

Below: An Mi-14PL manoeuvres over a roof to pick up 'casualties' during a major industrial accident exercise. In the SAR role the 'Haze' offers good cabin capacity, but is hampered by having only a small winch over the port side door.

OPLEV veterans

Kamov Ka-25Tz 'Hormone-B' (left): The Ka-25Tz is the over-the-horizon targeting variant of the 'Hormone', also providing limited AEW. OPLEV acquired one second-hand in 1984, and it was jovially referred to as the 'Bulgarian AWACS'. It was grounded in 1991 pending a major overhaul for which funds have not been forthcoming. It remains in hangar storage at Tchaika.

Mil Mi-4 'Hound' (below): OPLEV's first aircraft was a transport Mi-4, acquired in September 1960. In 1964/65 six Mi-4M ASW variants were delivered, serving until retirement in 1980, by which time two had been lost. This example, a utility transport used until the early 1980s, is in a museum at Varna.

Above: An Mi-14 rests on a Ukrainian oil rig in Bulgarian territorial waters. Patrols of the oil exploration region, as well as fishery protection and anti-drug smuggling operations, are routine for the OMEV fleet in the changed political climate since the end of the Cold War.

Above: The Mi-14 is an important element in Bulgaria's search and rescue effort, and often works with the nation's only dedicated civilian SAR/salvage vessel, the Perun. When the Mi-14 adopted the SAR role in the early 1990s, crew training altered accordingly. Water landings and take-offs became regularly practised as were single-engined, short-roll landings.

Right: The boat hull and pop-out floats make the 'Haze' truly amphibious, although pre-planned water landings require considerable preparation to ensure all joints are sealed, while after the flight the helicopter has to be washed down with fresh water and its engines washed through with a special emulsion. The Mi-14 was the world's first helicopter to demonstrate an auto-rotation on to water, and it can safely operate in sea states up to 4 (wave height 2 ft 6 in/0.75 m). It can water-taxi at up to 60 km/h (37 mph).

Above: The undernose radome houses the antenna for the Initziativa-2M search radar, which has a 220-km (137-mile) range against large surface targets and a 15-km (9.3-mile) range against periscope/liferaft-sized objects. The Mi-14s are often tasked with surveillance duties during naval vessel missile live firings.

Right: The Mi-14s are the most complex helicopters in Bulgarian service, in both handling and operational terms. Unlike Western types, Soviet helicopters are traditionally flown from the left-hand seat (although the recent Ka-60 has switched to a right-hand arrangement).

Below: In 1983 the OPLEV received two Mi-14BT 'Haze-B' mine countermeasures aircraft (811 and 812). The latter ditched in 1985 and was withdrawn from service. 811, meanwhile, was stripped of its minesweeping gear and was converted to serve as a passenger/cargo transport. If funds permit, the aircraft will be converted to the SAR-dedicated Mi-14PS 'Haze-C' standard.

Below right: In the late 1990s the OMEV Mi-14s began to exercise regularly with their former adversaries, including the navies of Black Sea neighbours Greece and Turkey, and with the US Navy. In Cooperative Partner 97, a NATO PfP exercise, OMEV helicopters exercised with CH-46 Sea Knights from HMM-261, including night formation work with NVGs. The 'Hazes' also performed deck landings on the CH-46s' 'home-plate' – the USS Ponce.

US Marine Corps

Although the USMC has a sizeable air arm, it is under increasing pressure to meet its commitments. New aircraft programmes, such as the MV-22 Osprey and JSF, are seen as vital to the future of the USMC's aviation organisation.

Rick Burgess

United States Marine Corps Aviation

The United States possesses not just one, or two, but three of the world's most powerful air arms. In addition to the global reach of the US Air Force and the forward-deployed prowess of the US Navy's carrier air wings, the United States has at its disposal the aviation elements of the US Marine Corps.

The primary role of Marine Corps aviation, which has been maintained since its inception, is to support Marine ground forces ashore and during amphibious operations. To carry out this role, the Marine Corps operates a potent force of tactical fixed-wing and rotary-wing aircraft – and soon tilt-rotor aircraft – to provide close air support, assault transport, air defence and electronic warfare support. As it has done frequently throughout its history, Marine Corps aviation augments Navy carrier-based aviation in projecting air power at sea or ashore.

Separate from, but closely aligned with, US naval aviation, Marine Corps aviation is a specialised force. Although distinct from the Navy, it is supported by that service, particularly the Naval Air Systems Command, in procurement, maintenance, logistics support, and training. Marine Corps aviation personnel receive their training from the Naval Air Training Command and the Naval Air Technical Training Center. USMC aviators and flight officers wear the same gold wings as their Navy counterparts, and Marine Corps jet pilots qualify to operate from aircraft-carriers.

Nine decades of glory

Marine Corps aviation traces its origin to 22 May 1912, the day First Lieutenant Alfred A. Cunningham reported for flight training at the Naval Academy in Annapolis, Md. Cunningham became Marine Corps aviator number 1 and naval aviator number 5. The number of aircraft and fliers grew slowly, but Marine Corps aviators participated in combat during amphibious landings at Tampico and Veracruz, Mexico, in April 1914. As Marine aviation grew, further action was seen in France during World War I, and in Nicaragua in 1927.

Many Marine aircraft were destroyed during the 1941 attack on Pearl Harbor, Hawaii, and during the valiant but unsuccessful defence of Wake Island. Marine fighters and dive-bombers then participated in the successful defence of Midway Island.

Marine Corps fighters, dive-bombers and, later, torpedo bombers formed the core of the 'Cactus Air Force' that defended the foothold on Guadalcanal in the Solomon Islands. For the remainder of the war, Marine flyers supported the advance up the Solomon chain and the isolation of the Japanese bastion at Rabaul, New Britain. They were instrumental in the Philippines and Okinawa campaigns.

The North Korean invasion of South Korea in June 1950 reversed the decline of Marine Corps aviation. Boosted by activated reserve squadrons, the Marine Corps entered combat in August 1950, flying close-air support missions from bases in Korea and from Navy carriers offshore, as well as fighter escort, interceptor and helicopter assault missions.

After the Korean conflict, Marine Corps aviation modernised with more jet aircraft, retiring its piston-engined F4U Corsairs and AD Skyraiders by 1959. Jet attack aircraft and supersonic jet fighters entered service during the late 1950s, followed by turbine-powered helicopters. More investment of resources was made into helicopter vertical envelopment forces, with some aircraft-carriers being converted to amphibious assault ships.

For the next decade, a substantial portion of Marine Corps aviation activity occurred in South Vietnam, where an intense effort was made to stem the Communist insurgency. Marine attack and fighter aircraft (A-4, A-6, F-4 and F-8), including some deployed onboard Navy carriers, flew mostly close air support and interdiction missions. Helicopter transports (UH-34, CH-37, CH-46 and CH-53) and gunships (UH-1, AH-1) gave Marines the mobility to carry the ground war to enemy strongholds and sanctuaries.

In the decades since the end of the Vietnam War, Marine Corps aviation has continued its modernisation, with improved tactical jet aircraft (such as the F/A-18 Hornet) and assault helicopters (CH-53E, UH-1N and AH-1T/W). The Corps also adopted the British-designed AV-8 Harrier V/STOL (vertical/short take-off and landing) attack aircraft as a front-line combat aircraft.

During the 1980s and 1990s, Marine Corps aircrews were frequently called into combat action or crisis response in various areas of the world. Helicopter crews participated in the aborted attempt to rescue American hostages in Iran in 1980, and duelled with Cuban anti-aircraft gunners during the 1983 invasion to thwart a Communist take-over of Grenada. AH-1T gunships countered Iranian boats threatening oil tankers in 1987-88 during the Iran-Iraq War. Helicopters performed numerous evacuations of Americans and other nationals from countries wracked by civil strife (Liberia in 1990; Somalia in 1991 and 1993; Albania, Congo and Sierra Leone in 1997); provided humanitarian aid to areas devastated by war or natural disaster (Kurdish northern Iraq, Bangladesh, and the Philippines in 1991); performed search and rescue missions (Bosnia in 1992 and 1995); and supported peacekeeping operations (Bosnia in 1992-1997, Cambodia in 1993 and Haiti in 1994). F/A-18 and EA-6B aircraft also supported United Nations and NATO peacekeeping efforts in Bosnia, including airstrikes flown in 1995.

By far the largest Marine Corps aviation deployment since World War II took place after the August 1990 Iraqi invasion of Kuwait. More than 70 per cent of Marine Corps aviation forces were staged in the Arabian peninsula or in amphibious assault ships offshore Kuwait as part of Operation Desert Shield. These forces formed part of the attack waves that drove Iraqi forces out of Kuwait in early 1991 in Operation Desert Storm. In the decade since, Marine Corps fighter-attack and electronic warfare squadrons have flown strikes into Iraq in support of Operations Northern and Southern Watch, and in Operation Desert Fox in December 1998.

Marine Corps aviation units were called into action in 1999 during Operation Allied Force, the NATO bombing campaign that forced a Serbian withdrawal from Kosovo. All-weather fighter-attack squadrons flew strike missions from Hungary; electronic warfare squadrons provided jamming support for NATO strikes; and Harriers and helicopters staged on amphibious assault ships supported the campaign from the Adriatic Sea.

The unrelenting tempo of crisis and combat operations during the 1990s since the end of Operation Desert Storm has kept Marine Corps aviation units at the forefront of activities, despite a significant decline in the force levels of Marine Corps fixed-wing aircraft during that time. Helicopter forces were not 'downsized' in the wake of the Cold War because they have never been sufficient to meet the needs of the Corps. The Corps has pressed ahead with its plan to decrease the number of different aircraft types in its inventory, phasing out such long-serving types such as the A-4 Skyhawk, A-6 Intruder, F-4 and RF-4 Phantom II, and OV-10 Bronco. The Corps has modernised its force with F/A-18C/D Hornets and remanufactured AV-8B Harriers, upgraded its old CH-46E Sea Knights, and is on the threshold of introducing the new MV-22B Osprey tilt-rotor assault transport into service. The Marine Corps looks forward to welcoming the remanufactured UH-1Y and AH-1Z helicopters into service, as well as the STOVL (short take-off/vertical landing) version of the Joint Strike Fighter.

In recent years, Marine Corps aviation has suffered material readiness problems with many of its ageing aircraft. Engine problems in the AV-8B Harrier II fleet caused many aircraft to be grounded and forced cancellation of deployments; CH-46E, CH-53E, AH-1W and UH-1N aircraft all have been grounded at least once for mechanical problems. Corrosion has forced the retirement of 40-year-old KC-130Fs. Two fatal mishaps have delayed production and service entry of the MV-22B.

Nevertheless, the Marine Corps has aggressively pursued and found solutions to these problems and is optimistic about the future of its aviation arm. More than any other US air arm, Marine Corps aviation, despite a constricted budget, has pushed farther in streamlining its force and its future procurement. By the end of the first quarter of the 21st century, Marine Corps aviation's front-line force will be composed of one type each of strike fighter, aerial tanker, tilt-rotor assault transport, heavy-lift helicopter and helicopter gunship.

As a replacement for the A-6 Intruder, the F/A-18D is used for multi-role taskings, including the all-weather delivery of precision-guided weapons. These two-seaters, with fully 'missionised' rear cockpit, are from VMFA(AW)-121 (with AGM-88 HARM, left), VMFA(AW)-225 (above) and VMFA(AW)-533 (below).

Above: This VMFA(AW)-224 aircraft is in RF-18D configuration, with ATARS reconnaissance equipment fitted in the nose. The cannon has to be removed to make way for ATARS.

Despite being assigned individual squadron codes, MAG-31's Hornets usually wear 'BM' codes (for Beaufort Marines). These F/A-18Ds are from VMFA(AW)-332: the assigned tailcode is 'EA'.

VMFAT-101 is the USMC's Hornet training squadron, based at Miramar. Part of VMFAT-101's syllabus is carrier qualification – here an F/A-18B from the unit lands on USS Abraham Lincoln.

VMFA-212 is the only forward-deployed Hornet unit, based at Iwakuni in Japan. It is augmented by rotations from US-based squadrons.

VMFA-115 (above) and VMFA-122 (below) are the last of the active-duty Marine squadrons to fly the F/A-18A. The aircraft below carries a rocket pod for fast-FAC duties.

Above: VMFA(AW)-242 aircraft wear the bat emblem on the insides of the fins. The F/A-18D has proved itself as an excellent laser-bomber over Bosnia and Kosovo, and has also been proven in the fast-FAC role. The overstretched fleet received a boost with the delivery of eight aircraft from the cancelled Thai order.

Below: VMFA-312 is one of two Beaufort-based USMC F/A-18 squadrons which are assigned to a carrier air wing. Miramar also has two units with a similar commitment.

Marine Corps Aircraft

To perform its premier mission of close air support, the Marine Corps currently operates two basic types of tactical jets, both built by Boeing (formerly McDonnell Douglas) – the V/STOL AV-8 Harrier II and the carrier-capable F/A-18 Hornet.

'Jump Jets'

The AV-8B Harrier II – which entered service in 1984 and eventually replaced the earlier, less capable AV-8A/C Harrier and many A-4M Skyhawks – is designed to operate from primitive airstrips, clearings and amphibious ships in support of Marines on the ground. For this role, AV-8Bs are armed with a 30-mm cannon, bombs (including laser-guided types), rockets, and AGM-65 Maverick missiles. The aircraft also have a limited air-to-air capability with AIM-9 Sidewinder missiles. AV-8Bs participated extensively in the 1991 Gulf War and, to a lesser degree, in Operation Allied Force. They routinely deploy in detachments onboard amphibious assault ships. In several recent international crises off Africa, they were the only strike aircraft on the scene.

The Harrier II fleet equips seven operational squadrons (down one from the Cold War era) and constitutes 40 per cent of Marine Corps 'Tacair'. It has passed through two avionics upgrades of the baseline version, and is currently undergoing a remanufacturing programme. The night-attack version, which equips four squadrons, includes upgrades such as a more powerful engine, a NVG-compatible cockpit, forward-looking infra-red (FLIR), a digital moving map, a fully integrated global positioning system (GPS), and triple the number of self-protection expendables, such as flares. The Harrier II+, which incorporates the night-attack upgrades and the APG-65 multi-mode radar, equips two squadrons beside the remaining baseline AV-8Bs.

A remanufacture programme for 72, now 74, aircraft is underway at Boeing's facilities in St Louis, Mo., and is more than halfway completed. (The remanufacture – which is 80 per cent the cost of a new Harrier II – is so extensive that the completed aircraft have been issued new Bureau numbers.) The programme involves replacing the Pegasus F402-RR-406 engine with the increased-thrust -408A version. (The two-seat TAV-8B, used by a Harrier replacement training squadron, is also scheduled to be refitted with the new engine.) The upgrade includes the APG-65 radar, the automatic target-handoff system (ATHS), NVG-compatible cockpit and exterior lighting, a missile-approach warning system, and a moving-map display. The Litening II IR navigation/laser-targeting system for the Harriers is undergoing tests, and the Harriers are being equipped to deploy the Joint Direct-Attack Munition (JDAM).

The Corps has been concerned with the safety record of the AV-8B, which has been grounded four times within the last year for engine problems. The remedy called for the rebuilding of 96 -408A engines by May 2001. The survivability of the Harrier in a hostile, intense air defence environment remains a concern because of the vulnerability to heat-seeking missiles of the engine exhaust nozzles, which are mounted amid the central fuselage.

In operations with amphibious ready groups in relatively benign air-defence environments, however, the Harrier is a formidable combat aircraft.

A swarm of Hornets

The Marine Corps' most potent aircraft is the Boeing F/A-18 Hornet, its front-line strike fighter, which entered service in 1982. This supersonic jet, like the F4U Corsair before it, is versatile as an air-superiority fighter and as a ground-attack aircraft. The F/A-18 carries a wide range of the aerial weapons in the Navy and Marine Corps arsenal, including the 20-mm cannon, the AIM-9 Sidewinder and AIM-7 Sparrow air-to-air missiles, the AGM-88 HARM, and a full range of other air-to-ground ordnance. Newer Hornets are capable of deploying the AIM-120 AMRAAM (Advanced Medium-Range Air-to-Air Missile) and the latest precision-guided weapons, such as JDAM, the AGM-154 JSOW (Joint Stand-Off Weapon), AGM-84E SLAM (Stand-off Land-Attack Missile), and AGM-84H SLAM-ER (Expanded Response).

The single-seat F/A-18A, which replaced the F-4 Phantom II and some A-4Ms, remains in service with two active-duty fighter-attack (VMFA) squadrons (based at MCAS Beaufort, SC), as well as four reserve VMFA squadrons. The Navy and Marine Corps have introduced the Engineering Change Proposal (ECP)-583 programme to update the combat capability of the F/A-18A with the AIM-120, AGM-154 and JDAM, as well as Link 16 and GPS, and to replace the APG-65 radar with the APG-73. The upgraded Hornet, called the F/A-18A+, is planned for all six F/A-18A squadrons. The upgrade of 76 Hornets is planned, with 44 funded to date through FY 2003. Four aircraft were modified in FY 2000; 15 will be modified in FY 2001; and 11 and 14 aircraft are slated for FY 2002 and FY 2003, respectively. The obsolescence of F/A-18A systems forced the Marine Corps to cancel the deployment of its two active-duty F/A-18A squadrons in support of Operation Allied Force in 1999, replacing them with two F/A-18D squadrons.

A few two-seat F/A-18Bs, similar to F/A-18As, serve in the replacement training role for the Hornet. For several years in the early 1990s, some reserve VMFA squadrons operated a single F/A-18B for crew proficiency training.

Six active-duty VMFA squadrons operate the single-seat F/A-18C Hornet, which is equipped with improved engines, avionics and weapons, including the AIM-120, AGM-154, AGM-84E/H and JDAM. F/A-18Cs produced since 1989 feature improved night-attack capabilities, including a FLIR pod, a raster HUD, NVGs, cockpit lighting compatible with NVGs, a digital colour moving map, and a multi-purpose colour display. Improved-performance engines were introduced in the mid-1990s. The F/A-18Cs are steadily being upgraded with a tactical FLIR/laser designator pod, ARC-210 anti-jam radios, GPS and a cockpit video recorder. Programmed upgrades to be completed by 2001 include Link 16 and the AIM-9X Sidewinder AAM. Further upgrades planned include advanced colour cockpit displays, satellite communications and the Block 6 version of the AGM-88 HARM.

Under an agreement struck during the mid-

1990s between the Commandant of the Marine Corps and the Chief of Naval Operations, four of the six F/A-18C VMFA squadrons are assigned permanently to Navy carrier air wings, replacing Navy squadrons that were disestablished because of the post-Cold War drawdown. These squadrons – two from MCAS Beaufort (VMFAs 251 and 312) and two from MCAS Miramar, Calif. (VMFAs 314 and 323) – sail with their Navy counterparts on regular six-month deployments. During the 1990s, these carrier-based squadrons flew combat missions over Bosnia and in support of Operation Southern Watch over Iraq. One carrier-based VMFA unit flew strikes over Iraq during Operation Desert Fox in December 1998, and in late 1999 an F/A-18C from VMFA-251 became the first aircraft to launch an AGM-84H SLAM-ER in combat. In 2000, VMFA-251 joined VFA-82 in becoming the first carrier-based aircraft to drop the JDAM in combat, during a Southern Watch strike.

All-weather Hornets

Six Marine All-Weather Fighter-Attack (VMFA(AW)) Squadrons are equipped with the two-seat F/A-18D, which replaced (though did not match in capability) the A-6 Intruder in Marine Corps service. Having a night-attack capability similar to that of the single-seat F/A-18C, the F/A-18D is assigned the FAC(A)/TAC(A) (forward air controller (airborne)/tactical air controller (airborne)) roles, in addition to the all-weather strike role. These aircraft are the most potent 'shooters' in Marine Corps inventory and are heavily tasked, a cause for concern among Marine Corps planners. During the mid-1990s, F/A-18Ds deployed to Aviano Air Base in Italy in support of NATO combat and peacekeeping operations in Bosnia. Two F/A-18D squadrons – VMFA(AW) 332 and 533 – deployed to Taszar, Hungary in 1999 for Allied Force (in place of two F/A-18A units) and flew 597 strike sorties over Serbia and Kosovo without loss. They expended more than 303,500 lb (137668 kg) of ordnance.

The Taszar-deployed squadrons brought the ATARS (Advanced Tactical Airborne Reconnaissance System) for its first operational deployment. ATARS restores to the Marine Corps a reconnaissance capability lost when the RF-4B Phantom II was retired in 1990. Interchangeable with the Hornet's cannon, ATARS features three EO and IR sensors linked to a ground site which can receive digital real-time or near-real-time imagery. The system can provide high-resolution vertical or oblique daylight imagery, or high-resolution infra-red imagery. The aircraft's APG-73 radar can transmit radar video or maps of the tactical area of interest to a ground site, as well. The Marine Corps plans to procure sufficient ATARS to equip each VMFA(AW) unit with four systems, plus extra systems for training and spares. However, funding for further procurement was deleted from the FY 2001 budget, thus delaying longer the full deployment of ATARS.

The heavy demand for F/A-18Ds has resulted in an agreement between the Navy and the Marine Corps under which the Navy will transfer some F/A-18Ds from its fleet readiness squadrons to the Marine Corps as the Navy acquires the F/A-18E/F Super Hornet. The misfortune of Thailand's economy in the late 1990s proved a boon for the USMC when

Above: VMFA-232 'Red Devils' forms part of MAG-11 at Miramar. Both of the Hornet MAGs have seven squadrons each, three of which fly the two-seat F/A-18D. Miramar has three F/A-18C units and the training squadron, while Beaufort has two with F/A-18As and two with F/A-18Cs.

VMFA-314 (above) and VMFA-323 (left) are the two Miramar squadrons with a carrier assignment. These units routinely spend about six months of the year afloat to augment the Navy's depleted F/A-18C force.

First Marine Aircraft Wing

Camp S.D. Butler, Okinawa

UNIT	NAME	TYPE	TAILCODE	BASE
MWHS-1	–	none	–	Camp S.D. Butler, Okinawa
H&HS Futenma	–	UC-12F, CT-39G	5F	MCAS Futenma, Okinawa
Note: CT-39G to be replaced by UC-35D by October 2001				
H&HS Iwakuni	–	UC-12F, HH-46D	5G	MCAS Iwakuni, Japan
Marine Aircraft Group 12				MCAS Iwakuni, Japan
MALS-12	–	none	–	MCAS Iwakuni, Japan
VMAQ-X	–	EA-6B	–	MCAS Iwakuni, Japan
VMFA-212	Lancers	F/A-18C	WD	MCAS Iwakuni, Japan
VMFA-XXX	–	F/A-18A/C		MCAS Iwakuni, Japan
VMFA(AW)-XXX	–	F/A-18D		MCAS Iwakuni, Japan
Note: XXX denotes units from other MAGs rotated to Japan on six-month deployments under the Unit Deployment Plan.				
Marine Aircraft Group 36				MCAS Futenma, Okinawa
MALS-36	–	none	–	MCAS Futenma, Okinawa
HMH-XXX	–	CH-53E	–	MCAS Futenma, Okinawa
HMLA-XXX	–	AH-1W/UH-1N	–	MCAS Futenma, Okinawa
HMM-262	Flying Tigers	CH-46E	ET	MCAS Futenma, Okinawa
HMM-265	Dragons	CH-46E	EP	MCAS Futenma, Okinawa
VMGR-152	Sumos	KC-130F	QD	MCAS Futenma, Okinawa
VMA-XXX Det	–	AV-8B	–	MCAS Futenma, Okinawa
Note: XXX denotes units from other MAGs rotated to Okinawa on six-month deployments under the Unit Deployment Plan.				
First MAW Air Support Element				MCAF Kaneohe Bay, Hawaii
MALSE	–	none	–	MCAF Kaneohe Bay, Hawaii
HMH-362	Ugly Angels	CH-53D	YL	MCAF Kaneohe Bay, Hawaii
HMH-363	Red Lions	CH-53D	YZ	MCAF Kaneohe Bay, Hawaii
HMH-463	Pegasus	CH-53D	YH	MCAF Kaneohe Bay, Hawaii
HMT-301 (RTS)	Wind Walkers	CH-53D	SU	MCAF Kaneohe Bay, Hawaii
Marine Wing Support Group 17				Camp Foster, Okinawa
MWSS-171	–	none	–	MCAS Iwakuni, Japan
MWSS-172	–	none	–	MCAS Futenma, Okinawa
Marine Air Control Group 18				MCAS Futenma, Okinawa
MASS-2	–	none	–	MCAS Futemna, Okinawa
MACS-4	–	none	–	MCAS Futenma, Okinawa
ATC Det.	–	none	–	MCAS Futenma, Okinawa
ATC Det.	–	none	–	MCAS Iwakuni, Japan
MWCS-18	–	none	–	MCAS Futenma, Okinawa
MTACS-18	–	none	–	MCAS Futenma, Okinawa
1st Stinger Batt.	–	none	–	MCAS Futenma, Okinawa

The EA-6B Prowler fleet is concentrated at Cherry Point and consists of four squadrons. Illustrated here are VMAQ-1 (left), VMAQ-2 (above) and VMAQ-3 (below). Like the Navy Prowler squadrons, the fleet is thinly stretched because of operational commitments (which include support for the US Air Force). Three of the four Marine Prowler units participated in Allied Force.

Below: As well as active jamming, the EA-6B is equipped to shoot back with the AGM-88 HARM missile, as displayed by this pair of VMAQ-4 aircraft. Marine Prowlers are also equipped to perform a limited electronic intelligence function.

81

Thailand cancelled an order for a batch of eight Hornets, which were diverted to the Corps. The last Hornet built by Boeing – an F/A-18D – was delivered to the Corps in September 2000. More F/A-18Cs will be made available to the Marine Corps as Navy VFA squadrons make the transition to the single-seat F/A-18E.

JSFs, not Super Hornets

The Marine Corps plans to continue to decrease the numbers of different aircraft types in service by replacing its AV-8Bs and F/A-18s from 2008 with the STOVL Joint Strike Fighter (JSF), a supersonic single-engined strike fighter that will be capable of strike missions, aerial combat, and suppression of enemy air defences. JSF STOVL concept development aircraft (Boeing X-32B and Lockheed Martin X-35B) flew their first test flights in 2001. The winning design of the competition – scheduled to be selected in September 2001 – will be the basis for a full-scale development JSF. The Marine Corps plans to procure 609 JSFs.

Any delay in the JSF programme or cancellation of the programme will pose a dilemma for Marine Corps planners. The Corps has declined to participate in the Navy's F/A-18E/F Super Hornet programme, choosing instead to husband its budget in order to afford the JSF. The decision was made easier because the Super Hornet production schedule was such that any aircraft for the Marine Corps would not have been available until about the time that the JSF entered production. The Navy acquisition of the Super Hornet eventually will free up low-time F/A-18Cs to replace older Hornets in the Corps. If the JSF is cancelled, it is conceivable that the Corps will change its plans and procure the Super Hornet, a move that would lower the unit cost of the aircraft for the Navy.

Jammers and HARMs

The ever-increasing importance of electronic warfare has been highlighted in recent years by the high level of demand on the Marine Corps' four Tactical Electronic Warfare (VMAQ) Squadrons equipped with Northrop Grumman EA-6B Prowlers. The carrier-capable EA-6B, which had replaced the EA-6A Intruder by 1992, is used to jam enemy radars and communications, and to attack enemy radars with AGM-88 HARMs (high-speed anti-radiation missiles). The current configuration of the EA-6B – the ICAP II (Increased Capability II) Block 89 – is almost identical to that of Navy EA-6Bs, one exception being the installation of TERPES (Tactical Electronic Reconnaissance and Processing System). TERPES is designed to provide tactical order-of-battle information and to allow theatre commanders to access electronically such sensors as satellites.

In 2001, the VMAQ squadrons began to receive the ICAP II Block 89A EA-6B, which features an upgraded AYK-14 mission computer, an integrated GPS/INS and two frequency-agile ARC-210 radios. The aircraft's wing centre-sections are being replaced as funds permit to alleviate the airframe limitations caused by stress cracks.

Department of Defense approval has been given to Northrop Grumman to develop an ICAP III Warfighter Upgrade System configuration, expected to enter service in 2005. ICAP III upgrades include installation of a new LR-700 receiver to replace the ALQ-99, improved low-band jamming capability, integration of the USQ-113 radio countermeasures set, and integration of sensor information from other EW platforms.

In the meantime, a variety of other upgrades is being integrated or are in development for the Prowler fleet: (1) multi-mission advanced tactical terminal/data modem; (2) digital storage memory unit; (3) low-band transmitter; (4) band 9/10 transmitter; (5) modified band 9/10 transmitter; (6) universal exciter upgrade; (7) night-vision lighting kits; and (8) spray-cool technology.

Although not designated expeditionary squadrons, Marine EA-6B units, together with Navy EA-6B squadrons, have assumed the electronic jamming role for the Air Force since the 1998 retirement of the EF-111A Raven. Marine EA-6Bs have been deployed routinely to MCAS Iwakuni, Japan and frequently to sites in Aviano, Italy (in support of UN and NATO operations over Bosnia), Incirlik, Turkey (in support of Operation Northern Watch over Iraq), and Prince Sultan Air Base, Saudi Arabia (in support of Operation Southern Watch). Three of the four VMAQ squadrons were deployed to Aviano in support of Operation Allied Force in early 1999, when, with Navy EA-6Bs, they flew combat missions for strikes in Kosovo and Serbia. The heavy Allied Force commitment has caused six-month gaps in deployments to Iwakuni. For several years until the mid-1990s, one VMAQ squadron was assigned to a Navy carrier air wing, until a Navy unit was established to replace it.

The EA-6B has been out of production since 1991, and the high level of defence commitments has strained the availability of this ageing aircraft, which is scheduled to serve until 2015. No successor for the EA-6B has been identified, but an analysis of alternatives is under way for the replacement, known as the Advanced Electronic Attack (AEA) aircraft. One possibility is an EW version of the JSF. Another is an EW version of the two-seat F/A-18F Super Hornet (F/A-18G 'Growler'); adoption of this platform would mean the acquisition of another distinct airframe for the Marine Corps, but would enable the replacement to be fielded sooner. If the Navy develops the 'Growler', a likely scenario would have the Navy pass its most modern EA-6Bs to the Marine Corps until a replacement aircraft is developed for the Marine Corps.

Herculean lifters

The Lockheed KC-130 Hercules has been used by the Marine Corps since 1960 as a long-range aerial tanker and, secondarily, as a transport. The KC-130 is used to refuel fixed-wing, tilt-rotor and rotary-wing aircraft in flight, and to refuel tactical vehicles and ground support equipment on the ground. As a transport, the KC-130 can carry 92 troops or 64 paratroops, or more than 38,000 lb (17235 kg) of cargo. The 34 KC-130F versions still in service are the oldest aircraft in front-line US naval service (with an average age of 39), and some recently have been struck from inventory because of corrosion.

The remainder of the active force is made up of 14 KC-130Rs that have served for two decades. The Marine Corps Reserve operates 28 modern KC-130T and stretched KC-130T-30 versions, the last of which was delivered in October 1996. Under an avionics systems improvement programme (ASIP), 13 older KC-130F/R versions ('core' aircraft to support the KC-130J transition) are being updated with the installation of GPS, night-vision lighting, ARC-210 radios and external wing tanks, among other upgrades. Eight KC-130Ts are equipped with DECM (defensive electronic countermeasures), as well as NVG-compatible exterior lighting.

On 14 June 2000, Lockheed Martin conducted the first flight of the new KC-130J, a version of the Hercules with new engines and six-bladed propellers, a 'digital' cockpit, head-up displays, night-vision lighting compatibility, aerial refuelling capability improvements, a 21 per cent increase in speed and a 35 per cent increase in range. The KC-130J, which is equipped with the Flight Refuelling Ltd Mk 32B-901E aerial refuelling system, has a 57,500-lb (26082-kg) fuel off-load capability using wing and external tanks, and can carry an additional 24,392 lb (11065 kg) in a tank in its cargo bay. Eleven KC-130Js have been ordered, to replace the KC-130Fs; the Marine Corps hopes eventually to acquire 51 KC-130Js. The KC-130J is scheduled to reach initial operational capability in FY 2002 when VMGR-252 fields six deployable KC-130Js.

The Marine Corps also operates one TC-130G (a former Navy EC-130G) to provide air show logistic support for the Naval Flight Demonstration Squadron, the 'Blue Angels'. This aircraft, *Fat Albert*, is also used to please crowds with demonstration of its rocket-assisted take-off capability.

At the heart of Marine Corps aviation is the support of ground troops, including providing mobility in the battlefield. A substantial number of Marine aircraft are assault transport helicopters, soon to be augmented by advanced tilt-rotor aircraft.

Heavy haulers

Competing with the KC-130 as the Marine Corps heavy hauler is the Sikorsky CH-53E Super Stallion, which succeeded the CH-53D on the Sikorsky production line. A larger, three-engined upgrade of the CH-53D, the CH-53E is capable of transporting 55 troops or 16 tons (16.25 tonnes) of cargo. A true heavy-lift helicopter, the CH-53E can carry externally the 26,000-lb (11793-kg) light armoured vehicle or any tactical jet aircraft in Marine Corps inventory. The CH-53E, armed with two 0.50-in machine-guns for self-defence, can be refuelled in flight from a KC-130.

Production of the CH-53E ended in 1999, but the helicopter is expected to serve until 2025, when a proposed replacement, the Joint Transport Rotorcraft, should supplant it. In the meantime, the Marine Corps is upgrading its Super Stallions with ARC-210 anti-jam radios, GPS, a ground-proximity warning system, a FLIR navigation set, an NVG HUD, crash-attenuating troop seats, and improved engine nacelles and fire detectors. The Marine Corps is planning to begin a service-life extension programme (SLEP) in 2005 to keep the CH-53E fleet capable through the first quarter of the 21st century. Planned upgrades include the modification of the airframe in critical structural wear points, improvement of the tail-rotor drive-shaft components, and replacement of older wiring. The Marine Corps is also consid-

Each of the three active-duty MAWs has a KC-130 squadron allocated for refuelling and transport duties. For the 1st MAW in Japan the squadron is VMGR-152 'Sumos', with KC-130F/Rs.

Left: A recent Marine Corps acquisition is the KC-130J, which entered service with VMGR-252 at Cherry Point in 2000. The 'J' has begun the replacement of the elderly KC-130F. Note the revised refuelling pods.

Above: A KC-130R from VMGR-352 demonstrates the art of refuelling with a pair of Hornets. The Marine Hercules are also routinely called upon to refuel CH-53 helicopters as well as tactical fighters.

MCAS Yuma houses four squadrons of AV-8Bs, including VMA-211 (above) and VMA-214 (below). The USMC fleet is a mix of radar-equipped Harrier II+ aircraft and standard night attack machines.

Above: VMA-223 'Bulldogs' is at Cherry Point flying the AV-8B+. The bulged canopy of the Harrier II gives the pilot excellent visibility, a distinct advantage in close air support operations.

Below: This trio of AV-8Bs is from VMA-513 'Nightmares'. When the gun is not fitted, large aerodynamic strakes are required instead to maintain recirculated lift in the hover.

Training for the Harrier community is conducted by VMAT-203 at Cherry Point. The schoolhouse operates all of the Corps' TAV-8B two-seaters. Limited weapons training is possible thanks to the TAV-8B's single pylon under each wing.

AV-8B Harrier II+ aircraft, like this gun-armed VMA-231 example, have the same APG-65 multi-mode radar as fitted to the F/A-18C.

Above: AV-8B of VMA-311 'Tomcats' at MCAS Yuma

Right: AV-8B+ of VMA-542 'Flying Tigers'.

ering replacing the helicopters' engines with the turboshaft engines used on the MV-22 Osprey.

The CH-53E equips five active and two reserve Marine Heavy Helicopter (HMH) Squadrons, as well as one Marine Helicopter Training (HMT) Squadron and Marine Helicopter Squadron One (HMX-1).

Medium lift

Once considered a heavy-lift helicopter, the twin-engined Sikorsky CH-53D Sea Stallion has been classed as a medium-lift helicopter since the CH-53E entered service in substantial numbers. Introduced in 1968, the CH-53D is used to lift troops, supplies and equipment (including small vehicles) to the battlefield. Armed with two 0.50-in machine-guns for self-defence, it can carry 37 troops or 8,000-12,000 lb (3628-5443 kg) of cargo.

All CH-53Ds are now based at Kaneohe Bay in Hawaii, where they equip three HMH squadrons and one HMT squadron. The earlier CH-53A versions were retired in the early 1990s, and the RH-53Ds (former Navy minesweeping helicopters) have also been retired, having been replaced in Marine Corps Reserve service by CH-53Es.

The CH-53D fleet is being modernised with GPS, ARC-210 anti-jam radios, and crash-attenuating troop seats. The Sea Stallion is scheduled to have been replaced by the MV-22B Osprey by 2008, although that replacement is likely to slip because of the delayed service entry of the MV-22B.

'Frogs'

The most numerous Marine Corps helicopter is the tandem-rotor Boeing CH-46E Sea Knight medium-lift helicopter, many of which are three decades old. The Sea Knight, which can be armed with two 0.50-in guns for self-defence, is assigned the role of transporting Marines and their equipment and supplies to the battlefield. The CH-46E fleet represents an upgrade from CH-46A/D/F versions, and is currently going through several upgrade programs to keep the 'Frog' flying until it can be replaced by the MV-22B tilt-rotor assault transport.

The Dynamic Component Upgrade (DCU) programme is designed to restore the CH-46E's original lift capability (24,300 lb/11022 kg), which has long been restricted by fatigue of the airframe and dynamic components. DCU involves the replacement of flight controls, rotor-heads, drive-train systems, hydraulic pumps and other dynamic components, and removal of engine exhaust-device plumbing.

Several OSIPs (Operational System Improvement Programs) are ongoing to ensure the airworthiness of the CH-46E fleet. These OSIPs include replacement of the utility hydraulic pump and upgrade of the engine condition control system and electrical system. The communications/navigation control system upgrade includes the installation of the ARC-210 radio, an NVG HUD, and an integrated GPS navigation system.

The CH-46E equips 14 active and two reserve Marine Medium Helicopter (HMM) Squadrons, as well as one replacement training squadron, HMM(T)-164. A few CH-46Es are used to support the presidential executive flight detachment of HMX-1. Nine HH-46D search and rescue versions are used by headquarters squadrons for air station rescue flights.

Advent of the Osprey

The long-awaited replacement for the CH-46E and CH-53D fleet is on the verge of achieving initial operational capability. The world's first operational tilt-rotor aircraft, the Bell Boeing MV-22 Osprey, entered low-rate initial production in 1997 after a protracted full-scale development period that was marred by two mishaps. It completed its operational evaluation in July 2000 in spite of a fatal mishap in Marana, Ariz., in which 19 Marines were killed.

The Osprey was required to complete an additional shipboard evaluation of its wing-fold mechanisms late in 2000 before a decision for full-rate production would be made. The shipboard period was successfully completed, but on 11 December 2000 another crash in North Carolina, in which four Marines were killed, resulted in the grounding of the Osprey fleet and an indefinite delay in a Department of Defense decision for full-rate production.

The Department of Defense initiated an independent panel to conduct a thorough review of the Osprey programme. The panel recommended a list of modifications and that the programme continue at the minimum rate of production necessary to sustain the factory line. The Department of Defense accepted the recommendations and decided to continue production at a minimum rate, said by some experts to be 11 or 12 aircraft per year. Thirty LRIP MV-22Bs had been authorised through FY 2000, 10 of which had been delivered before the fleet was grounded. Production of the MV-22B was expected to reach 30 aircraft per year and total 360 MV-22Bs by 2014. The timetable of the introduction of the Osprey is now conditional on its return to flight status and the time required to complete recommended modifications.

The MV-22B, with a crew of two, can carry 24 fully-equipped troops, or 12 litters, or 10,000 lb (4536 kg) of cargo internally or 15,000 lb (6804 kg) externally to a radius of 200 nm (370 km) (or farther with aerial refuelling). The Osprey can reach altitudes of 25,000 ft (7620 m) and speeds of more than 260 kt (481 km/h). The aircraft can range out to 1,820 nm (3370 km) with one aerial refuelling. The aircraft is stressed to handle 0.50-in guns for self-defence; a proposed nose-mounted Gatling gun has not yet been funded.

The four MV-22B EMD (engineering and manufacturing development) aircraft continued the test and evaluation programme initiated with the heavier V-22A versions, which have been retired. Two of the four EMD MV-22Bs have since been converted into the first two CV-22B special warfare versions for the USAF.

The Osprey replacement training squadron, Marine Medium Tilt-rotor Training Squadron 204 (VMMT-204), was redesignated from HMT-204 on 10 June 1999, one month after the first production MV-22B was delivered to the Marine Corps. Crew training commenced in mid-2000 at MCAS New River, NC. VMMT-204 is scheduled to receive 12 Ospreys.

Four HMM units at MCAS New River are scheduled to transition to the MV-22B, followed by four HMM squadrons at MCAS Miramar, Calif., then two HMM squadrons in Okinawa, three CH-53D-equipped HMM squadrons in Hawaii, three HMM squadrons at Camp Pendleton, Calif., and finally the last two HMM squadrons at New River. HMX-1 also is scheduled to receive 18 Ospreys between 2004 and 2012.

Hueys and Super Cobras

Versions of the Bell Textron UH-1 Iroquois (Huey) utility helicopter and AH-1 Cobra helicopter gunship have been in Marine Corps service for more than three decades. The AH-1J Sea Cobra has been retired, and all remaining AH-1Ts have been upgraded to AH-1W Super Cobra configuration. Production of the AH-1W for the Marine Corps closed in mid-1998, but remains open for foreign sales to Turkey. AH-1Ws and UH-1Ns serve together in Marine Light Attack Helicopter Squadrons (HMLAs).

The versatile AH-1W gunship is a powerful weapons platform with a size that belies is potency. The aircraft is armed with a turret-mounted M197 20-mm cannon and can carry 2.75-in and 5-in rockets, AGM-114 Hellfire and BGM-71 TOW anti-armour missiles, AGM-122 Sidearm anti-radiation missiles and AIM-9 Sidewinder air-to-air missiles.

The AH-1W fleet is going through an extensive avionics upgrade programme to improve its capability at night and in poor weather. The main feature of this upgrade is a night targeting system that includes an infra-red system, a low-light television system, laser-designation range finder, and – for the TOW missile system – an auto-track capability. Other components of the upgrade are the ARC-210 anti-jam radio, an integrated GPS/INS and a new TACAN (tactical air navigation) system.

USMC Aircraft Squadron Changes 1989-2000					
Activated		**Deactivated**		HML-776	1 Jul 1994
		VMFP-3	1 Oct 1990	VMO-4	30 Jul 1994
VMAQ-1	1 Jul 1992	VMA-133	30 Sep 1992	VMFA-235	30 Jun 1996
VMAQ-3	1 Jul 1992	VMA-322	30 Jun 1992	VMFA-451	31 Jan 1997
HMH-366	30 Sep 1994	VMA-331	30 Sep 1992	VMA-131	30 Dec 1998
VMU-2	15 Jan 1996	VMAQ-4*	1 Oct 1992	VMFA-124	1 Dec 1998
		VMFA-333	31 Mar 1992	HMH-366	1 Oct 2000
		VMFA-531	31 Mar 1992		
Reactivated		HMH-772 Det A	1 Apr 1993	**Redesignated**	
VMFA(AW)-225	1 Jul 1991	HMH-772 Det B	1 Apr 1993	VMA-142 to VMFA-142	21 Dec 1990
VMAQ-4*	2 Oct 1992	HMT-301	13 Dec 1993	VMA(AW)-121 to VMFA(AW)-121	8 Dec 1989
HMH-769	1 Apr 1993	VMO-1	31 Jul 1993	VMA(AW)-242 to VMFA(AW)-242	14 Dec 1990
HMT-301	30 Sep 1995	VMO-2	20 May 1993	VMA(AW)-533 to VMFA(AW)-533	1 Oct 1992
		HML-771	1 Aug 1994	VMA(AW)-224 to VMFA(AW)-224	5 Mar 1993

VMA(AW)-332 to VMFA(AW)-332	16 Jun 1993
HMA-773 to HMLA-773	1 Jul 1994
HMA-775 to HMLA-775	1 Aug 1994
HML-767 to HMLA-775 Det A	1 Aug 1994
VMA-124 to VMFA-124	15 Nov 1994
1st Marine UAV Co. to VMU-1	15 Jan 1996
SOES Cherry Point to VMR-1	17 Sep 1997
SOMS El Toro to VMR-2	1997
VMR-2 to H&HS Miramar	Jul 1999
HMT-204 to VMMT-204	10 Jun 1999
HMM-164 to HMM(T)-164	10 Jun 1999

VMAQ-4 was deactivated as a reserve unit on 1 October 1992 and reactivated as an active-duty unit on 2 October 1992

AH-1Ws and UH-1Ns operate in mixed squadrons. This Hellfire- and rocket-carrying 'Whiskey' (above) and FLIR-equipped Twin Huey (below) both serve with HMLA-167 'Warriors' at New River, North Carolina.

Camp Pendleton is the main base for the light attack helicopter fleet, with six squadrons (four active-duty, one reserve and one training). The UH-1N (above) flies with HMLA-169 while the AH-1W (left) serves with HMLA-267. The UH-1N is in full 'war fit', with FLIR, IR countermeasures and door gun/rocket mount.

Above and right: MCAS New River has two active-duty Cobra/Huey squadrons, including HMLA-269 which operates both this AH-1W and UH-1N.

Second Marine Aircraft Wing

MCAS Cherry Point, N.C.

UNIT	NAME	TYPE	TAILCODE	BASE
MWHS-2	–	none	–	MCAS Cherry Point, N.C.
H&HS Beaufort	–	UC-12B, HH-46D	5B	MCAS Beaufort, S.C.
H&HS New River	–	UC-12B	5D	MCAS New River, N.C.
VMR-1	–	C-9B, UC-12B, HH-46D	5C	MCAS Cherry Point
Marine Aircraft Group 14				MCAS Cherry Point, N.C.
MALS-14	–	none	–	MCAS Cherry Point, N.C.
VMA-223	Bulldogs	AV-8B	WP	MCAS Cherry Point, N.C.
VMA-231	Ace of Spades	AV-8B	CG	MCAS Cherry Point, N.C.
VMA-542	Flying Tigers	AV-8B	WH	MCAS Cherry Point, N.C.
VMAT-203 (RTS)	Hawks	AV-8B, TAV-8B	KD	MCAS Cherry Point, N.C.
VMAQ-1	Banshees	EA-6B	CB	MCAS Cherry Point, N.C.
VMAQ-2	Panthers	EA-6B	CY	MCAS Cherry Point, N.C.
VMAQ-3	Moon Dogs	EA-6B	MD	MCAS Cherry Point, N.C.
VMAQ-4	Seahawks	EA-6B	RM	MCAS Cherry Point, N.C.
VMGR-252	Heavy Haulers	KC-130F/R/J	BH	MCAS Cherry Point, N.C.
VMGRT-253 (RTS)	Titans	KC-130F	GR	MCAS Cherry Point, N.C.
VMU-2	Night Owls	RQ-2A	FF	MCAS Cherry Point, NC.
Marine Aircraft Group 26				MCAS New River, N.C.
MALS-26	–	none	–	MCAS New River, N.C.
HMH-461	Iron Horse	CH-53E	CJ	MCAS New River, N.C.
HMLA-167	Warriors	AH-1W, UH-1N	TV	MCAS New River, N.C.
HMM-261	Bulls	CH-46E	EM	MCAS New River, N.C.
HMM-264	Black Bulls	CH-46E	EH	MCAS New River, N.C.
HMM-266	Fighting Griffins	CH-46E	ES	MCAS New River, N.C.
VMMT-204 (RTS)	White Knights	MV-22B	GX	MCAS New River, N.C.
Marine Aircraft Group 29				MCAS New River, N.C.
MALS-29	–	none	–	MCAS New River, N.C.
HMH-464	Condors	CH-53E	EN	MCAS New River, N.C.
HMLA-269	Gunrunners	AH-1W, UH-1N	HF	MCAS New River, N.C.
HMM-162	Golden Eagles	CH-46E	YS	MCAS New River, N.C.
HMM-263	Red Lions	CH-46E	EG	MCAS New River, N.C.
HMM-365	Sky Knights	CH-46E	YM	MCAS New River, N.C.
HMT-302 (RTS)	Phoenix	CH-53E, MH-53E	UT	MCAS New River, N.C.
Marine Aircraft Group 31				MCAS Beaufort, S.C.
MALS-31	–	none	–	MCAS Beaufort, S.C.
VMFA-115	Silver Eagles	F/A-18A	VE	MCAS Beaufort, S.C.
VMFA-122	Crusaders	F/A-18A	DC	MCAS Beaufort, S.C.
VMFA-251	Thunderbolts	F/A-18C	DW	MCAS Beaufort, S.C.
VMFA-312	Checkerboards	F/A-18C	DR	MCAS Beaufort, S.C.
VMFA(AW)-224	Bengals	F/A-18D	WK	MCAS Beaufort, S.C.
VMFA(AW)-332	Moonlighters	F/A-18D	EA	MCAS Beaufort, S.C.
VMFA(AW)-533	Hawks	F/A-18D	ED	MCAS Beaufort, S.C.

Note: Since the mid-1990s, most MAG-31 squadrons used an unofficial tail code, BM., on their F/A-18 Hornets. The squadron's official code sometimes is carried on the inside of the vertical stabilizers. VMFA-251 and VMFA-312 use the codes of the carrier air wings (CVWs) to which they are assigned, currently AB (CVW-1) and AC (CVW-3), respectively.

Marine Wing Support Group 27				MCAS Cherry Point, N.C.
MWSS-271	–	none	–	MCALF Bogue Field, N.C.
MWSS-272	–	none	–	MCAS New River, N.C.
MWSS-273	–	none	–	MCAS Beaufort, S.C.
MWSS-274	–	none	–	MCAS Cherry Point, N.C.
Marine Air Control Group 28				MCAS Cherry Point, N.C.
MASS-1	–	none	–	MCAS Cherry Point, N.C.
MACS-2	–	none	–	MCAS Beaufort, S.C.
ATC Det.	–	none	–	MCALF Bogue Field, N.C.
ATC Det.	–	none	–	MCAS New River, N.C.
ATC Det.	–	none	–	MCAS Beaufort, S.C.
MWCS-28	–	none	–	MCAS Cherry Point, N.C.
MTACS-28	–	none	–	MCAS Cherry Point, N.C.
2nd LAAD Batt.	–	none	–	MCAS Cherry Point, N.C.

The Marine Corps has long used the Bell Textron UH-1N Iroquois for observation, utility, medevac and gunship roles. The Huey can be armed with M240D 7.62-mm machine-guns, GAU-17 7.62-mm Miniguns, GAU-15 0.50-in machine-guns and 2.75-in rockets. Like the AH-1W, the UH-1N fleet is going through an upgrade programme that includes installation of ARC-210 radios, satellite communication, a miniature GPS and an upgraded TACAN, as well as night-vision enhancements such as improved external lighting, an NVG HUD and the AAQ-22 NTIS (night thermal imaging system). The NTIS features a high-resolution FLIR, an autotracker, a laser rangefinder and a coupled-device camera. An upgrade to the AAQ-22 was introduced in 1999.

The Marine Corps also operates a few unarmed versions of the Huey as HH-1Ns. During the early 1990s, because of the increasing combat capability of the armed Hueys and the resulting avionics configuration, the Navy decided to redesignate unarmed UH-1Ns as HH-1Ns. These aircraft are used for replacement training with HMT-303 and for air station search and rescue duties.

Vipers and Venoms

When considering the need to upgrade its light helicopter fleet, the Marine Corps decided against upgrading to the Sikorsky Black Hawk, and opted instead for a remanufacturing programme for both the UH-1N and AH-1W, initially designated 4BW/4BN in recognition of one of the main improvements, a rotor with four composite-material blades rather than two. Airframe life will be extended by 10,000 flight hours. The upgrade, which aims to provide 85 per cent commonality in mechanical and avionics components, will also involve standardising the engines (T700-GE-401s), drive trains, hydraulic and fuel systems, crashworthy seats, and integrated avionics and software for both types. Both helicopter types will be fitted with the integrated helmet display and sighting system, and 'glass' cockpits featuring colour

multifunction displays, mission and weapon system computers, advanced digital navigation and communication equipment, and ribbonised wiring. The AH-1Z will also be equipped with the Lockheed Martin Hawkeye target sight system, which includes a third-generation IR detection system, a laser rangefinder, low-light colour television, and large-aperture optics.

The improvements embodied in the AH-1Z are expected to give it three times the range or twice the payload of an AH-1W in a typical close air support scenario. The UH-1Y is expected to have both twice the payload and twice the range of the UH-1N in a typical night-insertion scenario.

Plans call for 180 AH-1Ws and 100 UH-1Ns and HH-1Ns to be remanufactured into AH-1Zs and UH-1Ys, respectively. Two HH-1Ns are being remanufactured as UH-1Y development aircraft for the programme. Although the names have yet to achieve popularity, the Department of Defense has officially approved the names Viper and Venom for the AH-1Z and UH-1Y, respectively.

The first of three developmental AH-1Zs made its maiden flight on 7 December 2000 and is going through testing at NAS Patuxent River, Md. The first of two UH-1Y development aircraft is scheduled for its initial flight in November 2001. First deliveries of production aircraft are planned for 2003. The UH-1Y and AH-1Z are scheduled for initial operational capability in 2004 and 2006, respectively. A version of the AH-1Z known as the King Cobra is being offered for foreign military sales.

A proposed Joint Replacement Aircraft (JRA) is being considered to replace both the UH-1 and AH-1 in approximately 2020.

Radio flyers

One of the busiest aircraft in the Marine Corps over the last decade has been the RQ-2A Pioneer unmanned aerial vehicle (UAV). The radio-controlled aircraft, in service since the late 1980s, is used for battlefield reconnaissance, surveillance and target acquisition

(RTSA), as well as battle damage assessment.

Pioneers can be launched using RATO or pneumatic rails and can be recovered by net at sea or landed ashore in a 656 x 246-ft (200 x 75-m) unimproved field. The RQ-2A can carry a sensor payload weighing 65-100 lb (30-45 kg), consisting of a television or infra-red camera, on missions lasting more than five hours. Control of the UAV can be handed from one control station to another, thereby increasing the aircraft's range and allowing launch from one site and recovery at another. Controllers can pilot two Pioneers simultaneously, but the video downlink and positive control can be managed for only one vehicle at a time.

Pioneers were highly successful in Operation Desert Storm. They have been deployed extensively to Bosnia since the mid-1990s and were very active during Operation Allied Force in 1999 over Kosovo.

The Navy and Marine Corps have selected the RQ-8A Fire Scout vertical take-off UAV (VTUAV) to replace the RQ-2A. The Northrop Grumman Model 379, an unmanned development of the Schweizer 330SP light helicopter, was chosen in February 2000 for shipboard and land-based use, and approved for low-rate initial production in early 2001 (despite the crash of the first prototype). Designed to provide reconnaissance, surveillance, and targeting support, the Fire Scout will be able to provide continuous coverage for more than six hours at distances up to 110 miles (177 km) from its launch site. Payloads include EO and IR sensors, and a laser designator. The first three RQ-8As, as well as two ground control stations, a datalink suite, remote data terminals, and modular mission payloads, will be delivered by April 2002. The two services expect to procure 78 Fire Scouts, the first of which are scheduled to enter operational service in 2003.

Aggressive adversaries

The Marine Corps Reserve operates one squadron of Northrop F-5E (single-seat) and F-5F (two-seat) fighters as air combat manoeuvring adversary aircraft, used to train fighter crews of all services. The F-5s replaced Israeli Aircraft Industries F-21A Kfirs leased from Israel, which were withdrawn from service during the early 1990s. Plans to replace the F-5s have not been announced. (The Navy is procuring 14 F-16A/Bs from a group of 28 Fighting Falcons once destined for the Pakistani Air Force, but these are planned for the Navy's 'Top Gun' course, and none is earmarked for the Marine Corps.)

Logistics and liaison

The Marine Corps operates a small number of operational support airlift aircraft to support air station logistics, executive transport, and movement of squadron ground personnel and material for deployments. Two McDonnell Douglas C-9B Skytrain logistic aircraft have been in service for more than two decades. (It is possible that these aircraft eventually will be replaced by Boeing C-40A Clipper transports being procured by the Navy to replace its C-9s and DC-9s. The first of these aircraft was delivered to the Naval Air Reserve in April 2001.)

Several Raytheon Beech UC-12B Hurons are used for stateside air station liaison duties, and UC-12Fs are forward-based in Iwakuni, Japan, and Futenma, Okinawa. A single Rockwell

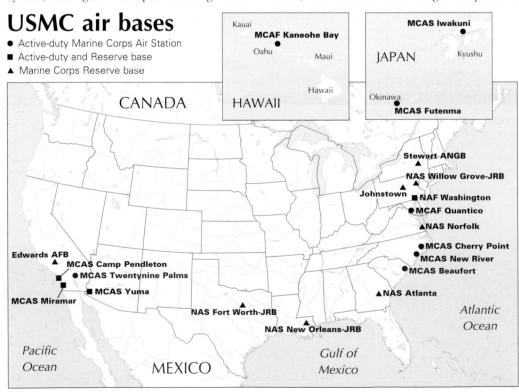

USMC air bases

- ● Active-duty Marine Corps Air Station
- ■ Active-duty and Reserve base
- ▲ Marine Corps Reserve base

Kauai
MCAF Kaneohe Bay
Oahu
Maui
HAWAII
Hawaii

MCAS Iwakuni
JAPAN
Kyushu
Okinawa
MCAS Futenma

CANADA
Edwards AFB
MCAS Camp Pendleton
MCAS Twentynine Palms
MCAS Yuma
MCAS Miramar
Pacific Ocean
MEXICO

Stewart ANGB
NAS Willow Grove-JRB
Johnstown
NAF Washington
MCAF Quantico
NAS Norfolk
MCAS Cherry Point
MCAS New River
MCAS Beaufort
NAS Atlanta
NAS Fort Worth-JRB
NAS New Orleans-JRB
Gulf of Mexico
Atlantic Ocean

Right: The AH-1W can be armed with either the BGM-71 TOW (illustrated) or AGM-114 Hellfire. This example is from HMLA-367 'Scarface'.

HMT-303 at Camp Pendleton is the schoolhouse for both Cobra (above) and Twin Huey. The squadron also trains Navy Twin Huey crews, and has some unarmed HH-1Ns assigned (below).

Right and below: Both the AH-1 and UH-1 are being upgraded with common engines and transmissions, and pilots will be able to fly either type. These examples are from HMLA-369 at Camp Pendleton.

Below: HMT-302 is the training unit for the H-53E, and in addition to Marine CH-53E crews, it also instructs Navy crews destined for the MH-53E fleet. Consequently, it has a few of the minesweeping variant in its inventory.

Over the years a number of helicopters have been assigned to station flights for base rescue duties. This UH-1N serves at Yuma, which is adjacent to a large and much-used training and weapons range complex.

Slated for replacement by the MV-22B, the CH-53D serves with three squadrons: HMH-362 (right), HMH-363 (above) and HMH-463 (below right). HMH-366 (below) deactivated in late 2000. The CH-53D community is concentrated at MCAF Kaneohe Bay in Hawaii, and includes an organic training squadron (HMT-301). Aircraft routinely deploy to CONUS for training exercises.

CT-39G Sabreliner remains in service for executive transport at Futenma but will be replaced by October 2001 by a Cessna UC-35D Citation Encore. Other CT-39Gs were replaced in late 1999 by two Cessna UC-35C Citation Ultras. Additional procurement of five more UC-35s is funded, and the Corps is planning to replace all of its UC-12s with UC-35s.

A single C-20G Gulfstream IV executive transport operated for Headquarters, Marine Corps, was severely damaged by a tornado in early 1998, but is expected to be restored for service by the end of 2001.

Presidential support

The Marine Corps has long been assigned the role of providing helicopter transportation to the President and Vice President of the United States, as well as to other senior government officials. To carry out this role, the Marine Corps operates two types not found elsewhere in its inventory: the Sikorsky VH-3D Sea King and the Sikorsky VH-60N Black Hawk. The ageing but well-maintained VH-3Ds, which long ago replaced similar VH-3As in presidential service, are routinely flown in Air Force C-5 transports to other fields to be ready for the President's visit. The VH-60Ns, based on the Army's UH-60A, are less spacious than the VH-3Ds, which are preferred by the executive passengers. Sikorsky Aircraft Company performs overhauls and modifications under contract on these executive aircraft.

Range support

A small number of Beech T-34C Turbo Mentor two-seat turboprop trainers are used by the Marine Corps's F/A-18 replacement training squadron (VMFAT-101) as target spotting aircraft for the squadron's weapons training.

United States Marine Corps Aviation organisation

Despite its size, Marine Corps aviation is not a separate organisation within the Marine Corps, but is integrated into every facet of Marine Corps training and operations. The Commandant of the Marine Corps, a four-star general headquartered at the Pentagon in Arlington, Va., has by tradition never been an aviator. The Assistant Commandant, also a four-star general, normally is an aviator. The senior officer directly responsible for aviation matters, the Deputy Chief of Staff for Aviation, is a lieutenant general (three-star).

Marine Forces Atlantic/Pacific

Marine Forces Atlantic and Marine Forces Pacific are the Marine Corps components equivalent to the Navy's Atlantic and Pacific Fleets, respectively. The three active-duty Marine Aircraft Wings are the aviation components of the Marine Forces commands.

Marine Aircraft Wings

Almost all active-duty Marine aircraft and aviation units are administratively assigned to the three Marine Aircraft Wings (MAWs), each of which is paired with one of the three active-duty Marine infantry divisions and one of the three force service support groups (FSSGs) to form a Marine Expeditionary Force (MEF).

The 1st MAW, headquartered at Camp Smedley D. Butler, Okinawa, Japan, supports III MEF – including the 3rd Marine Division – in the western Pacific from bases in Japan and Hawaii. The 1st MAW has permanently assigned groups and some permanently assigned squadrons, but draws much of its strength from squadrons and detachments from the other two MAWs on six-month deployments under the Unit Deployment Program (UDP).

The 3rd MAW supports I MEF – including the 1st Marine Division – from bases in southern California. Both the 1st and 3rd MAWs are

controlled by Marine Forces Pacific. The 2nd MAW, under Marine Forces Atlantic, supports II MEF – including the 2nd Marine Division – from bases in North and South Carolina.

Each MAW is supported by a Marine Wing Headquarters Squadron (MWHS), an administrative unit with no aircraft assigned. Each MAW is composed of several Marine Air Groups (MAGs), plus two groups of ground support personnel: one Marine Wing Support Group (MWSG) and one Marine Air Control Group (MACG).

In the event of a major conflict, such as Operation Desert Storm, MAWs deploy for combat operations as the Aviation Combat Element (ACE) of a standing Marine Expeditionary Force (MEF), the Marine Corp's largest Marine Air-Ground Task Force (MAGTF). As noted above, the Marine Corps maintains three standing MEFs, each of which includes a Marine Air wing, a Marine Division, and a Force Service Support Group.

Marine Expeditionary Units (MEUs) are smaller units that routinely deploy overseas as the Marine Corps combat force embarked in the ships of an amphibious task force, called an Amphibious Ready Group (ARG). The ACE of each MEU usually is a Medium Helicopter Squadron (HMM) (and, in the near future, a Medium Tiltrotor Squadron, or VMM) with 12 aircraft, reinforced by detachments of six AV-8B Harrier IIs, four CH-53Es, three UH-1Ns and four AH-1Ws drawn from other squadrons. Two KC-130 Hercules tankers normally are dispatched to airfields near the ARG's operating area to support the Harriers, Super Stallions and (soon) Ospreys assigned to the MEU.

Marine Aircraft Groups

Each MAW is comprised of several Marine Aircraft Groups (MAGs), equivalent in concept to Navy type wings. In the case of active-duty MAGs, each group typically includes all of the squadrons of a given type in the MAW. MAGs provide command, administration, training and maintenance support for the assigned squadrons. Some MAGs also command the replacement training squadrons assigned to the base at which the MAG is located.

Provisional MAGs are temporary commands that are formed for overseas crisis response – as in the case of Operation Desert Shield – in which the MAG commander will deploy and assume an operational role as commander of the provisional MAG.

Each MAG has a Marine Air Logistics Squadron (MALS) assigned for intermediate-level maintenance support for aircraft assigned

to the group. No aircraft are assigned to the MALS units, which previously operated aircraft as Headquarters and Maintenance Squadrons before they were redesignated. The 1st MAW aircraft based in Hawaii are supported by a 1st MAW Aviation Support Element (ASE).

MCAS/MCAF/H&HS/VMR

Most active-duty Marine Corps aviation units are based at a small number of air stations (MCASs), air facilities (MCAFs), and a few other installations. These bases and the assigned support squadrons provide the services needed to operate the tenant air groups and squadrons.

MCAS Cherry Point and MCAS New River in North Carolina, and MCAS Beaufort, in South Carolina, host all squadrons assigned to Marine Forces Atlantic. Bogue Field in North Carolina serves as an auxiliary landing field for East Coast units.

West Coast units (3rd MAW) are assigned to MCAS Miramar and MCAS Camp Pendleton in southern California, and MCAS Yuma, Arizona, as well as a few units at the Marine Corps Air-Ground Combat Center at Twenty-Nine Palms, Calif. MCAS Tustin and MCAS El Toro in California were closed in 1999. Units of the 1st MAW are based at MCAS Iwakuni in Japan, and at MCAS Futenma, Okinawa, Japan, as well as MCAF Kaneohe Bay, now part of Marine Corps Base (MCB) Hawaii. (Futenma is slated for closure because of local opposition and may be replaced by a new airfield in northern Okinawa or, less likely, an offshore mobile airfield.) MCAF Quantico, part of MCB Quantico, Va., hosts HMX-1, which maintains an executive flight detachment at NS Washington, DC.

Most air stations have a base flight and/or a SAR helicopter component, operated by Headquarters & Headquarters Squadron (H&HS), which until late 1999 were known as Station Operations & Maintenance Squadrons (SOMS) or Station Operations Squadrons (SOS). These units variously operate UC-12B, UC-12F, UC-35C/D, CT-39G, HH-1N and HH-46D aircraft. The Station Operations and Engineering Squadron (SOES) at Cherry Point, which operates the Corps' two C-9Bs, was redesignated Marine Transport Squadron One (VMR-1) in 1997. SOS El Toro operated for under two years as VMR-2 before being again redesignated H&HS Miramar at its new base.

Fighter-Attack Squadrons

Much of the Marine Corps' air combat power resides in its eight Marine Fighter-Attack (VMFA) Squadrons, which are equivalent to Navy strike fighter (VFA) squadrons. Four squadrons – two equipped with F/A-18As and two with F/A-18Cs – are based with MAG-31 at

US Marine Corps Aviation

Headquarters, US Marine Corps	Arlington, Va.
HMX-1 CH-46E, CH-53E, MV-22B (MX)	
	MCAF Quantico, Va.
Executive Flight Det. VH-3D, VH-60N (MX)	
	NS Washington, D.C.
MAWTS-1	MCAS Yuma, Ariz.
Marine Forces Atlantic	**NS Norfolk, Va.**
Second Marine Aircraft Wing	MCAS Cherry Point, N.C.
Marine Forces Pacific	**MCB Hawaii**
First Marine Aircraft Wing	Camp S.D. Butler, Okinawa
Third Marine Aircraft Wing	MCAS Miramar, Calif.
US Marine Corps Reserve	
Fourth Marine Aircraft Wing	NSA New Orleans, La.

For assault purposes, the Marine Corps' real muscle is provided by the three-engined CH-53E Super Stallion. As well as troop transport and heavylift, the type is also used for CSAR and retrieval of aircraft. These examples serve with HMH-461 (above) at New River, and HMH-462 (left) at Miramar.

The bulk of the CH-53E community is based at Miramar, with four squadrons, while two more are at New River as part of the 2nd MAW. These aircraft are from HMH-361 (above), HMH-464 (right, at Twentynine Palms) and HMH-465 (below).

Third Marine Aircraft Wing
MCAS Miramar, Calif.

UNIT	NAME	TYPE	TAILCODE	BASE
MWHS-3	–	none	–	MCAS Mir
H&HS Miramar Calif.	–	UC-12B, UC-35C	5T	MCAS Miramar,
H&HS Yuma	–	UC-12B, HH-1N	5Y	MCAS Yuma, Calif.
Marine Aircraft Group 11				MCAS Miramar, Calif.
MALS-11	–	none	–	MCAS Miramar, Calif.
VMFA-232	Red Devils	F/A-18C	WT	MCAS Miramar, Calif.
VMFA-314	Black Knights	F/A-18C	VW	MCAS Miramar, Calif.
VMFA-323	Death Rattlers	F/A-18C	WS	MCAS Miramar, Calif.
VMFA(AW)-121	Green Knights	F/A-18D	VK	MCAS Miramar, Calif.
VMFA(AW)-225	Vikings	F/A-18D	CE	MCAS Miramar, Calif.
VMFA(AW)-242	Bats	F/A-18D	DT	MCAS Miramar, Calif.
VMFAT-101 (RTS)	Sharpshooters	F/A-18A/B/C/D, T-34C	SH	MCAS Miramar, Calif.
VMGR-352	Raiders	KC-130F/R	QB	MCAS Miramar, Calif.

Note: Since the mid-1990s, VMFA-314 and VMFA-323 have used the codes of the carrier air wings (CVWs) to which they are assigned, currently NG (CVW-9) and NE (CVW-2), respectively.

UNIT	NAME	TYPE	TAILCODE	BASE
Marine Aircraft Group 13				MCAS Yuma, Ariz.
MALS-13	–	none	–	MCAS Yuma, Ariz.
VMA-211	Avengers	AV-8B	CF	MCAS Yuma, Ariz.
VMA-214	Black Sheep	AV-8B	WE	MCAS Yuma, Ariz.
VMA-311	Tomcats	AV-8B	WL	MCAS Yuma, Ariz.
VMA-513	Nightmares	AV-8B	WF	MCAS Yuma, Ariz.
Marine Aircraft Group 16				MCAS Miramar, Calif.
MALS-16	–	none	–	MCAS Miramar, Calif.
HMH-361	Flying Tigers	CH-53E	YN	MCAS Miramar, Calif.
HMH-462	Heavy Haulers	CH-53E	YF	MCAS Miramar, Calif.
HMH-465	Warhorses	CH-53E	YJ	MCAS Miramar, Calif.
HMH-466	Wolfpack	CH-53E	YK	MCAS Miramar, Calif.
HMM-161	Greyhawks	CH-46E	YR	MCAS Miramar, Calif.
HMM-163	Ridgerunners	CH-46E	YP	MCAS Miramar, Calif.
HMM-165	White Knights	CH-46E	YW	MCAS Miramar, Calif.
HMM-166	Sea Elk	CH-46E	YX	MCAS Miramar, Calif.
Marine Aircraft Group 39				MCAS Camp Pendleton, Calif.
MALS-39	–	none	–	MCAS Camp Pendleton, Calif.
HMLA-169	Vipers	AH-1W, UH-1N	SN	MCAS Camp Pendleton, Calif.
HMLA-267	Stingers	AH-1W, UH-1N	UV	MCAS Camp Pendleton, Calif.
HMLA-367	Scarface	AH-1W, UH-1N	VT	MCAS Camp Pendleton, Calif.
HMLA-369	Gunfighters	AH-1W, UH-1N	SM	MCAS Camp Pendleton, Calif.
HMT-303 (RTS)	Atlas	AH-1W, UH-1N, HH-1N	QT	MCAS Camp Pendleton, Calif.
HMM-268	Red Dragons	CH-46E	YQ	MCAS Camp Pendleton, Calif.
HMM-364	Purple Foxes	CH-46E	PF	MCAS Camp Pendleton, Calif.
HMM(T)-164 (RTS)	Knightriders	CH-46E	YT	MCAS Camp Pendleton, Calif.
Marine Wing Support Group 37				MCAS Miramar, Calif.
MWSS-371	–	none	–	MCAS Yuma, Ariz.
MWSS-372	–	none	–	MCAS Camp Pendleton, Calif.
MWSS-373	–	none	–	MCAS Miramar, Calif.
MWSS-374	–	none	–	MCAS Miramar, Calif.
Detachment	–	none	–	MCAGC Twentynine Palms, Calif.
Marine Air Control Group 38				MCAS Miramar, Calif
MASS-3	–	none	–	MCAS Camp Pendleton, Calif.
MACS-1	–	none	–	MCAS Yuma, Ariz.
ATC Det.	–	none	–	MCAS Miramar, Calif.
ATC Det.	–	none	–	MCAS Yuma, Ariz.
ATC Det.	–	none	–	MCAS Camp Pendleton, Calif.
MWCS-38	–	none	–	MCAS Miramar, Calif.
MTACS-38	–	none	–	MCAS Miramar, Calif.
3rd LAAD Batt.	–	none	–	MCAS Camp Pendleton, Calif.
Air-Ground Support Element			–	MCAGC Twentynine Palms, Calif.

Above: HMH-466 flies this CH-53E from Miramar. The rear ramp facilitates rapid loading and unloading of both troops and cargo, including light vehicles.

Right: Despite numerous problems, the USMC remains committed to the Bell/Boeing MV-22B Osprey as the replacement for its CH-46s and CH-53Ds. Training with VMMT-204 has been under way since mid-2000. This aircraft is on the strength of HMX-1, the Quantico-based test unit.

MCAS Beaufort, SC. The two F/A-18C units, VMFAs 251 and 312, are permanently assigned to Navy carrier air wings, CVW-1 and CVW-3, respectively.

Three VMFA squadrons, all equipped with F/A-18Cs, are based with MAG-11 at MCAS Miramar, Calif. Two of these squadrons, VMFA 314 and 323, are permanently assigned to Navy CVW-9 and CVW-2, respectively. The two VMFA squadrons at Beaufort and the single VMFA squadron at Miramar not assigned to Navy CVWs share rotating six-month deployments to MCAS Iwakuni, Japan, on UDP assignment to MAG-12 of the 1st MAW. As a result of the carrier commitment and the deactivation of four VMFA squadrons (235, 333, 451 and 531) during the early and mid-1990s, the Unit Deployment Program had come under such strain that the Marine Corps decided to move one unit, VMFA-212, permanently from MAG-11 in California to MAG-12 in Iwakuni, Japan.

Over the last decade, the four carrier-based VMFA units have participated in combat operations over Iraq (as part of Operation Southern Watch) and over Bosnia. VMFA-312 participated in Operation Desert Fox in Iraq in December 1998. In late 1999 and early 2000, VMFA-251 participated in naval aviation's first combat use of the AGM-84H SLAM-ER missile and the JDAM precision-guided bomb.

All-Weather Fighter-Attack

Grouped with the VMFA squadrons at MCAS Beaufort and MCAS Miramar are six All-Weather Fighter-Attack (VMFA(AW)) squadrons, three at each base, all equipped with two-seat F/A-18D Hornet strike fighters. In addition to close air support, these squadrons, all former A-6 Intruder operators, have the additional roles of forward air controller-airborne (FACA) and tactical air controller-airborne (TACA), and, with the Advanced Tactical Air Reconnaissance System, also undertake the imagery reconnaissance mission.

A VMFA(AW) squadron is rotated to MCAS Iwakuni, Japan every six months under the UDP to support the 1st MAW. For several years until 1997, VMFA(AW) units were deployed to Aviano AB in northern Italy in support of UN and NATO operations in Bosnia. Two squadrons, VMFA(AW)-332 and VMFA(AW)-533, deployed to Tazar, Hungary in support of Operation Allied Force, during which they conducted strikes against targets in Serbia and Kosovo. These squadrons were the first to introduce the ATARS into operation.

Fighter-Attack Training Squadron

Replacement training of pilots and maintenance personnel for the VMFA and VMFA(AW) units, plus weapon systems officers for VMFA(AW) units, is conducted by Marine Fighter-Attack Training (VMFAT) Squadron 101 at MCAS Miramar, Calif., and by two Navy VFA fleet readiness squadrons, VFA-125 at NAS Lemoore, Calif. and VFA-106 at NAS Oceana, Va. VMFAT-101 uses all basic versions of the Hornet (F/A-18A/B/C/D) and also operates a few T-34C Turbo Mentor trainers as target-spotting aircraft.

Attack Squadrons

Seven Marine Attack (VMA) squadrons operate the AV-8B Harrier II VSTOL attack aircraft for close air support missions. Four VMA

squadrons with MAG-13 at MCAS Yuma, Calif. fly the night-attack version of the AV-8B, while three VMAs with MAG-14 at MCAS Cherry Point, NC operate a mixture of basic AV-8Bs and radar-equipped Harrier II Plus versions (although the number of basic versions has been diminished by the remanufacturing programme.) One Harrier squadron, VMA-331 at Cherry Point, was deactivated in 1992. The remanufacturing programme, aircraft attrition and pilot shortages have resulted in the number of aircraft per squadron being reduced from 20 to 16 Harriers.

Harrier detachments from VMA squadrons routinely deploy as part of the MEU's ACE on each 'big-deck' 'Tarawa'-class (LHA) or 'Wasp'-class amphibious assault ship (LHD). The VMA detachment becomes part of the HMM squadron around which the ACE is formed, and the Harriers are marked with HMM squadron markings. A detachment of AV-8Bs (in recent years, usually from VMA-311) is normally rotated to MCAS Futenma, Okinawa, Japan every six months under the UDP for deployment with the 31st MEU's ACE. These detachments deployed onboard USS *Belleau Wood* (LHA 3) for several years until summer 2000, when USS *Essex* (LHD 2) exchanged homeports with *Belleau Wood*.

AV-8Bs participated in combat strikes in Kosovo during Operation Allied Force in 1999 from the decks of amphibious warfare ships. No aircraft were lost in action. AV-8B deployments ships were halted in 2000 because of the grounding of many Harriers for engine problems, but were to resume late in 2001.

Marine Attack Training Squadron

Harrier pilot and maintenance personnel training is conducted at MCAS Cherry Point, NC by Marine Attack Training (VMAT) Squadron 203, using AV-8B and two-seat TAV-8B aircraft. VMAT-203 makes extensive use of MCALF Bogue Field, NC for pilot training.

Tactical Electronic Warfare

The ability of Marine Corps combat aircraft to conduct warfare successfully is aided by the four Marine Tactical Electronic Warfare (VMAQ) squadrons, all based at Cherry Point with MAG-14. Each is equipped with five EA-6B Prowler electronic countermeasures aircraft, able to suppress enemy air defences with jamming and AGM-88 HARM missiles. Until 1992, the Marine Corps EA-6B fleet was operated in detachments by one active-duty squadron, VMAQ-1 at Cherry Point, and by one reserve squadron, VMAQ-4 at NAS Whidbey Island, Wash. A reorganisation divided VMAQ-1 into three squadrons (VMAQ-1, -2 and -3) and permanently activated VMAQ-4 as a regular squadron, moving it to Cherry Point. Until recently, these four units rotated in turn every six months under the UDP to MCAS Iwakuni, Japan. However, following Operation Allied Force, more than a year has elapsed since a VMAQ squadron deployed to Iwakuni, a result of heavy deployment commitments in Europe and the Middle East. Also, for a few years in the mid-1990s, one VMAQ squadron was assigned to a Navy carrier air wing, CVW-1.

VMAQ squadrons have been heavily committed to deployments in Aviano AB, Italy in support of UN and NATO operations in Bosnia, to Incirlik, Turkey in support of Operation

Northern Watch, and to Prince Sultan Air Base in Saudi Arabia. The VMAQ squadrons have been considered de facto expeditionary squadrons – in the sense that the Navy's four expeditionary VAQ squadrons have been – although they have not formally been designated as such. The retirement of the Air Force's EF-111A Raven electronic warfare aircraft has thrown the entire burden of electronic jamming onto the Navy and Marine Corps EA-6B units.

Three VMAQ squadrons were deployed to Aviano (one from Incirlik until relieved at Aviano by Navy EA-6Bs) during Operation Allied Force in 1999. These units provided vital electronic jamming support for NATO strikes into Kosovo and Serbia.

Marine Corps EA-6B aircrew and maintenance personnel training is conducted by the Navy's fleet readiness squadron, Electronic Attack (VAQ) Squadron 129, based at Whidbey Island.

Aerial Refueling Squadrons

Each active MAW has one Marine Aerial Refueler/Transport (VMGR) Squadron permanently assigned. These squadrons operate a mixture of KC-130F and KC-130R versions of the Lockheed Hercules. Although all are often engaged in routine transport missions, their primary mission is aerial refuelling of Marine Corps tactical jet aircraft and helicopters. This role is extended to include the refuelling of aircraft and ground support equipment on the ground. VMGR units deploy detachments in support of amphibious ready groups, for which they provide refuelling and logistics support.

VMGR-152 is permanently deployed to Futenma, Okinawa. VMGR-352 moved from MCAS El Toro, Calif. to Miramar in September 1998. VMGR-252 supports Atlantic area operations from MCAS Cherry Point, NC; this unit will be the first to receive the new KC-130J. Eleven KC-130Js were on order through FY 2001 to begin replacing the KC-130Fs.

Aerial Refueler/Transport Training

Replacement training for KC-130 crews is conducted by Marine Aerial Refueler/Transport Training (VMGRT) Squadron 253 at Cherry Point, using only the KC-130F version.

'Blue Angels'

The Naval Flight Demonstration Squadron, the 'Blue Angels', operates a single TC-130G for logistic support of the flying team. The Hercules also participates in air shows when it demonstrates rocket-assisted take-offs.

Medium Helicopter Squadrons

The Marine Corps operates a total of 14 Marine Medium Helicopter (HMM) squadrons, more than any other type. Although the number of tactical jet squadrons was reduced after the Cold War, no helicopter transport units were disbanded, for their numbers had always been inadequate. All HMM squadrons are equipped with the CH-46E Sea Knight helicopter. During 1998, deliveries began of the Dynamic Component Upgrade (DCU) version CH-46Es.

HMM squadrons routinely deploy onboard amphibious ships (LHAs or LHDs) for six-month cruises in the Mediterranean, Persian Gulf or western Pacific. When deployed, the detachments of CH-53s, AH-1s, UH-1s and

The CH-46E 'Sea Knight, better known as the 'Frog', is the backbone of the assault helicopter force, and provides the nucleus of the Marine expeditionary unit which deploys aboard assault carriers. These CH-46Es serve with HMM-161 (above left), HMM-162 (above) and HMM-163 (right).

The 'Knightriders' of HMM(T)-164 (above) act as the Sea Knight training unit. The aircraft below is from HMM-166 'Sea Elk', based at Miramar.

Above: The 3rd MAW Sea Knights are divided between Miramar and Camp Pendleton, located close to each other in the San Diego area. This aircraft is from one of the Miramar units, HMM-165 'White Knights'.

MCAS New River is home to six squadrons of CH-46Es, divided between two air groups. HMM-261 (above) is part of MAG 26, while HMM-263 (right) is with MAG 29.

HMM-264 (above) and HMM-266 (below) are part of MAG 26 at New River. East Coast squadrons routinely deploy to Twentynine Palms in California for large-scale exercises.

This CH-46E, of Camp Pendleton-based HMM-268 'Red Dragons', is equipped with infra-red countermeasures either side of the tail rotor pylon, and chaff/flare dispensers above the undercarriage sponsons.

Above: HMM-364 'Purple Foxes' also flies the CH-46E from Camp Pendleton. This aircraft is fitted with a winch on the starboard forward fuselage.

Below: The Sea Knight remains a common sight around Marine bases, but replacement by the MV-22B is under way. This aircraft is from HMM-365.

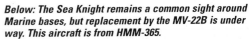

AV-8s assigned to the MEU become parts of the HMM and are marked accordingly for the duration of the deployment.

Two HMM squadrons are permanently assigned to MAG-36, based at Futenma, Okinawa. The squadrons were forward-deployed to Okinawa from Kaneohe Bay, Hawaii during the mid-1990s when all HMM squadrons at Kaneohe were moved from that base to make room for a consolidation of all CH-53D squadrons there. The basing of an amphibious assault ship – initially USS *Belleau Wood* but now USS *Essex* – at Sasebo, Japan made advantageous the permanent assignment in the western Pacific of an HMM squadron around which to form the core of an ACE for the assigned MEU.

The 3rd MAW has six HMM squadrons assigned, all formerly based at Tustin, Calif., which closed in 1999. The squadrons were moved to El Toro, Calif. as an interim measure, but by 1999, when El Toro closed, four units (HMM-161, -163, -165 and -166) moved to Miramar, Calif. and two (HMM-268 and -364) moved to Camp Pendleton, Calif. One other unit, HMM-164, moved to Camp Pendleton, but in June 1999 was redesignated HMM(T)-164 (see below).

The 2nd MAW has six HMM squadrons assigned, split between MAG-26 and MAG-29 at MCAS New River, NC. The number of HMM squadrons at New River will begin to diminish as they convert to the MV-22B Osprey (see below). HMM-264 was scheduled to begin transition in January 2001 as the first operational HMM squadron to switch to the MV-22B and be redesignated as a Marine Medium Tiltrotor (VMM) Squadron, but the delay in the operational introduction of the Osprey has pushed back the transition.

The current HMM/VMM transition plan calls for four squadrons at New River to adopt the Osprey, then three at Miramar, two at Futenma, three at Camp Pendleton, and finally the remaining two at New River.

Medium Helicopter training

When the CH-46E replacement training squadron at New River, Marine Helicopter Training (HMT) Squadron 204, was redesignated as the MV-22B training unit and became Marine Medium Tiltrotor Training (VMM) Squadron 204, CH-46E replacement training was shifted to HMM-164 at Camp Pendleton. HMM-164 was redesignated HMM(T)-164 (not HMT-164) on 10 June 1999.

Heavy Helicopter Squadrons

The Marine Corps operates nine operational Marine Heavy Helicopter (HMH) squadrons. Six units – two at New River (one each in MAGs 26 and 29) and four at Miramar (with MAG-16) – operate the CH-53E Super Stallion. The four units at Miramar moved from Tustin between September 1998 and May 1999.

HMH CH-53E squadrons routinely assign detachments as part of the MEU's ACE onboard amphibious assault ships (LHAs or LHDs). When deployed, these detachments are assigned to the embarked HMM squadron and are so marked. CH-53E-equipped HMH squadrons also participate in the Unit Deployment Program, deploying to Futenma, Okinawa, Japan; normally one HMH squadron so is deployed at any time.

During the mid-1990s the Marine Corps consolidated all remaining CH-53D Sea Stallion helicopters at MCAS (now MCAF) Kaneohe Bay, Hawaii. Four HMH CH-53D squadrons were assigned to the 1st MAW are based at Kaneohe, but HMH-366 was deactivated in October 2000 and its aircraft distributed to the remaining CH-53D squadrons. When the CH-53E fleet reached strength in substantial numbers, the HMH CH-53D units no longer deployed detachments with HMM squadrons assigned to ARGs. Even though the CH-53D is now considered a medium-lift helicopter, the CH-53D squadrons retain HMH designations. All three operational CH-53D squadrons are scheduled for transition to the MV-22B Osprey.

Light Attack Helicopter Squadrons

Six active Light Attack Helicopter (HMLA) squadrons provide the Marine Corps ground forces with helicopter gunship support, utility, and forward air controller support, using a mixture of AH-1W Super Cobra and UH-1N Iroquois ('Huey') helicopters. Two squadrons are based at New River (one each with MAGs 26 and 29), while four are assigned to MAG-39 at Camp Pendleton. One HMLA squadron from Camp Pendleton is normally deployed on six-month rotation to Okinawa, Japan, under the UDP.

HMLA detachments of both AH-1Ws and UH-1Ns routinely deploy onboard amphibious assault ships (LHAs or LHDs) as part of the MEU's ACE. When so deployed, the detachments are assigned to the deployed HMM squadron and their aircraft are so marked.

By 2006, the four-bladed AH-1Zs and UH-1Ys – remanufactured from AH-1Ws, UH-1Ns, and HH-1Ns – will enter service with HMLA squadrons.

Helicopter Training Squadrons

Replacement training for aircrews and maintenance personnel is conducted by three Marine Helicopter Training Squadrons (HMTs). HMT-301, formerly a CH-46E training squadron, was reactivated at Kaneohe in 1995 as the CH-53D replacement training squadron. Replacement training for the CH-53E is conducted at New River by HMT-302. (This unit also has MH-53E Sea Dragon minesweeping versions assigned, in which Navy MH-53E crews are trained.) HMT-303 at Camp Pendleton trains replacement personnel for HMLA squadrons using AH-1W, UH-1N, and HH-1N aircraft.

Replacement training for the CH-46E squadrons is conducted by HMM(T)-164 (see above).

Medium Tiltrotor Squadrons

Marine Medium Tiltrotor Squadron (VMM) is the designation chosen by the Marine Corps for the units that will fly the MV-22B Osprey tilt-rotor assault transport aircraft. These units will routinely deploy onboard LHAs and LHDs with Amphibious Ready Groups as the core unit of the ARG's ACE.

Current planning calls for the conversion of four HMM CH-46E squadrons at New River, three at Miramar, and two at Futenma, followed by three HMH CH-53D squadrons at Kaneohe, then three HMM squadrons at Camp Pendleton, and finally the last two HMM units at New River. HMM-264 at New River was scheduled to

commence transition to the MV-22B in January 2001 and be redesignated as the first VMM squadron, but the transition has been delayed by the Osprey's teething problems.

Medium Tilt-rotor training

On 10 June 1999, HMT-204 was redesignated Marine Medium Tilt-rotor Training Squadron (VMMT) 204. The squadron, assigned to MAG-26 at New River, started receiving its first MV-22B Osprey aircraft in 2000 and has begun replacement training for aircrews and maintenance personnel in the new aircraft. VMMT-204 is a joint squadron, and eventually will train Air Force personnel to fly and maintain the CV-22B special operations version of the Osprey.

Unmanned Aerial Vehicles

One of the most recent additions to Marine Corps aviation organisation is the Marine Unmanned Aerial Vehicle (UAV) Squadron, designated VMU. Both of the Marine Corps' VMUs fly the RQ-2A Pioneer UAV, and have seen extensive service during the 1990s in Bosnia and – in 1999 – over Kosovo during Operation Allied Force. Both VMUs were activated on 15 January 1996. VMU-1 was formerly designated as the 1st Marine UAV Company; VMU-2 was newly activated. Eventually the VMUs will retire their RQ-2As in favor of the Northrop Grumman RQ-8A Fire Scout.

Marine Helicopter Squadron 1

Marine Helicopter Squadron (HMX) 1, based at MCAF Quantico, Va., has two primary missions. One, using CH-46E, CH-53E and MV-22B aircraft, is to develop helicopter assault tactics under sponsorship of the Marine Corps Combat Development Command and the Navy's Commander, Operational Test and Evaluation Force. (HMX-1 participated in the operational evaluation of the MV-22B from November 1999 to July 2000.) The other mission, far more famous, is to provide executive transportation (and emergency evacuation) for the President and Vice President of the United States, members of the Cabinet, and other senior government officials. HMX-1 maintains a detachment at Naval Station Washington, D.C. (the site of the former NAS Anacostia) which flies VH-3D Sea King and VH-60N Black Hawk helicopters. The squadron's CH-46Es and CH-53Es also assist in VIP transport.

HMX-1 is not part of Marine Forces Atlantic, but reports directly to the Marine Corps' Deputy Chief of Staff for Aviation.

MAWTS-1

Based at MCAS Yuma, Ariz., Marine Air Weapons and Tactics Squadron (MAWTS) 1 develops aviation warfare tactics and provides

USMC Replacement Training Squadrons			
Unit	Aircraft	RTS	Site
VMA	AV-8B	VMAT-203	Cherry Point
VMAQ	EA-6B	VAQ-129	Whidbey Island
VMGR	KC-130F/R/T/J	VMGRT-253	Cherry Point
VMM	MV-22B	VMMT-204	New River
VMFA	F/A-18A/CD	VMFAT-101	Miramar
		VFA-106	Oceana
		VFA-125	Lemoore
VMFA(AW)	F/A-18D	VMFAT-101	Miramar
HMH	CH-53D	HMT-301	Kaneohe Bay
HMH	CH-53E	HMT-302	New River
HMLA	AH-1W/UH-1N	HMT-303	Camp Pendleton
HMM	CH-46E	HMM(T)-164	Camp Pendleton

Above: HMX-1 is at Quantico, close to Washington D.C. The unit operates the Executive Flight Detachment, equipped with VH-60Ns (illustrated) and VH-3Ds for Presidential transport. When the President is aboard the callsign 'Marine One' is used.

Among the more unusual types in USMC service is the Raytheon (Beech) T-34C Turbo-Mentor. A handful are assigned to VMFAT-101 'Sharpshooters', the Hornet training squadron, and are employed as range clearance aircraft and for target-spotting.

Support for the US Navy's 'Blue Angels' aerial demonstration team is the role for the USMC's sole TC-130G Hercules, although it also gets to perform in its own right during the RATO take-off display. The TC-130G is a demodified EC-130G TACAMO command post.

The Raytheon (Beech) UC-12B/F is the main liaison type, partially equipping station flights at all of the major Marine Corps bases. This aircraft is assigned to Yuma.

The USMC operates two numbered UAV squadrons equipped with the RQ-2A Pioneer. This Pioneer is assigned to the 'Night Owls' of VMU-2 at Cherry Point. VMU-1 'Watchdogs' is at Twentynine Palms.

Left: Two McDonnell Douglas C-9B Skytrain IIs are operated for logistic transport duties by VMR-1 at Cherry Point. The squadron also has UC-12s, and HH-46Ds for base rescue duties.

Gulfstream C-20G is allocated to the Marine Aircraft Support Detachment at Andrews AFB, Maryland. It was badly damaged in a storm at Miami on 2 February 1998.

Two squadrons within the USMC Reserve organisation fly the AH-1/UH-1 mix, both with permanent detachments at other bases. The UH-1N above is assigned to HMLA-773 'Red Dog', while the AH-1W (right) is with HMLA-775 'Coyotes'.

Above: The 4th MAW contributes two squadrons of CH-46Es, based at Edwards AFB (HMM-264, illustrated) and NAS Norfolk (HMM-774).

Right: Reserve heavy lift components are HMH-769 at Edwards (illustrated) and HMH-772 at Willow Grove. Both squadrons fly the CH-53E Super Stallion.

instruction in close air support and helicopter assault tactics to Marine Corps aircrews and those of other services. The squadron trains WTIs (Weapons and Tactics Instructors) from other squadrons and standardizes weapons training throughout Marine Corps aviation. MAWTS-1 has no aircraft assigned, but conducts training using aircraft assigned to units of the personnel being trained.

Marine Air Control Groups

Each MAW is assigned a Marine Air Control Group (MACG) for command and control of aerial operations. Each MACG controls several types of squadrons, none of which operate aircraft.

MACGs include Marine Air Control Squadrons (MACSs) that provide air traffic control and aerial surveillance for anti-air support for Marine combat forces. MACSs maintain air traffic control detachments at one or more airfields.

Marine Tactical Air Control Squadrons (MTACSs) provide planning and coordination of air operations for the MAGTF's Tactical Air Command Center (TACC).

Marine Air Support Squadrons (MASSs) control aircraft performing close air support or direct air support missions.

Marine Wing Communications Squadrons (MWCSs) provide communications support for the MAW and its elements.

MACGs also control the Low-Altitude Air-Defense Battalions (LAADs) – equipped with Avenger 'Humvees' and Stinger Batteries. (The last Light Anti-Aircraft Missile Battalion (LAAM) – which operated Hawk surface-to-air missiles – was phased out in 1998.)

Marine Wing Support Groups

Each MAW is also assigned a Marine Wing Support Group (MWSG). These groups, which have no aircraft assigned, control Marine Wing Support Squadrons (MWSSs). MWSSs provide a wide range of logistic and personnel services – including fuel, ground-support equipment, supply, medical services, and weather forecasting – to the MAW's units.

United States Marine Corps Reserve

The Marine Corps maintains a small but modern aviation reserve force that can be mobilised in times of national emergency.

Marine Corps Reserve aviation began shortly after the establishment of a Marine Corps Reserve in 1916. Many Marine Corps air reservists saw action during World War I, flying bombing sorties and anti-submarine patrols. Post-war demobilisation reduced Marine Corps Reserve aviation to a tiny force, but in 1928 a few reserve pilots were activated to revitalise the air reserve programme, which was strengthened by legislation during the 1930s that increased pay and training opportunities.

The reserve force maintained before World War II was able to mobilise 13 squadrons for service in the war. Marine Corps reservists fought alongside their active-duty counterparts in regular squadrons during the war.

Marine Corps Reserve aviation units, which operated aircraft shared with the Naval Air Reserve Training Command, were organised during the post-war demobilisation as part of Marine Air Reserve Training Command. The number of squadrons had grown to over 40 by the time war broke out in Korea. Few of the 11 reserve squadrons activated during the Korean conflict saw combat, but many Marine Corps reservists flew in combat with active-duty squadrons.

In 1962, all reserve aviation units were grouped under the newly reactivated 4th Marine Aircraft Wing. Although no reserve units were called to active duty during the Vietnam War, Marine Corps reservists flew with active-duty squadrons during the conflict.

The Navy's 1970 reorganisation of the Naval Air Reserve extended benefits to Marine Corps Reserve aviation in the form of revised force structure and more modern equipment, a trend that accelerated during the mid-1980s as reserve equipment closed the gap to near-fleet standard.

After the 1990 Iraqi invasion of Kuwait, several reserve units deployed to the battlefront as part of Operations Desert Shield/Storm, and several back-filled in Japan for active-duty units stripped from forward sites.

4th Marine Aircraft Wing

All Marine Corps Reserve aviation units are organised under the 4th Marine Aircraft Wing, headquartered at New Orleans, La. Four Marine Aircraft Groups (MAGs), one Marine Air Control Group (MACG) and one Marine Wing Support Group (MWSG) located around the country support the squadrons assigned to each location and, in some cases, in other locations. One important distinction in reserve groups is that they are organised more on geographical groupings than on common aircraft types or missions. Reserve groups might include, for example, a VMFA, an HMLA, an HMH and a VMGR squadron.

The aircraft assigned to the Marine Corps Reserve are mostly compatible with fleet-standard aircraft. However, many aircraft types -- including the AV-8B, TAV-8B, F/A-18C/D, EA-6B, MV-22B, C-9B, UC-12F, KC-130F/R/J, HH-46D, CH-53D and RQ-2A -- currently are not operated by the Marine Corps Reserve. Some types, such as the KC-130T and the F-5E/F Tiger II, are operated by the reserve but not by active-duty forces.

The Marine Corps Reserve aviation units are manned primarily by experienced aviators, naval flight officers, and enlisted Marines. A cadre of reservists on active duty in each unit trains the part-time personnel and runs the day-to-day operations of each unit.

Fighter-Attack Squadrons

The striking power of the Marine Corps Reserve resides in its four Fighter-Attack (VMFA) squadrons, all of which operate the F/A-18A Hornet strike fighter. (The upgraded F/A-18A, known as F/A-18A+, has started to arrive in Marine Corps Reserve VMFA squadrons.) If mobilised, these units would perform strike, close air support and air-defence missions. One unit, VMFA-142, is nominally assigned to the Naval Air Reserve's Carrier Air Wing 20 (CVWR-20) and would deploy onboard an aircraft-carrier with that wing if it were activated.

One reserve unit, VMFA-124, formerly Marine Attack (VMA) Squadron 124 (until its A-4M Skyhawks were retired in 1994 and the squadron moved to NAS Dallas, Texas), was deactivated in December 1998 before it received any F/A-18 aircraft. Another A-4M squadron, VMA-131 at NAS Willow Grove, Pa., was deactivated in December 1998 without ever being redesignated VMFA-131.

Aerial Refueling Squadrons

The Marine Corps Reserve operates two Aerial Refueling/Transport (VMGR) Squadrons,

which are heavily engaged in supporting both active-duty and reserve forces in aerial refuelling and transport roles. The two squadrons fly a mixture of KC-130T and stretched KC-130T-30 versions of the Hercules, more modern that the KC-130F/Rs operated by active-duty units.

Transport Helicopter Squadrons

The 4th MAW operates four Assault Transport Helicopter Squadrons with fleet-standard equipment. Two HMM squadrons fly the CH-46E Sea Knight and two HMH units operate the CH-53E Super Stallion, the latter recently having replaced its former Navy minesweeping RH-53Ds.

Light Attack Helicopter Squadrons

Two Marine Light Attack Helicopter (HMLA) Squadrons are operated by the reserve wing, and each unit also maintains a large detachment at a separate location. HMLA-773's detachment at NAS Willow Grove, Pa. was activated in 1997, and moved to a new facility at Johnstown, Pa. in 2001. Both HMLA squadrons operate a fleet-standard mixture of heavily-armed UH-1N Huey and AH-1W Super Cobra gunships.

Fighter Training Squadron

The 4th MAW operates the Marine Corps' only adversary squadron, Marine Fighter Training Squadron 401 (VMFT-401), based at MCAS Yuma, Ariz. This unit flies F-5E/F Tiger II fighters (which replaced IAI F-21A Kfirs) in the air-combat manoeuvring adversary training role for fighter units of all services.

Support Squadrons

Like its active-duty counterparts, the 4th MAW includes a number of support units that are not equipped with aircraft. Many of these units are widely dispersed around the country, some far from any aircraft-equipped units. Reserve units include Marine Aviation Logistics Squadrons (MALS), Marine Air Control Squadrons (MACS), Marine Wing Support Squadrons (MWSS) and Marine Air Support Squadrons (MASS). (See the active-duty Marine Corps section for an explanation of the roles of these support units.) The wing also includes a Low-Altitude Air-Defense Battalion (LAAD). The former Hawk-equipped Light Anti-Aircraft Missile Battalion (LAAM, later redesignated to Tactical Missile Defense detachments of an MACS), has been disbanded.

Fourth Marine Aircraft Wing
NSA New Orleans, La.

UNIT	NAME	TYPE	TAILCODE	BASE
MWHS-4	–	none	–	NSA New Orleans, La.
MASD	–	UC-12B, UC-35C	EZ	NAS New Orleans-JRB, La.
Marine Aircraft Group 41				NAS Fort Worth-JRB, Texas
MALS-41	–	none	–	NAS Fort Worth-JRB, Texas
VMFA-112	Cowboys	F/A-18A	MA	NAS Fort Worth-JRB, Texas
VMGR-234	Rangers	KC-130T	QH	NAS Fort Worth-JRB, Texas
Marine Aircraft Group 42				NAS Atlanta, Ga.
Det B	–	none	–	NAS Norfolk, Va.
Det C	–	none	–	NAS New Orleans-JRB, La.
MALS-42	–	none	–	NAS Atlanta, Ga.
HMLA-773	Red Dog	AH-1W, UH-1N	MP	NAS Atlanta, Ga.
HMLA-775 Det A	Coyotes	AH-1W, UH-1N	MM	NAS New Orleans-JRB, La.
HMM-774	Honkers	CH-46E	MQ	NAS Norfolk, Va.
VMFA-142	Flying Gators	F/A-18A	MB	NAS Atlanta, Ga.
Marine Aircraft Group 46				MCAS Miramar, Calif.
Det A	–	none	–	MCAS Camp Pendleton, Calif.
Det B	–	none	–	Edwards AFB, Calif.
MALS-46	–	none	–	MCAS Miramar, Calif.
HMH-769	Road Hogs	CH-53E	MS	Edwards AFB, Calif.
HMLA-775	Coyotes	AH-1W, UH-1N	WR	MCAS Camp Pendleton, Calif.
HMM-764	Moonlight	CH-46E	ML	Edwards AFB, Calif.
VMFA-134	Smoke	F/A-18A	MF	MCAS Miramar, Calif.
VMFT-401	Snipers	F-5E/F	(WB)	MCAS Yuma, Calif.
Marine Aircraft Group 49				NAS Willow Grove-JRB, Pa.
Det A	–	none	–	NAF Washington, Md.
Det B	–	none	–	Stewart ANGB, N.Y.
MASD	–	UC-12B, C-20G	5A	NAF Washington, Md.
HMH 772	Flying Armadillos	CH-53E	MT	NAS Willow Grove-JRB, Pa.
HMLA-773 Det A	Red Dog	AH-1W, UH-1N	WG	Johnstown, Pa.
Det A moved to Johnstown from NAS Willow Grove-JRB, Pa. in 2001				
VMFA-321	Hell's Angels	F/A-18A	MG	NAF Washington, Md.
VMGR-452	Yankees	KC-130T	NY	Stewart ANGB, N.Y.
Marine Wing Support Group 47				Detroit, Mich.
MWSS-471	–	none	–	NAS Fort Worth-JRB, Texas
Det A	–	none	–	Minneapolis, Minn.
Det B	–	none	–	Green Bay, Wis.
MWSS-472	–	none	–	NAS Atlanta, Ga.
Det A	–	none	–	Wyoming, Pa.
Det B	–	none	–	Detroit, Mich.
MWSS-473	–	none	–	MCAS Miramar, Calif.
Det A	–	none	–	Fresno, Calif.
Det B	–	none	–	NAS Whidbey Island, Wash.
MWSS-474	–	none	–	NAS Willow Grove-JRB, Pa.
Det A	–	none	–	Johnstown, Pa.
Det B	–	none	–	Westover AFB, Mass.
Marine Air Control Group 48				Ft. Sheridan, Ill.
MASS-6	–	none	–	Westover AFB, Mass.
Det A	–	none	–	MCAS Miramar, Calif.
MACS-23	–	none	–	Aurora, Colo.
TAOC Det	–	none	–	Aurora, Colo.
EW/C Det	–	none	–	Cheyenne, Wyo.
MACS-24	–	none	–	FCTC Dam Neck, Va.
TAOC Det	–	none	–	FCTC Dam Neck, Va.
TAOC Det	–	none	–	NS Norfolk, Va.
ATC Det A	–	none	–	NAS Fort Worth-JRB, Texas
ATC Det B	–	none	–	NAS Willow Grove-JRB, Pa.
MWCS-48	–	none	–	Ft. Sheridan, Ill.
Det A	–	none	–	Ft. Sheridan, Ill.
Det B	–	none	–	MCAS Miramar, Calif.
MTACS-48	–	none	–	Ft. Sheridan, Ill.
4th LAAD	–	none	–	Pasadena, Calif.
Battery A	–	none	–	Pasadena, Calif.
Battery B	–	none	–	NAS Atlanta, Ga.

Units stationed at Ft. Sheridan were scheduled to move to NTC Great Lakes, Ill., in early 2001.

Last US military users of the Northrop F-5E/F Tiger II, VMFT-401 'Snipers' at Yuma provides an organic adversary function. As well as air-to-air work, they mimic low-level ground attackers to train Marine ground air defence units.

The 4th MAW has two Hercules squadrons, both equipped with KC-130Ts. The fleet is a mix of standard-length aircraft (right, VMGR-234) and stretched KC-130T-30s (above, VMGR-452).

Below: VMFA-134 flies F/A-18As from Miramar. Several of the squadron's aircraft are painted in adversary colours.

The Hornets of VMFA-112 'Cowboys' fly from the Joint Reserve Base at Fort Worth, Texas.

VMFA-142's F/A-18As, based at Atlanta, are assigned to the US Navy's Reserve Air Wing 20.

All four USMCR Hornet squadrons operate the older F/A-18A. This aircraft is from Andrews-based VMFA-321.

Aérospatiale
SA 330 Puma

Sud Aviation followed the success of its Alouette designs with a fast and agile battlefield assault helicopter which is still in widespread use over 30 years after it entered service. This feature analyses the Turmo-powered SA 330 Pumas – in the following instalment the Makila-engined AS 332/532 Super Puma/Cougar will be examined in detail.

Above: The biggest operator of the SA 330 is the French Aviation Légère de l'Armée de Terre, and around 100 remain in service as the backbone of the assault transport force. This desert-camouflaged SA 330Ba is seen while operating with the Det ALAT in Djibouti.

Right: As well as regular air arms, the Puma has been sold to several quasi-military agencies. Germany's Bundesgrenzschutz (border police) has a large fleet. This aircraft exhibits two of the options for the basic Puma: enlarged sponsons for additional range and nose radar.

Development of the SA 330 began in the mid-1960s as a purely French programme, with Sud Aviation designing the aircraft as a *hélicoptère de manoeuvre*, a replacement for helicopters like the Sikorsky H-34, which the company had built under licence. The official requirement called for day/night, all-weather operation in all climates. In the event, this proved impossible to achieve due to the limited power available from the chosen engines and the difficulties inherent in installing a sufficiently capable radar for all-weather terrain avoidance.

Sud Aviation was not discouraged, and began drawing up the SA 330. Although it was of broadly conventional 'penny-farthing' (main rotor and anti-torque tail rotor) pod-and-boom layout, the SA 330 was an extremely clean and streamlined machine, using advanced structural design and manufacturing techniques to keep the weight down and to ensure the best possible performance. Unusually, the aircraft featured a fully-retractable tricycle undercarriage. These features ensured that the Puma would later gain a reputation as something of a 'GT Model' assault helicopter: extremely fast, agile and with excellent handling characteristics. On the other side of the coin, the lightly-built Puma attracted some derision from the pilots of some older and heavier helicopters, and there have often been worries as to the aircraft's supposed flimsiness.

The aircraft's designers may have been influenced by the Soviet Mil Mi-8 and/or the Sikorsky S-61, for they mounted the engines above the cabin to provide an unobstructed, full-height cabin. Sud Aviation designers provided two massive sliding doors, one on each side of the cabin, that allowed extremely rapid deplaning from the fore-and-aft rows of 15 troop seats. A row of seats lined each side of the cabin, facing inward, and there was a back-to-back central row of outward-facing seats along the centreline. A narrow passage linked the two-man cockpit to the cabin, giving direct access to the pilots for the crew-chief, loadmaster or the leader of the squad being carried. A collapsible seat for the loadmaster usually filled this space.

The SA 330 was much more than a mere troop transport, however. Combat experience in Algeria and Indo-China was carefully analysed, and the French designers ensured that the new helicopter – in addition to acting

Over the years many people, both civil and military, have had reason to thank the Puma and its crews. Speed of response, easy access through the large cabin doors and stability in the hover make it an excellent rescue platform. While most fly on standard SAR duties, like those of Spain (left), a few are dedicated to combat SAR, like the FLIR-equipped SA 330Bas of the French Armée de l'Air (above).

as a basic troop transport carrying a standard squad of up to 15 fully-equipped soldiers – would be able to operate as a casualty evacuation aircraft and as a medium-lift transport carrying underslung loads. It was even recognised that the aircraft might need to be able to provide its own suppressive fire, using door-mounted machine-guns. This versatility laid the foundations for the aircraft's later sales success. The importance of colonial, out-of-area operations ensured that the new helicopter was designed from the start to be capable of being airlifted in a variety of transport aircraft, saving long and time-consuming ferry flights.

Even before Sud Aviation could fly a prototype of its new SA 330, Britain and France set up a working group to prepare joint requirements for a range of future military aircraft.

These eventually included the Jaguar (then regarded principally as a trainer) and a stillborn variable-geometry strike attack aircraft, as well as helicopters. The working group was set up in 1964, and in March 1966 the helicopter sub-group began a detailed assessment of the SA 330 for possible use by the Royal Navy (for which the SA 330D designation was reserved) and the RAF (SA 330E).

RAF requirement

The RAF selected the SA 330E to fulfil its requirement for a new tactical medium transport helicopter to replace the ageing Bristol Belvedere and Westland Whirlwind helicopters then in service, just as production of the Wessex drew to a close. In many respects, continued production of the Wessex repre-

sented an obvious option for the RAF, since the aircraft was already in production and service, and its performance remained viable, if unspectacular. Like the SA 330E, the Wessex could carry 16 troops, albeit in even more cramped conditions, though it had only a single side door – effectively doubling the time it took to emplane and deplane. The aircraft had a number of other drawbacks, and its transmission was never able to cope with the full potential power output of its engines, limiting its load-carrying capabilities. Perhaps even more seriously, the Wessex was not well-suited to the rapid deployment role: it took 24 hours to strip down and prepare two Wessexes for transport aboard a Shorts Belfast, while it took only 14 hours to prepare two SA 330Es. Moreover, although a Belfast could accommodate only two Wessexes, it could carry four SA 330Es.

It was intended that the RAF would acquire as many SA 330Es as it could afford, and initial calculations indicated that 68 aircraft would be sufficient to meet the requirement. However, the defence economies that accompanied the then-Labour government's withdrawal from 'east of Suez' meant that funding could be found for only 48 aircraft, a figure subsequently reduced to 43 and, by the time a contract was signed, only 40.

The SA 330E acquisition formed a key part of the Anglo-French helicopter agreement, signed on 22 February 1967. Under this agreement, the RAF would purchase the SA 330E to meet its medium transport helicopter requirements, and the SA 341 (Gazelle) would be acquired for training use by all three British armed services, and as a light observation and reconnaissance

Above: For much of its RAF service the Puma has flown operationally in Northern Ireland, and continues to do so with Nos 72 and 230 Squadrons. Shown above is a No. 33 Squadron aircraft, landing at Bessbrook Mill in the 1970s. This is the barracks for the Armagh Roulement Battalion, and the main security forces base in the South Armagh district. Note the Westland Scout parked behind.

Right: A little known task for the RAF's Puma fleet is aerial surveillance, for which a handful of aircraft have been outfitted with a turret-mounted sensor which deploys through the lower hatch. The system may be covered by the codename 'Pleasant 4'.

The next hurdle was to name the three helicopter types involved in the agreement, which would obviously require names which meant the same in both languages. The French always favoured the name Puma, which was anathema to the British, who regarded 'big cat' names as suitable for more overtly aggressive aircraft types; they suggested, in order of preference, the names Machete, Atlas and Mistral. All were rejected by the British Ministry of Technology, as were the Deputy Chief of the Air Staff's further suggestions of Normandy or Consort. The name Puma was chosen in spite of RAF objections. The name of the manufacturer changed at the end of the 1960s, when Sud Aviation was absorbed into the new Société Nationale Industrielle Aérospatiale.

With only 40 aircraft (plus a later top-up attrition buy), the RAF was unable to use the Puma to replace its Wessexes, some of which are destined to serve until 2002. Under the Anglo-French agreement, Westland eventually produced 292 SA 341 Gazelle light helicopters and the French manufactured 40 Westland Lynxes. Fortunately, the French required an initial batch of 130 Pumas for the ALAT, and the type also proved popular with a range of export customers.

Puma construction

Nineteen RAF Pumas were deployed to participate in Desert Storm, accompanying the rapidly moving ground forces as they moved into Iraq and Kuwait and maintaining a steady flow of supplies. Temporary 'desert pink' was added, while the aircraft received missile approach warners and chaff/flare dispensers as part of the 'Granby fit'.

Portugal's aircraft have been successively updated – first to SA 330L standard and then to the unique SA 330S configuration. The Makila engines put them in the Super Puma class, although without the Super's ventral fin.

helicopter for the Army Air Corps. In return, France would buy the Westland WG.13 (Lynx) for the Aéronavale and to meet a requirement for an armed reconnaissance helicopter. In the event, neither side completely lived up to the spirit of the agreement. Britain's Puma buy failed to reach even 50 helicopters, and France preferred to develop new variants of the Gazelle for its army aviation (Aviation Légère de l'Armée de Terre) rather than to buy British army Lynxes.

Of all-metal semi-monocoque construction, the Puma made limited use of titanium alloy around the engine installation, but was otherwise entirely conventional in structural terms. The location of the engines above the cabin, with the flexible fuel tanks below the floor, left the cabin remarkably clear and unobstructed. The original French requirement was to carry 15 troops, though the RAF opted for 16 (later reducing this figure to 14, and then restoring the 16-seat fit), but the cabin is large enough that some operators have installed a high-density seating fit for up to 20 soldiers.

The floor was strengthened and provided with lashing points to allow freight to be carried with the seats stripped out (a procedure accomplished in minutes), while a removable

Right and below: French Pumas were first deployed to Saudi Arabia under Operation Salamandre, arriving in September 1990. Their main action came during the brief land war, supporting the French 6th Division as it raced northwards to cut off the Baghdad-Basra highway and shield the Kuwaiti theatre against Iraqi reinforcement. Saphir flare systems were added for Gulf operations, carried in racks aft of the wheel sponsons.

panel in the rear of the cabin (which doubles as an emergency exit on some export versions) allowed the aircraft to carry extra-long loads (such as spare rotor blades) that projected behind the cabin. A hatch in the floor directly below the rotor head allowed the installation of a load beam and external load hook for underslung loads of up to 2500 kg (5,511 lb) (more on later versions) using two-, three- and four-legged slings. Although underslung loads impose speed, range and manoeuvring limits on the aircraft, and increase the height at which it must be flown, they allow quick turn-around times at the landing point, and allow loads to be delivered where a helicopter can not land. They may also be jettisoned in emergency, giving great flexibility when carrying hazardous cargoes. The cargo hook hatch has also been used as a convenient aperture for the installation of FLIR and EO sensor turrets, although it does require the deletion of one fuel tank.

The cabin doors are large, aft-sliding and fully jettisonable, and later production SA 330s have additional cockpit entry doors on both sides. Early aircraft have jettisonable escape panels in this location. Troops can exit the cabin through the main doors on the ground, or from a low hover, and can also abseil or fast-rope from the aircraft, or even leave by parachute. A fixed or retractable winch can be rapidly installed in the starboard door for SAR or jungle operations, and some Pumas are able to use a Patrol Extraction Device. Away from the tactical arena, the cabin interior is spacious enough (and quiet enough) for the installation

The Puma has scored well in the export market. Brazil bought six SA 330Ls which flew with 3° Esquadrão/ 8° Grupo Aviação 'Puma' under the local designation CH-33. Like Brazil, many Puma operators went back to Aérospatiale/Eurocopter for the Super Puma/Cougar to augment or replace their SA 330 fleets.

of a properly furnished passenger fit, and some aircraft have airliner-type doors and incorporate retractable air-stairs for the VIP role. Some VIP aircraft also have a cabin air conditioning unit scabbed on to the port side of the forward fuselage, just behind the co-pilot's head.

Powerplant

Power is provided by a pair of Turboméca Turmo turboshaft engines, developments of the engine which powered the earlier Super Frelon. Power ratings vary from 985 to 1175 kW (1,320 to 1,575 shp), but all can accept a wide variety of fuels, fed from the usual fit of four self-sealing underfloor tanks (with a total capacity of 1029 kg/2,268 lb) and up to four overload tanks, each containing 370 kg (815 lb). The main gearbox, located behind the engines above the cabin, has two separate inputs from the engines and has five reduction stages. The first stage drives the alternator and

ventilation fan, as well as the two hydraulic pumps. The second stage synchronises both inputs on a single main driveshaft, allowing the drive gears to be rotated by a single engine or by the auto-rotating main rotor. With a turbine output of 23,000 rpm, the gearbox produces a main rotor shaft rpm of 265, with 1,278 rpm at the tail rotor. The aircraft includes a hydraulically-controlled integral rotor brake, which can stop the rotor 15 seconds after shutdown.

The Puma has a four-bladed main rotor, with a fully-articulated hub. The blade cuffs (with horns) are connected by link rods to the swash-plate, which is actuated via three twin-cylinder hydraulic servo control units. Each blade is attached to the hub by two pins, allowing quick and simple manual folding. The main rotor blades initially were formed around an extruded aluminium spar, milled to form the leading edge, and having a series of sheet metal pockets bonded to the rear face to form the trailing edge. They were of constant chord and of NACA 00 section. On later versions (and by retrofit on some early aircraft) the metal blades have been replaced by composite units which feature a glass-fibre roving spar, with a composite glass-fibre and carbon-fibre fabric skin, and a Moltoprene/honeycomb core. The leading edge has a stainless steel anti-abrasion sheath. The anti-torque tail rotor has five blades, with flapping hinges.

The Puma's retractable undercarriage has twin wheels on each unit, with dual-chamber oleo-pneumatic shock absorbers. The

South African troops ride nonchalantly in the doors of a Puma as it skims across the bush. In the 1970s and 1980s the Puma was the true warhorse of the South African Air Force, heavily involved in the fight against SWAPO guerrillas in what is now Namibia.

nosewheels retract rearward into a bay below the cockpit and forward part of the cabin (undercarriage doors are not fitted). The mainwheels (with differential hydraulically-actuated disc brakes) retract rearward into sponsons which are attached to the sides of the rear fuselage. Some Pumas have much enlarged sponsons, incorporating extra fuel tanks.

Emergency flotation gear may be attached to both sizes of sponson, as well as to a 'horse-collar' around the nose.

During the course of production (and afterwards), many improvements were made to the Puma. Increased engine power and the new composite rotor blades allowed a progressive but substantial improvement in load-carrying capability and 'hot-and-high' performance. Pumas have been equipped with the latest advanced navigation aids, defensive electronic countermeasure systems, night vision devices, and a range of equipment for specialised roles

ranging from combat SAR to reconnaissance. The provision of intake and blade de-icing systems on later aircraft made the Puma the first Western helicopter to be fully certificated for operation in all weathers, including flight in icing conditions.

Puma production

A total of 679 basic production SA 331 Pumas had been produced by the time French production ceased in 1987, including five of the 11 aircraft manufactured by IPTN/Nurtanio in Indonesia, and including all 48 of the aircraft built by Westland in the UK. Production continued in Romania, where an estimated 165 were manufactured. Even as the last Pumas rolled off the production line, manufacture of the closely-related AS 332 Super Puma continued apace.

The basic Puma airframe was fundamentally 'right' and this factor, coupled with the aircraft's competitive performance, gave it enormous potential. Apart from having its original nose contours cleaned up (a step taken on the second pre-production aircraft), the Puma underwent no major changes in external configuration until the introduction of the Super Puma, 13 years later. The last SA 330 to leave the production line at Marignane looked externally identical to the fourth prototype, and, apart from its nose and windscreen, to the first prototype.

Jon Lake

While the parent company concentrated on the Makila-powered Super Puma, it was left to licensee IAR in Romania to continue development of the Turmo-powered aircraft. Over 160 Pumas have been built in Romania, including some sold back to the French army. Although the armed Puma concept had been tested by Aérospatiale, it was not until IAR took up the reins that such an aircraft became operational. Following the lead of the Mi-8, several Romanian aircraft sport side-raced outrigger weapon pylons (right) and side-mounted cannon. Far more ambitious is the Socat programme (above), under which Elbit has integrated a modern weapon avionics suite to create a capable yet cheap combined assault/attack helicopter.

SA 330 Puma prototypes

Aérospatiale produced eight prototypes of the SA 330, these having been ordered in June 1963. The first (F-ZWWN) made its maiden flight on 15 April 1965, and the second (F-ZWWO) made the type's public debut at the Le Bourget air show in June that year. The remaining six SA 330 prototypes were officially designated as pre-production aircraft, and are sometimes referred to as SA 330As. The second

prototype later became an SA 330Z/AS 331 prototype for the Super Puma, retaining its original nose shape and airframe, but with Makila engines.

F-ZWWN was the prototype SA 330 (right), seen at Marignane without its nose data probe. Below it is seen leading the second and third aircraft, all of which featured the first nose shape.

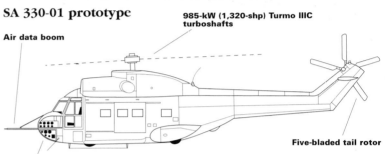

SA 330-01 prototype

Air data boom

985-kW (1,320-shp) Turmo IIIC turboshafts

Five-bladed tail rotor

Original rounded nose shape with more upright windscreen

SA 330A

The pre-production SA 330s introduced a slightly refined nose profile, with a more sloping windscreen. One of the prototypes was used to test a 10 wheeled landing gear, featuring four powered mainwheels on each side which allowed the aircraft to climb a shallow incline or cross a small trench under wheel power alone.

Generally, however, the six pre-production aircraft were identical to the initial production models that followed. The six aircraft were F-ZWWP, F-ZWWQ

(subsequently registered F BYAY, F-ZKCU and F-ZWWC), F-ZWWR (subsequently registered F-OCRK, and F-BRBU), F-ZWWS, F-ZWWT and F-ZJUX. F-ZWWR subsequently became the SA 330Z Fenestron tail rotor testbed.

F-ZWWQ was the fourth Puma, and the first to introduce the production nose profile with a more steeply sloping windscreen. With this aircraft the basic shape of the type was set, remaining unchanged throughout production. This aircraft later tested nose radar.

SA 330B

The initial production version for the French military was the SA 330B, which first flew in January 1969, followed by deliveries that spring to the Groupe de l'Aviation Légère's 7 Division at Habsheim Mulhouse. The SA 330B was powered by a pair of Turmo IIIC4 turboshafts, rated at 884 kW (1,185 shp) or 990 kW (1,328 shp) for take-off. Some 132 were procured for the Aviation Légère de l'Armée de Terre (ALAT, French army aviation). The only export customer for the SA 330B was Chad, which used two plus a single SA 330C.

Whereas there are significant external differences between the four basic standards of Super Puma/Cougar (if not between individual variants), all Puma versions look much the same, although there are differences between individual aircraft of the same basic mark, such as varying-sized sponsons, doors and antenna fit. Many SA 330s have been converted from one version to another, some Bs becoming Cs, and some Cs and Js becoming Ls. A handful of aircraft were even converted from L to J (eg, Brazilian aircraft being used by the Turkish police). Some Portuguese aircraft changed identity four times, being delivered as Cs, then successively converted to J, L and S-1 standards.

Above: Troops deplane from an ALAT SA 330B. In French army service the Puma was initially used solely in the assault transport role, although it later adopted other tasks such as air-mobile command post, casevac and mobile weather station. Most aircraft acquired intake filters above the flight deck, while the overall drab camouflage gave way to multi-tone European and desert schemes.

Left: The Dayglo panels on this Puma identify it as belonging to the EA.ALAT, the French army's training centre headquartered at Le Luc. France's Puma fleet has been brought up to SA 330Ba standard, equivalent to the SA 330H.

SA 330C

The SA 330C was the export version of the Puma. It was basically similar to the French SA 330B and the British SA 330E, but had slightly uprated 1044-kW (1,400-shp) Turmo IVB engines. The type was used by the air forces of Cameroon (one civil registered, one leased from South Africa), Chile (one), Ecuador (two), Gabon (four), Ivory Coast (two), Nepal (one), Nigeria (four), South Africa (20), Spain (two), Tunisia (one) and the Abu Dhabi element of the UAE air force (five), plus the Moroccan police (one). Zaïre used nine SA 330Cs, and the Belgian Gendarmerie used three,

upgrading two of them to L standards in service. In South Africa, the SA 330C was augmented by large numbers of

later variants, and the early aircraft were almost certainly upgraded to a similar standard in service.

South Africa was the first export customer for the Puma, buying 20 SA 330Cs (121 to 140) fitted with intake filters. They were followed by 18 SA 330Hs and 31 SA 330Ls.

SA 330D

The 'vacant' SA 330D designation was probably reserved for a SAR (or possibly even an ASW) version which was to have been offered to the British Royal Navy. The need for such an aircraft was obviated by the plentiful availability of redundant Whirlwinds and Wessexes displaced by new Sea Kings.

SA 330E/Puma HC.Mk 1

The SA 330E designation was used by Aérospatiale to describe the basic military utility variant built by Westland for the RAF. In its initial form, the RAF version was virtually identical to the Armée de l'Air (AA) and ALAT SA 330B. It was powered by a pair of Turmo IIIC engines, rated at 984 kW (1,320 shp) giving an MTOW of 6400 kg (14,109 lb) and a maximum speed of 151 kt (280 km/h; 174 mph).

The eighth Puma prototype (F-ZJUX) was supplied to Britain in late 1968 to serve as a pattern aircraft for Westland production of the SA 330E as the Puma HC.Mk 1. The aircraft subsequently served in the test and trials role (as XW241). An initial batch of 40 Pumas (XW198-237, equivalent to the Armée de l'Air SA 330B) was assembled at Westland's Hayes works, before being completed and test-flown at Yeovil.

The first RAF Pumas were delivered for trials work in January 1971, and No. 33 Squadron re-formed at Odiham to operate the type in June 1971. The second RAF Puma unit, No. 230 Squadron, converted in October 1972. The Puma also served briefly with No. 18 Squadron in RAF Germany (previously equipped solely with the Chinook) from 1992, and with a succession of training units.

A 'top-up' buy of eight attrition replacement aircraft was ordered in 1979, the first of which flew in May

1980. These aircraft were still basically SA 330Es, but were fitted with the new composite main rotor blades normally associated with later variants, and subsequently retrofitted to earlier RAF Pumas.

Another Puma was obtained in 1982 – captured from Argentine forces during the Falklands War. This aircraft, an SA 330L, was allocated the serial ZE449 but was put in storage at Fleetlands. The aircraft served as a ground instructional airframe, being moved to Odiham in 1991, before finally being sent to Westland at Weston Super-Mare where it awaited a decision on its future. The aircraft then began a thorough (if time-consuming) rebuild and refurbishment, reportedly entering service with No. 33 Squadron at Benson in March 2001. There have been suggestions that the aircraft will be used in the Special Forces support role.

The role of the Puma force generally has remained one of helicopter support, transporting men and material, including underslung loads. The role is much misunderstood, but the helicopter remains such a scarce and relatively vulnerable asset that direct assault, or transport directly into the battle area, is not part of that role. Instead, the Puma tends to be used to transport high-priority items like field guns and helicopter or Harrier spares and fuel to their operating sites, or to transport

specialised troops and air defence teams who may then be used to secure a road move, for example. The Puma would seldom have been deliberately flown close to the forward edge of battle area.

The end of the Cold War has altered the role somewhat, and in areas with a lower air defence and MANPADS (man-portable air defence system) threat, direct helicopter assault or troop insertion is again a possibility.

In addition to its transport and lift capabilities, the Puma can be used for a variety of other duties. *Jane's Weapons Systems* revealed that in Northern Ireland during the 1970s, for example, Pumas were among the types used for surveillance duties. These aircraft operated under the codename Pleasant 3 and carried a Ferranti/Barr and Stroud (later GEC) Type 221 thermal imaging surveillance system, outputting to 525- or 625-line TV/video. This system was mounted in the cabin, its sensor head

XW241 was an Aérospatiale-built SA 330E prototype which acted as the pattern aircraft for the Westland-built aircraft, and remained a trials machine throughout its career.

projecting down through the aperture usually used for the external load hook. The Puma may still carry out a surveillance role; one illustration shows a sensor turret projecting from the belly, which some sources suggest may be codenamed Pleasant 4.

Although the RAF's Pumas remain officially designated as HC.Mk 1s, they have received a succession of upgrades in service that have dramatically altered their external and internal appearance, and their combat capabilities.

Polyvalent (universal) air intake filters were fitted from about 1983, and ARI 18228 radar warning receivers began to be seen from 1995-96, with undernose and under-boom antenna fairings. An IRA MANPADS threat led to the

Left: ZA941 was one of the eight-aircraft 'top-up' purchase which featured composite rotor blades (retrofitted to the earlier aircraft). It served with the RAE at Farnborough but was later written off.

Below: The RAF Puma was optimised for duties in Germany, where this No. 230 Sqn aircraft was based. The type was a valuable asset for supporting the Harrier force in the field, among other tasks.

Puma HC.Mk 1

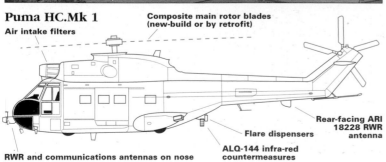

- Composite main rotor blades (new-build or by retrofit)
- Air intake filters
- Rear-facing ARI 18228 RWR antenna
- Flare dispensers
- ALQ-144 infra-red countermeasures
- RWR and communications antennas on nose

RAF Pumas are among the best defended, with an array of warning receivers and chaff/flare dispensers. This aircraft served with No. 27(R) Sqn, which acted as the OCU until the role was assumed by a flight of No. 33 Squadron.

installation of an AN/ALQ-144 infra-red jammer as part of the NI Fit, while M130 chaff/flare dispensers and AN/AAR-47 missile approach warning systems were installed for Operation Granby (Britain's part of Operations Desert Shield and Storm). An increasing emphasis on night operations and the use of night-vision goggles has resulted in improvements to cockpit NVG compatibility, and to the installation of an NVG covert external lighting fit.

In January 1993, a £3.5 million contract was signed with Racal Avionics covering a navigation system upgrade for 42 surviving RAF Pumas. The upgrade included dual Sextant Avionique LCD electronic horizontal situation indicator displays, RNS-252 Supertans, and other avionics improvements. The 39th aircraft was completed on 12 March 1996; the three remaining aircraft were damaged, and two of them received the upgrade during their rebuilds.

Most RAF Pumas share a common external configuration, although at least one has been fitted with the later, enlarged main undercarriage sponsons. Their use of a central underslung load hook means that RAF Pumas lack one of the standard underfloor fuel tanks, and the big sponsons were reportedly installed to give one aircraft an extended range capability, principally for use in the VIP transport role.

SA 330F

The first civilian version of the Puma was the SA 330F, which was fitted with 1070-kW (1,435-shp) Turmo IVA engines and which featured intake anti-icing as standard. The new engines gave an increased MTOW of 7400 kg (16,314 lb) and a maximum speed of 158 kt (293 km/h; 182 mph).

The standard Puma sliding doors were replaced by a narrower door with an integral air-stair. The first SA 330F made its maiden flight on 26 September 1969.

Although nominally a civil version, the SA 330F was used by a number of military customers. Chile acquired 12, Kuwait 12 (including at least one operated in police markings) and Morocco took 26 (some for the police). Five were delivered to the Abu Dhabi element of the UAE air force. The Madagascan air force took delivery of a single SA 330F, as did Pakistan.

SA 330G

The SA 330G was an improved civil variant, with further uprated 1175-kW (1,575-shp) Turmo IVC engines. The second pre-production SA 330A, F-ZWWQ, was converted to serve as the SA 330G prototype. Despite being a civilian version, the SA 330G also proved popular with a handful of military operators. Ivory Coast took three, Kenya four, Togo one, and Morocco 11.

The German Border Police acquired a number of Pumas for border and coastal patrols, inlcuding this SA 330G. It is fitted with nose-mounted Bendix weather radar and full flotation gear.

SA 330H

The SA 330H was an uprated military export version, with the same 1175-kW (1,575-shp) Turmo IVC engines as the SA 330G. Some were built for the French military as SA 330Bas, and all surviving French SA 330Bs were brought up to this improved standard.

The SA 330H served in the Congo Republic (one), Ethiopia (one), Gabon (two), Kenya (four), Malawi (two), Morocco (three), Nigeria (13), Senegal (three), South Africa (19), and Spain (one). Three South African SA 330Hs were subsequently sold to Romania.

This South African SA 330H is in SAR fit with winch and flotation gear.

SA 330Ba

The Armée de l'Air bought 37 new-build aircraft to the same standard as the export SA 330H, designating them SA 330Ba. The first such helicopter was F-MBAJ (c/n 1021). All 29 Pumas in current AdA service are now SA 330Ba sub-variants. These air force aircraft were joined by 15 new-build SA 330Bas for the ALAT, and by a small number of IAR-built aircraft delivered to the same standard. All surviving ALAT SA 330Bs (about 100 aircraft) were upgraded to the same standards.

Most ALAT Pumas are used in the support helicopter role, although a number of sub-variants perform more specialised duties. A handful of aircraft from the Détachement ALAT d'Opérations Spéciales at Pau (in southwest France) have a Chlio forward-looking infra-red turret under the belly, probably used for night observation and surveillance duties. Some SA 330Bas reportedly are equipped with nose-mounted ORB-37 radar, but details of these aircraft remain sketchy, and it is unknown which unit operates them. A few aircraft have a smaller Bendix weather radar mounted in their noses.

The ALAT has several Pumas fitted out as command posts. They have communications consoles in the cabin, and fittings for a large vertical antenna array above the starboard main undercarriage sponson. The aircraft do not operate as airborne command posts but, like Mi-6 and Mi-8 command post variants, act as mobile command posts, flying to dispersed locations where they set up with ground-based antennas. The Puma's cabin is augmented by the use of canvas awnings.

French army aviation also has a small number of SA 330Bas capable of carrying a modular weather station, with

This Armée de l'Air SA 330Ba serves with EH 6/67 at Solenzara. It has the large sponsons fitted for overwater SAR.

SA 330Ba

1175-kW (1,575-shp) Turmo IVC engines

Polyvalent intake filters

Most aircraft with small sponsons – some with large

Nose-mounted Bendix weather radar fitted to some SA 330Bas

powerful computers and satellite receivers.

At least one SA 330Ba (F-ZAGA) has been used as a test and trials aircraft in support of the Tigre HAP development programme, with a Helios radar installed in a radome above the co-pilot's cockpit roof. Another, the SA 330Ba DAV, has flown extensively with a DAV mast-

mounted air-to-air radar.

Like RAF SA 330Es, AdA and ALAT Pumas have been progressively updated and modernised in service. Most are now fitted with distinctive Polyvalent air intake filters, and have received a variety of new defensive systems, including Dassault Eléctronique EWR-99 radar warning receivers.

Although identical to other SA 330Bas, this radar-equipped aircraft was one of the small batch built for France by Romania. Within the ALAT the Puma equips eight regular Escadrilles d'Hélicoptères de Manoeuvre and a special forces EHM.

SA 330Ba Héron

Four SA 330Bas are operated by the Armée de l'Air's EHOM 68 from FAG 367, Cayenne-Rochambeau in French Guiana (covering the ESA space launch site at Kourou). These aircraft are

equipped with extensive long-range navigation aids, including IN/GPS, HF radio, and a Bendix weather radar in a thimble nose radome. They are known as Héron Pumas, from the acronym HERONS which stands for Hélicoptères Equipés pour la Recherche Opérationnelle en Navigation Solitaire.

SA 330Ba RESCO

The acronym RESCO (Recherche et Sauvetage en Combat) is the French equivalent to the US acronym CSAR (Combat Search and Rescue). It is used (perhaps unofficially) to describe the modified SA 330Bas used by EH 1/67 'Pyrénées' in the combat SAR role from Cazaux. Escadre de Hélicoptères 67 has five constituent Escadrons, three of which include Pumas on strength. Only EH 1/67 and EH 6/67 'Solenzara' are fully equipped with Pumas, and 1/67 is unique in being dedicated to the CSAR role. The squadron operates seven SA 330Ba helicopters, all extensively

modified for CSAR with IN/GPS, personnel locator system, a belly-mounted Thomson-CSF Chlio FLIR turret, an NVG-compatible cockpit, an auto-hover system, a large hoist in the starboard door, big undercarriage sponsons with extra fuel, armour protection for the crew and provision for a door-mounted GIAT AA-52 machine-gun in the port cabin door. The aircraft will be replaced by the new RESCO Cougar Mk 2 and Mk 2+, the first of which was delivered during 2000.

Visible beneath the cabin of this EH 1/67 Puma RESCO is the Chlio FLIR turret. Large sponsons and a heavy-duty winch are also fitted.

SA 330Ba Orchidée

The Orchidée (Observatoire Radar Cohérent Héliporté d'Investigation Des Eléments Enemis) programme of the 1980s was to have led to the procurement of 20 aircraft equipped for battlefield surveillance, using an advanced X-band radar with a rotating antenna below the rear fuselage, very much like that fitted to the EH-60B SOTAS (stand-off target acquisition system). When deployed, it limited speed to 100 kt (185 km/h; 115 mph) (110 kt; 204 km/h; 126 mph was demonstrated), although there was no speed restriction when the antenna was in the stowed, fore-and-aft, 'ferry' position. In this configuration, the helicopter could even carry out 60° banked turns. The antenna was designed to be jettisonable should it jam in the 'lowered' position.

A Puma-based demonstrator (F-ZKCQ) flew in 1986, although it was intended that the production system would be carried by the new Super Puma Mk 2 and that a Super Puma

The Orchidée radar was first taken aloft by this SA 330B. The aircraft carried a nose-mounted air data probe. Subsequently, the aircraft acquired a large search radar in a nose radome.

would serve as the Orchidée prototype. The aircraft originally was optimised to provide targeting data for systems like the MLRS, on NATO's central front, augmenting big-picture surveillance assets like the E-8 J-STARS.

By 1990, however, it was believed that Orchidée had been rendered surplus to requirements (or was at least a bearable potential defence cut) as a result of the end of the Cold War, and the programme was cancelled that year.

The sole Orchidée Puma was resurrected hastily and 'mobilised' for use in Operation Daguet. The deployment of the Orchidée Puma was known as Operation Horus, during which the aircraft flew five training/preparation sorties and 26 operational missions. The Puma was based at King Khaled Military City, and later at a forward strip north of Rafha, in the middle of the French army deployment area.

The aircraft carried a pre-Orchidée standard radar (with a range of only 60 to 70 km/37 to 44 miles, about 50 per cent of the production system's performance). It also lacked onboard processing power, limiting the size of the search area to a 20-km (12-mile) square (detecting, counting and

classifying vehicle targets by speed and direction), or a 40-km (25-mile) square if detection only was required.

The helicopter usually operated at 1,500 ft (457 m) and occasionally up to 4,000 ft (1219 m). It carried IFF Mod 4 so it could be identified by friendly AWACS platforms, and carried exhaust IR suppressors, RWRs, electronic countermeasures, and chaff/flare dispensers for survivability.

The Orchidée Puma operated in conjunction with French forces and US Army AH-64 Apaches, and was responsible for the destruction of large numbers of enemy tanks and vehicles. It encountered heavy hostile jamming

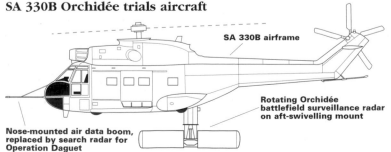

The cut-out in the rear of the fuselage housed the radar antenna mount when the sensor was stowed.

on two occasions, but on each occasion was able to use its antenna as a goniometer (a radio frequency interferometer) to pinpoint the source of the signals, which were then attacked by allied SEAD (suppression of enemy air defence) aircraft. The success of Operation Horus led to the reinstatement of a slimmed-down radar-equipped Cougar programme under the new designation Horizon (Hélicoptère d'Observation Radar et d'Investigation sur Zone).

SA 330B Orchidée trials aircraft

SA 330B airframe

Rotating Orchidée battlefield surveillance radar on aft-swivelling mount

Nose-mounted air data boom, replaced by search radar for Operation Daguet

SA 330J

The civil SA 330J introduced composite main rotor blades, and was cleared for operation at higher maximum take-off weights. One SA 330J operated by Sony was reportedly redesignated as the JA 330T.

Military and paramilitary operators of the SA 330J include the Burmese government (three), Ecuador (one), Malawi (one), Mexico (eight), Nepal (two), Oman (five), Pakistan (30), Sierra Leone (one), Spain (two for SAR and two for VIP duties) and the Turkish police (five). About 11 Portuguese SA 330Cs were upgraded to SA 330J standards, before becoming SA 330Ls and later SA 330S-1s. Indonesia took delivery of eight French-built SA 330Js before taking 10 built locally by IPTN.

An SA 330J, registered N330J, was used for VertRep trials by the US Navy.

Spain's SA 330Js were procured for VIP (illustrated) and SAR duties. The VIP aircraft served with 402 Escuadrón of Ala 48 at Cuatro Vientos.

This Fuerza Aérea Mexicana VIP SA 330J has flotation gear and nose radar. Note the passenger door, which has an integral airstair.

SA 330L

The SA 330L was the military equivalent of the SA 330J, with the same improvements. It was operated by Argentina (nine with the Army and three with the naval Prefectura), Brazil (six), Chile (three), Ecuador (one), Iraq (three), Lebanon (13), Malawi (one), Philippines (two), and Zaïre (two). About 11 Portuguese SA 330Js were upgraded to SA 330L standards, before becoming SA 330S-1s. Nine South African SA 330Ls were subsequently sold to Romania, and one Argentine aircraft was captured by the British during the Falklands campaign.

Chile bought a batch of three SA 330Ls (above) to add to its SA 330F fleet. Aérospatiale SA 330L demonstrator F-BRQK was used to test rocket armament (below).

This SA 330L is the last Puma operated by the Argentine army's Grupo de Helicópteros de Asalto 601 at Campo de Mayo. The variant also serves with the Prefectura Naval.

SA 330L

1175-kW (1,575-shp) Turmo IVC engines

Composite main rotor blades

Many SA 330Ls with large sponsons housing additional fuel

SA 330R

Some confusion surrounds the SA 330R designation, which is believed to have been applied to an early forerunner of the Super Puma, perhaps also known as the SA 331-001. Some sources describe this aircraft as having been no more than a simple re-engined SA 330, while others describe it as having had a stretched fuselage. The aircraft usually associated with the designation was SA 331 F-WZAT, converted from SA 330H c/n 1541.

SA 330S

Portugal was an early customer for the Puma, and most of its aircraft remain in service to this day. Several Portuguese SA 330Cs were upgraded to SA 330L standards, with new engines, composite rotors and other systems, and five were fitted with Omera

Portugal's Pumas began life with Turmo engines, but now have the Makila of the Super Puma.

ORB-31 Hercules search radar. These aircraft were among 10 Portuguese examples upgraded to SA 330S standards, with Makila engines. They do not feature the distinctive ventral tailfin of the standard Super Puma

SA 330S

Makila 1A turboshafts

Standard SA 330 airframe

Omera ORB-31 radar

Revised, strut-braced sponsons with flotation equipment

SA 330Z

The designation SA 330Z is usually associated with an aircraft (F-ZWWR) used to test a Gazelle-type Fenestron tail rotor, once planned to be a feature of the proposed Super Puma. The aircraft was converted from the fifth SA 330 prototype, F-BRBU. The SA 330Z designation was also used for a Makila-engined Super Puma pre-prototype (F-WZCY), which was converted from the second SA 330 prototype (F-ZWWO) flying for the first time in its new guise in June 1977.

SA 330Z

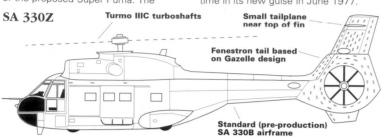

- Turmo IIIC turboshafts
- Small tailplane near top of fin
- Fenestron tail based on Gazelle design
- Standard (pre-production) SA 330B airframe

The SA 330Z remained a one-off trials conversion, and is seen here with the fenestron tail heavily tufted to allow observation of airflow patterns.

IAR 330L

The Puma was produced under licence in Romania, following a 1977 agreement. Under this agreement, 11 French-built Pumas were to be followed by 89 locally-built aircraft, the latter using the IAR 330 designation. Most (if not all) were built to SA 330L standards, and proved to be popular with the Romanian armed forces.

The Romanian company, IAR S.A. Brasov, also won export orders, being able to offer the aircraft at an extremely competitive price and without some of the diplomatic restrictions that were forced on Aérospatiale. Romanian-built Pumas were among those supplied to South Africa, and other customers included Ethiopia, the Guinea Republic

The Romanian military operates a large number of Pumas, including several armed versions. This IAR 330L carries outrigger pylons for rocket launchers, and also has a 20-mm cannon mounted on either side of the lower forward fuselage.

(one), Kenya (nine), Sudan (12-15), and the Dubai element of the United Arab Emirates air force (10).

Romanian production included a number of locally developed armed configurations, some simply having outrigger pylons outboard of the main undercarriage sponsons, carrying bombs, rockets, gun pods or AT-3 Sagger ATGMs. Some aircraft had 20-mm cannon 'scabbed on' to the sides of the forward fuselage, in

so-called 'cheek pods', fed via 540-round belts in boxes in the cabin.

The exact total of Romanian Puma production is unknown, although in 1991 it was reported to have reached 165 aircraft.

Left: Dubai (UAE) bought Pumas from Romania, this 'big-sponson' example being seen in Albania in 1999 during humanitarian relief operations. Note the wrecked Il-14s in the background.

After Romanian Puma production ended, IAR purchased a number of redundant SAAF Pumas from Denel to be refurbished and put into service in Romania. The total number of aircraft involved is believed to have been 12-18.

Below: Having received four SA 330Hs in 1977/78, Kenya later acquired a batch of IAR 330Ls for assault transport duties. Romanian-built aircraft usually have this early style of intake filter fitted.

IAR/Elbit IAR 330 SOCAT

A Romanian Puma upgrade proposal was first revealed at the 1992 Farnborough SBAC show. The Puma 2000, as it was then called, featured uprated engines and a new avionics suite, and Elbit was the prime avionics sub contractor. By the 1997 Paris Air Salon at Le Bourget, the upgrade had grown in scope and was offered as a joint venture between IAR-Brasov and Elbit, under the name IAR 330 SOCAT.

A Romanian Puma, coded '28', was displayed at the 1997 Paris air show, where details of the upgrade were revealed. The aircraft had a new MIL STD 1553B digital databus avionics architecture with hands on collective and stick (HOCAS) controls, and a new mission management system with a data transfer system to allow pre-prepared mission plans, DTEDs and other material to be uploaded directly by the crew. The MFLCD-dominated 'glass' cockpit was fully NVG-compatible, and the pilots could use helmet-mounted sighting systems and/or displays. The aircraft had a chin-mounted FLIR turret, and was capable of carrying an EO observation/targeting pod.

The SOCAT upgrade included provision for heavy armament, with a GIAT THL20 20-mm gun turret under the nose, and provision was made for rocket pods, NT-D air-to-ground missiles and air-to-air missiles on pylons.

It is expected that the SOCAT prototype will be followed by 24 'production' conversions for the Romanian air force. The first delivery was made in September 2000, with the remainder following at the rate of one per month. The SOCAT upgrade is being offered to other Puma operators, with and without the armament-related features.

The SOCAT upgrade represents a lot more than just an armed Puma. Internally the aircraft has a completely revised avionics system which includes state-of-the-art features such as 'glass' cockpit, hands-on weapon control, helmet-mounted sighting and data transfer systems. Similar aircraft are offered for export as the 'Puma 2000'. This SOCAT is one of the aircraft recently delivered to the Romanian air force's 61st Helicopter Group based at Titu/Boteni. It has the nose gun installed, and has outrigger pylons for rocket pods and anti-tank missiles.

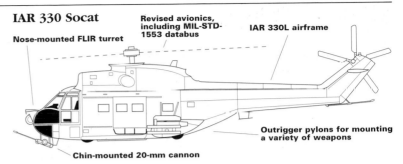

IAR 330 Socat

Nose-mounted FLIR turret · Revised avionics, including MIL-STD-1553 databus · IAR 330L airframe · Outrigger pylons for mounting a variety of weapons · Chin-mounted 20-mm cannon

IPTN NSA 330

Although some sources suggest that IPTN built 18 J and L models for the Indonesian armed forces, Indonesian production of the basic military Puma is believed to have totalled only 11 aircraft -- all J models, and two of these equipped as VIP transports.

IPTN produced 10 NSA 330Js for the TNI-AU. They serve on assault transport duties with Skwadron Udara 8.

Denel VIP 330

As well as the XTP-1 and Makila-powered Oryx, Denel (formerly Atlas) has also produced a number of less extensively modified aircraft, including a VIP transport. This has a neatly faired intake filter installation, and a luxuriously carpeted and upholstered, six-seat, leather-trimmed interior. A similar conversion may have been applied to at least one SAAF Puma, and may be applied to an Oryx.

Denel/Atlas XTP-1 Beta

The XTP-1 marked a stepping stone between the basic SA 330 Puma, and South Africa's indigenous Oryx 'Super Puma'.

Between one and three ex-SAAF SA 330Ls were sold or bailed back to Atlas for use in an indigenous attack helicopter programme, loosely based on the Puma. This followed the realisation that a planned attack helicopter based on Alouette III dynamics system components (and already preceded by the XH-1 Alpha technology demonstrator) would not be 'man enough' for the job.

Only one of the aircraft (177) was seen in public and in publicity photos, this initially flying (in 1986) with the doors sealed shut, but mounting new stub wings, and with a massive test instrumentation boom projecting from the starboard lower fuselage. Two more aircraft were reportedly used by Atlas under the designation FTB (189 and 190). The primary XTP aircraft subsequently gained an underbelly gun turret, a nose-mounted optronic sighting system, and carried a variety of lethal ordnance under and on the tips of its new stub wings. For many years, it was believed that the XTP-1s were prototypes of a planned Puma gunship conversion for the SAAF, and this impression was heightened by an opportunistic marketing campaign by

SA 330L 177 (right) was the principal XTP-1 test vehicle, seen here with rocket armament and characteristic air data boom. Aircraft 189 was also involved, and is seen below (with pylon censored) during a ground test launch of the V3B Kukri air-to-air missile.

Atlas for just such an aircraft.

The company described four alternative gunship configurations, one with an undernose Kentron TC-20 turret (with 1,000 rounds of ammunition) and a helmet-mounted sighting system, another adding provision for up to four 68-mm rocket pods, yet another adding a Kentron Helicopter Stabilised Optronic Sight, and a final variant with Kentron ZT-3 Swift ATGMs, too.

In fact, the XTP-1 Beta was intended as a technology demonstrator and trials

'hack' for the Rooivalk which, it was planned, would be based on Puma dynamics system components. As the XTP-1 flew with heavy warloads, it was felt expedient to increase installed engine power, and the aircraft received Makila turboshafts, which were also planned for the Rooivalk itself. With this higher power, it was only sensible to fit a Super Puma type ventral fin, and the XTP-1 became a potential prototype for an unarmed Puma upgrade, which emerged as the Oryx.

Meteorological Research Flight

From Spitfire to 'Snoopy'

Formed in 1942 as part of the High Altitude Flight, the Meteorological Research Flight has been the premier airborne weather research organisation in Europe for almost six decades. Its discoveries have made forecasting more accurate and contributed greatly to flight safety in all walks of aviation.

Since the earliest days of manned flight scientists have sought to analyse, forecast and utilise the prevailing weather conditions and phenomena that play a vital role in aviation.

In the second half of the 18th Century the success of the Montgolfier brothers and other balloon pioneers prompted huge interest from would-be aviators around Europe. For the first time scientists had a tool with which they could begin to analyse the earth's atmosphere. In 1784 an American physician living in England, named John Jefferies, conducted a series of flights in a gas balloon carrying rudimentary barometers, hygrometers and thermometers to heights exceeding 9,000 ft (2700 m), producing valuable data relating to temperature, humidity and pressure gradients in the lower atmosphere. By the early 1860s advances in the construction of gas balloons allowed Glashier and Coxwell to conduct a remarkable series of reconnaissance flights to again measure temperature, humidity and pressure, including one epic flight in an open gondola to height of some 29,000 ft (8840 m) which almost cost them their lives.

From 1898-1904 the first true meteorological research, rather than reconnaissance experiments, was conducted by the French scientist Teisserence de Bort. Measurements taken during nearly 600 flights at heights of up to 45,000 ft (13716 m) led to the discovery of the stratosphere.

The onset of fixed-wing flying in the second decade of the 20th Century attracted the interest of the Director of the Meteorological Office, who in 1913 proposed that equipment be developed to carry on aircraft including vanes to measure vertical air motion and an accelerometer to measure 'bumpiness'. However, World War I interrupted the development and little useful data came from these initiatives. In 1920 the Meteorological Office was officially absorbed into the Air Ministry and throughout the decade a number of experiments were conducted to analyse the growing number of weather-related hazards, such as airframe icing, which accompanied the rise in aircraft capabilities. In 1927 a meteorological research flight was established at Duxford, but lacking the expertise and specialised equipment, the flight had little success and was soon disbanded.

During the first two years of World War II

Brewer's concerns that the Boston had an inadequate ceiling for contrail research prompted the transfer of an ex-RAF Fortress to the HAF, primarily for Brewer's team. The hygrometer and thermometer were placed on small observation windows on the starboard side of the nose

Undoubtedly the most valuable type during the first 10 years of operations, the Mosquito was blessed with a high ceiling, long range and adequate room for a scientist observer. From 1944-46 HAF examples were modified to carry hygrometers and thermometers designed by Brewer himself (below). In 1946, with the establishment of the MRF, two Mosquito PR.Mk 34s were allocated, of which VL621 (left) is seen collecting contrail formation data at 30,000 ft (9144 m) in December 1952.

The MRF team poses in front of Halifax Met.Mk 6 ST817 in the spring of 1948 (above) at RAE Farnborough. The two Halifaxes were generally used for lower altitude research, complementing the high-altitude work of the Mosquito PR.Mk 34 (below, with Halifax).

Above: Two MRF scientists prepare their equipment in the nose section of the Halifax before another sortie in May 1948. Unheated and unpressurised, the Halifax was a less than ideal platform, and operating new and sensitive instrumentation in thick flying jackets and gloves in the cramped confines of the Halifax nose tested the scientists to the limit, particularly on long-endurance high-altitude sorties.

weather forecasting for combat operations was still rudimentary and unreliable, exacerbated by a lack of observations from the source of the majority of the UK's weather the Atlantic Ocean. The need for immediate solutions led to two initiatives. In November 1941 the Meteorological Research Committee (MRC) was established to form an organisation to conduct investigation and research into meteorological science. The second proposal was to establish met. reconnaissance flights at RAF stations throughout the UK to measure local wind, temperature, humidity and cloud cover, base and thickness. An immediate improvement in forecasts resulted, and during the course of the remainder of the war some 20,000 met. flights were made. In the late 1980s this comprehensive data was utilised during extensive research into helicopter rotor icing.

Early experiments

In the summer of 1942 the MRC arranged the transfer of scientists to the High Altitude Flight (HAF) at Boscombe Down. Led by Dr A. W. Brewer, their first task was to study the atmospheric conditions necessary for the formation of aircraft condensation trails. Contemporary science believed that a simple height/temperature plot formed the boundary at which contrails formed, however, pilots were reporting contrails outside these boundaries. Losses to Luftwaffe fighters, which homed in on the telltale contrails, were serious, and an accurate way of forecasting contrail altitudes was desperately required. The meteorological section 'loaned' aircraft from the HAF as required. Two Douglas Bostons and a Spitfire Mk VI became the first

types used in August 1942 and Brewer immediately began work devising new instruments and equipment. Initial experiments with the Bostons were largely unsuccessful. The hygrometers proved to be inaccurate when cloud was encountered and the aircraft itself, with a ceiling of just under 30,000 ft, could not reach the stratosphere where the trails were expected to occur. Although the Spitfire could reach these altitudes it could not carry the necessary equipment or the all-important scientific observer.

In 1943 many of these problems were alleviated when the HAF was allocated a B-17 Flying Fortress, one of six given as a personal present from Roosevelt to Churchill. All non-necessary equipment was stripped from the Fortress, allowing measurements to be taken for the first time in the stratosphere at 37,000 ft (11278 m). A new frost point hygrometer, developed by Brewer's team, provided accurate readings and led to the discovery that the upper troposphere was supersaturated with ice and ideal for contrail forma-

Right: In 1952 one Handley Page type replaced another when the MRF received two Hastings Mk 1s (TG618 and TG619) to replace the two Halifaxes. New instrumentation and equipment was adapted by MRF staff and installed by the RAE to ensure military safety procedures were met. By 1954 TG619 had a range of hygrometers, thermometers and aerosol detectors fitted beneath the nose, complementing the long instrumentation probe.

Below: Augmenting and finally replacing the Mosquitoes for high-altitude research was Canberra B.Mk 2 WJ582. Some of the first studies of ozone within the stratosphere were conducted in the late 1950s, with deployments made to Nairobi to investigate incidence of ozone and high-level cloud associated with outflow from the Indian monsoon (below right).

tion, whereas the stratosphere was extremely dry. By early-1944 various marks of de Havilland Mosquito, allocated to the HAF, were also being 'borrowed' by Brewer's team and experiments conducted with these aircraft reinforced earlier results. An accurate contrail forecasting method was devised, ultimately saving many Allied airmen's lives in the final 14 months of the war.

The successes of the meteorological research section of the HAF during World War II led to a change of name and location in 1946, along with additional staff and funds. Based at RAE Farnborough, the Meteorological Research Flight (MRF) was tasked with continuing the HAF's work in advancing meteorological science and providing research in weather related problems of aircraft design and operation as they arose. The Spitfire, Fortress, Hudson, Bostons and Mosquitoes were replaced by two Mosquito PR.Mk 34s (RG248 and VL621) and two Halifax Met.Mk 6s (ST796 and ST817). In the immediate post-war period aircraft were easier to acquire

Co-operation between the RAF aircrew and the civilian scientists has always been vital to the success of the MRF. Here the scientist observer briefs the aircrew on the precise objectives of the sortie, before strapping into his parachute and the unmistakable cartridge start of the engines. For longer range flights the aircraft could be fitted with tip tanks, allowing ozone measuring sorties to be flown well into the Arctic region. Note the RAE crest and inscription on the forward fuselage.

than trained meteorological scientists and the ratio of airframes to staff was around 1:1. The establishing of the MRF also saw regular postings of RAF aircrew to the flight – a system which continued until 1998. Although a posting to the MRF was something of a culture shock to the crews, they were soon heavily involved in the planning of the research, alerting the scientists to the ever-growing airspace constraints imposed over the British Isles. The aircraft themselves were serviced and maintained by RAE personnel, who also officiated over the installation of meteorological equipment, ensuring that the appropriate safety standards were met.

The two Mosquito PR.Mk 34s were tasked with conducting the majority of high-altitude research, with the Halifaxes conducting operations within the troposphere. The Mosquito was judged by Brewer to be the ideal met. reconnaissance platform, allowing close co-operation by the pilot and scientist sitting side-by-side in the aircraft's cabin. In 1954 an infra-red radiometer, developed by the Clarendon Laboratory of Oxford University (starting the MRF's long-standing association with the university), was installed on VL621, providing some of the earliest data on radiative heating throughout the troposphere.

A widespread change of equipment occurred in 1952 with the two Halifax Met.Mk 6s being replaced by two Handley Page Hastings and one

of the Mosquito PR.Mk 34s being replaced by Canberra B.Mk 2 WJ582. The Canberra provided the MRF with a valuable high-altitude platform with the ability, in favourable conditions, to be 'nursed' to 15000 m (49,200 ft). Soon after its introduction, the Canberra made the MRF's first official foreign deployment to Khartoum to study atmospheric humidity in tropical regions.

Cloud physics research

The Hastings' work during the 1950s concentrated on cloud physics research, for which a number of sensors were designed and fitted to the aircraft, including oiled slides to collect cloud droplets, hot-wire devices to measure cloud water content, aluminium foil instruments for detecting the impact of ice particles and drizzle droplets and an aerosol counter. These instruments were mounted beneath the nose section of the aircraft, or on an extended instrumentation boom which protruded forward of the nose. The measurements taken during the 1950s greatly improved the knowledge of the development of rain-producing clouds, and the crucial role played by ice particles in the process.

In 1958 Hastings TG619 was replaced by the first of two Vickers Varsity T.Mk 1s to be operated by the flight. With a spacious cabin, the Varsity was able to be configured to similar equipment levels as the Hastings, its twin-engined layout

was more economical and reliable and its tricycle-type undercarriage allowed a greater tolerance during crosswind operations. At the same time, the second Hastings underwent conversion to carry a weather radar, housed in a protruding radome mounted beneath the forward fuselage. The radar allowed the meteorologists to more accurately locate a particular weather feature they were interested in and gave some indication of the structure of certain cloud formations.

The Canberra's additional altitude allowed extensive studies of water content in the upper troposphere and the stratosphere, particularly in jetstreams. This data was particularly invaluable in studying the effects of nuclear weapon tests which were being conducted by the USA, United Kingdom and the USSR during the latter half of the decade. Radioactive particles from the test explosions penetrated the stratosphere and MRF studies allowed accurate prediction of the behaviour of the particles in the stratosphere. There was much concern that the radioactivity could travel many miles in the stratosphere before returning to earth as radioactive rain. However, the MRF studies concluded that these fears were largely misplaced, with the mid-stratosphere

Canberra B.Mk 2 crash - Scientist's miraculous escape

The high-altitude research work of the MRF came to an abrupt halt in February 1962 when the Canberra B.Mk 2 crashed on final approach to RAF Leuchars in Scotland. The aircraft had just completed a long flight measuring ozone and water distribution in the lower Arctic stratosphere and was on final approach when the pilot suddenly lost control. Both aircrew successfully ejected, leaving the unfortunate scientist, who was not equipped with an ejection seat, aboard the stricken Canberra. The aircraft pancaked into a few feet of water and slid along the beach, tearing off the cockpit section and the rear fuselage before severing the port wing as it came to rest. Miraculously the pilotless aircraft neither rolled or cartwheeled and the scientist was rescued alive from the wreckage. He did, however, sustain leg injuries and, as a testament to his miraculous escape, still walks with a limp today. The hiatus in high altitude research lasted until the following year when Canberra PR.Mk 3 WE173 was acquired as a replacement.

Following the transfer of TG619 to the RAE in 1958, TG618 became the sole Hastings in MRF service. The aircraft was fitted with a weather radar in a teardrop-shaped radome beneath the nose. Much of the data at this time was still recorded by hand by the scientists situated at their workstations in the aircraft's cabin.

acting as a 'storage tank' for these products.

In 1960 the Canberra was fitted with an ozone detector, developed by Dr Brewer at the Clarendon laboratory, for studying the distribution of ozone in the lower stratosphere. This issue would later become of great importance to governments and environmental groups and much of the data for the developing ozone holes in polar regions was gathered by the MRF.

The high altitude work of the MRF was interrupted in 1962 with the loss of the Canberra B.Mk 2 which coincided with the MRF moving to new permanent buildings at Farnborough.

High-altitude research resumed the following year when the MRF acquired an ex-RAF Canberra PR.Mk 3. Having previously served in the photographic reconnaissance role with Nos 540, 69 and 39 Squadrons, the PR.Mk 3 received modifications for the weather reconnaissance role including a long pointed instrumentation probe protruding from the front of the aircraft. The probe carried rapid response wind vanes linked to an inertial navigation platform positioned near the aircraft's centre of gravity. This system not only made it possible to extract the position at any time, but also allowed the onboard computer to automatically remove the aircraft's motions, allowing wind and turbulence data to be derived. The inertial navigation system and other associated equipment was used extensively by the Canberra in the late 1960s and early 1970s for detailed studies of high level clear-air turbulence and mountain waves. For this purpose, the Canberra was detached to Buckley Field, Denver, Colorado in March 1973 under the project name Wamflex.

Further equipment was added to the Canberra in 1975 in the shape of the prototype Selective Chopper Radiometer that was to be installed on the NASA Nimbus 5 satellite. Deploying to Dakar, Senegal, the aircraft calibrated the equipment as well as conducting valuable studies of radiation absorption rates in tropical latitudes.

In 1965 the Cloud Physics Department of Imperial College was transferred to the Met. Office and since this time this group has been the principle user of the MRF's aircraft. One of the department's first tasks was the development of dropsonde equipment that could be integrated into the MRF's larger aircraft. Taken from the french word *sonde* (meaning plumb line), the device consisted of a metal capsule containing sensors and a radio transmitter that descended vertically from the aircraft on a parachute, measuring various parameters on its descent and transmitting this data to a computer on the mother aircraft. These radiosondes were tested on the MRF's Hastings in 1966 before being used extensively by the Flight's second Varsity (which had replaced WJ906 in 1969) during Project Scillonia in 1970.

In 1967 the Hastings TG618 retired at the end of its design life, leaving the MRF with just two aircraft – the Varsity for lower altitude research and the Canberra PR.Mk 3 for high-altitude work.

Global experiments

This situation continued until the early 1970s when the UK was invited to participate in the international Global Atlantic Tropical Experiment (GATE) planned for 1974. With rapid advances in microchip and computer technology, the previous manual collection of data was becoming obsolete and with the Varsity approaching the end of its service life, the MRF was to be allocated a new aircraft. After some

deliberation it was decided that one of the RAF's fleet of Lockheed Hercules C.Mk 1s would be converted to the met. research role, incorporating the most recent technological advances in both sensor and computer technology.

The aircraft chosen for conversion was XV208, which had previously served with No. 48 Squadron, Far East Air Force, based at Changi, Singapore. From the outset it was intended that the Hercules would be the most capable met. research aircraft in Europe, if not the world, and the modifications would allow a host of new generation equipment to be incorporated. This included an extended nose boom, some 22 ft (6.71 m) in length, which carried a wind vane assembly at the tip for turbulence and gust measurements, along with experimental pitot and static pressure systems and fast response thermometers. Located at the base of the probe was the Ferranti miniature inertial platform for calibration of the readings. The installation of the probe necessitated the re-location of the aircraft's weather radar from the nose position (as on standard aircraft) to a teardrop-shaped pod mounted above the cockpit.

The sensitivity of early computer equipment necessitated the construction of a recorder 'van' or cabin. Fitted in the centre of the aircraft's cabin, the hermetically sealed 'van' was constructed with 4-in (10-cm) walls which reduced noise levels from 110 db to 80 db, and careful electrical bonding ensured that the 'van' became an electrically 'quiet' area. The 'van' was

Above: The radio dropsonde equipment was tested aboard TG618 before being successfully implemented on the Varsity, and subsequently the Hercules W.Mk 2. The Hastings was finally withdrawn from MRF service after some 14 years of service in 1968.

Left: The MRF's airborne assets of Hastings, Varsity and Canberra PR.Mk 3 line-up for a publicity photograph in the mid-1960s at RAE Farnborough.

Project Scillonia (1970)

As the main thrust of Met. Office cloud physics research moved away from ground-based laboratory studies towards the relationship between cloud microphysics and cloud dynamics, the role of the MRF's aircraft assumed paramount importance. The first major project involved Varsity WF425 deploying to RAF St Mawgan in 1970 for research into the structure of wind, temperature and humidity within active warm fronts approaching the British Isles. Under the project name Scillonia (most flying was conducted in the vicinity of the Scilly Isles), the aircraft was fitted with radiosonde ejection tubes releasing the sondes at an approximate altitude of 16,400 ft (5000 m). Providing a cross-section of the feature, the research led to several important discoveries in the structure of frontal zones and successfully proved the concept of sonde deployment from an aircraft for studying large-scale features.

The Varsity proved an ideal mount for lower altitude research, with a spacious cabin accommodating the growing equipment requirements (bottom centre) and easy access to the cockpit for liaison with the pilot in flight (bottom left). This was particularly important as changes to the pre-planned brief were a regular occurence in order to find the exact location of desired weather features. The original Varsity T.Mk 1, WJ906 (above left) served from 1958-1969 before being replaced by a second example (WF425).

Above: Varsity T.Mk 1 WF425, as with all MRF aircraft, was converted to carry a wide range of meteorological equipment. It was this aircraft which was fitted with the dropsonde equipment for Project Scillonia in 1970. This view shows nose-mounted field mill and conductivity tubes used to measure the electric field in clear and cloudy air during experiments in the early 1970s.

designed to accommodate four scientists plus the BAC data recording system, and the majority of monitoring displays and control panels for the plethora of sensors and instruments planned for the aircraft. The 'van' is one of two large removable cabins designed for UK Hercules', the other being the VIP transport cabin that was used to transport the then Prime Minister Margaret Thatcher to the Falkland Islands in the wake of the 1982 conflict. In reality the 'van' is only ever removed from the aircraft during major overhaul.

The aircraft's dropsonde ejector was incorporated into the rear loading ramp, along with a storage area for holding up to 66 radiosondes. This system was later replaced in use by a new dropsonde dispenser located in the rear of the cabin on the starboard side which utilises the new generation of smaller, less expensive sondes. Numerous other alterations and equipment installations were also completed, including forward-facing video cameras above the nose boom, forward- and downward-facing stills cameras, an air sampling boom, an automatic hygrometer, an air sampling pipe and the repositioning of the HF antenna. The cockpit of the aircraft was altered to allow the aircraft scientist to be accommodated as a fifth flight deck member (along with the two pilots, flight engineer and navigator). Located behind the first pilot's seat, the aircraft scientist liaises with the navigator, pilots and scientists in the cabin to ensure that the sortie is conducted to meet the particular requirements of the flight.

The conversion work was completed over a period of two and a half years by Marshall's of Cambridge before the aircraft made its maiden flight as a Hercules W.Mk 2 on 21 March 1973. The aircraft subsequently underwent service acceptance trials at Boscombe Down before being handed over to the MRF in January 1974.

After a number of preliminary research flights, the Hercules left Farnborough for Dakar on 24 June 1974 for participation in GATE. As one of only three aircraft from the participating nations to be equipped with a gust probe, all the sorties were flown below the boundary layer (5,000 ft/1524 m). The project's three phases were completed on 23 September, during which time the aircraft had flown 40 operational sorties with over 336 hours on task.

The experience gained during GATE highlighted the strengths and weaknesses of the

Modifications to the Canberra PR.Mk 3 included the addition of the distinctive nose instrumentation boom that was used to take measurements in undisturbed air forward of the aircraft. The Canberra is seen here in its original bare metal finish.

Above: XV208 rests on the tarmac at Bermuda airport alongside NASA's Convair CV 880 'Galileo II', during the microwave sounding project Camex in 1983.

Left: 'Snoopy' overflies Boscombe Down during its service acceptance trials in 1973. The addition of the nose probe and relocation of the weather radar necessitated a 4 kt increase in minimum control speeds and reduced crosswind take-off and landing limits.

modifications and allowed the team to evaluate the aircraft's optimum operating configuration. Despite a few minor teething problems, the system operated very successfully and the aircraft became widely accepted as the most capable met. research aircraft in the world. The W.Mk 2's on-board data-processing system recorded the data on magnetic tape, which could then be transferred to scientific institutions around the world. Data gathered proved conclusively that the mid-Atlantic cloud formations and thunderstorms have a significant effect on Europe's weather pattern and led directly to more accurate forecasting of the northern hemisphere's weather.

During the remainder of the 1970s the Hercules was used to carry out research in four main areas; cloud physics (for which Knollenberg optical probes were acquired for the aircraft), atmospheric turbulence, atmospheric chemistry and radiative transfer. In addition, the MRF was called on by various agencies to inves-

Hercules W.Mk 2 'Snoopy'

Specification
Powerplant: Four 4,508-ehp (3362-kW) Allison T56-A-15 turboprops
Crew: Two pilots, navigator, flight engineer, loadmaster and up to 14 scientists
Span: 132 ft 7 in (40.41 m)
Length: 119 ft 11 in (36.55 m)
Height: 38 ft 3 in (11.66 m)
Wing area: 1,745 sq ft (161 m²)
Cruise speed: 336 mph (540 km/h)
Mission speed: 224 mph (360 km/h)
Range: 3418 miles (5500 km) at 30,000 ft (9144 m)
Endurance: 12 hours with reserves
Service ceiling: 33,000 ft (10058 m)
Maximum payload: 38,800 lb (17600 kg) with maximum fuel

Diagram key
1 Pitot static head
2 Forward-facing video camera
3 Weather radar pod
4 Dew point hygrometer
5 Air sampling pipe
6 Counter-flow Virtual Impactor (CVI)
7 Isokinetic sampling intake
8 In-cloud temperature probe/ARIES
9 Maxi pod
10 Upper broad-band radiometers
11 Dropsonde dispenser
12 Obscurers
13 GPS/satellite communications aerial
14 Maxi pod
15 Scanning Airborne Filter Radiometer (SAFIRE)

16 Forward-scattering Spectrometer Probe (FSSP)
17 2-D cloud probe
18 Passive Cavity Aerosol Spectrometer Probe (PC ASP) or High-Volume Precipitation Sensor (HVPS)
19 Filter sampling
20 Air sampling pipes
21 Microwave Airborne Radiometer and Scanning System (MARSS)
22 Total water content meter
23 Liquid water content sensor
24 Gust probes

Below left: The fifth cockpit position is taken by the aircraft scientist (on left) and his HORACE screen.

Below centre: The maxipods on each wing can carry a range of probes, cameras and radiometers.

Below right: During radiosonde operations temperature, humidity, pressure and wind speeds are recorded at the dropsonde monitoring station.

Above: A Knollenberg console is used for water and ice droplet analysis.

Below: The dropsonde dispenser tube is fitted on the starboard side of the cabin.

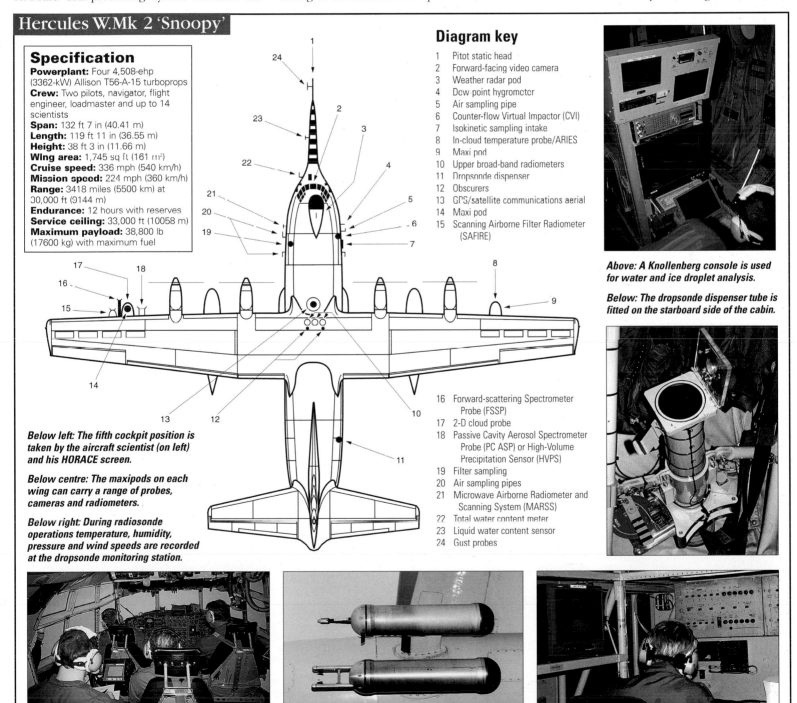

tigate particular weather related hazards in regard to aircraft operations and began its less publicised war role. As an RAF Strike Command asset, the aircraft would act as the principal NATO weather reconnaissance platform should war break out in Europe. The MRF's pilots and scientists were required to participate in annual NATO exercises, for which the aircraft would often deploy to Scandinavia.

Atmospheric sampling

Growing concern with atmospheric pollution, in particular the effects of acid rain, in the late 1970s led to the commencement of extensive atmospheric chemistry studies in conjunction with the Central Electricity Research Laboratories (CERL). To pursue the research, a range of chemical sampling equipment was installed, allowing the analysis of a wide range of airborne chemicals, including nitrogen and sulphur compounds and ozone. Flights were conducted over the North Sea within downwind plumes emitted by a major power station. The resulting data demonstrated the processes that produce acid rain and prompted the government to reduce sulphur emissions from the UK's power stations.

In 1981, cost-cutting saw the withdrawal from service of the Canberra PR.Mk 3, leaving the MRF without a high-altitude platform for the first time in its 39-year history.

In 1987 the Hercules participated in Project Fire – an investigation into marine stratocumulus off the coast of San Diego – in conjunction with NASA's Lockheed ER-2. This was followed the same year by one of the decade's most important frontal dynamics investigations, Project Fronts '87. A tri-national experiment with West Germany's DFVLR and France's Météorologie Nationale, vital research was conducted into the processes which produce the weather and rainfall associated with cold fronts. This in turn led to a successful follow-on study (Fronts '92) producing data which was available to research facilities around the world. By this time the Hercules On-board Recording And Computer Equipment (HORACE) had been installed, allowing scientists to monitor the data at screens positioned around the cabin and in the cockpit, as well as complete in-flight calculations comparing various parameters.

In the period to 1994, foreign experiments increased in frequency, with deployments made in support of a range of projects to locations as diverse as Bermuda, Senegal, Ascension Island,

In the 1970s the Canberra PR.Mk 3 adopted this smart red, white and grey colour scheme and 'barber's pole' nose probe. A larger version was subsequently adopted on 'Snoopy', seen here in a formation with the Canberra which marked the latter's retirement in 1981.

Canada, Morocco and the Solomons, along with a number of deployments to the USA and Europe.

With global warming and ozone becoming a major political issue, the aircraft's radiometers were upgraded in the mid-1980s with the addition of the Multichannel Radiometer and upward- and downward-facing radiative flux sensors. In 1988 Project Water conducted from Dakar made extensive use of these instruments and discovered that water vapour, rather than carbon dioxide was the significant contributor to the 'greenhouse effect' in tropical latitudes.

Along with continuing work in the areas of cloud physics and atmospheric chemistry, the MRF involvement in aspects of satellite meteorology expanded. Sensors intended to be installed in weather satellites were thoroughly evaluated aboard 'Snoopy', including the testing of equipment for the flagship ERS-1 satellite. Subsequently the MRF flew calibration-validation (cal-val) flights for this satellite following its launch in 1991.

Project Gulfex - Analysing Kuwaiti oil plumes

The most high profile project conducted by the MRF in the 1990s was Gulfex – environmental research into the effects of the pollution from the Kuwaiti oil fields set ablaze by the retreating Iraqi forces during the Gulf War. 'Snoopy' was the first met. research aircraft to arrive in-theatre and flew some 55 hours of operations during March 1991. At short notice the aircraft was fitted with the appropriate instrumentation and, using Sir Peter de la Billiere's BAe 125, OC MRF was dispatched around the Gulf states to acquire diplomatic permission to leave standard airway routes. Flying vertical profiles from 30,000 ft (9144 m) down to 50 ft (15 m) taking samples at every 50 ft, the exact composition of the plumes was determined. The research quickly established that the environmental impact was not as bad as some predictions and only moderate short-term regional environmental damage was expected, much to the relief of the politicians. The smoke was not entering the stratosphere to be circulated around the globe and some 125 miles (200 km) downwind the concentrations were similar to those found over industrial areas of Europe.

Above: Operating within the plume in near darkness presented a challenge to both crew and aircraft. The oily soot residue coated both the inside and outside of the Hercules, testing the robust nature of both equipment and scientists. With associated health risks, the aircraft carried a member from the Institute of Aviation Medicine who advised the crew when to don protective clothing and respirators.

Left: This view of the burning oil fields was taken from the Hercules in March 1991. Close liaison with the many military control assets, such as E-3 Sentries and NATO warships, was of paramount importance to allow them to follow the plumes.

As the threat of acid rain decreased during this period, the Hercules was fitted with sensors to measure ozone and the man-made substances which effect its formation and degradation. In addition, plumes of sulphur dioxide were still tracked to update the predictions of the Met. Office's Nuclear Accident Model. Already under threat from government cost cutting, the MRF increasingly flew sorties on behalf of research institutions and other funded organisations, helping the aircraft to become self-funding to some degree. One of the most important of these customers was the NERC which regularly used the aircraft for atmospheric chemistry research.

New location

In 1992 the MRF celebrated its 50th anniversary and, with the RAE planning to move its aircraft from Farnborough, a new base was sought. In March 1994 the aircraft was transferred to the place where it all began – Boscombe Down. Shortly after, the aircraft passed from RAF Strike Command ownership to the Met. Office and then on to DRA (later DERA) each time for a nominal £1. RAF aircrew were allocated under the auspices of the Experimental Flying Department of DRA until 1998, when the MRF lost its dedicated aircrew, replaced by personnel from the resident Heavy Aircraft Test Squadron.

Despite the end of the Cold War and the regular exercises hosted by NATO, the MRF has continued to conduct research for military customers, including CinC Fleet, the Maritime Warfare Centre and DERA. In 1999 an Defence Projects Scientist was allocated to help facilitate the needs of various military customers.

In 2000, the future of the 'Snoopy' again came under threat and this time the seemingly inevitable decision to remove the aircraft from service was taken. Examining the facts, this decision is hard to fathom. The aircraft itself has been constantly upgraded and can collect data in real-time before transferring the data to the Met.

Worldwide collaboration

From the 1970s the amount of collaborative projects in which the MRF has participated has gradually increased. By the mid-1990s much of the aircraft's funding was coming from international projects conducted in conjunction with numerous other met. research agencies. In 1997 the EU established the Scientific Training and Access to Aircraft for Atmospheric Research Throughout Europe (STAARTE) programme. Some 27 countries have participated in the scheme and its success has prompted a follow-on programme, Co-ordinated Access to Aircraft for Transitional Environmental Research (CAATER) employing assets including the Météo-France Metro and DLR of Germany's Falcon 20. In the future it is foreseen that European research will be centralised, using two pooled aircraft of differing capabilities available to all research groups. DERA has actively sought to offer the Hercules W.Mk 2 for this purpose and retains the hope that the aircraft may be selected for this role.

Throughout the 1980s and 1990s one of the MRF's main collaborative partners was the US National Oceanic and Atmospheric Administration (NOAA), which operates this pair of WP-3D Orions.

Left: 'Snoopy' is by no means the only met. research aircraft to feature a 'barber's pole' nose. In the early 1990s, the aircraft deployed to Australia working in conjunction with the CSIRO's modified Fokker F27.

Right: The Hercules often works as an airborne coordinator for types such as the DLR's Falcon 20.

Office in seconds using the aircraft's SATCOM system. The airframe has the lowest hours of any of the RAF's first-generation Hercules' and conservative estimates recognise that 'Snoopy' could have continued in the role for some 15 years. The aircraft itself is still regarded as the finest research platform in Europe and the experience of the flight crew working with scientists results in accurate data, usually at the first time of asking. With costs constantly being reduced by contract work from outside agencies, there seems little logic in the decision and both aircrew and

scientists alike remain somewhat disheartened and bemused by 'Snoopy's' demise. The aircraft was officially retired from service on 31 March 2001, leaving the MRF without a dedicated aircraft for the first time in its history.

To replace the Hercules, BAE Systems will convert a BAe 146-300 for the role. It will be funded directly from national and international research groups and maintained and flown by the civilian contractor, with the MRF obliged to 'buy time' on the aircraft. Serious doubts have been highlighted as to the workload on the two-man crew having to fly bearings and altitudes accurate within a few metres at the behest of the scientists who require new profiles to be initiated almost instantaneously, often in some of the worst weather conditions and within heavily restricted airspace. With allegedly further possible problems concerning the certification of the BAe 146, there remains the faint hope that 'Snoopy' could yet return to its rightful position as the UK's premier weather research platform. *Daniel J. March*

By the late 1990s the Hercules was under DERA ownership and had the organisation's logo and the MRF crest (awarded in 1993) applied to the tail fin. One of the aircraft's last major overseas deployments was to Namibia (left) for Project Safari in the autumn of 2000, investigating aerosol properties in the southern African atmosphere.

The withdrawal of the Hercules from service has left the UK without a specialised meteorological research platform until late 2002 at best. European research will rely on other assets such as the DLR Falcon 20 seen here formating with 'Snoopy' during a joint research project in 1998.

Aircraft operated by the HAF/MRF

Aircraft	Serial No.	Service
Spitfire Mk VI	BR287	1942-1945
Boston	-	1942-1944
Boston	-	1942-1944
Hudson	-	1943-1945
Fortress	-	1943-1945
Mosquito (various)	(various)	1943-1946
Mosquito PR.Mk 34	RG248	1946-1952
Mosquito PR.Mk 34	VL621	1946-1954
Halifax Met.Mk 6	ST796	1946-1951
Halifax Met.Mk 6	ST817	1946-1951
Hastings C.Mk 1	TG618	1952-1966
Hastings C.Mk 1	TG619	1952-1958
Canberra B.Mk 2	WJ582	1952-1962
Varsity T.Mk 1	WJ906	1958-1969
Canberra PR.Mk 3	WE173	1963-1981
Varsity T.Mk 1	WF425	1969-1975
Hercules W.Mk 2	XV208	1974-2001

B-58 Hustler
Convair's ultimate delta

Designed to meet a US Air Force requirement for a strategic bomber capable of speeds in excess of Mach 2, the Convair Model 4 Hustler is the fastest such aircraft to reach squadron service outside the Soviet Union. Delivered under the service designation B-58, it first flew in 1956, entered service in 1960 and was retired in 1970. Aside from one reconnaissance mission undertaken over Cuba during the October 1962 Missile Crisis, the Hustler is not known to have flown any operational missions within hostile airspace during its career with the US Air Force's Strategic Air Command.

Today it is almost a cliché to refer to the Convair B-58 as a milestone, but it truly was one of the most significant aircraft of the early days of high-performance jet aircraft. It was the world's first supersonic strategic bomber and arguably the most successful in terms of accomplishing the goals set for it. Despite this, the story of the Hustler ended with it being abruptly withdrawn from service after just a decade, without a replacement that could match its performance. After it was gone, Strategic Air Command would never again operate a strategic bomber – other than the FB-111 – that was capable of sustained supersonic speed.

Although it retired at a time of technologically 'lowered expectations', the B-58 was born in an era when the engineering prowess of American industry was perceived as being nearly omnipotent. Coming out of World War II, the guiding principle of military aircraft development in the United States was simply 'higher and faster'. The prevailing

attitude within the aviation industry was that anything was technologically possible and, to bend the old maxim, the sky was no longer the limit. Indeed, why should American industry not have been filled with a boundless optimism? The Yank planemakers may not have pushed the technological envelope as far as the Germans in 1939-1945, but they had accomplished the true miracle of backing their impressive technological achievements with an unmatched capability to produce exceptional aircraft in staggering quantity. Most of the German technological achievements existed on paper or as partially-completed prototypes that had no hope of ever going into production.

Going into the post-war years, the United States was in an enviable position. Britain had the technology, but no hope of matching the production levels. The Soviet Union had the production capacity, but nobody in the West took Soviet technology very seriously. The United States, it seemed, had it all. Looking at its wartime achievements

A B-58A of the 43rd Bomb Wing waits for take-off at Little Rock AFB, Arkansas, while another aircraft lands. The aircraft in the foreground is carrying the little-seen LA-331 photo-reconnaissance pod, as characterised by the window at the front. This pod was similar to the standard MB-1C pod, but incorporated a Fairchild KA-56 panoramic camera and associated equipment in the forward portion. Equipment included a scanner which automatically measured speed/height ratios and adjusted the camera accordingly to synchronise the frame rate with the relative motion of the image. Most reconnaissance missions were flown at low altitude and high speed. Only 43rd BW aircraft carried the pod, and a cadre of reconnaissance specialists was built up within the wing. Twenty-four B-58s received the full reconnaissance upgrade, while 10 LA-331 pods were produced.

from the vantage point of the autumn of 1945 – and against the backdrop of that guiding principle of 'higher and faster' – a smug American aircraft industry simply shrugged and asked, "How high and how fast?" The answer, coming from the aircraft buyers in that five-sided building on the Potomac, was that future combat aircraft should be jets, and supersonic jets as soon as possible after that. When World War II ended, all of America's aircraft manufacturers had military jet aircraft in development, and two already had been flight tested. The sound barrier was yet to be mastered, but engineers were already confidently working on the issues related to supersonic flight.

New generation of combat aircraft

In the late 1940s, the roadmap to future combat aircraft was clear: there were jet fighters for Tactical Air Command and Air Defense Command, and soon there would be jet bombers to project the might of Strategic Air Command. Then, there would be supersonic fighters, and as soon as possible thereafter, large, long-range, supersonic bombers. The first generation of subsonic jet bombers – the Douglas B-43, North American Aviation B-45, Convair B-46, Boeing B-47 and Martin B-48 – were already in development in 1945, and all had made their first flights by the end of 1947. Originally, the bomber designers, like their cousins the fighter designers, hung jet engines on familiar, straight-winged airframes. However, analysis of German aeronautical data led to a revolution in airframe design. Boeing was the first to adapt a swept wing to a bomber design and its

B-47 was the only swept-wing aircraft amid that first generation of jet bombers. The B-47 was also destined to be produced in larger numbers than any other American jet bomber.

Meanwhile, in San Diego, Convair was pioneering yet another wing design – the delta. The idea of the triangular, or delta, wing had been the brainchild of Germany's Dr Alexander Lippisch during the 1930s. He designed several aircraft types during World War II – notably the Messerschmitt Me 163 – and he built several delta-winged gliders. However, by the close of the war, a powered aircraft with true delta wings had yet to fly. As the war

With its four J79s in full afterburner the B-58 surged into the air. Fully loaded the B-58 could attain an initial climb rate of 17,000 ft (5180 m) per minute, and when nearly empty this figure rose to an astonishing 46,000 ft (14020 m) per minute. During SAC alert exercises B-58s demonstrated the ability to get airborne in less than three minutes.

ended, Lippisch and his work attracted the attention of the American military, and he was brought to the United States. Over the coming years, he would work for both the USAAF at Wright Field and the US Navy at the Naval Air Materiel Center.

Of all the American manufacturers that had access to the myriad of German wartime design studies that were spirited across the Atlantic, it was Convair that embraced the Lippisch delta. The first delta-winged aircraft was the XF-92, an experimental interceptor ordered by the USAAF in 1946. First flown on 18 September 1948 at Edwards AFB, California, the Convair XF-92A never entered production, but flight tests demonstrated that the stability and control characteristics of the delta-wing concept were practical. This flight testing would lead to the successful F-102 and F-106 supersonic interceptors, and to the B-58 bomber.

Defining the need for a supersonic bomber

Among the lessons that had been learned during World War II was that aircraft quickly became obsolete. Though it is hard to imagine today, when combat aircraft have useful lives exceeding two decades, in the late 1940s (and especially the 1950s) it was believed that aviation technology

was moving so quickly that aircraft would be obsolete within five years. Even if procurement funds were tight, an aircraft's successor had to be on the drawing board by the time it made its first flight. By 1947, the first generation of supersonic jet bombers was on the drawing boards at the major American airframe makers, including Boeing, Douglas, Martin and Convair.

The road that would lead to America's first supersonic strategic bomber began in October 1946 with the USAAF's Generalized Bomber Study (GEBO), which, as the name implies, was more of a general exploration of the limits of bomber technology than a specific study aimed at a specific aircraft type. The GEBO studies continued as the USAAF became the independent US Air Force in September 1947, and as the Soviet Union began to emerge as a serious threat to world stability with the Berlin Blockade of 1948.

Under GEBO II, which began in March 1949, the programme objectives came into sharper focus, and after the detonation of the first Soviet nuclear weapon five months later, the urgency increased. In April 1950, under GEBO II, the goal was an aircraft with a combat radius of more than 3,500 miles (5630 km) that was capable of attacking its target at speeds up to Mach 1.5, and of providing the basis for a reconnaissance variant with similar performance. Officially, the aircraft would be the High Altitude Bomber/Reconnaissance System. An initial operating capability with Strategic Air Command was targeted for 1958.

Just as swept wings had not necessarily been anticipated when the USAAF first sought jet bombers, nobody knew in the late 1940s what a supersonic jet bomber would look like. In the simplest terms, the US Air Force wanted a supersonic bomber, but didn't care how the potential contractors arrived at that end. In order to meet the longer range requirement, Convair initially studied the concept of a supersonic strike aircraft that would be carried and air-launched by the very long-range Convair B-36.

Most of the aircraft that reached the proposal stage were dart-shaped, swept-wing aircraft; Convair was working with a delta-wing design. Many of the airframe makers that

were working on potential supersonic bombers were also looking at designs in which the payload would be carried in an aerodynamic external pod, rather than an internal bomb bay.

By early 1951, only Boeing and Convair remained as serious competitors for the new supersonic bomber. Both companies were proposing aircraft with four turbojet engines, although many and various engine position configurations were explored – and wind tunnel-tested – by both contractors. A great many design studies were produced under Air Force 'MX' project designations. Boeing's proposals were given the company model number 484, and generally developed under the umbrella of Project MX-1712. These were designed with swept wings, while Convair's Project MX-1626 designs were, of course, delta-winged.

In December 1951, Air Research & Development Command issued a General Operational Requirement (GOR) that detailed precisely what was needed, and the two contractors went to work to finalise their proposals. Among the specifications in the GOR was that the aircraft would have to be capable of speeds above Mach 2; it would have to be not only fast, but very fast.

The two projects evolved into Boeing's Model 701, known to the Air Force as Project MX-1965, and Convair's MX-1964. In 1952, these two finalists received the official designations of B-59 and B-58, respectively.

Convair wins the contest

In October 1952, Air Research & Development Command picked the Convair MX-1964/B-58 over the Boeing MX-1965/B-59 for further development. Although no production contract was issued or implied for Convair, Boeing was now out of the running completely. In November, General Hoyt Vandenberg, the Air Force Chief of Staff, formally confirmed the Air Research & Development Command's choice, and by the end of the year his deputy for development had endorsed a tentative production schedule based on the four-year procurement of 244 examples.

Signed in February 1953, the initial B-58 acquisition contract called for two aircraft to be flight-ready by January 1956. It was originally planned that one would be an

XB-58 bomber version, and the other an XRB-58 reconnaissance version, and they were given the respective weapons system contract designations of WS-102A and WS-102L. The aircraft would also carry a designation of Convair Model 4.

The initial designation of the XRB-58 was changed subsequently to XB-58 and later to YB-58. After initial flight tests, it was modified to become a TB-58.

Convair spent all of 1953 refining the design of the MX-1964/B-58, and during this process an unpredictable, but major, design problem with the delta-wing configuration for supersonic aircraft had emerged. It affected both the MX-1964/B-58 and Convair's concurrent F-102 interceptor programme. Theoretically, smooth, sleek, pencil-straight fuselages with thin wings and powerful jet engines were assumed to be ideal for supersonic aircraft. However, in the early 1950s, the so-called 'transonic region' involving speeds from Mach 0.9 to Mach 1.1 had not yet been explored systematically in wind tunnels. Contrary to what was supposed intuitively, bullet-shaped aircraft were not ideal for supersonic flight.

The first hint of this had come during testing of the YF-102 at the National Advisory Committee on Aeronautics

Above: By carrying its warload, and much of its fuel, externally, the B-58 could be made extremely slim. However, pod carriage dictated the use of a long, stalky undercarriage. The undercarriage was complex, but in service proved reliable, unlike the tyres and brakes which proved to be problematic throughout the type's career.

Above left: B-58s progress down the huge Convair assembly line at Fort Worth, each identified by its construction number. At its peak, the B-58 programme involved nearly 5,000 companies. The Fort Worth plant, now owned by Lockheed Martin, currently produces the F-16.

Right: For its special trip to carry the B-58, B-36F 49-2677 had the propellers of its inner engines removed. It completed the flight on the remaining four piston engines and its four turbojets, which were kept running throughout.

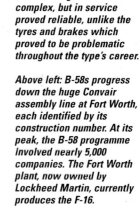

Below: The B-36 and its unique cargo departs Fort Worth at the start of a lumbering five-hour flight to Wright-Patterson, accompanied by a Fairchild C-119 chase plane. The B-36's undercarriage could not be raised because the B-58's wing was in the way.

Static test airframes

The fifth B-58 airframe, assigned construction number 4A, was pulled from the Convair line in February 1957 and transported under a B-36 to Wright-Patterson AFB, Ohio, for fatigue testing. The B-58 airframe weighed around 40,000 lb (18144 kg) and was hoisted into the B-36's bomb bay by means of a special shackle for the one-way trip. Once at Wright-Patterson, aircraft 4A had engines and fin fitted, and commenced structural loads testing, which ran until February 1962. It attained 135 percent of the aircraft design load, validating the soundness of the B-58's structure. In October 1959, a freshly completed B-58 (58-1022) was taken from the Convair flight test fleet and subjected to cyclic loading for five years before it finally succumbed.

'Ole Grandpappy' – first of the breed

The first of 116 Hustlers (later nicknamed 'Ole Grandpappy') was rolled out at Convair's Fort Worth plant on 1 September 1956, and undertook its first taxi trials on 29 October. It first flew on 11 November – Veterans Day – a 38-minute sortie which proved the general airworthiness of the design. On the aircraft's seventh flight on 30 December, '660 went supersonic for the first time. On its 24th flight on 29 June 1957, the aircraft was flown to Mach 2.03 with an MB-1 pod attached, validating the aircraft's design performance. The aircraft survived a lengthy test programme and became a ground instructional airframe at Kelly AFB, Texas, before being scrapped.

Above and above right: For its first flight the XB-58 was flown by Convair's experienced test pilot Beryl A. Erickson (who had also performed the first flight of the B-36), with flight test observer John D. McEachern in the second crew station and flight test engineer Charles P. Harrison in the third. Both of the rear crew stations had flight test equipment installed instead of the intended mission equipment. To reduce the chances of complex equipment failing, '660 was prepared for its first flight with the auto trim and inlet spikes deactivated, among other temporary safety measures. Little in the way of mission avionics was installed, as befitted the aircraft's prototype status.

(NACA) high-speed wind tunnel at Langley Field, Virginia. Convair aerodynamicists were sure their projectile-shaped aircraft would easily penetrate the sound barrier. By mid-1952, both Convair and the Air Force were committed to the construction of two YF-102 prototypes and a production line was being set up in San Diego to build hundreds more. However, wind tunnel tests were generating disturbing data suggesting that transonic drag (air resistance) for the YF-102 was so high that there was serious doubt that even the powerful Pratt & Whitney J57 engine could push the YF-102 through the sound barrier.

As the data was being reviewed, NACA aerodynamicist Richard Whitcomb and his team discovered that as the high-speed air flowed around the wind tunnel models, shock waves formed near the nose as expected – but they were startled to find additional strong shock waves established behind the trailing edges of the wings. The unexpectedly high drag was caused by the aircraft having to overcome the energy losses created by these extra shock waves, which were described as being like "aerodynamic anchors".

Whitcomb proposed his Area Rule, stating that the fuselage should be narrowest where the wings were attached and widened at the trailing edges. He suggested the radical idea that the pencil-straight fuselage should be replaced with a 'wasp waist' or 'Coke bottle' shaped fuselage, with a wide tail. The idea seemed bizarre, but the wind tunnel data convinced Convair engineers to redesign the YF-102 model. Wind tunnel testing conducted in October 1953 showed that a YF-102 – or a B-58 – designed according to the Area Rule would meet Air Force supersonic require-

ments. Early in January 1954, flight tests of a YF-102 in its original straight configuration proved the aircraft incapable of supersonic speeds in level flight. A new prototype with a 'Coke bottle' fuselage, designated YF-102A, broke the sound barrier on its first flight in December 1954. Using the Area Rule, the top speed of the YF-102A increased by about 25 per cent. By this time, the Area Rule had been applied to redesigning the B-58 as well.

A full-scale mock-up of the resulting Configuration II B-58 aircraft was unveiled in August 1953.

Configuration II

Another important design feature of Configuration II that was changed subsequently was the weapons pod. In most previous designs dating back to MX-1626 and before, the streamlined pod had conformed to the aircraft's fuselage. In other words, the contours of the two objects had been blended so as to appear as a single dart-shaped object. Indeed, that which appeared to be the tip of the aircraft's nose had actually been the tip of the pod, which was longer than the fuselage.

In October 1953, after evaluating Configuration II, Air Research & Development Command's Wright Air Development Center decided that the pod could be shortened and repositioned below the fuselage on a pylon.

One aspect of the 'large pod' concept seems particularly unwieldy and even dangerous. The size of the pod meant the nose gear had to be attached to the pod – not the fuselage – and jettisoned on take-off. Shortening and detaching the pod allowed Convair to use conventional nose gear.

Configuration II also finalised the flight deck layout. The crew of three – pilot, bombardier-navigator and defensive systems operator (DSO) – were to be accommodated in a tandem arrangement, each with a separate compartment and a separate ejection seat.

The Mach 2 General Electric J79 engine specified for the B-58 was nearing operational readiness, but still not available. In order to not hold up the B-58's progress, it was decided to equip the first 18 B-58 aircraft with the Mach-1 Pratt & Whitney J57-P-15 engines similar to those in use by Convair's F-102 programme. These aircraft could, it was supposed, be retrofitted with the proper engines later.

55-0660 overflies the Eglin range in Florida. This location was used for many of the B-58's armament trials. 'Ole Grandpappy' returned to Eglin AFB in August/September 1958 to conduct Project High Virgo, the use of the B-58 as a vehicle for a Lockheed Air-Launched Ballistic Missile. The four ALBM launches were conducted over the Cape Canaveral Space Range. In July 1959 '660 was used on a series of flights over NASA's Wallops Island facility which tested the effects of sonic booms on the ground, and which led to the establishment of restricted supersonic overland corridors.

The Configuration II aircraft also had its four engines paired into two underwing nacelles, the reason being an assumption that maintenance would be facilitated by this arrangement. However, wind tunnel tests indicated that the large nacelles caused an unacceptable amount of aerodynamic drag, so this layout was changed to four individual mountings in Configuration III, the mock-up of which was displayed in August 1954.

Configuration III

Following an October 1954 inspection of a full-scale Configuration III mock-up at Convair's Fort Worth, Texas facility, the US Air Force expanded the initial order for two XB-58 prototypes to add 11 YB-58 flight test aircraft.

Despite the green light represented by these orders, the response to the B-58 project within the US Air Force was divided. The opposite points of view were represented by the enthusiasm of Major General Clarence Irvine of Air Material Command, and the scepticism of General Curtis LeMay, Commander in Chief of Strategic Air Command. Irvine favoured the project because he believed that the leap in aeronautical technology inherent in the Mach-2 supersonic B-58 was worth its cost in terms of a proportion of the Air Force budget.

LeMay, who headed the command that would put the B-58 into operational use, was concerned about the B-58's range, which would be about half that of the long-range, long-endurance Boeing B-52 Stratofortress that was entering squadron service in the mid-1950s. The mission of Strategic Air Command was to attack strategic targets deep inside the Soviet Union in the time of war, and LeMay's experience in strategic bombing during World War II told him that, with distant targets, range was a more important characteristic for a bomber than speed. LeMay questioned the notion of earmarking a sizeable portion of the Air Force budget for developing and fielding a bomber with 'short legs'.

In 1954, internal Strategic Air Command planning papers even went so far as to exclude entirely the B-58, with its unit cost significantly higher than that of the B-52. Although LeMay did not fully embrace the B-58 programme, the advent of the KC-135 jet aerial refuelling aircraft helped to make the use of the B-58 somewhat more appealing to him.

The net result of LeMay's concerns was that Air Research & Development Command downgraded the urgency of the B-58 programme in 1954, emphasising it as a potential test aircraft, rather than as a potential production aircraft. LeMay had enough faith in the concept to support the B-58 as a technology demonstrator, but he did not want anything to interfere with his establishment of SAC's B-52 fleet.

Efforts to cancel the B-58 programme entirely continued until as late as August 1955, and the definitive contract for the first 13 aircraft (along with 31 MB-1 weapons pods) was not issued to the manufacturer until December of that year. A decision to order more than the initial 13 aircraft was deferred until 1956. As it turned out, an additional 17 Block

10 YB-58As were ordered in FY 1958; they were redesignated on the assembly line and completed as RB-58As.

These aircraft were intended to carry a reconnaissance pod, but most were used in test programmes along with the XB-58 and YB-58A aircraft. Most of the RB-58As were later adapted to B-58A production standards and used in operational units. One of these RB-58As was converted to a TB-58A trainer, one aircraft was retained for static stress and fatigue testing, and three aircraft were destroyed in test programme crashes between 1958 and 1960.

Keeping the designation prefixes straight is problematic, because nearly all of the first 30 B-58s were redesignated at least once – and some as many as three times – during their service lives.

One of the early B-58s was not designated at all. Built and delivered in 1957 after the fourth B-58, it was an incomplete airframe that was given no serial number and not included in the above totals. It was delivered, with no engines attached, to Wright-Patterson AFB, Ohio for static testing and was flown to Ohio bolted beneath a Convair B-36 bomber. This temporary, one-flight configuration was similar to that which had been imagined for the air-launched bomber studied nearly a decade earlier under GEBO II.

56-0660 made its 150th and last flight, to Kelly AFB, on 15 March 1960, having amassed 257 hours 30 minutes flight time. The early scheme was replaced by a gaudy red/white scheme (above and top) which became the Convair Hustler 'house' colours.

The second XB-58, 55-0661, joined the flight test programme on 16 February 1957, making its maiden flight with a pod attached. Later in the month it undertook the Hustler's first supersonic flight with the pod. Following trials with Convair it transferred to Edwards AFB, and was used extensively for ejection seat tests before being converted to TB-58A configuration.

The B-58's debut

The first XB-58 prototype (tail number 55-0660) was completed at Fort Worth in August 1956 and formally rolled out on 4 September. By this time, a prototype of the General Electric J79 engine was also ready, so the J57 was never used as an interim powerplant. The first run-up of the installed engines took place at the beginning of October, and taxi tests began at the end of the month.

The maiden flight of the first XB-58 took place on 11 November 1956, with veteran Convair test pilot Beryl Erickson at the controls. Convair systems specialist John McEachern and flight test engineer Charles Harrison flew in

the bombardier-navigator and defensive systems operator stations. Initially tested without the weapons pod, aircraft 55-0660 went supersonic for the first and second time in two separate flights conducted on 30 December, achieving a maximum speed of Mach 1.31 at 35,000 ft (10700 m).

The aircraft's intended high-speed capabilities had prompted people at Convair to refer to the B-58 unofficially as "a real hustler" for several years, and by the end of 1956, the Air Force had made the name official.

Flight test operations

During February 1957, the second Hustler (55-0661) joined the test programme and made the programme's first supersonic flight with the MB-1 weapons pod in place later in the month. The first flight at the required operational speed of Mach 2 occurred on 29 June 1957, with aircraft 55-0660 carrying the MB-1 pod at 43,350 ft (13200 m).

Meanwhile, the first two YB-58As, aircraft 55-0662 and 55-0663, had been completed and sent to Kirtland AFB at Albuquerque, New Mexico for tests involving the dropping of the weapons pods. Although the aircraft flew from Kirtland, the actual test drops were made at the Holloman AFB range adjacent to the US Army's White Sands Missile Range, also in New Mexico. Aircraft 55-0662 made the first subsonic drop on 5 June 1957, followed by the first supersonic drop – from an altitude of 40,000 ft (12200 m) – on 30 September. The first Mach 2 release of the MB-1 was made on 20 December from 60,000 ft (18300 m).

Flight testing of the Hustlers, which was conducted mainly at Edwards AFB, California, also demonstrated the aircraft's ability to sustain a supersonic cruising speed for in excess of 90 minutes. On 15 October 1959, a YB-58A (58-1015) flew from Seattle, Washington to Carswell AFB in 70 minutes at an average speed of nearly 1,320 mph (2124 km/h) in the Hustler's first sustained Mach 2 flight.

The vitally important issue of inflight refuelling was addressed in a series of trials with KC-135s that began in June 1958. The Hustler proved itself to be especially suitable for these operations, which would enhance its mission capability by lengthening its 'legs'.

Teething troubles

Despite the successes in achieving the desired performance levels, flight tests highlighted serious problems with the first-generation J79-GE-1 engines. Uneven fuel management caused more fuel to remain in a tank on one side of the aircraft than on the other, meaning the weight of the aircraft was asymmetrical. This, in turn, resulted in problems of balance and stability that were magnified when the aircraft flew at Mach 1 or above. Not only was this a potential danger for the crews, it was seen to be resulting in fatigue cracks in the aircraft. Many of these problems were solved with the retrofit of the J79-GE-5 engines, which were first delivered to the factory in September 1957.

All but the first seven Hustlers were flown with General Electric J79-GE-5A or -5B engines, which, at sea level, were rated at 9,700 lb (43.14 kN) of continuous thrust, with a maximum thrust rating of 15,600 lb (69.38 kN). This

122

Above: YB-58 55-0665 was the first aircraft to be delivered to the ARDC's 6592nd Test Squadron, arriving at Edwards on 15 February 1957.

Right: Five XB/YB-58s are seen in the Fort Worth flight test facility. As well as flying trials, Convair was also busy training ground personnel for the growing B-58 fleet.

Flight test programme

The B-58's flight test programme was divided into three phases. Phase I was undertaken by Convair and was concerned with basic flying characteristics and the operation of aircraft systems. Phase II, begun by Convair and completed by the USAF, looked at system development and evaluation, while Phase III (USAF only) examined and developed weaponeering techniques and procedures. The tests examined every facet of the aircraft but, naturally, focussed on the novel aspects of the design – chiefly the ASQ-42 nav/bomb system, J79 powerplant and the pod release system. The large B-58 trials fleet encompassed all of the FY55 and FY58 aircraft (although 11 of the latter were subsequently modified under the Junior Flash-Up programme for operational duty) and several of the early FY59 aircraft. Tests were centred on Carswell AFB and Edwards AFB.

compared to 8,900 lb (39.59 kN) and 14,500 lb (64.49 kN), respectively, for the original J79-GE-1.

The 14th Hustler, and the first B-58A production aircraft (59-2428), was delivered to the Air Force early in 1959, but the programme was running behind schedule. A number of bugs had yet to be wrung from the flight test aircraft, as well as from the AN/ASQ-42 bombing and navigation system and the AN/ALQ-16 electronics countermeasures system.

Meanwhile, three fatal in-flight accidents between December 1958 and November 1959 were attributed to control problems, as was a fatal accident on take-off from Fort Worth. A fifth Hustler was lost in a fire at the factory during this period, and another two fatal in-flight losses occurred during the first half of 1960. The rate of accidents and crashes in 1959 and 1960 was such that Strategic Air Command postponed taking over the programme from Air Research & Development Command from 1959 to 1960 – and it restricted the fleet to subsonic flight for nearly a year while control system problems were addressed.

The crew losses pointed out that the Convair ejection

Inflight refuelling trials were first undertaken on 11 June 1958 using 55-0661. 55-0664, seen here, continued the trials. '664 was heavily instrumented for collection of air loads data, and had its third crew station filled with instrumentation. On 7 November 1959 the aircraft broke apart during Mach 2 asymmetric engine tests when it yawed to 15°. Following this incident the Hustler fleet was restricted to subsonic flight for nearly a year.

NB-58A – the five-engined Hustler

In July 1959 Convair began the modification of an early test Hustler to the unique NB-58A configuration. The aircraft had served with the ARDC and was chosen to be a flying testbed for the General Electric J93 engine, which was the intended powerplant for North American's F-108 Rapier fighter and XB-70 Valkyrie bomber projects. The aircraft was completed by late August and was ferried to Edwards AFB for use by General Electric's flight test operation. The NB-58A made several flights with the podded engine, with tests exploring a number of facets such as afterburner operation, air starts, compressor stalls and ground handling difficulties. The project was terminated before it had run its full course due to the down-scaling of the F-108 and B-70 programmes. The aircraft returned to other test work before being converted to a TB-58A.

Two views show 55-0662 with the massive J93-GE-3 engine installed in a special pod. The engine weighed around 6,000 lb (2722 kg) and developed 31,500 lb (140.17 kN) thrust at sea level. With the J93 generating roughly double the power of the J79, the NB-58A could easily reach Mach 2 with its stock J79s operating at less than full power. Sorties were relatively short as all five engines drew on the B-58's internal fuel capacity.

Tyre and brake problems plagued the B-58, as demonstrated by this aircraft landing at Edwards. On 30 March 1958 55-0662 suffered the dubious honour of being the first Hustler to blow all its tyres on landing. A cooling blower and shrapnel cage, which could be placed round the wheels after a 'hot' landing, was developed to minimise damage and danger to the emergency crews.

seats were inadequate to permit a crewman to escape safely at supersonic speeds. This led to the B-58 being redesigned with an 'escape capsule' system. Developed by the Stanley Aviation Corporation in Denver, the capsules had airtight clam-shell doors and independent pressurisation and oxygen supply systems. In this way, the crew could use the capsules as survival aids in the event of cabin depressurisation. The pilot's capsule operated in such a way that he could continue to fly the aircraft when it was closed. When the crew did punch out, the capsules were directed away from the aircraft by a rocket motor and dropped to earth via parachute. In the event of a water landing, flotation cells could be inflated manually, turning the capsules into life rafts. These capsules went into service, replacing the ejection seats, from 1962.

As the B-58 flight test programme evolved, maintenance issues developed and costs began to exceed estimates. Against this backdrop, US Air Force headquarters ordered Strategic Air Command to scale back the planned deployment. In December 1959, General Thomas Power, who had succeeded General LeMay as Commander in Chief of Strategic Air Command in July 1957, reduced the total number of B-58s from the 290 on the production schedule

to just 148. This total would be slashed again and, ultimately, only 116 Hustlers would be built.

Interestingly, one of the elements in the decision by LeMay and Power to go ahead with deploying the B-58 was that it would force the Soviet Union to invest in the development of a Mach 2 interceptor to counter it.

Flight testing of the YB-58A aircraft officially concluded in April 1959, although production flight testing continued until the delivery of the last three of 116 B-58 aircraft on 25-26 October 1962. Coincidentally, this occurred during the Cuban Missile Crisis

Project Flash-Up

In February 1960, as the long-awaited and often-delayed moment of the B-58's initial operating capability finally neared, the US Air Force undertook the Junior Flash-Up project, which was aimed at converting low-time pre-production and flight test aircraft to operational status by upgrading their avionics and retrofitting equipment. These included eight YB-58As that were converted as operational dual-control TB-58A trainers, the first of which was delivered in May 1960.

A batch of 17 Block 10 YB-58As later became RB-58A aircraft, and the first YB-58A (55-0662) was briefly redesignated as NB-58A when employed to test the J93-GE-3 turbojet that was designed to be used in the North American Aviation XB-70 and XF-108 programmes. The J93-GE-3 had twice the thrust of the Hustler's J79-GE-5, and the huge XB-70 was to have been the supersonic successor to the B-52, the B-58's 'big brother'. Only two XB-70s were built, and no production series B-70As were ordered. The XF-108 was cancelled without reaching the prototype stage.

An additional Flash-Up project undertaken in 1960 was Senior Flash-Up, an effort to standardise the existing B-58 fleet. After four years of testing, modification and retrofitting, it could be said that no two Hustlers were alike, and this presented a maintenance and operational nightmare. Senior Flash-Up was intended to correct this situation by introducing a measure of commonality so that the existing

Hustlers could become useful members of the Strategic Air Command force. At the same time, upgraded Tactical Air Navigation (TACAN) systems were added. The first Senior Flash-Up B-58 was delivered on 7 November 1960.

TB-58 trainer variant

As noted above, there were TB-58 trainer conversions after the initial deployment of the bomber. When the Hustler was being developed, the requirement for a dedicated trainer variant seemingly had not been apparent, but as the aircraft inched toward its operational debut, this need became unmistakable. The Hustler had no provision for a co-pilot, and the pilot was physically isolated from the other crew members. There was an access tunnel between the middle and aft crew positions, but none between the pilot's compartment and the middle crew compartment – meaning that it was impossible for an instructor to be present with a student. Anyone who flew the Hustler soloed in the aircraft on his first flight!

This shortcoming was solved by completely revamping the middle crew station of eight YB-58As (including the second Hustler to be built), and installing a second set of flight controls. A ninth was to have been converted, but it was lost in an accident before being retrofitted. These eight aircraft, redesignated as TB-58As, were all assigned to 'schools' run by operational units rather than to dedicated training squadrons.

In the TB-58 conversion, the second pilot position was offset slightly to allow some forward visibility. The aft compartment was often not used during TB-58 missions. Theoretically, a third pilot could be accommodated here, and he could trade places with the pilot in the middle position. In practice, however, the tunnel between the two positions was so narrow and cramped that it was almost never used in any of the Hustler variants.

Becoming operational

The first operational B-58A Hustler to go to a SAC unit was delivered on 15 March 1960 to the 43rd Bomb Wing, which had just been relocated from Davis-Monthan AFB, Arizona to Carswell AFB, Texas. The latter base, which shared a runway with Convair's Fort Worth factory where the Hustler was being produced, previously had been

TB-58A pilot trainer

Eight ex-test B-58s were modified with dual controls to become TB-58A trainers. The first, 55-0670, entered Convair's rework facility on 5 October 1959, and made its first flight from Carswell on 10 May 1960, flown by Val Prahl, Earl Guthrie and Grover Tate. In August the aircraft was delivered to the 43rd Bomb Wing to begin its operational career. Additional TB-58s were delivered as they were modified, including the first aircraft for the 305th BW (55 0664) in July 1961. The last was handed over to the air force on 13 April 1964. As well as the additional side glazing for the second pilot (instructor), the TB-58s also had a large glazed overhead panel. With the front pilot's seat offset to port, the instructor's seat was offset to starboard to provide a measure of forward visibility. A glazed panel separated the two compartments, although the flight controls were linked mechanically. All tactical systems, including the nav/bombing system, were removed.

home to the Convair B-36s of the 7th Bomb Wing that had also been produced at Convair's Fort Worth facility. On 1 August, when Strategic Air Command officially assumed control of the B-58 programme from Air Material Command, 12 B-58s were operational with the 43rd Bomb Wing at Carswell.

In December 1960, the 305th Bomb Wing at Bunker Hill AFB (known as Grissom AFB after 1968) in Indiana – the only other Strategic Air Command wing to become operational with the Hustler – began to receive its B-58As. Both of these wings eventually had three medium bomb squadrons equipped with 12 Hustlers each, comprising the 63rd, 64th and 65th at the Texas base, and the 364th, 365th and 366th in Indiana. Training was conducted in TB-58 trainers by the 43rd and 305th Combat Crew Training Schools, which were co-located with the bomb wings of the same numbers.

The 43rd Bomb Wing remained at Carswell AFB until 1964 when it was moved to Little Rock AFB in Arkansas, which had been under consideration as a Hustler base since the beginning of the programme. Meanwhile, overseas deployments were conducted to sites in Britain, Okinawa and Guam that would function as advance operating bases in time of war.

Although it had docile handling, the high landing speed of the Hustler made it a particularly 'hot ship'. The provision of a trainer allowed novices to take to the air with the security of an experienced pilot behind them, even though forward visibility from the second cockpit was poor.

Far left: While most of the pre-production aircraft had no tail gun fitted, 55-0667 was employed as the main test bed for the defensive armament system. Trials were conducted at Eglin in 1959, using an F-104 as a target. No rounds were fired, the tests involving a camera to record the system's accuracy. '667 was also the first aircraft to be powered by the YJ79-GE-5 engine.

Left: With a Piasecki H-21 Retriever standing by to provide swift rescue in the case of an emergency, a B-58 kicks up the spray during wet runway tests at Edwards.

As the B-58 neared operational capability, the test fleet demonstrated the type's range and speed capabilities in several notable flights. On 15 October 1959, this ARDC-assigned aircraft (58-1015) performed the first sustained Mach 2 flight, flying for 70 minutes between Seattle and Carswell at an average speed of almost 1,320 mph (2125 km/h).

Above: On 22-23 March 1960, aircraft 55-0671 made the longest flight ever undertaken by a B-58, the crew of Lt Col Leonard Legge, Captain Andrew Rose Jr and Captain Raymond Wagener staying aloft for 18 hours 10 minutes, during which they covered around 11,000 miles (17700 km).

While the B-58 had been designed initially for nuclear strike missions to be conducted at altitudes from 35,000 to 55,000 ft (10700 to 16800 m), advances in Soviet radar and surface-to-air missiles led to new tactics. Thus, in addition to training for the original high-altitude scenario, SAC B-58 crews also conducted training for supersonic low-level strike missions.

One of the most important non-training missions ever undertaken by the Hustler was a low-level photo-reconnaissance mission. It involved surveillance of the damage caused by the March 1964 Alaska earthquake,

which at the time was the strongest earthquake to have been recorded in the United States. Flying below cloud cover at 500 ft (150 m), two B-58As were able to complete the mission so quickly that the finished photography was available for review in Washington, DC just 14 hours after the aircraft had been assigned the task.

Although it was created for high-altitude operations, the Hustler also proved reliable in high-speed low-level operations in which structural stress is a potential problem. The aircraft was constructed of aluminium honeycomb with a chemically-bonded aluminium skin, designed to make it remarkably light and rigid. It had the highest ratio of payload weight to overall gross weight of any bomber yet placed in service, but it had the structural rigidity to withstand routine operations at Mach 2 to Mach 2.2 – as well as in the turbulent air at low altitudes.

The MB-1 weapons pod

In contrast to the conventional and nuclear-capable bombers which had preceded it in Strategic Air Command fleet, the B-58 was the first strategic bomber designed to drop just a single weapon – the jettisonable weapons pod. Of course, the kilotonnage present in that single weapon was vastly greater than any bomb bay full of conventional bombs.

The operational MB-1C pod contained a W39Y1-1 nuclear weapon as well as jet fuel in tanks placed at both ends of the pod for balance. In a strike mission, the bomber would draw fuel from these tanks en route to the target, so that the whole unit could be dropped. This would leave the B-58 much lighter and capable of a fast exit from the target area.

The pod was about 5 ft (1.5 m) in diameter, so the B-58's landing gear had to be especially long to guarantee sufficient clearance. This was a particularly daunting engineering task which Convair engineers accomplished quite successfully.

The unguided MB-1C weapons pod was actually the second choice for a weapons system. Until quite late in the development process, it had been intended that the primary offensive weapon would be a guided missile rather than the free-fall pod that was eventually deployed. Often referred to in the literature as a "pod", the MA-1C missile was the same size as the MB-1C and slightly lighter, at 27,108 lb (12296 kg). It was to have been powered by one Ball Aerospace LR-81-BA-1 rocket which delivered 15,000 lb (66.71 kN) of thrust for 65 seconds of flight time. It was to have been directed over its 160-mile (260-km) range by a Sperry guidance system.

The idea of stand-off weapons made sense theoretically,

Among the 40 B-58s initially allocated to the 43rd Bomb Wing were 11 test aircraft brought to full operational configuration under Project Junior Flash-Up. Modifications included the replacement of the undercarriage to raise gross weight from 153,000 lb (69401 kg) to the full 160,000-lb (72576-kg) limit.

Into Strategic Air Command service

Having received its first aircraft on 15 March 1960, the 43rd Bomb Wing was not declared fully operational until August 1962, with the first aircraft going on nuclear alert in September. The 305th Bomb Wing received its first aircraft on 11 May 1961, and joined the 43rd in being declared to SAC for alert duties at the same time. The considerable delay was caused by ongoing technical problems, the heavy training commitment and the need for ongoing Phase III flight trials. Even after operational capability had been achieved, the B-58 fleet was in some disarray, resulting in the Senior Flash-Up programme which brought all in-service B-58s to a common standard. Later, Project Hustle-Up added the ability to carry four Mk 43 nuclear weapons on wingroot pylons.

59-2429 from the 43rd BW is seen at Bergstrom AFB during the September 1960 bombing competition, in which the two B-58 crews acquitted themselves extremely well. This was a remarkable performance given that the wing had only received its first aircraft five months before.

and a number of air-launched ballistic missile (ALBM) concepts were developed during the 1950s, of which the MA-1C was one. There were problems with guidance system accuracy, however, and it was not until the 1980s that microprocessors made ALBMs and other cruise missiles practical.

Although the powered and guided MA-1C was cancelled in favour of the free-fall MB-1C in May 1957, other ALBM options remained under study for as long as the Hustler was in service.

In 1958, as the MB-1C weapons pods that would equip the first B-58s were in production, Convair began development of the two-component pod, best known by its acronym of TCP. The 37,970-lb (17223-kg) gross weight pod was designed in two sections so that the fuel tank component could be dropped before the weapon. This would leave just the lighter weapons component, which contained barometric sensors as well as the BA53-Y1 variable-yield weapon. Offensive action was co-ordinated through the Sperry AN/ASQ-42 bombing and navigation system. The TCP was designed to fit the same bracketing system as the MB-1C, although the pair of components was shorter and heavier than the previous pod.

The first drop of the lower section occurred in May 1960 and of the upper (with an inert weapon, of course) in December 1960. Fuel leak problems in the MB-1Cs led to the operational equipping of the B-58 force with TCPs soon after the test drops.

During the B-58's development, no serious consideration was given to it having a conventional bombing capability, but in 1959 Convair made such a proposal during an effort to sell a version of the Hustler to the Royal Australian Air Force. The Australian proposal went nowhere, but in the late 1960s the US Air Force studied – and even tested – using the Hustler to carry 'iron' bombs on hardpoints beneath the fuselage.

Other Hustler-launched ballistic missiles

Although the MA-1C guided missile system was cancelled in 1957, the idea of the B-58 as an ALBM carrier did not go away. Air-launched strategic missiles had interested Strategic Air Command planners since the early 1950s, and, by 1960, two missile systems were being earmarked for deployment aboard the B-52 fleet. These included the jet-propelled North American Aviation Hound

Dog, which was flight tested in 1959, and the longer-range, rocket-propelled Douglas Skybolt, which was first test-launched from a B-52 in 1961. Neither of these was seriously considered for the B-58. Having rejected the MA-1, Convair and the US Air Force agreed to develop another unique missile system for the Hustler.

At the same time that the B-58 was working its way toward the start of its operational career, Convair was developing the Atlas intercontinental ballistic missile for Strategic Air Command. The B-58/ALBM projects were undertaken in co-operation with other aerospace companies, especially Lockheed, and not with Convair missiles. Among the systems that Lockheed brought to the table were variations on its X-17 experimental vehicle and its Polaris, a compact submarine-launched missile that was being developed for the US Navy's first generation of ballistic missile submarines.

The X-17 was chosen as the basis for the B-58/ALBM test weapon, and the Air Force conducted four test firings from a B-58 between September 1958 and September 1959

The third Hustler, 55-0662, was a hard-working aircraft. A veteran of many trials programmes (including the J93 engine tests) by the time it was converted to TB-58A standard, it was used at Edwards AFB as a chase-plane for the XB-70A Valkyrie programme, and is seen here during that period. It subsequently joined the 305th Bomb Wing as a trainer, before being scrapped at Tucson, Arizona, with the rest of the Hustler fleet.

ALBM tests - the missile-launching Hustler

The XB-58 prototype, 55-0660, was the chosen vehicle for the air-launched ballistic missile tests, which were flown from Eglin AFB in Florida under the codenames High Virgo and Snap Shot. The Hustler carried the Lockheed-developed missile, which had a Thiokol XM-20 rocket motor rated at 50,000 lb (222.5 kN) thrust, on a specially designed pylon. During one flight the rocket achieved an altitude of 250,000 ft (76200 m) and a speed of Mach 6. The four tests were as follows:

Date	Launch alt.	Launch speed	Remarks
5 September 1958	40,500 ft	Mach 1	test terminated due to rocket oscillations
19 December 1958	35,000 ft	Mach 1.6	successful flight of 280 seconds
4 June 1959	?	?	successful 240-second flight with inertial system employed
22 September 1959	37,500 ft	Mach 2	rocket carried camera package to photograph satellite; communication with missile lost and cameras not recovered

A 43rd Bomb Wing aircraft is seen at an air show in the early 1960s. The aircraft displays typical initial operational markings, with a red arrow fin marking and a black mask around the cockpit. Other black patches denoted the location of antennas. The grey circle at the apex of the flight deck area above the national insignia was the antenna for the ARC-57 UHF command radio.

Pod test drops were conducted primarily at the White Sands/Holloman range complex. These two views show an MB-1C pod, which was first released on 5 June 1957. By the end of the year drop speeds and altitudes had reached the design figures of Mach 2 and over 60,000 ft (18288 m). In May 1960 a pod was dropped with an inert Sandia Mk 53 warhead.

Right: 58-0111 is seen at Edwards with both pod types. The TCP on its trolley is in the process of assembly, demonstrating how the the BLU-2/B-1 upper component slotted into the BLU-2/B-2 lower section.

under Project Snap Shot. The fourth and last of these missions involved a camera-equipped missile that was intended to photograph a NASA Explorer satellite.

Other ALBM projects that were never developed into actual hardware included Project Hook Shot, an anti-ballistic missile (ABM) concept, and Project Close Shot that envisioned using a missile launched from a B-58 at Mach 2 to place an object into space. The latter was a precursor to the Pegasus system of three decades later.

The notion that the single pod carried by the Hustler could and should be a powered missile of some sort remained alive and well for the life of the aircraft. Many systems were considered and some were tested, but the free-fall MB-1C remained as the standard operational weapon.

Other offensive weapons

The weapons pod was an integral part of the overall B-58 system from the beginning. The Hustler was designed, quite simply, to carry a single nuclear weapon to a single high-priority target. During the early 1950s, Convair and Air Research & Development Command looked at various types of pods, but neither seriously considered an offensive weapon other than what was carried in the pod.

Of course, as almost invariably happens with complex weapons systems, new needs and possibilities presented themselves after deployment. Almost as soon as the first squadrons became operational, Strategic Air Command began to consider operational requirements demanding additional flexibility that would not be possible with the original 'single weapon/single target' circumstances.

With this in mind, between 1961 and 1963 the B-58 fleet was retrofitted to allow each aircraft to carry four Mk 43 or Mk 61 nuclear bombs outside the pod on underfuselage hardpoints near the wingroots.

The B-58 was also used to test fire the Hughes AIM-47 air-to-air missile, although the weapon was never intended for operational deployment aboard the Hustler. In the late 1950s, the US Air Force was working toward the development of an interceptor capable of speeds exceeding Mach 2, and needed an existing Mach 2 aircraft to test the weapons system intended for such an interceptor.

For a time, the leading contender for this interceptor was the North American Aviation XF-108 Rapier, although the winner was the Lockheed YF-12 that evolved into the SR-71 Blackbird. Eventually, the AIM-47 evolved into the

Testing the Two-Component Pod

Following on from the extensive and successful MB-1C pod drop tests which began in June 1957, the test force geared up for TCP tests, which were flown from Kirtland AFB, New Mexico. Pods were released over the White Sands range near Holloman AFB in New Mexico, or the Tonopah Test Range in Nevada. Testing began with a subsonic lower component drop on 24 May 1960, followed by a low-level upper component drop on 19 November. A supersonic upper component drop was made on 11 December, while a Mach 2 drop was made on 10 February 1961. In April both components were dropped, paving the way for the final milestone: a Mach 2 lower component drop on 8 August 1961.

The first few TCP tests were undertaken by 55-0663, crewed by Earl Guthrie, Grover Tate and O.D. Lively. Other crews joined the programme, as did aircraft 59-2435, which is seen here releasing the lower component. The rear dorsal strut of the component formed a pivot during release, forcing the discarded pod down and away from the aircraft. The antenna from the aircraft's tailcone was for a datalink system to transfer test information back to a ground station during test launches.

AIM-54 Phoenix, which was deployed on the US Navy's Grumman F-14 Tomcat fleet interceptor, while the YF-12 never entered service as an interceptor with the US Air Force.

Other pod concepts

With its offensive pod-carrying capability, the B-58 was considered for a variety of pod systems other than those with which it was actually deployed. In the early stages of the programme, it was planned that the RB-58 aircraft would carry a specifically-designed reconnaissance pod. Fairchild Camera & Instrument was asked to develop the MC-1 reconnaissance pod, whose outside shell would have the same dimensions as the MB-1C pod. Inside, the MC-1 would have carried 13 cameras weighing a total of 998 lb (453 kg). However, the project was cancelled in 1955 at a time when the Air Force had decided against an RB-58 variant. When the RB-58 concept was later revived, some MB-1 pods were retrofitted with cameras and/or sensors for low-level reconnaissance operations.

As the MC-1 was being developed, there was a parallel effort, at Convair's suggestion, to develop an MD-1 electronic warfare pod. A single MD-1 was built, but it is not known to have ever been flight tested.

The first serious revival of the RB-58 concept emerged early in 1956, when the Air Force contracted with Hughes Aircraft to develop a side-looking airborne radar (SLAR) system that would be compatible with the B-58 and its external pod attachments.

It should be remembered that, while aircraft technology made great strides during the 1950s, radar technology was still relatively primitive during this time period. One measure of this was in the area of miniaturisation. In contrast to optical systems involving cameras, the Hughes

'Snoopy' – the Hustler 'fighter'

55-0665 was chosen as a test vehicle for the Hughes ASG-18 long-range fire control radar and its associated GAR-9 (AIM-47) missile, which had been developed for the F-108 and F-12 interceptors. A single missile was housed in a bay in a special underfuselage pod, while the massive radar was shoehorned into a grossly extended nose, which gave rise to the nickname 'Snoopy'. The first missile launch was undertaken on 25 May 1962. Several more were fired by the B-58, the last in February 1964. Subsequently, the YF-12A took over test firings, the first on 18 March 1965.

The 40-in (101.6-cm) diameter radar antenna for the ASG-18 (left) made it one of the largest ever fighter radars, and the extended radome resulted in 'Snoopy' gaining an extra 7 ft (2.1 m) in length. During the test programme the aircraft was also fitted with infra-red sensors on either side of the nose, as intended for the F-12A interceptor. Missile launches were conducted with varying degrees of success against a number of targets

AN/APQ-69 SLAR system was enormous, with an antenna section alone that was nearly 50 ft (about 15 m) in length. This meant that it required virtually the entire internal volume of the pod, which in turn meant that there was no room for fuel, and the range of the AN/APQ-69-equipped RB-58 would be less than an RB-58 with an optical MC-1 system. The unwieldy shape of the huge SLAR was such that its aerodynamic drag prevented the Hustler from carrying it above subsonic speeds.

The first of two-dozen AN/APQ-69 flight-tests was conducted in late December 1959, about 10 months after Hughes delivered the first system. While the 50-mile (80-km) range and 10-ft (3-m) resolution of the AN/APQ-69 was impressive for 1959, the overall bulkiness of the system led to the system's cancellation in favour of a derivative of the Goodyear AN/APS-73 X-band synthetic aperture radar.

Quick Check

Work on this system began in June 1958 at the Wright Air Development Center under the project name Quick Check. The AN/APS-73 proved to have a half-again greater range than the Hughes system, although its resolution was poorer at that range. It was, however, small enough to allow the use of a modified MB-1 pod and it did allow room within the MB-1 for a modest fuel tank.

'Snoopy' only carried one of the massive Mach 6+ GAR-9 missiles, accommodated in a specially-built pod. Double-hinged doors opened and the missile was lowered on pylons before firing. Cameras to record missile firings were housed in high-speed fairings under the outer engine nacelles.

One of the drawbacks of the original Hustler design was its 'single-shot' capability. To provide the B-58 with multi-weapons capability, Convair designed four wingroot pylons which could carry B43 (or B61) laydown weapons. The pylons were first tested on 59-2456, while on 7 February 1962 aircraft 59-2435 made the first multi-weapon drop. The same aircraft performed a supersonic drop on 19 June, and a Mach 2 release on 2 August. The external pylons were fitted on the production line from the 87th aircraft (61-2051), and were retrofitted to earlier machines.

The ninth Hustler delivered (56-0668), a YB-58 that was originally and coincidentally ordered as an RB-58, is believed to have been used to test both the Hughes SLAR and the Quick Check system. After the former project was terminated, the aircraft was re-modified for the latter and handed over to the Quick Check project in May 1961.

It is believed that no other aircraft ever carried the Quick Check pod and that the system was not used operationally after the conclusion of the test programme. However, it was used operationally at least once during the flight test programme. The Cuban Missile Crisis, which occurred in October 1962, brought 56-0668 into action on an emergency basis.

SLAR testbeds

Two of the most remarkable Hustler test programmes involved the use of 55-0668 as a testbed for giant side-looking airborne radars for stand-off reconnaissance. The first involved the Hughes APQ-69 radar, which was housed in a 50-ft (15.2-m) pod. The radar was a real-aperture unit, hence the enormous size of the pod. In its new configuration, 55-0668 first flew on 24 December 1959. An unusual side effect of the pod fitment was that the bow wave created by the pod stopped the nose gear from retracting normally. A 0.5-g bunt manoeuvre during gear retraction was adopted to overcome this. Results from the APQ-69 were quite good, although the aircraft was limited in range and to subsonic speeds. Advances in radars – particularly of synthetic aperture technology – resulted in the Goodyear APS-37 SLAR, which was mounted in the modified nose of a converted (fuel-carrying) MB-1C pod, and which could be carried at supersonic speeds. The nose of 55-0668 was also fitted with a Raytheon high-resolution forward-looking radar in an enlarged radome, while a special astro-navigation system was installed, resulting in a revised hatch fairing over the second crew station. The project was known as Quick Check and was flight-tested from July 1961.

During the Missile Crisis there was an urgent need for reconnaissance operations over the island, and both the US Air Force and the US Navy used their best assets. In the case of the former, the use of the supersonic B-58 was seen as an important way to get the needed information. Ironically, the only Hustler ever to fly an operational mission in hostile air space was a test aircraft.

One of the more unusual pod concepts – and one certainly not flight tested – was a passenger pod that would have accommodated up to five people. This proposal was suggested as a means for delivering highly important government or military personnel anywhere in the world quickly, though hardly economically. The concept also was seen as a possible test environment for the development of a commercial scale supersonic transport (SST). Every major airframe maker in the United States was studying the SST concept during the 1960s. Convair's study concept, the 52-passenger Model 58, was based on the Hustler and is discussed later.

Defensive systems

During World War II, the theory of defensive armament for bombers followed the idea that the more gun turrets, the better. However, with the advent of jet bombers, it was believed that speed was in itself a defensive weapon, and that turrets should be located only in the tail, where they would be useful in defending against an interceptor aircraft chasing the bomber.

The Hustler's speed meant it was considered unlikely that an interceptor could attack from any direction other than straight on, from the front or the tail. In the former situation, because of the tremendous speeds of aircraft approaching one another at Mach 1 or faster, an interceptor pilot would have so little time to aim that it could be considered a virtually impossible shot.

The B-58 was designed with a single tail-mounted cannon that would be operated by a defensive systems operator (DSO) facing forward and sitting in the forward part of the aircraft, aft of the bombardier/navigator and the pilot. Originally, a twin-barrelled T-182 gun was among those considered, but by 1954 Convair and the Air Force had settled on the General Electric 20-mm T-171E (M61) six-barrelled rotary Gatling gun cannon, with fire control directed by an Emerson MD-7 radar unit. The gun had a

Record-setting flights

During the early years of the B-58's operational career, it was used for a number of record-breaking flights that demonstrated its capabilities and its potential. These were also seen as good public relations for the Air Force and for Convair. On 23 March 1960, shortly after the initial Strategic Air Command delivery, a B-58A crewed by Lieutenant Colonel Leonard Legge, Captain Andrew Rose and Captain Raymond Wagener conducted an 18-hour, 11,000-mile (17700-km) flight that ranks as the longest Hustler flight ever made.

On 12 January 1961, the B-58 began a year in which it established a number of important world speed and payload records. On this date, under Operation Quick Step I, Major Henry Deutschendorf, with Captain William Polhemus and Captain Raymond Wagener of the 43rd Bombardment Wing, established six such records, including a speed record of 1,061 mph (1707.467 km/h) over a 2000-km (1,242-mile) closed-circuit course and 1,200.194 mph (1931.472 km/h) over a 1000-km (621-mile) course. Both records were set with a 2000-kg (4,409-lb) payload.

Two days later, Lieutenant Colonel Harold Confer, Lieutenant Colonel Richard Weir and Major Howard Bialas earned the Thompson Trophy for carrying a 2000-kg (4,409-lb) payload over a 1000-km course at 1,284.73 mph (2067.52 km/h).

On 10 May 1961, a B-58 flying from Edwards AFB and crewed by Major Elmer Murphy, Major Eugene Moses and Lieutenant David Dickerson captured the esteemed Bleriot Trophy with a sustained speed of 1,302.07 mph (2095.42 km/h) over a 1073-km (667-mile) course. Louis Bleriot, the noted French aviator who was the first man to fly the English Channel, had established the trophy in 1930 to be awarded permanently to any aircraft flying for at least half an hour at an average speed of 2000 km/h (1,243 mph).

Two weeks later, on 26 May, it was time for Strategic Air Command to display its new prize performer at the most prestigious of all aviation gatherings, the Paris air show. A 43rd Bomb Wing B-58 called Firefly, commanded by Major William Payne and crewed by Quick Step veterans Polhemus and Wagener, flew from New York to Paris in a record time of just under three hours and 40 minutes, averaging 1,089 mph (1753 km/h). This flight earned the crew and the Hustler both the Harmon Trophy and the McKay Trophy.

The return flight on 3 June was scheduled to be flown by the Bleriot Trophy-winning team of Murphy, Moses and Dickerson. Shortly after take-off, however, the crew attempted a low-level demonstration that proved too low, and Firefly crashed. All three crewmen were killed.

As the B-58s were entering squadron service with Strategic Air Command, they continued to set new speed records. On 5 March 1962, a Hustler crewed by Captains Robert Sowers, Robert MacDonald and John Walton set a United States transcontinental speed record of 1,214.71 mph (1954.83 km/h) eastbound from Los Angeles to New York, and 1,081.77 mph (1740.89 km/h) on the return. The round trip took four hours and 41 minutes, less time than a commercial one-way flight, even to this day. The previous record-holder for the flight had been a McDonnell F-4 Phantom. The latter leg of the flight is notable for having been the first ever to have been completed in a faster time than the rotation of the earth.

On 18 September 1962, the Hustler won its second Harmon Trophy in as many years when an aircraft crewed by Major Fitzhugh Fulton, Captain W.R. Payne and Convair flight test engineer C.R. Haines carried a 5000-kg (11,023-lb) payload to 85,360.84 ft (26017.98 m).

In October 1963, a 305th Bomb Wing Hustler crewed by Major Sidney Kubesch, Major John Barrett and Captain Gerard Williamson – in an exercise appropriately nicknamed Greased Lightning – flew from Tokyo to London at an average speed of 938 mph (1510 km/h) to set yet another speed record. This flight, in addition to being a record flight, was seen as tactically important because it demonstrated the B-58's range capability in Arctic airspace where operational missions would have been flown in the event of a nuclear war.

Above: Road Runner (59-2441) was the aircraft used to capture the 1000-km closed circuit speed record in the 0-, 1,000- and 2000-kg load classes on 14 January 1961.

Right: The ill-fated Firefly (59-2451) was the aircraft which took the Bleriot Trophy, and then set a New York-Paris record, winning the McKay and Harmon trophies in the process.

59-2458, better known as the Cowtown Hustler, set an out-and-back transcontinental speed record on 5 March 1962, beating the previous records on both legs. The crew won the prestigious Bendix and McKay Trophies.

Above: One of the lesser known record-breakers, 59-2456 was the aircraft employed for the 18 September 1962 payload-to-altitude flight which reached over 85,000 ft with a 5000-kg load, winning the crew the 1962 Harmon trophy.

Right: Major Sidney Kubesch, Major John Barrett and Captain Gerard Williamson talk in front of 61-2059 (Greased Lightning), in which they established an over-the-Pole Tokyo-London time of 8 hours 35 minutes. After the fifth and last refuelling, one afterburner would not light, forcing the crew to complete the flight subsonically and adding over an hour to the flight time.

Above: Having been used to capture the Bleriot Trophy outright (which called for an aircraft to fly for at least 30 minutes at more than 2000 km/h), and having set a New York-Paris speed record, Firefly was justifiably the sensation of the 1961 Paris Air Show. Tragedy struck soon after the aircraft departed le Bourget on 3 June, 59-2451 crashing during a low-level aerobatic routine minutes after this photograph was taken.

The Hustler's return to Paris for the 1965 show was no less tragic than its debut. On 15 June 59-2443 (ironically named Bye Bye Birdie) landed short of the runway, killing the pilot although the navigator and DSO survived. This aircraft, 61-2069, was at the show as a back-up.

A 43rd BW B-58A rolls out after a dusk landing at Little Rock in 1967. Although the TCP was the preferred weapon choice, the MB-1C remained in use throughout the Hustler's career.

Avionics systems

Among the avionics, the Sperry AN/ASQ-42 bombing and navigation system was the most important. It was designed to accomplish the typical tasks of such a system – with the added variable of supersonic speed and what that velocity would mean to the trajectory of the unpowered weapons pod when it was released at speeds up to Mach 2.

In the defensive avionics suite were the AN/ALR-12 radar warning system, the AN/ALQ-16 radar jamming system – which was designed to confuse enemy ranging systems – and an AN/ALE-16 chaff dispenser. Also in the defensive array was the AN/APX-47 Identification Friend or Foe (IFF) communicator.

UHF communications systems included the AN/ARC-34 and the AN/ARC-57 radios, as well as the AN/ARC-74 emergency communications system and the AN/ARN-50 VHF system.

A high level of mishaps

No discussion of the Hustler's record-setting successes would be complete without a mention of the B-58's dark side. Of the 116 that were built, 21 of them, or 18 per cent, crashed. An additional five were destroyed or damaged in ground accidents, and only one of the damaged aircraft was repaired. Thirty-three aircrew members and two ground crewmen were killed.

The aircraft loss rate remained relatively constant through the entire service life of the B-58. With three exceptions, two or three aircraft were lost every year from 1959 through 1969, the last full year of service. The exceptions were 1963, 1964 and 1966, when only a single Hustler was lost each year, and 1962, when there were four aircraft losses and seven crewmen killed in three fatal incidents.

Systems malfunctions, mainly in the control systems, were the leading cause, accounting for 11 B-58 losses and possibly a 12th. Landing gear or tyre problems were responsible for three aircraft losses and one Hustler was lost in 1961 due to an engine flame-out. Weather was a factor in two incidents in 1960 and 1967. The single damaged Hustler to be restored to flight status had suffered a structural failure during taxiing in 1967.

Pilot error was the principal factor in six losses, five of them between 1963 and 1966. Of these, two involved hard landings, two involved missing the runway, and one occurred during low-level training operations.

The B-58 also had the dubious distinction of having suffered not one, but two, fatal crashes at the Paris air show. The first occurred in 1961, and the second happened

rate of fire of 4,000 rounds per minute, although only 1,200 rounds could be accommodated.

The fire control system could be operated by automatic target acquisition (ATA) or manual target acquisition (MTA). In the former, the system automatically searched a set pattern, acquired and tracked a target, displaying the target on the radar scope and indicating to the DSO when to fire the gun. In manual operation, the DSO selected the target and fired.

One of the more interesting problems encountered in aiming and operating the gun was that the forward motion of the aircraft at Mach 2 was faster than the muzzle velocity of the gun, so, theoretically, as a round left the barrel, it would actually be travelling backward relative to the ground. An interceptor pursuing the B-58 at that speed would have to run into the cannon shells, rather than vice versa. The B-58's gun was never fired in anger.

in June 1965 when the crew undershot the runway at Le Bourget airport.

Accidents by year

Year	Fatal accidents	Fatalities	Non-fatal accidents
1956	0	0	0
1957	0	0	0
1958	1	1	0
1959	3	5	0
1960	2	5	0
1961	1	3	1
1962	3	7	1
1963	1	2	0
1964	1	1	0
1965	3	2	1
1966	1	3	0
1967	2	4	1
1968	1	3	1
1969	0	0	2
1970	0	0	0

Later B-58s

Only the B-58A production model was built, although both a B-58B and a B-58C were considered, and one B-58B aircraft was ordered. These would have had larger weapons pods and provisions for additional weapons, including ALBMs. Different engine configurations, and side-by-side seating for the pilot and the bombardier-navigator, were also studied.

The B-58B would have been powered by a more powerful version of the General Electric J79 turbojet, designated J79-GE-19. This aircraft would have had canard surfaces mounted forward of the wing that were similar to, but smaller than, those seen on the XB-70. The single B-58B was cancelled shortly after it was ordered in 1960, although metal was cut for some components.

A larger aircraft than the B-58A or B-58B, the B-58C (also known as BJ-58) was conceived in part as Convair's proposed alternative to the North American Aviation XB-70. In retrospect, it would have been an amazing aircraft, powered by the same 32,500-lb (144.54-kN) thrust Pratt & Whitney J58 turbojet engines that Lockheed used for the YF-12/SR-71 series. Like the SR-71, the B-58C would have hit speeds in the Mach 3 environment and would have cruised at Mach 2 and above 70,000 ft (21300 m).

As with the XB-70 programme, the idea of developing the B-58C was a victim of the Defense Department's decision that fast, high-altitude penetration bombers were a thing of the past. The B-58C died in 1961 with no such aircraft having been funded or built.

Less fully evolved were studies for the B-58D and the B-58E, and the designations were not officially assigned. Both were efforts by Convair to adapt the B-58 for roles other than that of a strategic bomber. The twin-engined B-58D concept was Convair's answer to the need for a longer-range, supersonic interceptor similar to the Lockheed YF-12. The B-58E, also proposed with two engines, was a tactical bomber. If the B-58A was a medium-range strategic bomber, the range of the B-58E would have seemed long in the context of a tactical mission.

The tactical 'B-58E' was a child of the 1960s, undertaken at the time the Defense Department was exploring its controversial Tactical Fighter, Experimental programme, best remembered by the acronym TFX. This project was a

59-2432 Regal Beagle of the 43rd BW refuels from a KC-135A. The Hustler was considered an easy aircraft to refuel as it was very stable behind the boom. The position of the receptacle was ideal for visibility. Very early Hustlers had the receptacle located much further forward.

A characteristic feature of the B-58 was the long overwing fairing, necessary to accommodate the main landing gear. This is the 43rd BW's 59-2434.

failed attempt to build one aircraft that could function as both a fighter and bomber for both the US Air Force and the US Navy. Ultimately, the TFX was built only as a bomber (although it carried the 'F for fighter' designation), and only for the US Air Force. Designated as F-111 and FB-111, these aircraft were products of Convair's parent company, General Dynamics, and were manufactured on the same Fort Worth assembly line as the B-58A Hustlers.

Unproduced derivative projects

As noted earlier, it was axiomatic in the weapons planning paradigm of the 1950s that an aircraft's successor should be on the drawing board by the time it made its first flight. Such was the case with the Hustler. A Super Hustler, with a performance envelope significantly better than that of the B-58A, was considered very early on.

Beginning to take shape early in 1957, the Mach 4 Super Hustler was a distinctly different aircraft and a distinctly different concept. It was much smaller and much faster than a B-58A, and it was initially intended to be air-launched from a B-58A. When the B-58 mothership had achieved a speed of Mach 2 at a predetermined distance from the target, the Super Hustler parasite would fire up its ram-jet engines and separate from the host vehicle.

In this air-launch scenario, the size of the aircraft was governed by the need for the Super Hustler to fit under the Hustler's fuselage with the same ground clearance as the MB-1C weapons pod. Various Super Hustler configurations were studied, most involving a multi-stage vehicle composed of two or three dart-shaped vehicles 40 to 50 ft (12 to 15 m) in length, or slightly shorter than a Convair F-102. A two-man crew would sit side-by-side in one vehicle, while the second and/or third component would be a powered fuel and/or weapons section(s) that could be jettisoned.

Although the Super Hustler was never built, it evolved into the Project Kingfish reconnaissance proposal. Just as an interceptor derivative of the B-58 was passed over in favour of the Lockheed YF-12, the Kingfish was rejected in favour of the YF-12's nearly identical sister, the SR-71.

Another buzz that was heard in the halls of America's aircraft companies during the 1960s was the notion of the supersonic transport (SST). It was predicted – even assumed – that commercial air travel at speeds greater than sound would be routine by the end of the 1970s. Design studies for an aircraft to make this possible were a high

priority at Boeing, Douglas, Lockheed, North American Aviation and, of course, Convair. Early in the 1960s, both North American Aviation and Convair had something of a head start, insofar as both companies had practical experience with large supersonic aircraft – the XB-70 and the B-58, respectively.

Convair's Hustler-derived SST was developed under the company designation Model 58 (the B-58 was the Convair Model 4). The ultimate Model 58 proposal was the Model 58-9. The Dash 9 would use the same wing and tail as the Hustler, although Pratt & Whitney J58 turbojet engines were specified as substitutes for the General Electric J79s.

At the same time that the Model 58 programme was on the drawing boards at Convair in Fort Worth, the company's San Diego facility was producing and flight testing two subsonic jetliners, the 880 (Model 22) and 990 (Model 30). The people involved in these two programmes, for which first flights occurred in 1959 and 1961, respectively, had little contact with the people involved in the Hustler programme in Texas, and the jetliners had minimal influence on the design of the Model 58.

Stretched Hustler

The Hustler had been designed for the performance envelope imagined for the Model 58, and the latter's fuselage was to have been a stretched Hustler fuselage, rather than a passenger cabin borrowed from either the 880 or the 990. As such, it would have been only 80 in (203 cm) wide, or about half the width of its commercial cousins. This would have permitted no more than two-abreast seating, as contrasted with the five-abreast configuration of the 880 and 990. As a footnote, it is worth mentioning that the 880 and 990 were, themselves, narrower than their competitors,

the Douglas DC-8 and Boeing 707, which offered the six-abreast seating that became the industry standard.

To compensate for the narrowness of the fuselage, the pencil-like fuselage of the Model 58 was designed to be longer than either of the Convair jetliners. The Hustler's 96-ft 9.4-in (29.49-m) fuselage would be stretched to 150 ft (45.72 m) in length. This compared to 129 ft 4 in (39.42 m) for the 880, and 139 ft 5 in (42.49 m) for the 990. These dimensions would have given the Model 58 a passenger capacity of 52, compared to maximums (in all-economy configuration) of 130 and 149, respectively, for the 880 and 990. Even assuming that the 52 passengers would pay extra for the supersonic speed, the economics of the Model 58 were more of a stretch than its fuselage length.

In the event, the only American SST on which metal was cut was the Boeing 2707, which would have accommodated more than 250 passengers depending on configuration. The Anglo-French Concorde, the only SST ever to see consistent, long-term service, had a passenger capacity of up to 144 passengers.

The Convair Model 58 programme never progressed beyond design studies. As it turned out, the company lost so much money on the 880 and 990 that they were the last production aircraft of any kind that the company built.

Late operational career

During the 1960s, the 'higher and faster' doctrine of military aircraft operations was qualified with a resounding 'not exactly'. As was dramatically illustrated by the May 1960 downing by the Soviet Union of the U-2 piloted by Francis Gary Powers, advancements in air defence systems rendered high-flying aircraft vulnerable. This led to the adoption of low-level tactics for strategic aircraft. Until well

Above: This Hustler is carrying an LA-331 camera pod. Although the reconnaissance capability was little called-upon, it was practised and routinely inspected with missions launched against unknown targets with little notice. In general, the results gained were excellent – largely a function of the combined talents of the Hustler crews and the state-of-the-art navigation suite.

Far left: Inflight refuelling was essential to the Hustler's strategic mission.

Below: The nature of the strategic deterrent mission required SAC crews to be at readiness all day, all year. That often meant working in appalling conditions, as evidenced by this B-58 sitting out an ice-storm. In the background are the open-ended shelters, known as 'Hustler Huts', usually used to house the aircraft.

Clutching its TCP to its belly, 59-2454 lifts off from Little Rock. This aircraft, named Patches, suffered a major forward fuselage structural failure while taxiing, but was rebuilt. Take-off in the B-58 was exhilarating, but required forward stick pressure throughout as the B-58 used nosewheel steering. Rapid checks of speed were required during the roll until decision speed (about 140 kt/260 km/h) was reached. Rotation to 12° was at about 185 kt (342 km/h), and lift-off occurred at about 203 kt (376 km/h). At 200 ft (61 m) the pilot pressed the brake pedals to stop wheel rotation and then raised the gear. The B-58 accelerated to its normal climb speed of 425 kt (787 km/h).

after B-52s and B-58s had been deployed, SAC had never imagined they would be used for such operations.

As for the 'faster' aspect of the equation, the US Air Force had a rude awakening in Vietnam, where slower aircraft were an asset – not only in the ground attack role, but in air-to-air combat, where few of the 'experts' could have predicted it. That fast was best had always been assumed to be a given, and air superiority fighters were always designed to be faster than their predecessors. When American fighter pilots went to war in Vietnam, the McDonnell F-4 Phantom II was the epitome of the 'higher and faster' fighter. In reality, North Vietnam's Soviet-built MiG-21s could literally fly circles around the F-4. They were slower, but they were lighter and more manoeuvrable. It was a stunning wake-up call.

Conventional bomber

Strategic Air Command's contribution to the war in Southeast Asia – other than its fleet of KC-135 tankers – was the slower B-52, not the supersonic B-58. Why? Because the speed was unnecessary and the B-52 had a huge conventional bomb capacity. The B-58 had been designed

An enduring part of Hustler mythology was the rumour that one received tactical camouflage in trials for potential participation in the conflict in Southeast Asia. While the B-58 was certainly tested with conventional weaponry, there is no firm evidence to support the idea that the 'Camo Hustler' was ever anything more than a paper proposal. This impression shows what such a beast might have looked like.

with no conventional bomb-carrying capacity; its nuclear weapons pod was part of the design of the aircraft itself.

Vietnam was the type of war on which American military planners had focussed little attention during the 1950s and, as a result, the United States found itself adapting high-tech weapons to low-tech operations. For the US Air Force, this meant adapting nearly every aircraft in its inventory to fit a role in Southeast Asia. Although it did not actually serve, even the B-58 was considered.

In 1967, the Air Force's Project Bullseye studied the feasibility of using the B-58 with conventional high-explosive ordnance. The United States service had never given much thought to such an idea before, but this arrangement had been the subject of a short-lived proposal made by Convair to the Australian government nearly a decade earlier.

Under Bullseye, the four external hardpoints that had

Hustler training

To enter the Hustler programme pilots were required to have more than 1,000 hours, of which 500 had to be in command of a multi-jet aircraft. Initially, most came from the B-47 community. Navigators needed 500 hours, while DSOs required 200 hours. Training was overseen by the Combat Crew Training Schools within each wing. Pilots began with an intensive instrument course on T-33s at Perrin AFB, where they also acquired delta-wing skills in the TF-102A. Navigators and DSOs underwent a special B-58 course at Mather AFB. Only after a lengthy ground course did the pilots then proceed to the TB-58A, in which roughly seven sorties were made before they flew an operational aircraft. The trainers were assigned to both the 43rd (right) and 305th (above) CCTS.

been retrofitted for additional nuclear weapons were adapted for conventional iron bombs. Up to 3,000 lb (1360 kg) of such weapons were dropped in successful low-level tests flown from Eglin AFB in Florida.

In simulated strike missions – which some say involved at least one B-58 painted in SEA camouflage colours – Hustlers flew both pathfinder operations with other strike aircraft and solo bombing missions. Almost all of the drops were visual, with the AN/ASQ-42 system rarely being used.

Due to their speed and manoeuvrability, the Hustlers were found suitable in the conventional role, but the fear that the B-58s' integral wing tanks would make them vulnerable to ground fire during low-altitude attacks led to the abandonment of the Bullseye programme. Another reason for the Hustler not being deployed was, reportedly, that the Defense Department feared the negative publicity that might come with the loss of a B-58 on a tactical mission.

This was essentially the B-58's last hurrah. The tactical lessons and the high cost of the war in Southeast Asia led to a major shift in American strategic thinking. Expensive, high-tech systems were being heavily scrutinised.

At the same time, United States Secretary of Defense Robert McNamara was on a crusade to change the way that the American armed forces operated. He had come to office in 1961, touted as one of President John F. Kennedy's 'whiz kids', a management genius who would revolutionise weapons procurement. For the US Air Force, this meant cancellation of the major vehicles that had been on its roadmap for the future.

In 1961, McNamara terminated the production variant of the hypersonic North American Aviation XB-70, the successor to the B-52, as well as the Douglas Skybolt ALBM. In 1963, he killed the Boeing X-20 Dyna-Soar, which could have flown in 1965 as America's first space shuttle. In December 1965, just 26 months after the final B-58A delivery, the Secretary ordered Strategic Air Command to plan for the phase-out of the Hustler by the end of the decade. There would be no need for a supersonic bomber, McNamara reasoned, when intercontinental ballistic missiles could do the job.

For its part, Strategic Air Command, which had argued against the B-58 in the beginning, asserted that the aircraft should be retained – at least until 1974 – to give the strategic service more flexibility in meeting the demands of its mission.

McNamara stood by his decision, although it was his successor, Melvin Laird, who presided over the final termination of B-58 operations during the first year of Richard Nixon's presidency.

Withdrawal from service

The decision to withdraw the B-58 from service has always been controversial. On one hand, the Hustler had achieved its design goals and it was the fastest strategic bomber to serve with the US Air Force. On the other hand, Strategic Air Command had never fully embraced the Hustler because of its limited range, and its service career coincided with a serious debate within the US Air Force over whether the role of nuclear deterrence was better performed by manned bombers or intercontinental ballistic missiles.

Another important and inescapable issue was the cost – especially at the peak of the war in Southeast Asia – of maintaining an aircraft so sophisticated and with so many unique parts. Maintenance was inescapably complex and expensive, and it involved specially-trained crews that were always in short supply. The engines, designed for performance over durability, were also problematic, and thoughts of re-engining the Hustler fleet were not pursued because the Defense Department had already made up its mind to phase out the B-58.

Although there had been plenty of warning, the end of the B-58's career came abruptly. It was announced in October 1969 that both Little Rock AFB and Grissom AFB would be closed and that the entire B-58 fleet would be mothballed within three months. This process began within a few weeks of the announcement, and most of the roughly 80 surviving B-58s were flown to Davis-Monthan AFB in the six weeks between mid-December and the end of January 1970. Here, they were put into indefinite storage at the Military Aircraft Storage & Disposal Center – known affectionately as the Davis-Monthan 'Boneyard'.

A routine feature of strategic forces was the minimum-interval take-off (MITO), usually undertaken during Operational Readiness Inspections (ORIs). Here six B-58s taxi out at Little Rock for a MITO in July 1968. Launching 15 seconds apart, MITOs often involved up to 20 aircraft launching on simulated Emergency War Order (EWO) missions. Quite apart from the logistical effort of getting that many B-58s into the air, the pilots had to contend with near-blind take-offs thanks to the smokescreen laid down by the preceding aircraft.

Operation Bullseye – conventional bomb trials at Eglin

In April 1967 a number of 305th BW B-58As were sent to Eglin AFB to conduct a series of trials with various conventional free-fall bombs (up to 3,000 lb/1361 kg in weight) mounted on the external wingroot racks. Triple and Multiple Ejector Racks were used, as well as direct pylon mounting. The B-58s also flew with F-105s and F-4s, acting as navigation leaders. The results proved that the B-58 could easily drop conventional weapons, but achieved only a small increase in accuracy compared to regular fighter-bombers.

Above: Various sizes of conventional bomb can be seen next to this 305th BW aircraft (61-2055), which has weapons mounted under the wingroot pylons. Most of the conventional tests were flown at low altitude, with the result that one aircraft was slightly damaged by exploding bomb fragments.

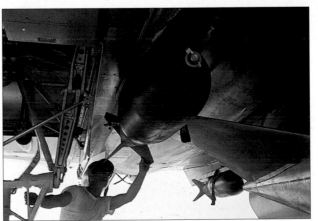

Left: An armourer checks the installation of a bomb during Bullseye tests. The aircraft also carries the upper component of the TCP.

B-58 production summary

Model	No. built	Serials
XB-58-CF	2	55-0660, 55-0661
YB-58A-CF	11	55-0662 to 55-0672
YB/RB-58A-CF	17	58-1007 to 58-1023
B-58A-10-CF	36	59-2428 to 59-2463
B-58A-20-CF	20	60-1110 to 60-1129
B-58A-30-CF	30	61-2051 to 61-2080
Total	**116**	

Conversions

NB-58A-CF	1	55-0662
TB-58A-CF	8	55-0661 to 55-0663,
		55-0668, 55-0670 to
		55-0672, 58-1007

Individual aircraft assignments

As the first B-58 wing to form, the 43rd was assigned aircraft in the FY58 and FY59 serial blocks, while the 305th which followed mostly operated the FY60 and FY61 machines. As well as full production aircraft, the 43rd operated the Flash Up aircraft, which were upgraded to operational status after early trials. The following is a listing of wing allocations. Italicised entries are those aircraft which were lost in accidents.

43rd Bomb Wing
B-58A – 58-1010, 58-1011, 58-1013, 58-1014, 58-1015, *58-1016*, *58-1017*, 58-1018, 58-1019, *58-1020*, 58-1021, 59-2428, 59-2429, 59-2431, 59-2432, 59-2433, 59-2434, 59-2435, 59-2436, *59-2437*, 59-2438, 59-2439, 59-2440, 59-2441, 59-2442, *59-2443*, 59-2444, 59-2445, 59-2446, *59-2447*, 59-2448, 59-2449, 59-2450, *59-2451*, 59-2452, 59-2453, 59-2454, 59-2455, 59-2456, 59-2457, 59-2458, *59-2459*, 59-2460, 59-2461*, 59-2463, 60-1122, 61-2066, 61-2078
TB-58A – 55-0668, 55-0670, 55-0671, 55-0672, 58-1007

305th Bomb Wing
B-58A – 59-2430, 59-2461*, *59-2462*, 60-1110, 60-1111, 60-1112, 60-1113, 60-1114, 60-1115, *60-1116*, 60-1117, 60-1118, *60-1119*, 60-1120, 60-1121, 60-1123, 60-1124, 60-1125, 60-1126, 60-1127, *60-1128*, 60-1129, 61-2051, 61-2052, 61-2053, 61-2054, 61-2055, *61-2056*, *61-2057*, 61-2058, 61-2059, 61-2060, *61-2061*, *61-2062*, *61-2063*, 61-2064, *61-2065*, 61-2066, 61-2067, 61-2068, 61-2069, 61-2070, 61-2071, 61-2072, *61-2073*, 61-2074, 61-2075, 61-2076, 61-2077, 61-2079, 61-2080
TB-58A – 55-0661, 55-0662, 55-0663

*As far as is known, only one aircraft served with both units, transferred from the 43rd to become the first aircraft for the 305th.

The following aircraft remained in test status throughout their careers, or were lost before being given Flash Up or TB-58 modifications: 55-0660, *55-0664*, 55-0665, 55-0666, *55-0667*, *55-0669*, *58-1008*, 58-1009, *58-1012*, 58-1022, *58-1023*

wered by the General Electric YJ79-GE-1
ssentially prototype engines and suffered from
aircraft were powered by the J79-GE-5A or 5B,
eliability and extra thrust. The J79 had a 17-stage
stages of which employed variable stator vanes (a first in
compression ratio was 12.2:1. The compressor was driven by a
exhaust had two variable-area nozzles: the primary was the first ejector
ust, while downstream was the secondary (visible) nozzle which also
when the secondary flaps were open (during idle and afterburner operation).
hits which optimised engine configuration, the pilot's throttle levers
f fuel flow, engine speed, (up to 7,460 rpm), variable inlet guide position,
ary and secondary nozzle area, and afterburner flow.

Convair B-58A-20-CF Hustler

305th Bomb Wing
Bunker Hill AFB, Indiana

The B-58 Hustler was designed to penetrate hostile airspace at high speeds (up to Mach 2.2) and high altitude (up to 70,000 ft/21336 m). Unlike the B-52s, which flew Chrome Dome airborne alerts, the B-58 fleet was maintained on ground alert. Each crew had a specific target assigned under the Emergency War Order, and they carefully studied the ingress/egress routes and tanker tracks. Initially, the standard high-level profile involved an acceleration to 600 kt indicated, going through Mach 1. The aircraft climbed until Mach 1.72 was reached, when the aircraft was put into 'overspeed' (max afterburner plus 103.5 percent rpm). Mach 2 was attained at about 47,000 ft (14325 ft). After that the Hustler climbed to the mission height of around 55,000 ft (16764 m). Later, another profile was introduced, in which the pilot went straight into 'overspeed' at 30,000 ft (9144 m). By the late 1960s, the threat of Soviet SAMs dictated that virtually all penetration missions were to be flown at low level. After a high-level transit, the B-58 would drop down to around 1,000 ft (305 m) AGL some 30 to 45 minutes out from the target. The descent began at a predetermined IP (initial point). During the final run-in to target, which would be flown at 500 ft (152 m) or lower, it was the navigator who actually had control of the aircraft, feeding precise positional data into the nav/bombing system which was interfaced with the autopilot.

Although most B-58 operations were flown from the two US bases, the force also had a Reflex commitment, under which B-58s could be forward deployed. The first B-58 Reflex base was Zaragoza in Spain, which became operational on 1 July 1963. Later, B-58 Reflex capabilities were established at Upper Heyford in England, at Kadena on Okinawa, and at Andersen on Guam.

Defensive systems

For its day the B-58 was very well protected, and pioneered the radar track breaker (deception electronic countermeasures). The overall defensive electronic suite consisted of three main elements. The ALR-12 radar warning receiver, with antennas in the inner wing leading edges and fin, detected activity in the D to J bands (1 to 12.5 GHz) and provided both an aural and visual warning at the DSO's station. Furthermore, it could be set up to automatically activate the ALE-16 chaff dispensers. Five dispensers were mounted in each wing, and they could dispense various types of chaff at varying intervals and sequences. The ALQ-16 radar track breaker was an impressive deception ECM system with antennas situated either side of the nose, in the wingroot leading edges, under the rear fuselage and at the tip of the fin. The system received the transmitted radar signal, and with minimum time delay captured the range gate, allowing the signal to be returned to the ground radar, but with deceptive angle and range information added. The ground radar's antenna would then be wrongly positioned, and give false range and position information to its operator.

For defence aginst fighter attack, a rearward-firing gun system was installed. Designed by Emerson, the system consisted of an MD-7 Ku-band fire control radar which detected and tracked targets out to a range of 22,500 ft (6858 m) and computed lead and windage. Control could be effected either automatically by the system computer, or manually by the DSO. The radar's 'view' encompassed +/-50° in azimuth and +42°/-18° in elevation. The gun itself was the 20-mm General Electric T-171E-3 (later designated M61) Vulcan cannon, a six-barrelled Gatling weapon firing at up to 4,000 rounds per minute. 1,200 rounds were carried, fed by flexible chute from an ammunition box. Spent cases were ejected through a hatch underneath the turret. The gun could travel through +/- 30° in both azimuth and elevation, and could traverse at a rate of up to 60° per second. Effective range of the cannon was 4,500 ft (1372 m). The gun was mounted in an articulated tailcone which consisted of interlocking concentric rings. These were spring-loaded, and allowed the gun to move freely to the limits of its travel while maintaining the aerodynamic integrity of the tailcone.

Engine nacelles

Designed to offer minimum frontal cross-section, the nacelles were attached to the wings on pylons (vestigial for the outboard pair). An engine change could be accomplished in about 3 hours. The moveable inlet spike was an integral part of the nacelle, as was a cooling system which took ram air from two scoops in the intake and fed it around the engine core, the flow re-entering the hot core air to be exhausted through the engine's nozzle.

Powerplant

Early test aircraft were p
turbojet but these were
frequent failures. Servic
offering much improved
compressor, the first six
turbine technology). The
three-stage turbine. The
handling just engine exh
handled (bypass) airflow
Through engine control u
controlled the functions
stator blade position, prir

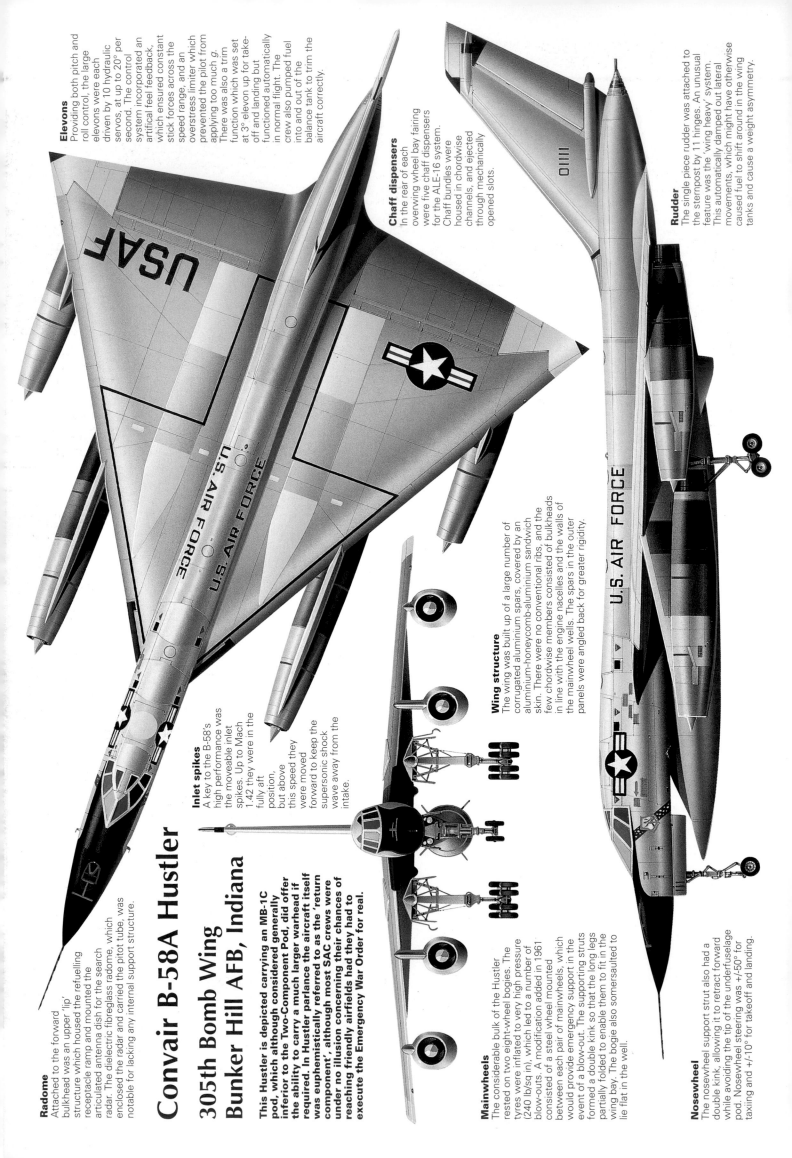

Radome
Attached to the forward bulkhead was an upper 'lip' structure which housed the refuelling receptacle ramp and mounted the articulated antenna dish for the search radar. The dielectric fibreglass radome, which enclosed the radar and carried the pitot tube, was notable for lacking any internal support structure.

Convair B-58A Hustler

305th Bomb Wing
Bunker Hill AFB, Indiana

This Hustler is depicted carrying an MB-1C pod, which although considered generally inferior to the Two-Component Pod, did offer the ability to carry a much larger warhead if required. In Hustler parlance the aircraft itself was euphemistically referred to as the 'return component', although most SAC crews were under no illusion concerning their chances of reaching friendly airfields had they had to execute the Emergency War Order for real.

Elevons
Providing both pitch and roll control, the large elevons were each driven by 10 hydraulic servos, at up to 20° per second. The control system incorporated an artifical feel feedback, which ensured constant stick forces across the speed range, and an overstress limiter which prevented the pilot from applying too much g. There was also a trim function which was set at 3° elevon up for take-off and landing but functioned automatically in normal flight. The crew also pumped fuel into and out of the balance tank to trim the aircraft correctly.

Inlet spikes
A key to the B-58's high performance was the moveable inlet spikes. Up to Mach 1.42 they were in the fully aft position, but above this speed they were moved forward to keep the supersonic shock wave away from the intake.

Chaff dispensers
In the rear of each overwing wheel bay fairing were five chaff dispensers for the ALE-16 system. Chaff bundles were housed in chordwise channels, and ejected through mechanically opened slots.

Rudder
The single piece rudder was attached to the sternpost by 11 hinges. An unusual feature was the 'wing heavy' system. This automatically damped out lateral movements, which might have otherwise caused fuel to shift around in the wing tanks and cause a weight asymmetry.

Wing structure
The wing was built up of a large number of corrugated aluminium spars, covered by an aluminium-honeycomb-aluminium sandwich skin. There were no conventional ribs, and the few chordwise members consisted of bulkheads in line with the engine nacelles and the walls of the mainwheel wells. The spars in the outer panels were angled back for greater rigidity.

Mainwheels
The considerable bulk of the Hustler rested on two eight-wheel bogies. The tyres were inflated to very high pressure (240 lb/sq in), which led to a number of blow-outs. A modification added in 1961 consisted of a steel wheel mounted between each pair of mainwheels, which would provide emergency support in the event of a blow-out. The supporting struts formed a double kink so that the long legs partially folded to enable them to fit in the wing bay. The bogie also somersaulted to lie flat in the well.

Nosewheel
The nosewheel support strut also had a double kink, allowing it to retract forward while avoiding the tip of the underfuselage pod. Nosewheel steering was +/-50° for taxiing and +/-10° for takeoff and landing.

Above: The cockpit was fairly cramped but considered comfortable for long-endurance flights. Principal flight instruments occupied the left-hand side of the dashboard, with engine dials to the right.

Left: Better known as the engine for the F-4 Phantom II, the General Electric J79 offered an exceptional power to weight ratio of 4.37 (at sea level in afterburner). In the GE-5A version it weighed 3,570 lb (1619 kg) and was 16 ft 10 in (5.13 m) long.

Convair B-58A Hustler

1 Pitot head
2 Instrumentation boom
3 Glassfibre radome
4 Long-range communications system antenna
5 Antenna coupler
6 Search radar scanner
7 Scanner tracking mechanism
8 Inflight retuelling receptacle
9 Incidence probe
10 Radar modulator
11 Radar and nosewheel mounting bulkhead
12 Landing light
13 Nose undercarriage leg strut
14 ILS glideslope aerial
15 Twin nosewheels, aft retracting
16 Steering jacks
17 Nosewheel doors
18 Hydraulic retraction jack
19 Oxygen bottles, port and starboard
20 Cockpit front pressure bulkhead
21 Rudder pedals and control column
22 Instrument panel shroud
23 Windscreen panels
24 Overhead windows
25 Pilot's upward hingeing entry hatch
26 Pilot's seat and integral escape capsule
27 Canopy hydraulic jack
28 UHF command antenna
29 Navigational system gyro platform

30 Navigator's instrument console
31 Modular navigation system computer
32 Avionics equipment racks
33 Ventral pod integral fuel tank
34 MB-1C combined fuel and weapons pod
35 Mk 43 free fall nuclear weapon, wingroot pylon mounted
36 Pod integral munitions bay
37 Navigator's escape capsule
38 Navigator's entry hatch
39 TACAN aerial
40 Defensive electronics control module
41 Radar track breaking antennas
42 Radar warning antennas
43 Defensive system operator's escape hatch
44 Entry hatch
45 Forward fuselage integral fuel tank
46 Astro navigation tracker unit
47 Starboard main undercarriage, stowed position
48 Main undercarriage bay fairing
49 Starboard inboard engine nacelle

50 Nacelle pylon
51 Outboard engine nacelle
52 Outboard nacelle stub pylon
53 Starboard navigation light
54 Static dischargers
55 Outboard elevon
56 Linked inboard elevons
57 Mainwheel housing tail fairing
58 Centre fuselage integral fuel tank
59 Rear fuselage ventral equipment bay
60 Radar track breaker unit
61 Rear fuselage integral trim/balance fuel tank
62 Doppler transmitting antennas
63 Doppler electronics package
64 Doppler receiving antennas
65 Fin root attachment joint
66 Position indicating beacon transmitter
67 Rendezvous beacon transmitter

68 IFF transmitter
69 Multi-spar fin structure
70 Remote compass units
71 Anti-collision light
72 IFF aerial
73 Rendezvous beacon antenna
74 VOR localiser aerial
75 Static dischargers
76 Rudder
77 Position indicator transmitting antenna
78 Radar equipment module
79 Lower anti-collision light
80 Fire control radar antenna
81 Remotely controlled M61 20-mm Vulcan cannon
82 Cannon gimbal mounting
83 Fire control system tracking unit
84 Ammunition magazine, 1,120 rounds

85 Ventral brake parachute doors
86 Fuel jettison
87 Strike camera
88 Wingroot fillet fairing
89 Radar warning antenna
90 Port elevon panels
91 Elevon hydraulic actuators

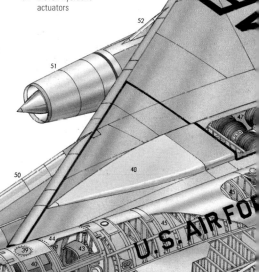

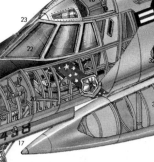

Fuel system

The B-58 employed a complex fuel system consisting of four main internal tanks. The forward tank occupied a section of the forward fuselage and the forward part of the wings, and held 3,202 US gal (12121 litres). The aft tank occupied the central fuselage and the aft part of the wing structure, and contained 6,122 US gal (23174 litres). The reservoir tank was situated in the fuselage just aft of the forward tank, and provided 640 US gal (2423 litres), while the balance tank was in the rear fuselage and contained 1,261 US gal (4773 litres). In addition to these figures must be added 4,314 US gal (16330 litres) for the MB-1C pod or 3,962 US gal (14998 litres) for the TCP. Due to centre of gravity considerations these capacities were not fully available to ground-filled aircraft, but could be used when inflight-refuelled. Indeed, a fully inflight-refuelled aircraft weighed more than the maximum permissible taxi weight.

Nav/bomb system

Due to the high speed and high altitude of the B-58, a complex nav/bomb system was required to provide the desired level of accuracy. Sperry Gyroscope integrated the various elements into the ASQ-42 system. Ground mapping was provided by a Raytheon Ku-band Doppler radar in the nose, which proved to be highly accurate. Under the rear fuselage were six antennas for the APN-113 downward-looking Doppler system which provided accurate ground velocity and drift information, while a Kollsman KS-39 astro-tracker was provided for celestial navigation. A radio altimeter provided accurate height information and inertial systems provided attitude/acceleration data. Systems for using both civil and military navigation aids were installed. The nav/bomb system was designed to provide great accuracy for long periods of time without radiation. Occasional use of search radar fixes against known features and altimeter readouts were used to update the system and refine its position.

Convair history

For the purpose of this article, the manufacturer which built the B-58 is referred to simply as Convair. However, the name 'Convair' was never officially assigned to an independent entity. It originated as the shortened nickname of Consolidated Vultee Aircraft, Inc., which was formed by the 17 March 1943 merger of Consolidated Aircraft Corporation of San Diego and the 'Vultee' company of Downey, California.

Consolidated was founded in 1923 by Reuben Hollis Fleet, and Vultee was actually the Aviation Corporation (AVCO). It was created by Errett Lobban Cord, who owned the Auburn, Cord and Duesenberg automobile companies as well as the Stinson Aircraft company. The namesake was that of designer and AVCO vice president Gerard Freebairn 'Jerry' Vultee, who was killed in a crash in 1938. The merger process began in 1941 with the purchase of Fleet's Consolidated stock by AVCO, and became final in 1943. Though widely used, the name 'Convair' was never officially registered by Consolidated Vultee Aircraft, Inc.

In April 1954, Consolidated Vultee Aircraft, Inc. was acquired by the two-year-old General Dynamics Corporation. General Dynamics then registered the name 'Convair' as the official name of the division that contained all of the former Consolidated Vultee assets. General Dynamics was created by John Jay Hopkins, a lawyer and financier who was president of the Electric Boat Company from 1947 to 1952, when he used the 53-year-old Electric Boat as the nucleus of the new enterprise, which also contained Canadair, Canada's leading aircraft manufacturer. Hopkins saw General Dynamics as a new kind of company deliberately designed and created not merely as a business, but as a national defence service to wage the Cold War more effectively. In an address to the Convair Astronautics Management Club in February 1959, Frank Pace Jr, President of the General Dynamics Corporation, spelled this out. "Convair men and women are among this nation's foremost contributors to the safety of the free world. We are involved in a 'chancy' business. We have to take chances to succeed. I see our efforts directed more toward competition with the USSR, which would destroy our way of life, than with other business firms. And we must pursue this problem of survival relentlessly. Where we are today is important. But where we are heading is even more important."

General Dynamics was a pioneer in the weapon system concept which provides for the design and production, not just of aircraft or ships or missiles, but of entire integrated weapon systems. Of the 63,000 workers who now took home a General Dynamics paycheck, 45,000 worked for the Convair Division. It was the Convair Division that built the B-58.

In 1995, General Dynamics officially closed the Convair Division and most of its original facilities in San Diego were torn down. General Dynamics sold the Fort Worth factory complex where the B-58 had been built – and where the F-16 Falcon was then in production – to Lockheed Martin.

MB-1C pod

The operational MB-1C pod contained a variable-yield W39Y1-1 nuclear warhead, as well as 4,172 US gal (15793 litres) of jet fuel in tanks placed at both ends of the pod for balance. In a strike mission, the bomber would draw fuel from this tank en route to the target, so that the whole unit could be dropped. This would leave the B-58 much lighter and capable of a fast exit from the target area. The MB-1C had a design weight of 2,500 lb (1134 kg), with the W39Y1-1 weighing an additional 6,050 lb (2744 kg) and the fuel tank having a maximum capacity of 27,537 lb (12491 kg). The pod was 57 ft (17.37 m) long, or nearly 60 percent of the length of the aircraft itself. It was attached with three hooks – one forward and two aft – and was released by pneumatic action to ensure clean separation. The fins of the pod were slightly offset so that it span during its trajectory. In the nosecone was equipment necessary to arm and fuze the weapon. Prior to launch the system was activated by the crew, a pitot tube being extended from the pod's nose. This provided a pressure source for the barometric arming system. The MB-1C pod suffered throughout its career from fuel leaking into the warhead section, leading to the hasty introduction of the TCP.

The MB-1C pod design served as the basis for several special pods. The LA-331 low-altitude photo-reconnaissance pod had a camera installed in the nosecone in place of the nuclear arming system. The pod retained its fuel capacity, but had ballast in place of the W39 warhead. This was required to maintain the correct centre of gravity. Other MB-1 pods were used for various test programmes, including downward-firing ejection seats and side-looking radars.

With the pod removed, the B-58's centre of gravity was critical on the ground. Aircraft parked in the 'return component' configuration thus usually had a weight added to either the nosewheel strut or forward pod connection point to prevent any inadvertent tipping back.

Two-component pod

Weighing 37,970 lb (17223 kg) fully loaded, the TCP (as carried by this aircraft) was actually two separate pods. The TCP's BLU-2/B-2 lower fuel tank component was 54 ft (16.45 m) long and 5 ft (1.52 m) in diameter. It weighed 1,900 lb (862 kg) empty and accommodated 24,100 lb (10932 kg) of fuel in two sections separated by a bulkhead. The BLU-2/B-1 upper section also carried some fuel along with a variable-yield BA53-Y1 (Mk 53) nuclear weapon. This component weighed 11,970 lb (5430 kg) fully fuelled and 7,700 lb (3493 kg) with just the weapon. Designed to conform to the convex surface of the lower pod, the BLU-2/B-1 was 35 ft (10.67 m) in length and 3 ft 6 in (1.07 m) in diameter.

When all the fuel in the lower component had been consumed, it was discarded. It was attached to the upper component by single connections fore and aft. The single fin at the extreme tail was attached to the underside of the aircraft and served as a fulcrum point about which the pod rotated during release. The much lighter B-58 then continued to bomb release point, where the upper component was released. On release the upper component deployed a ventral fin to aid stability during its ballistic trajectory. Like the MB-1C, this had a pitot tube in the nose which served the bomb's arming/fuzing system. The Mk 53 warhead had more varied fuzing options than the W39. As the lower component neared its intended target, the rear-section fuel tank was discarded, leaving the forward portion, with warhead and associated equipment, to continue its free fall. Fuzing options included impact or, more usually, a low-altitude air burst.

Crew accommodation

The three-man crew sat in tandem, although the pilot's seat was offset to port for optimum forward vision. There were crawlways between the cockpits, although that between the pilot and the navigator/bombardier's station was used only for maintenance. Early Hustlers (and TB-58s) used the SACseat, a conventional ejection seat designed by Convair and first tested on the ground in February 1956. This seat was optimised for crew comfort on long-endurance sorties, but required the crew to wear MC-2/3 partial pressure suits for high-altitude missions. The parachute was contained in a back pack, while the seat pan contained rudimentary survival gear.

It was realised at an early stage that the SACseat offered insufficient protection for the crew at the B-58's operational speed and altitude, leading to the development of the escape capsule by Stanley Aviation. On initiation of the ejection sequence, shutters stowed above the head extended to enclose the occupant in a pressurised environment, offering complete protection against the supersonic blast and the effects of high altitude. Each capsule had a small window in front of the occupant's face to provide some outside visibility, and before the shutters closed the knees had to be brought up to allow the shutters to completely enclose the seat. The capsule was stabilised during ejection by a drogue chute and automatically deployed its main recovery chute. The pilot's capsule differed from the others by having the flight control column enclosed. This allowed him to maintain control of the aircraft in an emergency situation with the capsule fully closed. The pilot's capsule was mounted on slightly canted rails to counter the offset position of his seat. To soften landing, the capsule had crushable cylinders and collapsible strakes. Once on the ground, the capsule provided shelter and contained a comprehensive survival kit with plenty of food and equipment. In the case of a water landing, flotation bags were inflated to allow the capsule to function as a liferaft. The capsule could be used at any altitude, but required 100 kt (185 km/h) airspeed.

Ground tests of the capsule began in 1959, and later air drops were made from a North American T-28 and a Boeing B-47. Tests with B-58s began in October 1961, using 55-0661. These began with high-speed taxi ejections, followed by subsonic inflight ejections. At first the capsule was ejected empty from the second crew station. In January 1962 a chimpanzee was successfully ejected in a subsonic test, leading to the first human test on 28 February. In March the first supersonic tests were successfully undertaken, using a small bear as passenger. The Stanley capsules were fitted across the operational B-58A fleet. Meanwhile, 55-0661 continued its ejection seat trials, using an MB-1 pod modified to carry downward-firing ejection seats.

Markings

Operational B-58s were universally left in natural metal finish apart from the black nosecone and anti-glare panel ahead of the windshield. Smaller black dielectric panels covered antennas in the fin and wingroots. SAC's 'Milky Way' sash usually adorned the forward fuselage, with the command badge to port and wing badge to starboard. This aircraft also features the winged '2' to denote assignment to the 2nd Air Force. National insignia were usually worn on the forward fuselage sides (located lower down on the TB-58As) and above the port wing. The MB-1C and TCP pods were usually painted in silver. Many of the B-58s were given nicknames.

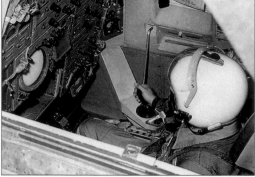

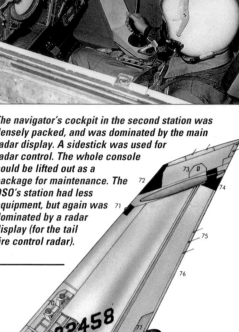

The front cockpit of the TB-58A (above) was similar to that of the operational aircraft. However, the second (instructor's) cockpit (below) was less well-equipped. The flight controls in both cockpits were linked.

The Stanley escape capsule provided protection in high-speed, high-altitude ejections and could function as a makeshift shelter or liferaft (above). The capsule was first fitted to 61-2062 (below). Sadly it could not save the three crew members who perished in the aircraft in a post take-off crash in June 1968.

The navigator's cockpit in the second station was densely packed, and was dominated by the main radar display. A sidestick was used for radar control. The whole console could be lifted out as a package for maintenance. The DSO's station had less equipment, but again was dominated by a radar display (for the tail fire control radar).

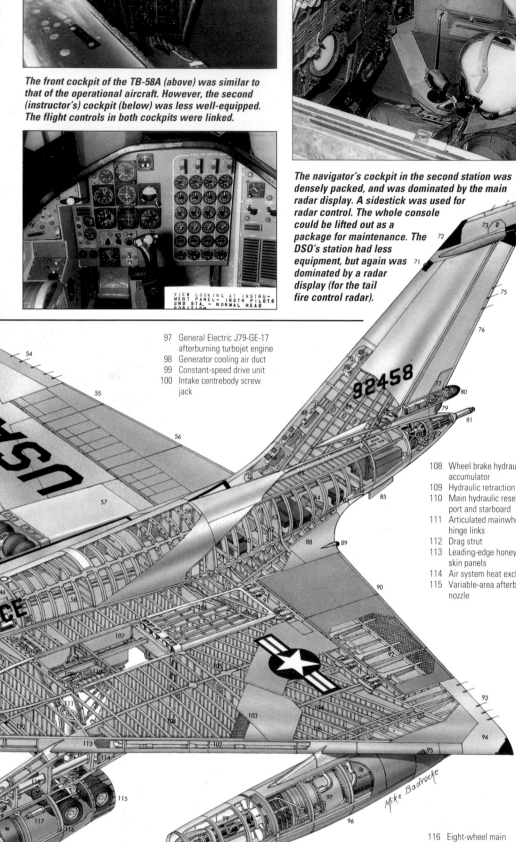

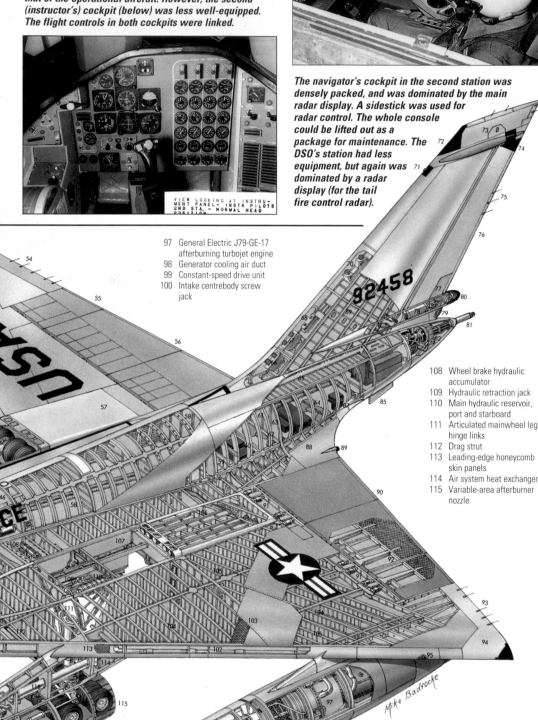

97 General Electric J79-GE-17 afterburning turbojet engine
98 Generator cooling air duct
99 Constant-speed drive unit
100 Intake centrebody screw jack

108 Wheel brake hydraulic accumulator
109 Hydraulic retraction jack
110 Main hydraulic reservoir, port and starboard
111 Articulated mainwheel leg hinge links
112 Drag strut
113 Leading-edge honeycomb skin panels
114 Air system heat exchanger
115 Variable-area afterburner nozzle

92 Honeycomb trailing-edge panels
93 Static dischargers
94 Fixed wing tip segment
95 Port navigation light
96 Port outboard engine nacelle

101 Moveable intake centre body
102 Leading-edge bleed air ducting
103 Honeycomb wing skin panels

104 Multi-spar wing panel construction
105 Port wing integral fuel tank bays
106 Chaff stowage/launch chutes
107 Port main undercarriage wheel bay

116 Eight-wheel main undercarriage bogie
117 Afterburner nozzle control jack
118 Heat exchanger air ducting
119 Engine bleed air ducting
120 Inboard J79-GE-17 engine
121 Hinged lower cowling panels
122 Intake ducting
123 Intake bleed air duct
124 Variable-area engine intake

Mike Badrocke

B-58A Specifications

Powerplant: four General Electric J79-GE-5A or -5B engines rated at 9,700 lb (43.16 kN) of continuous thrust, with a maximum thrust rating of 15,600 lb (69.42 kN) with afterburning

Performance
cruising speed: 611 mph (983 km/h)
design maximum speed: Mach 0.9 (below 25,000 ft/7620 m) or Mach 2 (at 40,000 ft/12192 m)
structural integrity maximum speed: Mach 2.2 (for short intervals)
unrefuelled ferry range: 4,715 miles (7588 km)
cruising altitude: 38,450 ft (11720 m)
target area altitude: 55,900 ft (17040 m)
combat ceiling: 63,400 ft (19324 m)

Weights (B-58A)
empty: 55,560 lb (25202 kg)
empty, with MB-1C pod: 64,115 lb (29083 kg)
maximum gross: 176,890 lb (80237 kg)

Weights (TB-58A)
empty: 52,400 lb (23769 kg)
maximum gross: 158,000 lb (71669 kg)

Dimensions
span: 56 ft 9.9 in (17.32 m)
length: 96 ft 9.4 in (29.50 m)
fuselage height (at pilot's hatch cover): 13 ft 9 in (4.19 m)
tail height: 29 ft 11.1 in (9.12 m)
wing area (less elevons): 1,364.69 sq ft (126.78 m²)
total wing area: 1,542.53 sq ft (143.30 m²)

Armament
Offensive: MB-1C weapons pod with a W39Y1-1 nuclear weapon; or a two-component 'TCP' pod with a BA53-Y1 nuclear weapon; and/or four Mk 43 or Mk 61 nuclear bombs outside the pod on underfuselage hardpoints
Defensive: General Electric T-171E (M61) six-barrelled 20-mm rotary cannon

B-58 Hustler weapons

Above: 59-2456 shows the B-58's principal weapons in its later career: the TCP (with BA53-Y1 warhead in the upper component), four Mk 43 laydown weapons and the T-171E-3 tail gun. The latter could be removed as a package, complete with the MD-7 fire control radar.

Left: 59-2435 Shackbuster was one of two TCP trials aircraft. This view emphasises the hollow in the lower component into which the upper component snugly fitted. Both this aircraft and the one above were used during the multi-weapon (Mk 43) drop trials in late 1961 and 1962.

Left: The MB-1C was the standard single-component free-fall pod. Many of the early pods were instrumented for trial drops.

Right: The first pod envisaged for the B-58 was the MA-1C, which had small wings, nose-mounted control fins, folding ventral fin and pop-up dorsal fin. It was rocket-powered, giving the B-58 a stand-off capability of up to 160 miles (257 km).

The B-58 had never attracted the loyalty and support enjoyed by other aircraft types, despite its capabilities. When the end came, the fleet was dispatched to the 'boneyard' with almost unseemly haste. An unavoidable issue was the huge cost – it was no exaggeration to say the aircraft had cost more than their weight in gold, and the running costs of two B-58 wings would have kept six B-52 wings in the air.

Freshly arrived for processing, B-58s line a taxiway at Davis-Monthan AFB in January 1970. The aircraft were stripped of engines and other useful parts, Spraylatted and parked out in the desert.

Only four intact aircraft escaped the 'Boneyard'. Three were dispersed to be preserved as museum pieces, being flown to Strategic Air Command headquarters at Offutt AFB, Nebraska, Chanute AFB, Illinois and the Air Force Museum at Wright-Patterson AFB, Ohio. The fourth remained at Grissom AFB as a permanent static display.

Two abandoned B-58 hulks that were deemed not to be worth moving also remained behind. One was a damaged aircraft at Little Rock AFB that was written off as not worth repairing, and the other was a discarded Air Research & Development Command test aircraft at Edwards AFB.

For nearly six years, the bulk of the Hustler fleet rested in the high and dry Arizona desert, each aircraft theoretically ready to be restored to flying condition. Finally, in October 1976, the Defense Department officially sold them for scrap metal value at a sealed-bid scrap auction. The fleet lasted through the winter before finally being cut up between May and August 1977 by Tucson-based Southwest Alloys.

Two of the 'Boneyard' B-58s sold at the scrap auction were saved. One – interestingly, the last Hustler ever built – was purchased by the Pima County Air Museum. This private organisation located adjacent to Davis-Monthan AFB is dedicated to preserving an example of each aircraft type that passes through the 'Boneyard'. The other was transported back to where it started, to become part of the permanent collection of the Southwest Aerospace Museum at Fort Worth.

This writer recalls having heard a story told at an Air Force function in Washington, DC in the early 1980s which, if true, would thicken the plot of the B-58 disposition. The probably apocryphal tale was that when the Reagan administration took office in 1980, the incoming Defense Department under Secretary Caspar Weinberger considered bringing the B-58 fleet out of retirement and retrofitting them with turbofan engines to augment the planned B-1B fleet. It was only after the plan won official approval that it was discovered the previous administration had already disposed of the Hustlers.

Today, the six aircraft that were intentionally preserved still remain, and the hulk at Little Rock AFB was moved to Barksdale AFB in Louisiana for restoration. The only theoretically flyable B-58 is the one located at the Air Force Museum, where an effort is made to maintain all aircraft in perfect, ready-to-fly condition. It has not, however, been flown in many decades, and it almost certainly will never undergo so much as an engine run-up. This aircraft is of particular note, being the specific B-58A to have won the Bendix Trophy.

These seven aircraft and one derelict are all that remain of one of aviation history's truly legendary aircraft.

Bill Yenne

Eight Hustlers escaped the scrapman's torch, of which six are on museum display. This aircraft is one of two TB-58As to have survived, and now guards the gate at Grissom AFB, Indiana. It was retained by the base for display after the rest of the fleet had been dispatched to Davis-Monthan. The other TB-58A was rescued from 'D-M' and was transported by C-5 Galaxy back to Fort Worth.

Right: Without doubt the best example remaining of a B-58 is the USAF Museum's 59-2458, restored to virtual airworthy condition. It was the machine which was used for the Bendix Trophy-winning transcontinental speed record.

Hustlers – the final reckoning

Crashed	21	Scrapped	82
Lost in ground accidents	4*	Museum display	6
Destroyed in fatigue testing	1	Derelict	2

* a fifth damaged B-58 often listed as lost was repaired and put back into operation

The B-58 was the ultimate expression of the conventional delta wing, and while it enjoyed the great benefits of the concept (structural sturdiness, low thickness:chord ratio and high sweepback for low supersonic drag, and high internal fuel volume), it also suffered from the drawbacks (high landing and take-off speeds, high energy bleed in turns, trim/controllability problems at low speed, and lack of stability in the rolling plane). Only much later, with the advent of fly-by-wire control of unstable deltas in designs such as the Mirage 2000, were these drawbacks largely overcome. A feature of the Hustler, obvious in this view, was its 'wasp waist' area-ruled fuselage, adopted to reduce transonic drag.

AIR RESEARCH & DEVELOPMENT COMMAND

Although the US Air Force's Air Research & Development Command was deeply involved in the early development of the B-58, the programme was not officially turned over to the Air Force by Convair until January 1958, more than a year after the aircraft's first flight. For the next two years, the B-58 programme was administered jointly by a board that included representatives of Air Research & Development Command, Strategic Air Command and Air Materiel Command.

Over the years, the US Air Force and its predecessor organisations have vacillated over the issue of having both their logistics and supply activities, as well as their research and development activities, combined into a single major command. The functions were originally separate, but were merged into the Materiel Division of the US Army Air Corps when the latter was created in 1926, and remained as such when the Air Corps became the US Army Air Forces (USAAF). In 1941, immediately after the United States entered World War II, they were separated as the Air Technical Service Command and the Air Service Command. These, in turn, were merged into a single Air Materiel Command in 1944, and it remained as such when the USAAF became the US Air Force in 1947. Air Research & Development Command was officially created in February 1950 when the research and testing function was spun off from Air Materiel Command. The activities of both agencies spread across the globe, but were centred at Wright Field (later Wright-Patterson AFB), near Dayton, Ohio. As a practical matter, the two commands worked together closely and many of their activities overlapped, although the attention of Air Materiel Command was focussed primarily on providing support for aircraft after they had been 'researched and developed'.

As the US Air Force developed new aircraft during the 1950s, the Air Research & Development Command was the agency doing the developing, although this work was always done on behalf of an operational command that would be the ultimate 'customer' for the aircraft. In the case of the B-58, Strategic Air Command was the ultimate customer, but Air Research & Development Command had the job of running the programme on behalf of the end user until the B-58 was ready for operational use. Theoretically, new aircraft were 'owned' by Air Research &

By the time that ARDC became Air Force Systems Command in April 1961, there were few Hustlers left in the test/trials fleet. One was TB-58A 55-0662, seen here with the AFSC badge on the nose.

Development Command from their earliest conceptual stage through at least a portion of flight testing. In general terms, it can be said that Air Research & Development Command operated the aircraft with 'X' and 'Y' prefixes, and these prefixes were dropped as the aircraft were ready to go to work for the end user.

During the development and test phase, it was not necessarily a foregone conclusion that an operational command would ultimately assume a programme, even if it was being developed to meet a specific requirement defined by an operational command. If the need was not being met, an operational command would not necessarily sign on. A great many aircraft were built and tested, but neither deployed nor put into production; this was especially true in the 1950s. Such aircraft spent their entire lives with Air Research & Development Command.

Between January 1958 and August 1960, Air Force B-58 operations were officially assigned to the 6592nd Test Squadron, which was jointly 'owned and operated' by Air Research & Development Command and Strategic Air Command. On 1 August 1960, all B-58 operations, including Category II and III evaluations, were officially transferred to Strategic Air Command.

In April 1961, Air Research & Development Command became Air Force Systems Command, while Air Materiel Command became Air Force Logistics Command. In 1992, the two merged to form Air Force Materiel Command – an entity that had the equivalent function of the pre-1950 Air Materiel Command.

One Hustler, a YB-58 (55-0665), remained with Air Research & Development Command/Air Force Systems Command when the rest of the programme was officially turned over to Strategic Air Command. It was employed in testing systems intended for use in the operational fleet, as well as systems intended for other supersonic aircraft programmes. The latter included the AN/ASG-18 fire control radar and AIM-47 air-to-air missile, as well as other systems intended for use in the North American Aviation XF-108 and the Lockheed YF-12. This aircraft was abandoned, its engines removed, on the Edwards AFB range, where it still remains, resting in a sea of sagebrush.

58-1015 Ginger is seen during its time at Edwards AFB. It carries ARDC's badge on the nose, under which is the legend 'Air Force Flight Test Center'. On the fin is the shield of the 6512th Test Wing. Forward of the ARDC badge is a logo consisting of a Hustler silhouette and the words 'Flight Test'.

STRATEGIC AIR COMMAND

The B-58 was tailored specifically to the mission of Strategic Air Command, which was formed in March 1946 to operate and manage all USAAF (US Air Force after September 1947) strategic assets. The US Air Force never considered any other operational command for the B-58. SAC assumed executive responsibility for the B-58 programme on 1 August 1960. This event was to have occurred during 1959, but the high accident rate in 1959 and early 1960 led to the delay.

Reductions in the number of B-58s delivered to the command accompanied the delays to the programme. On 11 June 1959, the Air Force announced that it planned to purchase 290 B-58s: including the 30 pre-

Rise and decline of operational B-58s in the SAC inventory

Date	No. of B-58s	Proportion of bomber force
December 1960	19	1.0 percent
December 1961	66	4.0 percent
December 1962	76	4.5 percent
December 1963	86	5.7 percent
December 1964	94	7.8 percent
December 1965	93	11.5 percent
December 1966	83	12.0 percent
December 1967	81	12.1 percent
December 1968	76	11.6 percent
December 1969	41	7.5 percent
December 1970	0	0 percent

production and test aircraft, this number would have allowed for five operational Strategic Air Command bomb wings. In December 1959, the total number was reduced to 148 in three wings, and ultimately only 116 aircraft were built. At various points in the planning, varying numbers of operational wings were discussed, but just two wings of three squadrons each became B-58 operators. Each wing was allocated around 40 aircraft (squadron assignment was 12). SAC's commander, General Thomas Power, reportedly wanted a third wing established at Little Rock AFB in Arkansas, and planning proceeded accordingly. However, the wing that was activated there was moved from Carswell AFB, Texas, rather than being a new wing.

3958TH OPERATIONAL TEST AND EVALUATION SQUADRON

Technically the first Strategic Air Command unit to have any contact with the Hustler programme, the 3958th was created at Carswell AFB, which was located directly across the runway from the Convair Fort Worth factory where the Hustlers were being built. The squadron was activated in March 1958, more than a year after the B-58's first flight, but two years before the first delivery of the Hustler to an operational

unit. The unit in turn became the 3958th Combat Crew Training Squadron and was officially absorbed by the 43rd Bombardment Wing in March 1960.

Delivery of operational B-58s to SAC got under way in 1960. At this point the work of the 3958th OT&ES came to an end. The squadron had overseen the pre-operational training effort.

43RD BOMBARDMENT WING

In March 1960, the 43rd Bombardment Wing, then commanded by Colonel James K. Johnson, became the first operational unit to receive the B-58. The 43rd, which had been at Davis-Monthan AFB near Tucson, Arizona, was deliberately relocated to Carswell AFB to be close to the Convair Fort Worth factory.

The 43rd was originally formed in November 1940 as the 43rd Bombardment Group, with the 63rd, 64th and 65th Bombardment Squadrons and the 13th Reconnaissance Squadron assigned to it. Activated in January 1941 at Langley Field, Virginia, its wartime activities began nearly a year later and consisted of patrol missions along the Eastern Seaboard. Between February and August 1942, the assigned squadrons were sent to the Pacific Theatre piecemeal, and the group became active as a B-17 unit within the Fifth Air Force in the autumn of 1942. The group took part in many important actions, including the Battle of the Bismarck Sea in 1943, and earned numerous awards, including the Philippines Presidential Citation.

Disbanded after World War II, the 43rd Bombardment Wing was re-established at Davis-Monthan AFB on 3 November 1947 as the 43rd Bombardment Wing, Very Heavy, a designation implying that it operated Boeing B-29 Superfortresses. On 1 August 1948, as the B-29 was redesignated as a medium bomber, the 43rd was reactivated as a Bombardment Wing, Medium. Subsequently, Boeing B-50 'Super'

Superfortresses and Boeing B-47 Stratojets were also assigned. It is worth noting that the 43rd Bombardment Wing 'owned' the B-50, *Lucky Lady II*, which made the first non-stop, round-the-word flight in 1949.

Initially, the 43rd Bombardment Wing was assigned to the Eighth Air Force, but it was transferred to the Fifteenth Air Force in April 1950. Both of these Air Forces were components of Strategic Air Command.

Technically, the 43rd Bombardment Wing was used by SAC for strategic bombardment training, a function that continued as the wing made the transition to Hustlers. The proximity to the Convair factory made sense in this context. From March 1960 to July 1961, the wing conducted Category II and III evaluations of B-58s – including the TB-58s and RB-58s – while operating a

combat crew training school to train Strategic Air Command aircrews in Hustler operations. The evaluations continued until July 1962, at which time the 43rd Bombardment Wing became operational in support of SAC's strategic bombing mission. This continued until January 1970. The wing moved from Carswell AFB to Little Rock AFB, Arkansas in September 1964, where it remained until B-58 operations were terminated six years later.

The 43rd Bombardment Wing had always had aerial refuelling components assigned to it, but it later operated primarily in that role. The wing was inactivated as a bomb wing at the end of January 1970 when the B-58s were withdrawn from service. However, it was reactivated in April 1970 as an aerial refuelling wing and designated as

59-2444 Lucky Lady V *continued a 43rd BW tradition in having an aircraft bearing this name. It displays the unit badge on its starboard side. The blue and yellow design incorporated a falling bomb. The wing's motto was 'Willing, Able, Ready'.*

the 43rd Strategic Wing. As such, it replaced the 3960th Strategic Wing at Andersen AFB, Guam, flying KC-135s in support of B-52 Arc Light bombing operations in Southeast Asia.

During the 1960s, the 43rd's three original bomb squadrons – the 63rd 'Sea Hawks', the 64th and the 65th 'Lucky Dicers' – were all operational as medium (B-58) bomb squadrons. A fourth wartime squadron, the 403rd 'Mareeba Butchers' Bombardment Squadron, was never a B-58 unit.

305TH BOMBARDMENT WING

The 305th Bombardment Wing received its first B-58 in May 1961, 14 months after the first Hustler was delivered to the 43rd Bombardment Wing.

The 305th Bombardment Wing originated during World War II as the 305th Bombardment Group, which was activated at Salt Lake City Army Air Base, Utah in March 1942. After training at various locations in the United States, the 305th was sent to England in September 1942 as a B-17 heavy bomber component of the USAAF Eighth Air Force. Its first mission against the enemy came on 17 November. The commander of the 305th through May 1943 was Colonel Curtis LeMay, who later, as a four-star general, would command Strategic Air Command at the time the B-58s were assigned to the 305th. The group's wartime bases were at Grafton Underwood and Chelveston in southern England. In July 1945, the 305th was transferred to the Ninth Air Force and moved to St Trond, Belgium, where it was involved in the Project Casey Jones aerial mapping survey of Europe and North Africa. It was officially inactivated on Christmas 1946.

The 305th was re-established as a medium bomb wing on 20 December 1950 and activated two weeks later at MacDill AFB, Florida for the purpose of training B-29 crews for operations in Korea. Conversion to an operational B-47 unit began late in 1952, and the wing made three overseas deployments to Europe and North Africa through 1957 as part of Strategic Air Command's demonstrations of global readiness. In June 1959, the wing's home base was relocated to Bunker Hill AFB (known as Grissom AFB after May 1968) in Indiana.

After 1961, in addition to flying B-58s as part of SAC's strategic bombing mission, the 305th Bombardment Wing also operated a combat crew training school with TB-58s.

In 1966, the 3rd Airborne Command & Control Squadron was attached to operate EC-135s in the Post Attack Command & Control System (PACCS) mission. These aircraft would have had the grisly task of conducting the post-mortem in the event of a B-58 strategic attack against the Soviet Union.

As with the 43rd Bombardment Wing, the 305th was relieved of its B-58s and its strategic bombing mission in January 1970. Also like its sister

305th Hustlers are represented here by a TB-58A (right) and TCP-carrying B-58A (below). In the 'Hoosier Hustler' era the wing badge consisted of a winged bomb, but was later changed to a KC-135's refuelling boom to reflect the post-1970 mission. The motto was short and to the point – 'Can Do'.

wing, the 305th had operated an aerial refuelling component to support its B-58 operations, and this became the wing's primary focus after the bombers were retired. However, the PACCS mission continued as the 305th became the 305th Air Refueling Wing in January 1970.

The three medium (B-58) bomb squadrons within the 305th

Bombardment Wing during the 1960s had originated with the 305th Bombardment Group during World War II as heavy (B-17) bomb squadrons. They were the 364th Bombardment Squadron, the 365th Bombardment Squadron and the 366th Bombardment Squadron. Another wartime unit, the 422nd Bombardment Squadron, was never a B-58 unit.

'Impending Danger West'

The Luftwaffe's response to the D-Day landings

By mid-May 1944 the two resident Western Front jagdgeschwader (JG 2 and JG 26) were scattered around airfields all over France. Kommandeur of JG 26, 'Pips' Priller, warned his superiors of such folly at a time of immenent danger, however his fears were ignored. Weeks later these underequipped and underprepared units were to face the might of Allied air power over the fields of Normandy.

When reconnaissance pilot Leutnant Adalbert Bärwolf of 3./NAGr 13 lifted off from his Laval base shortly after first light on the morning of 6 June 1944, he was not sure what he was going to find. For the last two hours reports had been trickling in to Gruppe HQ at Chartres of enemy airborne landings close to the mouth of the River Orne northeast of Caen in Normandy. A precautionary Stage II Alert had been transmitted to all Luftwaffe units in the area. At 04.30 Bärwolf and his wingman, Obergefreiter Maurer, were ordered to 'fly up there and have a look.'

As the two Bf 109G-8 reconnaissance fighters raced northwards at 280 mph (450 km/h) low across the Normandy countryside rain beat against their armoured windscreens. Shortly before Caen Bärwolf signalled to Maurer to jettison their ventral fuel tanks and the pair sank lower still, barely brushing the treetops as the city slid by on their right. A slight turn to starboard, across the twin streams of the Orne canal and river, and there, littering the meadow beyond, was the confirmation they were seeking: the abandoned carcasses of well over a

hundred enemy assault gliders.

Bärwolf captured the incredible scene with his two wing cameras; the drab camouflage of the gliders compromised by their strikingly unfamiliar black and white stripes. Then, pushing the throttles to the firewall to escape the attentions of patrolling Allied fighters, the two G-8s roared out over the estuary at more than 375 mph (600 km/h). Looming out of the murk just off the coast another sight met their eyes – a flotilla of some 40 to 50 ships of all shapes and sizes; destroyers, transports and landing craft. There could be little doubt. This had to be the long expected invasion!

So why, Bärwolf demanded after the pair's return to Laval, was the General Alarm not sounded? This was the question General der Jagdflieger Adolf Galland was also asking. It is now known that the German armoured divisions in the west, whose early intervention might have proved decisive, had not moved against the Allied beachheads because they were strictly forbidden to do so without the express permission of the Commander-in-Chief of the armed forces, Adolf Hitler. And the Führer was a notoriously

Top: Calm before the storm: the relaxed nature of the armourer, with ordnance lying around him, and the fact that this III./SG 4 Fw 190A-7 is exposed on the airfield at St Quentin-Clastres, date this photograph in the weeks preceding D-Day. The armourer is seen tightening the locking ring of one of the bomb's two fuses.

Above: Representative of the fate of many Luftwaffe fighters in the weeks following D-day, this Fw 190 is caught on the gun film of a pursuing Allied fighter. More used to countering the high-altitude threat of US Eighth Air Force bombers, the jagdgruppen were underprepared for low-level combat over the fields of Normandy. Some 100 Bf 109s and Fw 190s were lost in two days alone (7 and 12 June), with 48 pilots being posted as missing or killed in action.

Above: Soon to be a luxury of the past, Major Erich Hohagen, Gruppenkommandeur of I./JG 2, having arrived at dispersal in his own staff car (wearing the Kommandeur's pennant) conducts a leisurely warm-up of his Fw 190A-6 before another sortie. After D-day the Luftwaffe's fighters sought the protective camouflage of trees and specially erected nets.

Right: As commander of JG 26, Oberstleutnant Josef 'Pips' Priller (on right) was one of the two pilots who strafed Sword beach on the morning of D-day. He is seen here in the spring of 1944 showing his Fw 190 (carrying personal markings beneath the cockpit) to Generalfeldmarschall Erwin Rommel, who had by this time assumed responsibility for the defence of northern France.

late riser. He had gone to bed at the Berghof, his Alpine mountain retreat, at 3 a.m. – nearly three hours after the first British paratroops began to descend over the Orne. But his adjutants were reluctant to rouse him on the strength of 'unconfirmed reports'. It was not until 10 a.m. that he was finally woken.

The Luftwaffe was under no such constraint. Here the delay was caused by Generalfeldmarschall Hugo Sperrle, the GOC of Luftflotte 3, who was still undecided as to whether or not this was the invasion proper. After all, had not the Führer himself declared that any attempt at an invasion would almost certainly be preceded by feint landings elsewhere to draw attention away from the actual area of assault (which many members of the German High Command remained convinced would be in the Pas de Calais). By mid-morning, however, any lingering doubts had been dispelled and Sperrle finally authorised the sending of 'Dr. Gustav West'.

'**Dr G**ustav **W**est' was the code signal for '**Dr**ohende **G**efahr **W**est' ('Impending Danger West'). Its transmission to Luftwaffe units throughout the Reich and beyond was to set in motion long-laid plans for the large-scale reinforcement of Luftflotte 3, the command which controlled all Luftwaffe units stationed in occupied western Europe.

Fighters fly west

The bulk of the aircraft involved in this mass transfer would be single-engined fighters: 19 jagdgruppen in all, plus a further two staffeln and five geschwaderstäbe (HQ staffs) – a strength on paper of well over 900 machines. The importance attached to combatting the Allied invasion of France may be gauged from the fact that this movement all but denuded the Defence of the Reich organisation of its entire day-fighter strength.

In addition, two geschwaderstäbe and eight gruppen of night-fighters, one stab and two gruppen of ground-attack aircraft, five gruppen of bombers and two staffeln of reconnaissance machines were also earmarked for transfer to Sperrle's Luftflotte 3.

To accommodate this sudden influx the Luftwaffe had some 100 airfields and landing strips available within a radius of approximately 300 miles (500 km) from the invasion beaches. These were located mainly inland, in a broad swathe stretching from the Netherlands to the French Biscay coast. At the army's insistence most of the airfields along, and on, the Channel coast – which the Luftwaffe had occupied during its heydays of 1940-41 – had been rendered unusable. They were regarded as being too vulnerable to air and sea bombardment and would be at risk of early capture and use by the enemy in the event of invasion.

At first Luftwaffe chief Hermann Göring had favoured the construction of what he termed 'Luftwaffe Fortresses'. These were to be modelled on the RAF's bases on Malta (which had

Luftflotte 3 Order of Battle – as of 25 May 1944

Unit	Base	Type	Allocated/ In service
DIRECTLY SUBORDINATE UNITS			
Stab FAGr 123	Toussus le Buc	Ju 188, Ju 88, Fw 190	-/-
4.(F)/123	Cherbourg	Bf 109	10 – 6
5.(F)/123	Monchy-Breton	Bf 109, Fw 190	12 – 6
1.(F)/121	Toussus le Buc	Me 410	6 – 2
Sond.Aufkl. St 123 *(1)*	Paris-Orly	Ar 240, Ju 88	-/-
II. FLIEGERKORPS (Compiègne)			
Stab NAGr 13	Dinard	Bf 109, Fw 190	4 – 3
1./NAGr 13	Dinard	Bf 109, Fw 190	14 – 9
3./NAGr 13	Laval	Bf 109, Fw 190	15 – 10
III./SG 4 (exc 9.)	St Quentin-Clastres	Fw 190	40 – 27
IX. FLIEGERKORPS (Beauvais-Tille)			
3.(F)/122	Soesterberg	Ju 188, Ju 88	10 – 4
6.(F)/123 *(2)*	Cormeilles	Ju 188, Ju 88	5 – 0
Stab KG 2	Zeist	Ju 188	2 – 1
I./KG 2	Hesepe	(re-equipping)	-/-
II./KG 2	Münster-Handorf	Ju 188	9 – 6
III./KG 2	Achmer	Do 217	7 – 4
Stab KG 6	Melsbroek	Ju 188/Ju 88	1 – 0
I./KG 6	Bretigny	(re-equipping)	-/-
II./KG 6	Le Culot	Ju 88	5 – 4
III./KG 6	Ahlhorn	Ju 88	15 – 11
I./SKG 10	Rosières	Fw 190	35 – 17
Eins.St.KG 101 *(3)*	Couvron	-	3 – 2
Stab KG 30	Zwischenahn	Ju 88	1 – 1
II./ KG 30	Zwischenahn	Ju 88	3 – 1
III./KG 30	Varel	Ju 88	5 – 3
Stab KG 51	Dreux	Me 410	-/-
I./KG 51	St André, Dreux, Evreux	Me 410	-/-
II./KG 51	Soesterberg, Eindhoven	Me 410	23 – 18
Stab KG 54	Marx	Ju 88	2 – 1
I./KG 54	Wittmundhafen	Ju 88	8 – 4
III./KG 54	Marx	Ju 88	8 – 8
I./KG 66 (exc 3.)	Avord	Ju 188	16 – 3
X. FLIEGERKORPS (Angers)			
Stab FAGr 5	Mont de Marsan	Ju 290	
1./FAGr 5	Mont de Marsan	Ju 290	14 – 5
2./FAGr 5	Mont de Marsan	Ju 290	
4.(F)/5 *(2)*	Nantes	Do 217, He 111	3 – 1
3.(F)/123	Rennes	Ju 88	9 – 4
1.(F)/SAGr 129	Biscarosse	Bv 222	2 – 1
Stab KG 40	Bordeaux-Mérignac	Fw 200	-/-
I./KG 40 (exc 3.)	Orléans-Bricy	He 177	23 – 8
II./KG 40	Bordeaux-Mérignac	He 177	30 – 11
III./KG 40	St Jean d'Angely, Cognac	Fw 200	-/-
2. Fliegerdivision (Montfrin)			
1.(F)/33	St Martin	Ju 188, Ju 88	6 – 4
2./NAGr 13	Cuers	Bf 109, Fw 190	12 – 9
2./SAGr 128	Berre	Ar 196	14 – 8
9./SG 4	Le Luc	Fw 190	-/-
III./KG 26 (LT) *(4)*	Montpellier, Valence	Ju 88	35 – 19
Stab KG 77	Salon	Ju 88	1 – 0
I./KG 77(LT) *(4)*	Orange-Caritat	Ju 88	27 – 19
III./KG 77(LT) *(4)*	Orange-Caritat	Ju 88	23 – 13
4. & 6./KG 76	Istres	Ju 88	11 – 5
6./KG 100	Lezignan	Do 217	8 – 4
III./KG 100 (exc 8.)	Toulouse-Francazals	Do 217, He 177	29 – 11
II. JAGDKORPS (Chantilly)			
4. Fliegerdivision (Metz)			
(Jafü 4/St.Pol-Bryas)			
Luftbeob.St 4 *(5)*	Juvincourt	(forming)	-/-
Stab JG 26	Lille-Nord	Fw 190	3 – 2
I./ JG 26	Vendeville, Denain, Lille-Nord	Fw 190	39 – 22
III./JG 26	Nancy, Lupcourt	Bf 109	58 – 36
6./JG 26	St Dizier	(re-equipping)	-/-
Stab NJG 4	Chenay	Bf 110	1 – 1
I./NJG 4	Florennes	Ju 88, Bf 110	23 – 10
III./NJG 4	Juvincourt	Bf 110, Do 217	18 – 11
I./NJG 5	St Dizier	Bf 110, Me 410	11 – 8
III./NJG 5	Athies-sous-Laon	Bf 110, Do 217	14 – 11
5. Jagddivision (Jouy en Jousas)			
(Jafü 5/Bernay)			
Stab JG 2	Creil	Fw 190	6 – 2
I./JG 2	Cormeilles	Fw 190	32 – 16
II./ JG 2	Creil	Bf 109	51 – 23
III./JG 2 *(6)*	Cormeilles	Fw 190	26 – 14
II./NJG 4	Coulommiers	Bf 110, Do 217	19 – 10
(Jafü Bretagne/Brest)			
Stab ZG 1	Lorient	Ju 88	2 – 1
I./ ZG 1	Lorient, Vannes	Ju 88	34 – 24
III./JG 2	Fontenay le Comte	Fw 190	26 – 14
(J.Abschn.Fü Bordeaux/Bordeaux-Mérignac)			
II./JG 26 (exc 6.)	Mont de Marsan	Fw 190	25 – 10
Eins.St. JG 101 *(7)*	Pau	-	-/-
III./ZG 1 (exc 8.)	Cazaux	Ju 88	21 – 12
(Jafü Südfrankreich/Aix)			
Stab JGr Süd *(8)*	Orange Caritat		-/-
1./JGr Süd	Orange-Caritat	-	-/-
2./JGr Süd	Avignon-West	-	-/-
3./JGr Süd	Nîmes	-	-/-
4./JGr Süd	Avignon-East	-	-/-
JLehrerGr (Eins.) *(9)*	Marignane	-	-/-
JLehrerGr (Ausb.) *(10)*	Orange-Caritat	-	-/-
8./ZG 1	Salon	Ju 88	-/-

(1) Special recce staffel		*(6)* In transit to Fontenay	
(2) Radio jamming staffeln		*(7)* Fighter school (operational)	
(3) Bomber school staffel		*(8)* Operational training unit	
(4) Torpedo-bomber gruppen		*(9)* Fighter school (operational)	
(5) Night observation staffel		*(10)* Fighter school (training)	

obviously not escaped the Germans' notice!) and would consist of two or more existing and neighbouring airfields being enlarged and expanded to allow their common surrounding road networks to be used as additional runways and linking taxiways. The Reichsmarschall issued orders for four such 'fortresses' to be established in the west: one north of Venlo in Holland, and three in France in the areas east of Laon, to the northeast of Orléans, and near Orange in the far south. But saner minds prevailed, pointing out that a programme of this size would be both labour-intensive and time-consuming – two commodities at a premium with the spectre of invasion already looming large. It was also argued that a so-called 'fortress' would concentrate too much of the Luftwaffe's strength in one relatively small area and thus invite inevitable attention from the enemy.

Hidden operating bases

Instead, a system of 'airfield groups' was devised. These 'groups' were made up of two or three existing airfields in one region, each of which was, in turn, to be provided with two to four new, carefully camouflaged landing strips in its immediate proximity. Carved out of virgin French countryside, each of these hidden airstrips rejoiced in its own exotic code-name, such as 'Boar's Haunt' and 'Dragon's Heath'. A 'group', which could comprise anything up to 12 individual strips, was designed to house either a gruppe, or a complete geschwader, depending upon its size. Although not all of the planned 'groups' had been completed by 6 June, those that were in operation proved their worth; preserving their occupants from total annihilation and keeping their losses on the ground to the merely prohibitive!

As the largest body of reinforcements sent to France, the fighters were distributed in three main areas. Those units initially scheduled for use as fighter-bombers (eight gruppen of JGs 1, 3 and 11) were to be deployed on fields south of Normandy between the Seine and the Loire. They were thus the closest to the invasion beach-heads, a position dictated by their intended role, which involved the attachment of temporary ventral bomb racks in place of the fighters' more usual long-range fuel tanks. Another eight jagdgruppen would be based further back on air-fields around, and to the east of Paris. Lastly, further east still, JG 27's three gruppen would form a kind of 'aerial longstop' some 100 miles (160 km) beyond the French capital.

But the delay in transmitting the 'Dr Gustav West' signal, which most units stationed in the Reich did not receive until mid-morning, meant that the first reinforcements would not begin arriving in France until the evening of 6 June – and then under only the most difficult of circumstances – and none would be ready to commence operations in earnest until D+1.

It thus fell to Luftflotte 3's two resident jagdgeschwader, JG 2 'Richthofen' and JG 26 'Schlageter', to bear the full brunt of the opening D-Day assault alone. These two units had been the sole guardians of the Channel coast for more than three years. JG 26's area of operations had covered the eastern sector from the Dutch border approximately to the line of the Seine. JG 2's zone extended westwards from the Seine to the Biscay. Together they had protected Belgian and French airspace against the inexorably growing weight of Allied air power, from

Bf 110 night fighters

On D-Day the Luftwaffe's night fighter assets in the west comprised NJG 4 and two gruppen of NJG 5 equipped with Bf 110s, Ju 88s, Do 217s and Me 410s. By mid-June these had been joined by I. and II./NJG 2 with Bf 110G-4s.

Bf 110G-4
Major Paul Zorner, Gruppenkommandeur of III./NJG 5, flew this FuG 220 SN-2 radar- and schräge Musik-equipped Bf 110G-4 at the time of D-Day. Marked with 42 kills, Zorner's total eventually reached 59 by the end of the war.

Bf 110G-4
A similarly-equipped Bf 110G was flown by Oberleutnant Martin Becker of 2./NJG 4 from Florennes. The schräge Musik twin 30-mm upward-firing cannon was installed in the rear of the aft cockpit at an angle of 60-70° from the horizontal.

the RAF's first tentative 'lean into France' in 1941 to the incursions by hundreds of US heavy bombers being mounted by the spring of 1944.

Given their importance as the first line of defence along the north-western ramparts of what Hitler claimed to be his Festung Europa (European Fortress), it seems almost incredible in retrospect that all but one of the geschwaders' six component gruppen should be withdrawn from the regions they had guarded for so long just at the time of greatest danger. The Germans were certainly not unaware of Allied intentions. One of the last successful cross-Channel reconnaissance sorties, flown on 25 April, had reported no fewer than 264 vessels concentrated in the Portsmouth and Southampton areas, and had even discovered the presence of 'large landing stages', estimated to measure some 225 ft x 65 ft (68 m x 20 m) – these latter presumably being parts of the pre-fabricated Mulberry harbour.

Yet withdrawn the Luftwaffe fighters were, despite the protestations of their commanding officers. In mid-May II. and III./JG 26 had retired to southern and eastern France respectively. More extraordinary still, all three of JG 2's Gruppen vacated their bases only a matter of days before the invasion was launched. The Fw 190s of III./JG 2 departed Normandy for the French Biscay coast late in May. At the same time the pilots of II. Gruppe, only recently returned from a brief but costly deployment to Italy, left by road and rail for Germany and re-equipment with new Bf 109s.

Lastly, on 3 June – even as Allied invasion troops were converging on their ports of embar-cation along England's southern coast, and less than seventy-two hours before the first of them would be storming ashore on the beaches of Normandy – I./JG 2 were ordered to move out of that very area (the gruppe's airstrips around Cormeilles were little more than 30 miles (48 km) from Sword, the easternmost of the five designated landing beaches) and redeploy on airfields to the south of Luxembourg.

This meant that the only Luftwaffe fighters anywhere within even the general vicinity of the beachheads on the morning of D-Day were the three Fw 190s of the Geschwaderstab JG 26, commanded by Oberstleutnant Josef Priller, at Lille Nord (nearly 200 miles; 320 km distant) plus some two dozen serviceable Focke-Wulfs of Hauptmann Hermann Staiger's I./JG 26 close by at Lille-Vendeville.

Famous mission

At 08.00 Josef Priller and his wingman, Unteroffizier Heinz Wodarczyk, took off for their now famous low-level strafing run of Sword beach. This exploit has been immortalised in post-war literature and featured prominently in the Hollywood film *The Longest Day*. But in seeming to suggest that this was the Germans' sole aerial response to the D-Day landings, something of a disservice is done to the rest of the Luftwaffe units involved. In all, aircraft of Luftflotte 3 mounted 269 individual sorties during the daylight hours of 6 June (compared to almost 15,000 put up by the Allies), of which 172 were flown by II. Jagdkorps' fighters, claiming 19 Allied fighters shot down.

I./JG 26 had followed their Kommandeur westwards from Lille. Making temporary use of JG 2's fields at Creil and around Cormeilles, they undertook their first operational missions shortly after midday. But it was not until evening that Oberleutnant Franz Kunz, the Staffelkapitän of 2./JG 26, scored the Geschwader's only D-Day success by bringing down a P-51 near Caen.

Meanwhile, JG 2's two Fw 190 gruppen had also been returning post-haste to the bases they had so recently vacated. Arriving back at Creil, pilots of I./JG 2 had to wait for two hours while underwing rocket tubes were fitted to their fighters before taking off to attack shipping off Gold beach. After the mission they landed not

Arriving at Beauvais on the evening of D-day, II./JG 11 were immediately in the thick of the action. On 7 June (D+1) they suffered at least four pilots killed, one missing, three wounded and one PoW. The latter was 6. Staffel's Unteroffizier Rudolf Strosetzki, who crash-landed his Bf 109G-6, 'Yellow 7', in a field only 5 miles (8 km) inland from the beaches, after tangling with P-47s.

Major Kurt Bühligen, JG 2

Geschwaderkommodore of JG 2 during the Normandy invasion, Major Kurt Bühligen was to become the top-scoring ace of the western front with an eventual total of 112. This did, however include 40 kills made during II./JG 2's deployment in Tunisia. His century of 'kills' was brought up by the first of two P-47s downed on the evening of 7 June. On landing he was presented with garlands and a placard reading 'We congratulate you on the 100th kill' while still wearing his lifejacket (right). His Fw 190A-8 (below) wore non-standard Kommodore markings of double chevrons and horizontal bars along with the stylised black 'zig-zag' around the exhaust louvres common to many of JG 2's fighters. As a command machine the aircraft was fitted with additional antennas beneath the wing and the fuselage.

In the face of constant Allied fighter-bomber raids the Luftwaffe gruppen took to the woods surrounding their bases, using the trees as camouflage. By the end of June 136 Luftwaffe fighters had been destroyed on the ground, plus another 216 damaged. Above a late-production Bf 109G-6, fitted with an Erla canopy, is pushed back into its woodland dispersal while in a similar hideaway (left) a groundcrewman checks over a Bf 109G-6 'Gunboat' (note the underwing cannon gondolas).

at Creil, but on one of their several contingency airstrips: a racecourse in the grounds of a small chateau near Senlis.

Shortly before midday Major Kurt Bühligen, the Kommodore of JG 2, shot down a P-47 south of the Orne estuary. It was his 99th victory of the war – and the first of 18 enemy fighters his geschwader would claim before the day was done. Over half of that number were despatched during one hectic 30-minute period between 20.35 and 21.05, including an entire flight of four ground-strafing P-51s bounced by a mixed formation of I. and III./JG 2 Focke-Wulfs north of Evreux. A trio of RAF Typhoons was also shot down in the same area.

Single-day ace

Hauptmann Herbert Huppertz, the Kommandeur of III. Gruppe, was alone responsible for five of JG 2's D-Day kills. On the debit side JG 2 and JG 26 each reported a single pilot fatality. Both had fallen victim to 'friendly' Flak, south of Rouen and over Abbeville, respectively.

Luftflotte 3's fighter-bomber and ground-attack Fw 190s experienced similarly mixed fortunes. One source credits 3./SKG 10 with the first four aerial victories of the day: a quartet of RAF Lancasters shot down in the space of three minutes just after 05.00. All but one had fallen to the guns of Staffelkapitän Hauptmann Helmut Eberspächer. (During the night of 5/6 June Bomber Command had set a new operational record with the despatch of over 1,200 aircraft. The vast majority targeted coastal defence batteries in the area of the coming morning's landings; losing eight of their number in so doing.)

On the other side of the coin, Major Weyert's III./SG 4 suffered significant casualties. At least six of the unit's ground-attack Focke-Wulfs were

brought down by US fighters during the course of the day. Four pilots were killed, including Gruppen-Adjutant Oberleutnant Johann Pühringer. To make matters worse, many of the Fw 190s had been caught while moving forward from St Quentin-Clastres to fields closer to the Normandy landing beaches, and most aircraft were also carrying their chief mechanics stowed in the rear fuselage. The Gruppe's sole victory – a P-51 claimed by Hauptmann Mihlan, Staffelkapitän of 8./SG 4, north of Le Mans – was poor recompense for the losses sustained.

But III./SG 4's trials were as nothing compared to those undergone by the jagdgruppen transferring in to Luftflotte 3 from the Reich. The majority of these had received the 'Dr. Gustav West' signal by mid to late morning. This authorised unit commanders to open sealed orders, and only then did they learn of their destinations. Every gruppe was allocated a number of Ju 52 transports to fly advanced parties of key ground personnel to their assigned bases in France. The first such parties, some accompanied and escorted by their own fighters, began touching down on their French airfields during the evening of 6 June. Others would continue to arrive over the course of the next three days.

This mass movement did not go unchallenged by the Allies. Already enjoying near total air superiority, standing patrols of American and British fighters wrought considerable carnage among the incoming Luftwaffe machines, destroying not only many of the vulnerable Junkers, but also inflicting severe losses on the German fighters (over 60 of the newcomers would be shot down in the first 72 hours of the invasion). The constant threat of Allied air attack, combined with the unseasonably poor weather

conditions, plus the inexperience of many of the young Luftwaffe pilots, transformed every transfer flight into an odyssey. No gruppe escaped unscathed, but some suffered more than others.

II./JG 3, for example, did not set out from Sachau, their base in Germany, for Evreux until 7 June. Led by Gruppenadjutant Oberleutnant Max-Bruno Fischer, the unit's Bf 109s were scheduled to make a refuelling stop en route at Frankfurt-Eschborn. All had gone according to plan up until that point. But bad weather during the second and final leg of the flight completely scattered the formation. Ten fighters crashed or forced-landed. The remaining pilots, many straight out of flight school and sketchily trained at best, put down where they could. Oberleutnant Fischer was the only one to arrive at Evreux!

III./JG 54's 22 Focke-Wulfs fared little better. They had taken off from Cologne shortly after 20.00 on 6 June. Approaching Paris, with the weather deteriorating and darkness beginning to fall, they ran into an Allied fighter-bomber raid. Separated and disorientated, the German pilots – again, many of them with insufficient flying experience – sought the sanctuary of the ground, only to write off their machines in the process. Just two touched down at their proper destination, Villacoublay. On D+1 III./JG 54 reported itself ready to commence operations – with one serviceable Fw 190!

A gruppe faced with one of the longest transfer flights was I./JG 27, which departed Fels am Wagram in Austria for Vertus (one of the 'longstop' fields close to the Marne) in the early evening of D-Day. Staging via Echterdingen and St Dizier, the unit left 15 Bf 109s in its wake, all force-landed in open country and damaged to varying degree.

Despite their considerable material losses, the above gruppen had suffered few casualties. II./JG 53 were not so lucky. They, too, had a long transfer flight ahead of them, being ordered to vacate their Defence of the Reich bases in the Frankfurt area for Vannes on the French Atlantic coast, from where they were to operate against the western (US-held) half of the Normandy beachhead. The length of this journey also necessitated two intermediate stops, at Nancy and Le Mans. It was while landing at the latter airfield, at about 07.45 on

Fitted with drop tanks beneath their wings and a single bomb under the fuselage, a trio of Fw 190G-8s of I./SKG 10 has its foliage camouflage removed prior to a mission against the advancing Allied armies. Already strapped into his parachute, one of the pilots makes his final preparations for combat.

Fighter reinforcements

Fw 190A-8/R8
In response to the call for increased fighter assets the specialised bomber-destroyer 'Sturmböcke' Fw 190A-8s of IV.(Sturm)/JG 3 were briefly deployed to Dreux. This aircraft, the mount of Unteroffizier Willi Maximowitz, is believed to have flown operations between 7-13 June.

Me 262A-2a/U1
In mid-July the Me 262 made its combat debut in the hands of Einsatzkommando Schenk. Detailed to fulfil the fighter-bomber role, fitted with two 250-kg (551-lb) SC 250 bombs, the unit opoerated from Châteaudun, Etampes and Creil before pulling back to Juvincourt in late August.

7 June, that the gruppe was attacked by P-47 fighter-bombers. Four of their Ju 52 transports were shot down in flames and a pilot of the escorting 4. Staffel was killed. Another pilot, of 6./JG 53, was lost to roving P-51s later in the morning. And shortly after midday a second attack by P-47s resulted in a further three Ju 52s being destroyed on the ground and a number of fighters suffering damage. The survivors finally arrived at Vannes on the evening of D+1.

Desperate losses

The attempts to reinforce Luftflotte 3 did not get any easier, or better, in the days ahead. If anything, the situation worsened. The last gruppe to fly in during June was II./JG 5, recently re-equipped in Germany with new Bf 109G-6 'Gunboats'. Fifty-three of these fighters departed the Reich on 20 June; their destination Evreux, west of the Seine. Despite enjoying the luxury of a pair of twin-engined aircraft to provide navigation and act as guides, many of II./JG 5's young pilots became hopelessly lost. Two were killed in crashes, nine belly landed, thirty-nine put down on fields all over eastern France ... and exactly three landed as ordered at Evreux!

It was this last fiasco which prompted the staff of the General der Jagdflieger to consider instituting court-matial proceedings against some of the officers involved in the transfer flights from Germany. Among those called before hearings were Oberleutnants Hans Tetzner, the Gruppenkommandeur of II./JG 5, and Max-Bruno Fischer, the Adjutant of II./JG 3. In the event, few, if any, of the hearings resulted in further action being taken.

It is, perhaps, a reflection of just how out of touch Hermann Göring had become with the day-to-day working of his Luftwaffe that he should have issued a special Order of the Day, dated 14 June, thanking all those engaged in the measures set in motion by the 'Dr. Gustav West' signal for their "smooth and exemplary execution"!

A III./KG 2 Dornier Do 217E, equipped with underwing search radar, receives its bombload at its Soesterberg base in early spring of 1944. By D-day the unit had received the improved K and M variants of the Do 217 which were used, with only marginal success, against Allied maritime targets.

While the main emphasis of Luftflotte 3's reinforcement had been aimed at building up the air fleet's fighter strength, its offensive striking power had not been ignored entirely. Generalfeldmarschall Hugo Sperrle's bomber forces were divided into three separate subordinate commands.

The largest of these was IX. Fliegerkorps, whose gruppen were deployed on bases in north-eastern France, the Low Countries, and north-west Germany. But it was this command which had recently been engaged in Operation Steinbock (Ibex), a series of costly and ultimately abortive night bombing raids on the British Isles. As a consequence, almost all units were desperately under strength, with the serviceability returns of most gruppen being in single figures.

IX. Fliegerkorps was to be reinforced by some 40 Ju 88s of LG 1. But these aircraft had to fly in from Italy. And with the command's own machines in process of redeployment on to the westernmost airfields in its sector,

IX. Fliegerkorps managed to mount only 24 individual operational sorties on D-Day, almost all of which were flown under cover of darkness.

Among the units involved were I. and III./KG 54, whose combined strength of some dozen serviceable Ju 88s provided the core of this 'maximum effort' on the part of the Luftwaffe's bombers. Ordered to attack Sword beach with 500-kg (1,100-lb) bombs, five of the gruppen's aircraft failed to return. KG 2 also lost two bombers, a Ju 188 and a Do 217, on the night of 6/7 June. The 3. Staffel Junkers had been shot down by German Flak. The combination of 'friendly' fire and Allied night-fighters would decimate the Korps' meagre bomber strength in the days (more accurately, nights) and weeks ahead. By the end of June II./KG 2 did not have a single Ju 188 left. Although losses were continually being made good, this only served to prolong the agony. The two months following D-Day saw the virtual demise of the Luftwaffe's bomber force in the west.

After three nights bombing the beaches and

Above: 2. Fliegerdivision's main strike force consisted of torpedo-equipped Ju 88s based in southern France. Here a mirror-wave camouflaged, radar-equipped example from KG 77 carries a pair of long-range fuel tanks in place of its two torpedoes.

Top: Formed in the spring of 1943 with Do 217s, I./KG 66 was a specialised pathfinder gruppe. Shortly after D-Day it transferred from Montdidier to Avord and re-equipped with Junkers Ju 88s and Ju 188s (seen here). Tasked with pathfinder duties over the invasion front, the gruppe's serviceability figures rarely, if ever, reached double figures and its effectiveness proved minimal.

As the D-Day landings were taking place IX. Fliegerkorps's KG 6 was in the process of replacing its Ju 88Ss (seen here in night camouflage) with Ju 188s. The unit's Ju 88s saw limited action in the days following the invasion and by the end of June had been completely replaced by the newer type.

offshore shipping, and with only the sinking of the frigate *Lawford* to show for it, IX. Fliegerkorps had redirected its attention to mining the Bay of the Seine. On the night of 9/10 June 49 bombers laid 122 mines off the Cotentin peninsula. Four nights later they dropped a further 94. Although this produced some results, the mining campaign was nowhere near as successful as the claims made by Luftflotte 3 at the time (which included the sinking of 1 heavy cruiser, 4 destroyers and over 100,000 tons of merchant shipping!).

The air fleet's other bomber Korps had virtually no effect at all on the D-Day landings. The Biscay-based X. Fliegerkorps had, until just two months earlier, been operating as the Fliegerführer Atlantik. As this title implies, it was engaged almost exclusively on long-range anti-shipping and maritime reconnaissance duties far out over the Atlantic. Its aircraft, mainly four-engined, had no part to play above the Normandy beachheads. The He 177s of KG 40 did put in a brief appearance over the western Channel, attacking a US convoy off Falmouth with Henschel Hs 293 glide-bombs on 10 June, but with conspicuous lack of success. Any further danger from this quarter was promptly neutralised by three heavy daylight bombing raids on KG 40's airfields, which destroyed 15 He 177s and damaged many others.

Luftflotte 3's third and last bomber compo-

nent was 2. Fliegerdivision based in southern France. This, too, was primarily an anti-shipping force, composed mainly of twin-engined torpedo-bombers and engaged in operations over the Mediterranean. Attempts were made to employ the division's four torpedo gruppen (two each of KGs 26 and 77) by night against Allied shipping in the Channel, but the difficulties involved were formidable.

Torpedo bombers

Firstly the heavily-laden Junkers had to traverse the length of France, from south to north, which necessitated intermediate refuelling stops at airfields in the Dijon-Chalons area. Having run the gauntlet of enemy night intruders, the bomber crews then needed precise knowledge of a target convoy's location, course and speed, plus reports on the local weather conditions – information which the northern-based reconnaissance units, nailed to the ground by Allied air superiority, were rarely able to supply. It is little wonder that the results they achieved were negligible. Their one notable success occurred in the early hours of 13 June when an attack on a convoy off Portland resulted in the sinking of the destroyer *Boadicea*.

With Luftflotte 3's night-fighters rendered all but ineffective by the same enemy intruders which were taking such a heavy toll of the kampfgruppen during their nocturnal missions,

the main responsibility for the defence of Normandy fell squarely on the shoulders of the fighters of II. Jagdkorps. But even before the battle for the beachheads had developed into the Battle of Normandy proper, it was a battle already irretrievably lost.

By the evening of 9 June (D+3) 15 of the 19 jagdgruppen expected by Luftflotte 3 had arrived in some shape of form. Added to the six gruppen of the resident JGs 2 and 26, this gave II. Jagdkorps a theoretical establishment of some 1,000 fighters. But the reality on the ground was very different. On 10 June the Korps was able to mount just 326 sorties. Although this was nearly double the number put up on D-Day itself (172), it still meant that the Luftwaffe's fighters were facing an enemy who enjoyed a numerical superiority of close on 20:1.

To make matters worse, that same D+4 saw Allied air power gain a foothold in France with the establishment of the first airstrip in the beachhead, close to the hamlet of St Croix-sur-Mer. Many more such strips were bulldozed out of the Normandy countryside in the next two weeks. Luftflotte 3 estimated that the enemy were now mounting 6,000 fighter sorties a day. The constant air umbrella over the landing beaches was so efficient that the command was forced to call a halt to its ad hoc fighter-bomber operations on 13 June. The use of the eight ex-Defence of the Reich jagdgruppen in the Jabo role had proved a

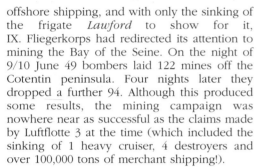

Above: Based on the Biscay coast, the Focke-Wulf Fw 200s of X. Fliegerkorps' KG 40 played no direct part in Normandy operations, their only contribution being shadowing Atlantic convoys bringing supplies and reinforcements. In danger of being cut off in western France by the Allied advance, KG 40's gruppen had transferred to Luftflotte 5 in Norway by the end of June.

Below: Six Heinkel He 177A-5s of II./KG 40 prepare for a mission in June 1944 from their Bordeaux-Mérignac base. The four aircraft on the left are carrying a Henschel Hs 293A radio-controlled glide bomb beneath each wing. To neutralise the threat of the He 177s the Allies mounted three large bombing raids on the airfield of which the effects of the first is in evidence by the severely damaged hangars.

Despite flying 9,162 individual sorties in June, and a further 10,728 by the end of July, the Luftwaffe's fighters could not prevent the inevitable and in August the retreat from Normandy began. But the Allies still had to be wary. This Fw 190A-8 of II./JG 26, abandoned at Melsbroek in early September, was reportedly booby-trapped when a bomb buried beneath its nose exploded as the aircraft was moved.

costly failure. But the young pilots, more used to combatting high-flying US heavy bombers, were little better suited to the new task awaiting them: the low-level protection of their own troops and lines of supply.

Even as more Allied squadrons began to occupy their new beachhead airstrips, the Luftwaffe's fighters were being driven from their own landing grounds. They had long been bombed from the major bases which formed the nucleus of each 'airfield group'. Now marauding bands of Allied fighter-bombers were seeking out their hiding places among the trees bordering the meadows which served as the 'groups" peripheral strips.

Facing near insuperable odds in the air, and hunted remorselessly when on the ground, it is little wonder that their losses were escalating rapidly. But despite all their difficulties, individual pilots were still claiming victories. The Kommodores of JGs 2 and 26, Major Kurt Bühlingen and Oberstleutnant Josef 'Pips'

Priller, both achieved their centuries during this period: the former being credited with a P-47 near Caen on D+1, and the latter bringing down a B-24 south of Chartres eight days later.

At least four pilots scored double figures over Normandy during June. The most successful of all was III./JG 54's Hauptmann Emil 'Bully' Lang who claimed 14, the last a Spitfire shot down over Bernay on the 26th. Shortly before this, the night-fighters had scored a rare and spectacular success when NJG 2 destroyed 10 Lancasters without loss in the early hours of 25 June. Over 700 heavies of Bomber Command had attacked V-1 flying bomb sites in northern France on the night of 24/25 June. Twenty of their number failed to return.

Coincidentally, this same night also witnessed the first operational Mistel sorties. Five of these bizarre weapons, which comprised a single-engined fighter mated atop an unmanned Ju 88 bomber packed with explosives, attacked shipping in the Bay of the Seine. Four hits were

claimed, but remain unconfirmed.

Another revolutionary weapon to make its operational debut in the skies of Normandy was the Me 262 jet. A small Kommando of these twin-engined machines would begin to fly fighter-bomber missions out of Juvincourt towards the end of July. But so minimal was their impact that the Allies were completely unaware of their presence above the battlefield.

Such novelties aside, it was the young, inadequately trained pilots of the Bf 109s and Fw 190s who bore the brunt of the overwhelming Allied air assault which accompanied the Normandy landings. And it was they who paid the price. II. Jagdkorps' records indicate that 35 to 40 of them were killed for each combat-experienced veteran lost. For although they contributed to the 537 aircraft claimed by the jagdgruppen before the end of June, theirs are the unknown names which dominate the daily casualty returns.

In the 25 days from 6 to 30 June 1944 II. Jagdkorps lost over 900 fighters – the equivalent of almost an entire jagdgruppe every day! Although the war would continue for another eleven months, the Luftwaffe fighter force in the west would never fully recover from the battle for the Normandy beachheads.

Glossary/translation	
Geschwader – Wing	SG – Ground-attack wing
Gruppe – Group	LG – Bomber wing
Staffel – Squadron	FAGr – Long-range recce group
JG – Fighter wing	SAGr – Maritime recce group
NJG – Night fighter wing	NAGr – Short-range recce group
ZG – Long-range fighter wing	Jafü – Fighter leader
KG – Bomber wing	Stab – Staff flight
SKG – Fast bomber wing	

Luftflotte 3 Order of Battle – as of 26 June 1944

Unit	Base	Type	Allocated/In service
SUBORDINATE UNITS			
Stab FAGr 123	Toussus le Buc	Ju 88, Fw 190	-/-
4.(F)/123	St André	Bf 109	9 – 1
5.(F)/123	Monchy-Breton	Bf 109	8 – 7
1.(F)/121	Toussus le Buc	Me 410	6 – 2
II. FLIEGERKORPS (Chartres)			
Stab NAGr 13	Chartres	Bf 109, Fw 190	-/-
1./NAGr 13	Chartres	Bf 109, Fw 190	11 – 4
3./NAGr 13	Laval	Bf 109, Fw 190	10 – 7
III./SG 4	Clermont-Ferrand, Avord	Fw 190	52 – 29
IX. FLIEGERKORPS (Beauvais-Tille)			
3.(F)/122	Soesterberg	Ju 188	7 – 5
6.(F)/123 (1)	Cormeilles	Ju 188, Ju 88	6 – 0
Stab KG 2	Gilze-Rijen	Ju 188	4 – 4
I./KG 2	Gilze-Rijen	Ju 188	10 – 5
II./KG 2	Gilze-Rijen	Ju 188	0 – 0
III./KG 2	Hesepe	Do 217	6 – 5
5./KG 3	Gilze-Rijen	Ju 88	-/-
III./KG 3	Hesepe	He 111	-/-
Stab KG 6	Melun-Villaroche	Ju 188	0 – 0
I./KG 6	Melun-Villaroche	Ju 188	16 – 13
II./KG 6	Melun-Villaroche	Ju 188	-/-
III./KG 6	Melun-Villaroche	Ju 188	7 – 5
I./SKG 10	Tours	Fw 190	19 – 7
Stab KG 30	Tours	Ju 88	0 – 0
II./KG 30 (2)	Leck/Le Culot	Ju 88	20 – 10
II./KG 51	Soesterberg, Gilze-Rijen	Me 410	14 – 12
Stab KG 54	Eindhoven	Ju 88	2 – 1
I./KG 54	Eindhoven	Ju 88	14 – 8
III./ KG 54	Eindhoven	Ju 88	13 – 12
I./KG 66	Montdidier	Ju 188, Ju 88	6 – 5
Eins.St.IV/ KG 101 (3)	St Dizier	Mistel	6 – 4
Stab LG 1	Melsbroek	Ju 88	1 – 0
I./LG 1	Le Culot	Ju 88	13 – 11
II./LG 1	Melsbroek	Ju 88	13 – 11

Unit	Base	Type	Allocated/In service
X. FLIEGERKORPS (Angers)			
Stab FAGr 5	Mont de Marsan	Ju 290	
1./FAGr 5	Mont de Marsan	Ju 290	15 – 7
2./FAGr 5	Mont de Marsan	Ju 290	
4.(F)/5 (1)	Nantes	Do 217, He 111	4 – 3
3.(F)/123	Corme Ecluse	Ju 88	7 – 2
1.(F)/SAGr 129	Biscarosse	Bv 222	4 – 2
Stab KG 40	Bordeaux-Mérignac	Fw 200	-/-
I./KG 40 (exc 3.)	Toulouse-Blagnac	He 177	12 – 7
II./KG 40	Bordeaux-Mérignac	He 177	12 – 3
III./KG 40	St Jean d'Angely, Cognac	Fw 200	23 – 8
2.Fliegerdivision (Montfrin)			
1.(F)/33	St Martin	Ju 88, Me 410	11 – 3
2./NAGr 13	Cuers	Bf 109, Fw 190	10 – 7
2./SAGr 128	Berre	Ar 196	4 – 2
Stab KG 26	Montpellier	Ju 88	-/-
II./KG 26(LT) (4)	Valence	Ju 88	27 – 18
III./KG 26(LT) (4)	Montpellier, Valence	Ju 88	22 – 12
Stab KG 77	Salon	Ju 88	1 – 0
I./KG 77(LT) (4)	Orange-Caritat	Ju 88	18 – 10
III./KG 77(LT) (4)	Orange-Caritat	Ju 88	16 – 9
6./KG 77	Istres	Ju 88	8 – 6
4. & 6./KG 76	Istres	Ju 88	7 – 4
Stab KG 100	Toulouse-Francazals	Do 217, He 177	2 – 0
III./KG 100	Toulouse-Francazals	Do 217	26 – 10
II. JAGDKORPS (Chantilly)			
4. Fliegerdivision (Metz)			
(Jafü 4/St.Pol-Bryas)			
Stab JG 1	St Quentin-Clastres	Fw 190	3 – 0
I./JG 3	St Quentin-Clastres	Bf 109	14 – 5
I./JG 5	Mons en Chaussée	Bf 109	14 – 9
II./JG 11	St Quentin-Clastres	Bf 109	19 – 5
I./JG 301	Epinoy	Bf 109	13 – 13
Stab JG 27	Champfleury	Bf 109	6 – 3
I./JG 27	Vertus	Bf 109	39 – 24
III./JG 27	Connantre	Bf 109	32 – 22
IV./JG 27	Champfleury	Bf 109	31 – 19
Stab NJG 4	Chenay	Bf 110	2 – 1
I./NJG 4	Florennes	Ju 88	38 – 12

Unit	Base	Type	Allocated/In service
III./NJG 4	Juvincourt	Ju 88	18 – 11
Stab NJG 5	Hagenau	Bf 110	-/-
I./NJG 5	St Dizier	Bf 110	15 – 11
III./NJG 5	Athies-sous-Laon	Bf 110	-/-
5. Jagddivision (Jouy en Jousas)			
(Jafü 5/Bernay)			
Stab JG 2	Creil	Fw 190	2 – 2
I./JG 2	Creil	Fw 190	16 – 5
II./JG 2	Creil	Bf 109	46 –17
III./JG 2	Creil	Fw 190	18 – 8
Stab JG 3	Evreux	Bf 109, Fw 190	3 – 2
II./JG 3	Guyancourt	(re-equipping)	-/-
III./JG 3	Mareilly	Bf 109	23 – 15
II./JG 5	Evreux	Bf 109	51 – 18
Stab JG 11	Le Mans	Fw 190	-/-
I./JG 11	Le Mans	Fw 190	19 – 14
10./JG 11	Le Mans	Fw 190	-/-
I./JG 1	Alençon	Fw 190	17 – 5
II./JG 1	Alençon	Fw 190	0 – 0
Stab JG 26	Guyancourt	Fw 190	3 – 2
I./JG 26	Guyancourt	Fw 190	27 – 9
II./JG 26	Guyancourt	Fw 190	12 – 5
Stab NJG 2	Coulommiers	Ju 88	4 – 2
I./NJG 2	Chateaudun	Ju 88	10 – 6
II./NJG 2	Coulommiers	Ju 88	24 – 10
III./NJG 4	Coulommiers	Ju 88	13 – 6
(Jafü Bretagne/Brest)			
II./JG 53	Vannes	Bf 109	32 – 9
(J.Abschn.Fü Bordeaux/Bordeaux-Mérignac)			
Stab ZG 1	Bordeaux-Mérignac	Ju 88	1 – 1
I./ZG 1	Corme Ecluse Chateauroux	Ju 88	14 – 9
III./ZG 1	Cazaux	Ju 88	7 – 6
(Jafü Südfrankreich/Aix)			
JGr 200	Orange-Caritat, Avignon	Fw 190	34 - 28
JLehrerGr (Eins.) (5)	Marignane	-	-/-

(1) Radio jamming staffeln	(5) Torpedo-bomber gruppen
(2) In transit	(6) Fighter school (operational)
(3) Bomber school staffel	

Supermarine Scimitar

In the twilight of its front-line career, the Scimitar served aboard HMS Eagle with No. 800B Squadron, primarily as an air-to-air refuelling asset for the mother squadron's Buccaneer S.Mk 1s. In typical nose-high launch configuration, XD274 is attached to Eagle's catapult in late 1965 as a Wessex HAS.Mk 1 from No. 820 Squadron stands on 'Plane Guard' duty, with rescue crewmen poised for action in the open cabin door.

Designed as an interceptor for the Fleet Air Arm, the Supermarine Scimitar, nicknamed 'The Beast', ultimately spent the majority of its operational career in the naval strike role. Although procured only in small numbers, the aircraft achieved several claims to fame, including being the largest and fastest British single-seat fighter at the time of its first flight, and the first Royal Navy aircraft to carry a nuclear device. Plagued by a high loss-rate, the Scimitar had a brief front-line career of some eight years, before being replaced by the Blackburn Buccaneer.

Supermarine is a name that will forever be associated with the Spitfire, Britain's most famous fighter. But after the war Vickers-Armstrong Ltd (Aircraft Section) (Supermarine Division), to give the full title, slowly but steadily lost its position as the premier British fighter company to Hawker Aircraft, which had produced the Hurricane. The less than successful Spiteful and Seafang were developed from the Spitfire, before the firm's first jet fighter, the Attacker, saw limited service with the Royal Navy. Through a series of prototypes, the Attacker evolved into the Swift as a competitor to Hawker's Hunter for the RAF's transonic swept-wing fighter requirements for the 1950s. The Swift was produced in numbers for the RAF, but cancelled amid major political controversy before all of its flaws were rectified. Before becoming part of the British Aircraft Corporation in 1960, the busy Supermarine team were to put into production just one more fighter – the Scimitar

Type 508 prototypes

In February 1945, N.E. Rowe, the Director of Technical Development (DTD) at the Ministry of Supply, requested from Joe Smith, Supermarine's Chief Designer, a proposal for an advanced jet propulsion interceptor, the

Ministry having studied new project ideas for both the Royal Air Force and Fleet Air Arm (FAA). The result was a radical undercarriage-less project for the FAA, designated the Type 505. It was felt great advantages would be forthcoming through the use of a landing 'carpet' in respect to saving of undercarriage weight, to make possible a very real improvement in performance. Power was provided by two Rolls Royce AJ.65 engines, after much investigation of single engine and rocket powerplants.

In August 1946, the decision was taken not to order the aircraft, mainly because flexible deck trials were yet to take place and the converted carriers would not be ready for the production aircraft. A new requirement for a naval fighter in the 1947/48 development programme was brought forward a year, as the idea of converting the Type 505 into a conventional fighter with an undercarriage was attractive. A hedge against possible failure of the Hawker N.7/46 (later the Sea Hawk) was needed, and Supermarine produced a new brochure for the Type 508, a project initially near identical in appearance to the 505 except for a larger wing area and the addition of an undercarriage.

The 508 was a big aeroplane, particularly for a ship-borne fighter, with a near straight wing (8° sweep on leading edge) and a distinctive

butterfly or V-tail that performed a dual role of tailplane and fin. Three prototypes were ordered in August 1947 to the new Naval Staff Requirement NR/A.17 and Specification N.9/47 issued in April. Weight had increased appreciably over the Type 505 with four 30-mm Aden cannon fitted below the air intakes, although only the second aircraft actually received the guns. Two Rolls-Royce Avon RA.3 engines of 6,500 lb (28.97 kN) thrust were used. The Type 508's span was 41 ft (12.50 m), length 50 ft (15.24 m) and normal loaded weight 18,850 lb (8,550 kg).

Joe Smith had seriously considered fitting a tail wheel instead of the nose wheel, as the latter had such an enormous load thrown onto it after engaging the arrester wire, but ultimately chose the tricycle arrangement to assist pilot view. A mock-up was officially examined in September 1948, and construction of the first prototype, VX133, began in mid-1949. A contract for three prototypes (VX133, VX136 and VX136), placed to Specification N.9/47, was signed in 1950. The first engine runs were made at the Hursley Park site in June 1951, before the aircraft was transported by road to Boscombe Down to commence the flight test programme. The aircraft's successful maiden flight, made from Boscombe Down in the hands of Mike Lithgow, occurred on 31 August 1951.

Early flight tests, conducted from the main flight test airfield at Chilbolton, evaluated leading- and trailing- edge flap combinations and

Both the Type 508 (left) and Type 529 (above) underwent deck landing trials aboard HMS Eagle. The former is seen during the first of these trials in May 1952, fitted with two cameras on the underside of the fuselage to record undercarriage oleo compression and the behaviour of the arrester hook. Above, the launching bridle of VX136 drops away during catapult acceleration and take-off handling trials during November 1953, just days before the aircraft's flying days were ended by a landing accident at Chilbolton.

resulted in an interconnection such that full trailing-edge flap was accompanied by 10° of leading-edge flap. Full testing was planned in this condition, but was seriously interrupted by aileron flutter just prior to high speed and Mach number examinations. Take-off and climb performance proved to be excellent, but maximum speed was only 603 mph (970 km/h) at 30,000 ft (9144m). The main criticism came with certain lateral and directional characteristics, some of which appeared to be inherent with the butterfly tail.

On 5 December 1951, the only major inflight incident during the test programme occurred. At some 450 kt (884 km/h), with Mike Lithgow at the controls, VX133 experienced violent accelerations following an uncontrolled pitch-up. After disengaging the elevator power system, the aircraft entered a vertical upward roll, pulling in excess of 11 g and causing Lithgow to black out. On regaining control, he made a successful landing back at Chilbolton, the aircraft having suffered Cat 3 damage including the loss of both wingtip pitot heads. The problem was subsequently attributed to an inadvertent opening of the port undercarriage chassis

door. The problem was solved by a small modification – or so they thought!

The second prototype (VX136) joined the flight test programme after its maiden flight on 29 August 1952. By this time, the many interior modifications and the fitting of cannon armament prompted the decision to re-designate this aircraft as the Type 529.

Initial deck-landing trials on HMS *Eagle* were conducted by VX133 in May 1952, with both aircraft returning to the carrier in November 1953 for follow-on trials. The first test comprised seven landings, all by Lithgow, who felt the 508 presented few difficulties and a pilot used to the Attacker would find it a far easier proposition thanks to light and effective ailerons and elevator, excellent throttle response and the tricycle landing gear. VX136 was employed on tail-down landing and catapult acceleration trials, before being transferred to RAE Bedford for use by the RN Test Squadron. However, its flying career was to be short-lived as it was damaged beyond economic repair in an emergency landing on 2 December 1953, attributed again to the chassis door problem Supermarine thought it had solved. During its period of test flying, the

Type 529's maximum performance reached 607 mph (977 km/h), or Mach 0.92, at 30,000 ft (9144 m).

The Type 508 had a longer career, continuing its test flight work until 1956, before finally being scrapped, after employment as a fire practice airframe at RNAS Culdrose.

N.113 and blown flaps

By mid-1955 plans were underway for further developments. The question had arisen of ordering more N.9/47 prototypes, as the Type 525 did not appear to be fully meeting the specification (see box). A new document, N.113D, was drawn up and Supermarine's response, the Type 544, was a full redesign utilising a reshaped wing-body junction and subtly shaped wingtips to postpone the onset of compressibility drag rise, a combination which pushed up

Supermarine's chief test pilot, Mike Lithgow, formates with the company's Type 535 Swift prototype during the SBAC show at Farnborough in September 1951. The aircraft had made its maiden flight only 11 days earlier and with barely 10 hours of development flying having been completed, the aircraft's flying demonstrations were understandably sedate.

Above: By the mid-1960s, the Type 508 had its outer wings removed and was being used by the School of Aircraft Handling at RNAS Culdrose. Here, a tractor driver receives training for deck handling techniques in the summer of 1966. At the end of the decade, this unique prototype was transferred to Predannack, where it met an ignominious end on the fire dump.

Right: Developments in aircraft-carrier catapult and arresting gear, and high-lift devices for swept wing aircraft, prompted Supermarine to issue its own specification (the Type 525) for a swept-wing naval fighter. Seen here in its original form, with a swept butterfly tail, the Type 525 was eventually built with a conventional empennage.

the maximum speed a fraction. It had a longer nose, but did not encompass area-ruling, and really resembled the Type 525 only in appearance.

The Director of Military Aircraft Research and Development was disappointed that the swept N.9 differed so much from the final N.113 and did not propose, therefore, to use up effort clearing up any problems peculiar to just the 525, despite a request for Boscombe Down to make a quick pre-view check. In the event, the 525 spun into the ground and was destroyed on 5 July 1955, after 61 hours flying, causing a

major delay in the investigation and development of flap blowing techniques. Modification of the 525 to provide the supersonic blowing of air over the flaps had been approved in May 1954, the air being bled from the engine compressor and projected as a thin sheet through a tiny slot along the trailing edge slightly ahead of the flap.

The concept of blowing very high velocity air over extended flaps is to re-energise the airflow, ensuring it remains in contact with the wing and flap upper surfaces, instead of letting it break away. Lift is improved and thus, stalling speed

is reduced. Without blowing, the upper surface airflow can break up and become turbulent at low speeds, so leading to a loss of lift and increase in drag. The technique was pioneered in America by NACA (the National Advisory Committee for Aeronautics) under the leadership of John D. Attinello and the 'Attinello flap' was taken on board several contemporary American aircraft. In Britain, some early bound-

Supermarine Type 525 – Scimitar takes shape

Well before the Type 508's first flight, a meeting, held by Supermarine and the Air Ministry in April 1950, examined the N.9/47 specification and agreed to embody swept back wings and reheated engines in the third prototype, in order to obtain the best possible performance from the project as soon as possible. A redesign, called Type 525, had already been proposed by Supermarine in June 1949, with both wing and butterfly tail highly swept, followed shortly after by the de-navalised Type 526, offered to the F.3/48 Hawker P.1067 (Hunter) specification, which the Air Ministry considered an appreciable improvement over the Kingston design. Go-ahead was given for the Type 525, but initial design work revealed the swept V-tail was a problem structurally and a cruciform tail, with all-flying horizontal surfaces, was substituted. The high sweep-back of the wing, without dihedral, resulted in the tips being too close to the ground and the oleos were raised by 15 in (38 cm). The aircraft's larger wing area, twin engines and double-slotted trailing-edge and full-span leading-edge flaps would reduce the aircraft's landing speed to within limits for operations from aircraft-carriers. This was later further improved with the addition of boundary layer control (BLC), otherwise known as 'supercirculation' or 'flap-blowing'. Additionally, air brakes would be fitted to the underside of the fuselage and to the upper and lower surfaces of the wings. A pair of Rolls-Royce Avon RA.7s, each of 7,500 lb (33.4 kN) thrust, was fitted but the planned addition of reheat never took place.

In 1952, work began in earnest in converting the third Type 508 to meet this new specification. Despite few of the workforce being spared for the project, progress was relatively rapid with the airframe substantially complete by the end of 1953. By mid-April 1954, the Type 525 emerged ready for transportation on a low-loader (with its undercarriage raised and outer wings removed) from the factory at Hursley to Boscombe Down for initial flight tests. It was, at the time, the largest single-seat fighter being produced by the British aviation industry, with a span of 37 ft 2 in (11.34 m), length of 53 ft (16.15 m), normal loaded weight of 19,910 lb (9031 kg) and maximum overload weight of 28,169 lb (12777 kg). The maiden flight of VX138 took place, in the

In the hands of Supermarine's chief test pilot Mike lithgow, the Type 525 made its maiden flight at Boscombe Down on 27 April 1954. At this time the aircraft remained unpainted, yet to receive the all-cream paint scheme in which it graced the SBAC show at Farnborough in September.

hands of Mike Lithgow, on 27 April 1954. Despite the great amount of installed thrust, the Type 525 was still subsonic at its maximum speed of 647 mph (1041 km/h) or Mach 0.954, at 30,000 ft (9,144 m). It could, however, go supersonic in a shallow dive and reached Mach 1.08 by 1 November. Time to height was, however, below expectations and there were some problems with handling. Flight testing revealed serious trouble with engine surging and pitch-up characteristics and modifications to the fin, rudder and control circuit were made to assist directional stability. After further flight tests examining the effect of the 'flap-blowing', the aircraft was lost in a fatal accident on 5 July 1955. Although the inquiry eventually revealed the flap-blowing had nothing to do with the accident, the loss of the aircraft dealt a tremendous blow to the programme and effectively delayed N.113 development by some two years.

Above: The Supermarine 525 sits on the tarmac at Boscombe Down around the time of its maiden flight. The high angle-of-attack during landing and rotation (also a feature of the later Scimitar) necessitated the need for a prominent retractable tail buffer, to prevent the rear fuselage from striking the runway or deck.

Left: With many of HMS Centaur's complement watching, Mike Lithgow makes the first carrier touchdown by the Type 525 on 8 June 1955, during a 'shop window' demonstration of the effects of flap-blowing. By this time the aircraft had acquired a naval scheme of dark sea grey upper and sky lower surfaces.

Below: WT854 was the first prototype Supermarine Type 544 and, after being transported by road from the construction hangar at Hursley Park to A&AEE Boscombe Down, made its maiden flight on 20 January 1956. One of the key figures in the evolution of the Scimitar was Supermarine chief test pilot Mike Lithgow, who not only conducted the first flights of all the prototypes, but completed a large proportion of the development flights.

Above: Making its maiden flight on 22 June 1956, the second Type 544 (WT859), like the first, was initially fitted with a large nose boom carrying a pitot head and yaw vanes, which were visible to the pilot from the cockpit. WT859 incorporated single-slotted trailing-edge flaps and had provision for the flap-blowing (supercirculation) system, although this was not activated before the aircraft's Rolls-Royce Avon RA.28 engines were replaced by the definitive Avon 202 in October 1956.

ary layer control research had been undertaken for Supermarine by Westland before the fighter firm carried out another investigation in October 1953. Two schemes looked at either blowing out of the flap shroud or suction applied at the flap leading edge, and the former was selected as the more promising.

The Type 525 first flew with blow operating in June 1955, and preliminary results showed a reduced approach speed of about 12 mph (19 km/h) and much improved stability and control at low speeds, but detailed assessment was prevented by the crash. In April 1955 it was decided to fit blown flaps to production N.113 aircraft in place of double-slotted flaps. When first flown, however, the first Scimitar prototype had the slotted flaps fitted for use during carrier trials on HMS *Ark Royal*; these were held to satisfy an urgent need for deck handling experience. A few years later another FAA aircraft, the Buccaneer, took 'flap-blowing' a stage further in spanning the whole wing plus the tail, which reduced the size of both horizontal surfaces quite markedly, an important benefit for a carrier aircraft.

Refining the specification

Specification N.113D had been issued on 16 July 1951 for a prototype swept-wing fighter capable of 720 mph (1,158 km/h) at sea level without reheat and carrying four Aden cannon,

an air-to-air rocket battery and Blue Sky or Red Dean missiles. The whole question of armament was so fluid that the only known fitting was the cannon; the guided weapons and air-to-air rockets were to be installed during production. It was resolved that the Type 544, as Supermarine designated the aircraft, should have four wing hardpoints which could accept the missiles and any other weapons introduced later. Two Rolls-Royce Avon RA.7s were specified, but the plan to fit reheat was, in due course, dropped. Spec. N.113P followed in May 1953 to cover production aircraft and included RA.23 engines (switched to Avon 202s on manufacture) and the additional capability of long-range low-level bombing and strike.

Construction of all three Type 544 prototypes was conducted at the Hursley Park design centre's experimental hangar. With the delays caused by the loss of the Type 525 uppermost in their minds, the Supermarine engineers rapidly assembled the first aircraft, WT854, in the latter half of 1955. Following the usual route, the aircraft was transported by road to Boscombe Down on 14 January 1956, in preparation for its first flight. This was achieved six days later on 20 January 1956, with Mike Lithgow again in control for a brief 10-minute general handling flight, being observed by Dave Morgan in Swift FR.Mk 5 WK277. Further handling flights were carried out in the follow-

ing days, before the aircraft transferred to Chilbolton. Here, the prototype was used for inertia coupling investigation and the development of the wing fences adopted for production machines. In April, it made 29 deck landings on HMS *Ark Royal* where cockpit view on approach was considered adequate, yet close to being judged marginal. All take-offs were conducted without the use of the catapult, and one take-off on 9 April was made in error with the parking brake still on. With the mainwheels locked for the entire length of the deck, the aircraft practically fell off the end of the ship at barely 100 kt (185 km/h). Initially using the 'ground effect' of the sea, the aircraft staggered into the air for a safe landing back on deck and a tyre change! The pilot of this incident was Lt Cdr Colin Little of the A&AEE, and the *Ark Royal* sported two black parallel streaks, as testament to his escape, for months afterwards

The others prototypes were WT859 (flown 22 June) and WW134 (10 October), the former becoming the development aircraft for the flap-blowing system, while the latter, with RA.24 engines, undertook further deck landing trials on *Ark Royal* in January 1957. WW134, complete with full wing and tail modifications and flap blowing, showed that approach speed had been reduced by about 21 mph (34 km/h) at a given weight relative to the first prototype. The difference between blow-on and blow-off

By March 1956 WT854, minus its nose probe, had been delivered to RAE Bedford for arrester gear trials. This involved the aircraft taxiing into an arrester wire, representative of those fitted on the Royal Navy's aircraft-carriers, at increasing speeds. Strain gauges fitted to the arresting gear measured the forces employed, and from this it was determined how the aircraft would behave when making actual carrier landings at various weights and wind speeds.

Above: A vision of things to come. The first Type 544, in the hands of Mike Lithgow, rotates from the deck of HMS Ark Royal during its initial carrier trials in the English Channel, which commenced on 5 April 1956. Parked alongside is the third prototype de Havilland DH.110 (XF828), which evolved into the Sea Vixen, a type that later served operationally alongside the Scimitar on this very ship.

Right: Initial carrier trials involved free, unassisted take-offs, as the aircraft had not yet received the clearance from RAE Bedford for catapult launches. However, trial manoeuvring of WT854 on to the catapult was carried out and is seen here, in typical nose-high launch attitude, conducting a full-power run-up.

on approach was around 10 mph (16 km/h). Slot widths of 0.25, 0.15 and 0.10 in (6.4, 3.8 and 2.5 mm) were flown but exhibited little difference, so the thinnest was chosen, as more thrust remained available for catapult take-offs and overshoot situations. Some 5 per cent of engine mass flow was ducted away but with full 'blow' on, a landing overshoot was still possible.

Early problems

This early development flying revealed high Mach number 'pitch-up' worse than the Type 525, in other words normal acceleration (g) was increased more than expected from the applied back stick thanks to air-flow separation and subsequent high-speed tip stall. Also manifest was longitudinal instability at low speeds. As a result, a single saw tooth on the leading edge plus a boundary-layer fence were added to the wing. Also by changing the tailplane's 10° dihedral to 10° anhedral, lowering the tips by 3 ft (0.9 m), the longitudinal instability which occurred a few knots below the original approach speed prior to the introduction of blowing was practically eliminated; in fact, stability was improved throughout the speed range. Setting the tail higher than the wing to avoid the jet efflux had proved bad for preventing high-speed pitch up and by now fighters were appearing with low-set tails.

Limited production

Approval was given for the fighter to be named Scimitar in March 1957. Initial plans for 100 aircraft received financial approval but, in the event, only 76 were built, receiving serials XD212-250, XD264-282 and XD316-333. XD334-357 were the cancelled airframes. The first series aircraft (XD212) flew on 11 January 1957. Earlier Supermarine jets had been tested at Chilbolton, but once the Scimitar was ready, the equivalent work was switched to the Vickers test airfield at Wisley. Production was completed at South Marston in Wiltshire in September 1960 and deliveries to the Navy were concluded the following March.

This battleship of an aeroplane had an 8 per cent thick cantilever wing swept 45° at quarter chord. The wing was manufactured mainly in light alloy, but its three-spar structure was produced in high tensile steel, a material also used in the most heavily stressed areas of wing and tail. A pair of large flaps was placed under the fuselage in line with the 'blown' trailing-edge flaps. The full-span leading-edge flaps were hydraulically operated, all flaps being linked to the all-moving slab tailplane which deflected 4° when the flaps were lowered. The ailerons had duplicated power controls with artificial spring feel, the tailplane the same but with combined q-feel and spring feel, this being the first time that fully powered controls were used in a Royal Navy type. Power control on the rudder was unduplicated with manual reversion. For storage the wing folded hydraulically in just one position.

The fuselage had a light alloy semi-monocoque structure, and the complete nose ahead of the cockpit hinged for radar access and to reduce length. Hydraulically operated air brakes were placed on each side of the fuselage aft of the wing. Chemical etching of aluminium panels (the selective removal of metal with caustic soda) was introduced to give a smooth accurate surface and better fatigue characteristics, a feature so important in low-altitude operations, while it was also the first to have titanium. Each Scimitar used around 270 lb (122 kg) of the 'new' metal in the flap blowing air ducts and other areas that needed heat protection. The main undercarriage wheels retracted laterally into the fuselage, the nosewheel rearwards and there was also a retractable tail bumper.

Total internal fuel was 1,064 Imp gal (4,837 litres) but another 800 Imp gal (3,637 litres) was available in four drop tanks and a flight refuelling probe could be fitted in the nose. Like its partner, the de Havilland Sea Vixen, the Scimitar could act as a 'buddy' flight refuelling tanker,

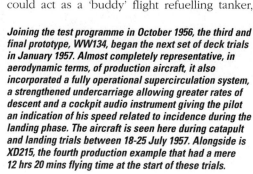

Joining the test programme in October 1956, the third and final prototype, WW134, began the next set of deck trials in January 1957. Almost completely representative, in aerodynamic terms, of production aircraft, it also incorporated a fully operational supercirculation system, a strengthened undercarriage allowing greater rates of descent and a cockpit audio instrument giving the pilot an indication of his speed related to incidence during the landing phase. The aircraft is seen here during catapult and landing trials between 18-25 July 1957. Alongside is XD215, the fourth production example that had a mere 12 hrs 20 mins flying time at the start of these trials.

During the eight-day carrier trials aboard HMS Ark Royal in July 1957, WW134 and XD215 (seen here) completed a total of 148 landings and catapult take-offs flown by six pilots, with all but 13 of the take-offs using 'flap-blowing'. The 94 deck landings achieved by XD215 alone, was in excess of the number expected by an entire operational squadron over a similar time scale. By this time, XD215 had joined WT854 in having a dummy air-to-air refuelling probe fitted for tanking trials, the former having initiated the programme in January alongside a drogue-equipped Vickers Valiant and EE Canberra.

carrying a Flight Refuelling Ltd Mk 20 pod with retractable drogue on the inner starboard pylon and fuel tanks on the other three that could supply Sea Vixens, Buccaneers and other Scimitars. Four 30-mm Aden cannon were located in the bottom of the intake fairings, and missiles and stores were carried on the four wing pylons to satisfy the various Scimitar operations.

The original role of day fighter was satisfied by the cannon and 96 unguided air-to-air rockets, but by 1962 the aircraft had been adapted to carry four Sidewinder infra-red homing air-to-air missiles. In the event the Sea Vixen took on most of the Navy's interception duties, leaving the Scimitar for strike work, but the Aden cannon were retained. Other duties for this 'jack of all trades' comprised ground attack with Bullpup air-to-surface guided missiles, rocket projectiles or 1,000-lb (454-kg) bombs, and photo-reconnaissance using oblique cameras in an interchangeable nose fairing. The PR role was raised to fill a short gap before the Buccaneer S.Mk 1 entered service.

LABS and Red Beard

The most secretive of the Scimitar's roles, however, was that of nuclear strike. Equipped to carry the Target Marker Bomb (Red Beard), initial trials began in the first week of June 1959. The delivery method was known as the Low Altitude Bombing System (LABS), and the majority of trials were conducted by XD218 on the instrumented range at West Freugh. The system involved approaching the target at low-level and a speed of 600 kt (1112 km/h). At a designated identification point (IP) the Scimitar would initiate a 4-g loop releasing the weapon at an attitude of some 45°. The bomb would then travel around 24,000 ft (7315 m) from the release point towards the target on a ballistic course. The looping manoeuvre was then continued over the vertical until the aircraft had a 40° nose-down attitude on the reciprocal heading. At this point, the pilot completed a half roll and descended to low level for a maximum speed egress. Alternatively the weapon could be released at 60° attitude, which reduced the

distance by 3,000 ft (914 m), but increased the duration of the bomb's flight by 11 seconds. When no IP could be identified, the instruction was to release the bomb directly over the target at 10° beyond the vertical. The bomb would then travel vertically upwards, reaching some 18,000 ft (5486 m), before descending onto the target. Although this method reduced the separation distance from the launch aircraft, it was still allegedly sufficient to prevent it being destroyed in the nuclear blast.

Red Beard-designated aircraft required a number of modifications to enable them to perform the role. A LABS indicator replaced the gun sight, consisting of a simple but accurate horizontal and vertical needle linked to the Blue Silk Doppler navigation aid. At the IP the horizontal needle dropped to the bottom of the scale and, as the 4-g loop was initiated, the pilot attempted to return and keep the 'crosshairs' in the centre of the dial. This instrument markedly improved the accuracy of delivery. Additional

changes included the deletion of the cannon and installation of LABS control switch boxes, roller map display and ballast weights to counteract the missing cannon. The Blue Silk equipment was mounted on the cockpit coaming, reducing the visibility from the cockpit.

Testing

Service clearance was the function of A&AEE, Boscombe Down, and prototype WT854 was assessed during October 1956 after the anhedral tailplane, saw tooth and fences were fitted. Handling qualities were generally good over the speed range tested, with apparently docile transonic behaviour. There was, however, a lack of precision in longitudinal control, particularly in the climb, and difficulty in maintaining lateral level at high weights and high indicated airspeeds. Improvement on both these counts was essential. Pitch-up still occurred at high Mach numbers, but at high altitude and within a relatively narrow Mach range. This was easily

Above: By the time of the maiden flight of the first production Type 544, on 11 January 1957, it had been rumoured that the type was to be named Scimitar. What was not known was that this day also heralded the demise of Supermarine, as new Prime Minister Harold Macmillan appointed Duncan Sandys as Defence Secretary. Three months later, Sandys would produce his White Paper which will forever be linked with the decimation of the British aircraft industry.

Below: After a gap of some four months the second production Scimitar (XD213) flew in May 1957, marking a rapid rise in the rate of production, with an average of two aircraft completed each month for the remainder of the year. XD213 performed demonstrations at both the Paris and Farnborough shows in 1957.

With pressure mounting on the British aviation manufacturers, the SBAC show at Farnborough in 1958 was an important event in which to showcase new designs. No. 803 Sqn was selected to represent the navy's newest and largest aircraft, and began perfecting a six-ship display routine. After a rehearsal period at RNAS Ford in Sussex (that prompted irate calls about the deafening noise from the locals), the show went without a hitch. Here, one of the six Scimitars concludes the display with a maximum speed low-level run. At high transonic speeds, vapour clouds would often envelope the aircraft, particularly in moist air conditions.

Scimitar weapons

Intended initially as a fighter, the Scimitar's main armament comprised four 30-mm Aden Mk 4 cannon, positioned in pairs in the underside of each engine bay. The ammunition boxes were positioned in the wing roots, with each gun having a maximum load of 160 rounds. The rate of fire was in the region of 1,200 rounds per minute, with all ammunition able to be fired in a four-gun, eight-second burst. Dispensed ammunition cases were fed to a collecting tank fitted between the gun bays in the forward fuselage. On firing, a scoop on the underside of the fuselage opened, the airflow cooling the gun bays and clearing them of gases and debris. The pilot fired the guns using a trigger-button positioned on the front of the control column and incorporating a safety catch.

Deemed unsuitable in the high-altitude fighter role, the Scimitar was much more at home in the ground-attack role. Four 1,000-lb (454-kg) bombs (right) could be carried (one on each of the underwing pylons) and trials were carried out with two 2,000-lb (907-kg) bombs. Unguided rocket projectiles were also regularly carried (right below), usually fired in 'ripple' bursts.

Following trials conducted in the early 1960s, the Scimitar was cleared to carry the US-supplied Bullpup air-to-ground missile (bottom right). Controlled via a radio link, the Bullpup weighed 570 lb (258 kg), measured 10 ft 6 in (3.20 m) in length and was fitted with a 250-lb (113-kg) warhead. Up to four missiles could be carried although, in reality, two (along with two drop tanks) was a more normal load. The Scimitar could launch the missile at speeds of up to Mach 0.95 and dive angles of 45°. Guidance was achieved by the pilot using a switch mounted on the left side of the cockpit. The system was rudimentary with only singular up, down, left or right commands able to be transmitted at one time. On its journey to the target the missile could dispatch two parasite flares that were used by the pilot for target alignment, provided he maintained a steady course following release.

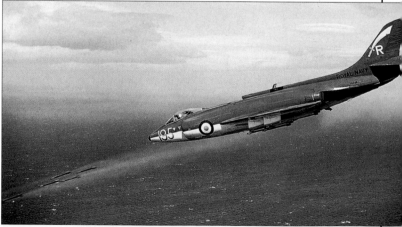

Lacking radar, and with gun armament rapidly becoming obsolete for air-to-air encounters, the Fleet Air Arm acquired the infra-red homing version of the AIM-9 Sidewinder missile, which was cleared for use on the Scimitar in early 1963. Already well refined and tested, the missile was easily integrated and was usually carried on the outboard underwing pylons. When the missile had locked onto an infra-red source, the pilot would hear an audio 'growl' in his headphones indicating that the missile was ready.

Shrouded in secrecy, the Scimitar was the first Royal Navy aircraft to be assigned the nuclear strike role. In an attempt to hide its real identity the weapon was referred to as the 'Target Marker Bomb' (TMB), but was actually the OR.1127 Red Beard 25-kiloton nuclear free-fall bomb (later used by the Buccaneer). A relatively crude device, accidental dropping or banging could result in an inadvertent explosion in the region of 1 kiloton. For that reason, Scimitars carrying Red Beard were never allowed to land on a carrier. The weapon was deployed using the LABS technique (described in the main text) and was operational on the aircraft from late 1963. A dummy Red Beard was displayed on a No. 803 Squadron aircraft at the Leuchars air day in September 1964 (below).

controllable, although the feature had to be eliminated as this had implications at lower altitudes regarding considerations of airframe strength. By the date of these tests, the change of the Scimitar's primary role to strike had been made and, on the evidence of this testing, it potentially showed great promise.

Handling tests by Mike Lithgow in May 1957 showed satisfactory all-up stall characteristics with full warning coming from acute buffeting. The Scimitar showed no natural tendency to spin whatsoever, its spin was mildly oscillatory and showed no untoward characteristics for a swept-wing aircraft. An Indicated Mach Number of 1.25 (1.32 true) was achieved in the dive during November. Later tests revealed that the Scimitar's configuration was such that greater than predicted inertia cross coupling effects in rolling manoeuvres had to be considered. It was found that sideslip angles, in the neighbourhood of the structural limit, were sometimes

recorded in very harsh rolling manoe-uvres, but the risk of structural damage was small.

Inertia coupling (coupling between pitch, roll and yaw at high speeds to create sideslip with excessive loading and possible structural failure) had recently been brought to the fore by the crashes of F-100 Super Sabre fighters in America, modern aircraft with a concentration of weight in the fuselage and short wings being particularly susceptible. After a thorough investigation by Supermarine and discussion with A&AEE, normal rolling was limited to 360° and rolling pull-outs to 5 *g* and full aileron. Clearance for service trials of the Bullpup and Sidewinder missiles were also made at A&AEE during 1961 through to the end of 1962, using XD268. Bullpup carriage limits were Mach 1.1 and 6 *g* (or 5 *g* in rolling pullouts) with no rapid rates of roll.

The allowance for carrying Sidewinder Mk 1A, both in flight and for catapulting and

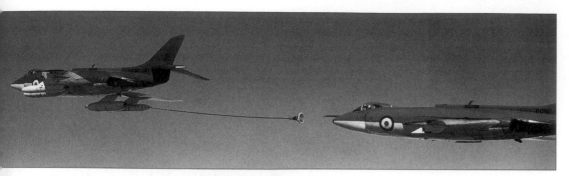

arresting, actually reached the aircraft's full limits; the missile could also be fired up to the aircraft's speed limits, but within *g* limits of -1.5 to +4.0 and a maximum dive angle of 65°. Early production aircraft XD212, XD213, XD214 and XD218 were used by the contractor for trials: several more including XD216, XD217, XD219, XD226 and XD228 found their way direct from manufacture to A&AEE for armament trials. XD219, for example, used just over 20,000 rounds clearing the Aden for air firing, and confirmed even the worst condition scenario did not surge the engines. XD214 and XD227 undertook tropical trials at El Adem, while XD229 was to spend its entire career (1960 to 1967) as a development aircraft with RAE Farnborough where it was painted light blue and white. In this role it made many high-speed

weapon delivery runs over the West Freugh test ranges.

Operational service

Over 12 years had passed since presentation of the initial Type 505 proposals, but the Scimitar's service life was to last just another eight. Service trials and training for the new type were first carried out by No. 700X Intensive Flying Training Unit formed at RNAS Ford on 27 August 1957, before full entry into service as the Scimitar F.Mk.1 came with No. 803 Squadron on 3 June 1958 at Lossiemouth. No. 803 went to sea on HMS *Victorious* three months later. The next unit to get the new machine was No. 807 Squadron, again at Lossiemouth on 1 October 1958. It was not until March 1960 that it went to sea on *Ark Royal*, transferring just over a year

later to HMS *Centaur*.

Tours on both ships were spent in the Mediterranean, before *Centaur* was sent to the Persian Gulf in mid-1961 for No. 807 to begin policing patrols off Kuwait following some intimidation from Iraq. This was the closest the Scimitar ever came to active service in a conflict and sand became a source of trouble to the type during these operations. A Far East tour on *Centaur* followed before disbandment at Lossiemouth on 15 May 1962. History was made by No. 807 at Grand Harbour, Malta, on 12 November 1960 when the 'Ark' launched two Scimitars while in harbour, the first occasion this had been done with jet aircraft.

The final front-line recipients were No. 800 Squadron from 1 July 1959 and No. 804 from 1 March 1960, both at Lossiemouth. No. 800

Within a year of its reformation with the Scimitar in October 1958, No. 807 Squadron had earned a reputation for the excellence of its squadron display team. The pilots adorned their helmets with the squadron 'Scimitar' symbol for the 1959 SBAC air show (above), where they made such an impression that the CO was invited to appear on the TV programme 'What's my line?'. The aircraft displayed without drop tanks and with only a single weapons pylon beneath each wing, shown as the formation enters a loop during practice over the Moray Firth (left). The aircraft were adorned with the code 'R' for their allocated carrier HMS Ark Royal, on which they eventually embarked for the first time in March 1960.

Below: By 1962, the Scimitar fleet was certainly not uniform in fit. Some aircraft were fitted with refuelling probes (as shown by two of this trio of No. 736 Sqn aircraft), some were fitted with the Blue Silk Doppler navigation role associated with LABS, while others were configured for the 'buddy' tanking role.

Above: The Scimitar and Sea Vixen were the Royal Navy's premier front-line aircraft in the early 1960s. Smoke generators were fitted to both types for the 1962 SBAC show at Farnborough, the Scimitars being represented by No. 736 Squadron which was the conversion unit for the type.

embarked on HMS *Ark Royal* for passage and a tour to the Far East, where shore-based detachments spent time at Tengah, Singapore. The unit amalgamated with No. 803 on 25 February 1964. No. 804 Squadron kept its Scimitars for a shorter period than any other operational squadron, being disbanded on 15 September 1961 after Far East and home deployment on HMS *Hermes*, again including time at Tengah. One of its last duties was representing the Fleet Air Arm at the 1961 Farnborough Show, a formation of nine aircraft performing an immaculate display.

Final operations

No. 803 Squadron was to be the longest and last user of the Scimitar. Its period in the Mediterranean on *Victorious* was mixed with returns to the UK before departure with the ship to the Far East for most of 1961. In 1962, No. 803 returned to the Mediterranean and the Far East, this time with *Hermes*, before a final Far East tour in *Ark Royal* during 1965 and 1966. This final Scimitar squadron was disbanded, and

the aircraft therefore withdrawn from the front-line, on 1 October 1966, to be replaced by the Buccaneer. No. 800B's aircraft were the only examples to embark on HMS *Eagle*. This was a special tanker flight formed to allow Buccaneer S.Mk 1s to take-off with a full bomb load in hot weather. The latter's Gyron Juniors were insufficient to allow a catapult take-off in such conditions with both bombs and maximum fuel, so 800B's Scimitars departed first to allow the Buccaneers to refuel immediately after leaving the carrier. These Scimitars really proved their worth during the 1966 Beira Patrol.

Lossiemouth was the home base for all Scimitar squadrons when not at sea, and repair and maintenance facilities were also established at Tengah/Sembawang, to assist overseas deployments. Operational pilot training was also concentrated at Lossiemouth and was the task of No. 700X until February 1959. As the Naval Air Fighter and Strike School, No. 736 Squadron filled the training role until it was disbanded on 26 March 1965.

An interesting aside to the aircraft's operational career was the participation by No. 807 Squadron Scimitar XD268, piloted by Commander I. H. F. Martin, in the 1959 *Daily Mail* Bleriot Air Race between London and Paris. In early 1959, the Royal Navy entered two teams, one using the Scimitar, the other the Sea Vixen. After the team's strategies had been worked out, the event commenced on 15 July, along with entrants from the RAF and the French. The journey started from the control point on Avenue d'Iena, Paris, with Martin riding pillion on a motorbike, driven at speeds of over 70 mph (113 km/h), through the Paris traffic to the heliport at Issy. Here, he jumped aboard a Royal Navy Whirlwind for the transit to Villacoublay, where the Scimitar awaited him, engines running. A 20-minute dash to Wisley ensued, with the pilot egressing down a specially modified canvas slide to save a few precious seconds. From here another Whirlwind took him to Cadogan Pier on the Thames River, where he alighted on a motor launch to cross

Left: From 1959 trials were conducted to assess the suitability of the Scimitar for the target-towing role using the Dart target. A specially designed extended A-frame, carrying a forked hook, was attached to the aircraft's arrester gear assembly. The target itself could be jettisoned by pressing the camera button on the control column. Trial pick-ups were made from both land and HMS Victorious, although the assembly prevented the aircraft landing aboard the ship. The aircraft demonstrated it could perform the role at heights in excess of 40,000 ft (12192 m) and speeds in the vicinity of Mach 1, however, the Scimitar was eventually deemed unsuitable for the role and the experiment was officially abandoned in 1961.

Above: Photo-reconnaissance was always intended as a secondary role for the Scimitar and a number of aircraft were fitted with the 'PR nose' (note aperture on port side of nose), this was easily interchangeable with a standard nose section. Attached to the RAE Weapons Flight, this aircraft (XD268) is seen at the SBAC show in 1960, where it was used to photograph the crowd at the beginning of the air demonstrations, having the photographs on display before the show's end. The aircraft had previously conducted Bullpup firing trials, and for this purpose had an additional camera underslung beneath the forward fuselage.

Left: The nose-high attitude of the Scimitar during the landing phase was disconcerting to pilots at first. With airbrakes and 'flap-blowing' employed the aircraft had to be positively 'flown onto' the runway or deck, as initiating a flare could actually increase the rate of descent.

Right: A No. 803 Squadron Scimitar 'tucks up' its undercarriage at RAAF Butterworth, Malaysia, during a detachment from HMS Victorious in the spring of 1961. The aircraft regularly deployed to Butterworth, Changi and Tengah during Far East cruises, often using the nearby ranges for weapons firing practice.

Below: From 1960, the Sea Vixen FAW.Mk 1 began replacing the Sea Venom on the decks of the Royal Navy carriers, and worked in conjunction with the Scimitar until the latter was replaced by the Buccaneer from 1963.

the river to a Royal Marines motorcycle, for the final sprint to the finishing line in Marble Arch. On the final run on 19 July the techniques had been perfected and a French motorcycle champion enlisted for the first leg. On arrival at Wisley in the Scimitar Martin threw the aircraft into a tight 7-*g* turn to rapidly reduce speed before touching down. Everything else ran smoothly, and the time from the centre of Paris to Marble Arch was reduced to 43 mins 11 secs. Unfortunately, the time was just beaten by the RAF entry, although much debate still rages today about the RAF helicopter 'cheating' by transitting through restricted airspace!

Heavy losses

Of the 76 aircraft built, no less than 37 were lost in crashes or accidents, claiming the lives of nine pilots. After withdrawal, 16 aircraft were passed to Airwork FRU, at Bournemouth (Hurn), for Fleet Requirement work; the pilots being trained to fly Scimitars by No. 764(B) Squadron (specially formed from No. 736), until it disbanded in November 1965. This work comprised simulated fast low-level attacks against surface ships for defence training and air traffic and direction work, to assist the training of new controllers at Yeovilton. This came to an end at the close of 1970, signalling also the end of the aircraft's flying career.

Two of the prototypes, WT854 and WT859, served with the School of Aircraft Handling at Culdrose until 1969, while the third, WW134, was fired off the forward catapult of HMS *Victorious* during underwater ejection trials in the Mediterraneam in June 1962. Twelve aircraft became ground instructional airframes in 1968 while WT854 and some production airframes

A Scimitar of No. 736 Squadron tops up its tanks from a 'buddy'-equipped Sea Vixen during trials in 1963. Notoriously 'short-legged', the Scimitar had an unrefuelled endurance of about 40 minutes without drop tanks. Even with auxiliary tanks the aircraft would have to be refuelled for longer range strike missions.

went to the target ranges at Foulness during 1969 to 1971. The final contribution made by the Scimitar was as a test vehicle for braking trials at RAE. The increasing weights of new military and particularly civil aircraft necessitated research into the behaviour of aircraft on snow-covered, wet and slippery runways and two Scimitars became the aerodynamic guinea pigs. For the initial tests XD248 was loaned to Farnborough for high-speed runs over a variety of surfaces, the tests being made in the first months of 1968. XD219 replaced XD248 at the end of the year for more experiments. No flying was required and the outboard wing sections were removed, the aircraft completing nearly 150 trials before a spectacular end on 9 January 1973. Missing the arrester wire at over 120 mph (193 km/h) it careered on to hit a concrete plinth.

At the end of their flying careers, the remaining Scimitars were either sent to the scrapyards, armament ranges or the Proof & Experimental Establishment at Shoeburyness. It was here that the Scimitars, along with the corpses of innumerable other retired aircraft (including such rare airframes as the TSR-2, Bristol 188 and Fairey Delta), were subjected to live ammunition trials assessing the effectiveness of modern weapons against different materials. Many of the airframes were simply tested to destruction, including the majority of the aircraft which

latterly had served with Airwork FRU. By the late 1980s only a handful of airframes remained at Shoeburyness, with the remains purchased by a local scrapyard, or by the MoD for use as targets on the Aberporth and Pendine armament ranges.

Further designs

There were numerous proposals for second generation Scimitars. One was the Type 556 two-seat all-weather fighter of March 1954. An adaptation to carry two Red Dean or four Blue Jay (Firestreak) air-to-air missiles, four cannon or a Blue Jay/cannon mix, the 556 had a larger nose to take the Ferranti Airpass radar. A single prototype, XH451, was ordered to Specification NA.38 in September, but cancelled the following July because the DH.110 (Sea Vixen) was already ordered to this requirement. The Navy had actually requested strike versions before the Scimitar became a strike aircraft. Their requirement NR/A.19 was raised in 1947 to which, among other projects, was proposed a conversion of the straight-wing Type 508 called Type 522. When the swept 525 appeared, a new swept conversion was requested in January 1950 and the submission, complete with V-tail, carried a 2,000-lb (907-kg) or two 1,000-lb (454-kg) bombs or two Red Angel bombs and was designated Type 537. The aircraft was ordered but the prototypes were suspended in April for a lack of cash, while the subsequent progress with the Scimitar pushed the project aside.

The Type 558 was a Scimitar Mk 2 project of April 1955, with developed Avon RA.24 engines. Wing span was increased and the main weapons were Firestreak plus two cannon. Type 561 was a low-level atomic strike aircraft with RA.28s; Type 564 received two de Havilland Gyron Junior PS.43 engines with blown flaps and ailerons, the Target Marker Bomb and Ferranti Blue Parrot radar; Type 565 was a two-seat tactical bomber for the RAF to the embryonic GOR.339 'Canberra Replacement' requirement.

Supersonic Scimitar proposals under Type 576 were submitted in December 1958, to a new requirement for a naval fighter replacement. However, Naval Staff considered an all-new aircraft was the way ahead. The 576 had the two Avons reheated or supplemented by two de

Above: A pair of Scimitars from No. 807 Squadron blasts low along the Scottish coastline from their Lossiemouth base in November 1958. Although intended as a fighter, the aircraft was subsonic and lacked manoeuvrability at high altitudes. It did, however, find its niche as a low-level strike platform combining excellent speed and acceleration with a rock-steady ride.

Right: On December 1965, the Scimitar commenced its last operational tour as a strike aircraft, when No. 803 Squadron embarked on HMS Ark Royal for a cruise to the Far East. During the deployment, the squadron was called on to fly operations in support of the blockade of Mozambique, known as the Beira Patrol.

Havilland Spectre rocket boosters, to give a Mach 1.8 capability at 65,000 ft (19812 m). In the fighter role it carried four Firestreak or Red Top missiles. Several two-seat Scimitars were proposed, but none was built, which is curious as the Buccaneer clearly benefited from having an observer. In the end, any Scimitar development would have been a futile exercise since the Buccaneer was to take the Navy's strike role, while the Sea Vixen had already filled the all-weather fighter need.

Opinions differ between pilots but in general the Scimitar seems to have been well liked. The fuel balance system and hydraulics were complex and their operation may have influenced some judgements. High-speed handling at altitude was certainly pretty poor, but supersonic speed could be maintained in the dive and, on occasions, Mach 1.3 was reached. Many considered it a pilot's aircraft but it had to be

Above: Having served as a trials aircraft for a large part of its service career, it was appropriate that XD219 spent its final days at RAE Farnborough. From March 1971 it was operated by the Western Squadron with its outer wings cropped for wet runway braking/aquaplaning trials (as seen here). On 9 January 1973 it ran off the runway during a high-speed run and was terminally damaged. The wreckage was later transported to the Proof & Experimental Establishment, Shoeburyness.

Scimitar F.Mk 1, XD268
No. 800B Flight, Fleet Air Arm
September 1964-July 1965

No. 800B Flight operated the Scimitar between September 1964 and August 1966. Allocated four aircraft, No. 800B's *raison d'être* was to provide inflight refuelling for the embarked Buccaneer S.Mk 1s, which lacked the thrust to take off with full fuel and warload. The distinctive froth-laden tankard symbol was in recognition of the unit's friendly bond with the Whitbreads brewery. This unofficial 'sponsorship' providing a valuable source of alcohol, particularly on long cruises to the Far East. Such was the rate of consumption aboard *Eagle*, that on one 71-day cruise, the ship's complement got through 426,000 cans of beer. High-ranking naval officers made various attempts to get the tankard removed from the aircraft, but the symbol endured until the unit was disbanded in August 1966. The photograph shows Scimitar XD268 being guided by the Flight Deck Director onto the catapult for a launch during duties aboard HMS *Eagle* in the winter of 1964/65. In November of that year the aircraft crashed during single-engined circuit practice at Lossiemouth, the pilot, Sub Lt A. C. Hill, successfully ejected suffering minor injuries.

treated with respect at all times as mistakes would be penalised, unlike, for example, the Sea Hawk. The crash list rather backs this up. Manoeuvrability was not helped by the weight, but the machine was adopted for formation aerobatics at SBAC Farnborough and other air shows and displayed an excellent 540°/sec rate of roll which permitted the development of the 'Twinkle Roll' routine.

Raw power

Most pilots were surprised by the phenomenal power and take-off acceleration, particularly those switching from the Hawker Hunter, and it has been stated that at low level a Scimitar, with one engine shutdown, could outpace a F-4 Phantom with both engines running at maximum dry thrust.

With no two-seat conversion aircraft available, transition was not always easy and a simulator was brought into use once No. 700X Flight was up and running. It was a heavy lander, but the undercarriage was strong enough to withstand this. No export orders were ever won by the aircraft, however, a de-navalised variant,

designated Type 563, was prepared for the Swiss Air Force in the late 1950s. The Swiss undertook in-depth studies of several aircraft, including the Saab 35 Draken, to replace their de Havilland Vampires and Venoms, before the French Mirage III was declared the winner.

A handsome machine, the Scimitar was the first single-seat swept-wing fighter, the first supersonic aeroplane, the first equipped with nuclear weapons and the biggest and heaviest single-seat fighter in the Fleet Air Arm. Designed to replace the Sea Hawk, it represented quite an improvement on that highly successful product, but nowhere near as many were built. Attack capability was dramatically increased placing heavy demands on crew training. The engine, the Avon 202, was good, but the Scimitar would surely have benefited from a thinner wing. Perhaps the Americans sum it up best by observing that 'Only the British could put 22,500 lb (100.3 kN) of thrust into an aircraft and keep it subsonic', yet on entering service it was the UK's fastest fighter.

Scimitar was an immensely noisy beast and did suffer some fatigue cracking in the rear fuse-

This fine study of XD322, captured in March 1970, shows this aircraft, and indeed the Scimitar itself, in its final few months of service. Operated by the Airwork Fleet Requirements Unit, it was the penultimate Scimitar to make the short flight to Southend, for onwards transportation to the P&EE at Shoeburyness for ordnance trials. Despite their age, the FRU Scimitars had a remarkably good service record, with only one aircraft being lost in over three and a half years of operations.

lage and tail from acoustic vibration. Unlike some of its contemporaries, it was not delayed by major changes of policy or a nasty crash, but development was slow for a number of reasons and by the time it entered service it had been made a little antiquated by supersonic machines such as the McDonnell F4H Phantom. Supermarine, of course, had to give priority and so much time to the numerous problems plaguing their Swift. The Scimitar was the last new aircraft to be designed and built by Supermarine, the government's White Paper, of 1957, signalling the beginning of the end of both Scimitar development proposals and the company itself.

Tony Buttler, AMRAeS

Scimitar survivors

Only three complete Scimitars survived the scrapyard and all are now in the hands of museums. The best preserved example is XD317 which resides at the Fleet Air Arm Museum, RNAS Yeovilton. Having ended its flying career with the FRU at Bournemouth, it was acquired by RAE Farnborough before delivery to the FAA Museum in August 1969. Placed in storage in 1970 by the FAA Museum, XD220 was acquired by the USS *Intrepid* Air and Space Museum, New York in the mid-1980s as part of a swap deal involving an ex-US Marine Corps F-4 Phantom, and is currently undergoing refurbishment. The final whole example is XD332, owned by the Southampton Hall of Aviation and in open storage in the museum car park. Additionally, three nose sections have survived, most notably that of WT859, the second prototype, which is housed at the Brooklands Museum, Surrey. Parts of various other Scimitars may still be extant on the Pendine and Larkhill Ranges and at a number of scrapyards around the UK.

Left: XD317 is currently on display at the FAA Museum and is painted in the markings it wore when serving with No. 800 Sqn between Jan 1963-Feb 1964.

Below: Its flying days over, XD243 is seen with the AES at Lee-on-Solent in June 1967 (left). It was transported to the P&EE in 1970, before the rear fuselage was transported to the Pendine Ranges, Dyfed in 1983. The RAE's 'Wingless Wonder', XD219, survived longer than most, serving as a crash rescue airframe at Yeovilton (right) from 1990-94 being sold for scrap.

Scimitar Operators

No. 700 Squadron

Stationed at RNAS Ford, No. 700 Sqn reformed in August 1955 as a Trials and Requirements Unit from the constituent parts of Nos 703 and 771 Squadrons. Equipped with a wide variety of contemporary types, including various marks of Gannet, Sea Hawk, Sea Venom and Whirlwind, No. 700 received its first Scimitar (XD226) on 12 March 1958. Two further examples were added (XD220, XD221) when No. 700X Squadron disbanded on 27 May. Deck trials were conducted aboard HMS *Victorious* between 29 August

XD226 ('510') was the first Scimitar to join the unit, and is seen here landing at its RNAS Yeovilton headquarters in October 1959.

and 4 September, testing the arrester gear and catapults, prior to the first carrier deployment by No. 803 Squadron later in the month. In mid-September the unit relocated to RNAS Yeovilton and continued to operate the type until 20 February 1959. Codes 510-512.

No. 700X Squadron

A pair of No. 700X Scimitars transits past The Needles, Isle of Wight, during a training sortie from their base at RNAS Ford in early 1958. Note the 'FD' tail code on XD221 ('801').

Tasked with ensuring the Scimitar entered service able to perform and sustain operations in its designated roles, No. 700X Intensive Flying Trials Unit (IFTU) formed at RNAS Ford on 27 August 1957. The first aircraft (XD221) arrived on 25 September and the unit eventually operated with a complement of seven aircraft. Among the unit's tasks were confirming the manufacturer's performance figures for the aircraft, establishing guidelines for weapon delivery profiles, weapons release and air-to-air combat, extensive evaluation of the aircraft's maintainability especially during intensive operations and forwarding all recommendations to the operational units. The squadron completed almost 1,000 sorties in the eight months of operations, before the unit was disbanded on 27 May 1958. Codes 800-806.

No. 736 Squadron

As part of the Naval Air Fighter and Strike School, No. 736 Squadron received its first Scimitars at Lossiemouth in May 1959, joining the Sea Hawks already on strength. Operational conversion and weapons training for the Scimitar had, until then, been performed by No. 807 Squadron and the original intention was for No. 764 Squadron to adopt Scimitar Operational Flying School (OFS) Part II training as No. 807 relinquished this role. However, a change of plan saw No. 764 receive Hunters and No. 736 Squadron was assigned the role in its place. Originally allocated six aircraft, the OFS Part II course lasted 14 weeks, and on the successful completion trainee pilots were allocated an operational squadron. The Sea Hawks had been re-allocated to No. 738 Squadron by July 1960 and Scimitar strength was increased to eight and subsequently 10 aircraft. A total of 41 OFS courses was conducted by No. 736 Squadron between June 1958 and March 1965, with the majority of operational squadron pilots passing through the unit during the seven-year period. In 1964, a French Navy exchange pilot was placed on the OFS prior to joining No. 803 Squadron, cementing a close relationship with the French Etendard IV training unit. The squadron devised an impressive five-day display routine for the 1962 Farnborough Air Show, establishing a reputation for formation demonstrations which continued until the unit was disbanded on 26 March 1965, its role and remaining aircraft being transferred to No. 764B Squadron. On the same day No. 736 reformed as the training squadron for the Buccaneer S.Mk 1. Codes 608 618.

Above: The first production Scimitar, XD212, served with the unit from July-September 1961 before being destroyed in a fatal accident.

Left: No. 736's display team pull into a loop during the summer of 1962.

Far left: In 1960, the 'LM' code, initially applied to No. 736's aircraft, was replaced by a blue lightning flash on a white fin, as shown by Sidewinder-equipped XD239 in May 1962.

No. 764B Squadron

No. 764B retained its predecessor's codes and markings, as demonstrated by XD215 in May

Taking over Scimitar training duties from No. 736 Squadron on 26 March 1965, No. 764B Sqn completed two OFS courses at Lossiemouth (training pilots for Airwork FRU), before disbanding in on 23 November 1965 on completion of its tasks. Codes 611-621

No. 800 Squadron

No. 800 Squadron became the third front-line Scimitar squadron on 1 July 1959 and spent the following eight months undergoing intensive flying training, before embarking on HMS *Ark Royal* with six Scimitars, for its first cruise on 3 March 1960. The unit spent the majority of the following year deployed on the carrier, operating in the Mediterranean, the North Atlantic and the Arctic Ocean, until returning to Lossiemouth on 27 February 1961. The unit was chosen as the Royal Naval Display Team and, naming themselves 'The Red Blades', performed some 19 displays during 1961, including the Paris Air Salon and a nine-ship display at Farnborough. In the autumn of 1961 the squadron's complement was increased from six to 12 aircraft, all of which underwent the modification programme to allow the firing of Bullpup and Sidewinder missiles. In late 1961, the squadron conducted work-up operations from *Ark Royal* before embarking in March 1962 for a major Far East deployment. The cruise lasted nine months and included detachments to RAF Tengah, Singapore and RAAF Pearce, Australia and exercises with the Royal Marines and the navies of Australia, USA, Thailand, New Zealand and Pakistan. During exercises off Okinawa, the squadron became the first front line Royal Navy unit to fire the Bullpup missile. On the return to the UK, the squadron's aircraft were called on to mount combat air patrols during counter-insurgent operations in the Radfan area. After elements from the squadron conducted exercises in the English Channel during early 1963, the whole 14-aircraft complement embarked on 4 May for the unit's final major cruise with

the Scimitar. Again deployed to the Far East, the squadron participated in major exercises off Singapore and in the Gulf of Oman, and made detachments to Tengah, Singapore and Embakasi, Kenya, before participating with the US and Pakistan navies in Exercise Midlink 6 which involved the Scimitars defending the ship from low-level mock attacks by Pakistani air force F-86 Sabres. The squadron departed *Ark Royal* on 31 December 1963 and disbanded at Lossiemouth on 25 February 1964. Codes 100-113

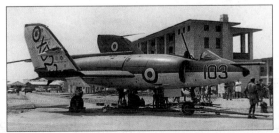

Left: XD239 at RAF Khormaksar in May 1963 after ditching in Aden harbour during an aborted approach. The projecting rail from the cockpit is evidence of Sub Lt Legg's successful ejection, the aircraft ending up in 6 ft (1.83 m) of water.

Left: No. 800 Sqn aircraft carried a white letter 'R' on a red painted fin.

Right: The squadron put up this impressive nine-ship display team for the 1961 SBAC show.

Left: A Buccaneer S.Mk 1 of No. 800 Sqn prepares to take on fuel from an 800B Flight Scimitar, while operating from HMS Eagle in 1965.

Right: During operations, the Scimitars would launch first, before rendezvousing with the Buccaneers during their transit to the target area.

No. 800B Squadron

Associated with, but separate from No. 800 Squadron, No. 800B formed on 9 September 1964 with the main task of investigating air-to-air refuelling techniques, particularly with the former squadron's Buccaneer S.Mk 1s which were unable to take-off from a carrier with a full fuel and weapons load. On 2 December 1964, No. 800B's four aircraft and pilots joined HMS Eagle for a cruise to the Far East. The Scimitars not only 'topped-up' the Buccaneer' but also refuelled No. 899 Squadron Sea Vixens and other NATO aircraft. By the end of the cruise in May, the squadron had perfected 'insurance for beyond diversionary range' operations with one aircraft as tanker, one as a 'tanker CAP' and a third on deck at five minutes' notice. On returning to the Mediterranean in May 1965, the Scimitars were involved in additional exercises, including photography and strafing on Libyan ranges. After spending the summer of 1965 at Lossiemouth, the squadron re-embarked aboard Eagle on 27 August, conducting exercises in the Mediterranean and off the coast of Aden, before transitting to the Far East in November. Further exercises were conducted in the Singapore/Penang areas and off the coast of Mombasa before, in March, the carrier was ordered to the Mozambique Channel to participate in the Beira Patrol – the British embargo on oil to Southern Rhodesia. Relieved by HMS Ark Royal on 30 April, the carrier returned to the Far East for further exercises before heading for the Indian Ocean. On 31 July, Eagle began its voyage home, and on 14 August No. 800B's Scimitars departed the carrier in the Mediterranean and flew to RNAS Yeovilton, where the unit was immediately disbanded. Codes 111-117.

No. 803 Squadron

As the first and longest serving of the front-line Scimitar squadrons, No. 803 reformed at Lossiemouth on 3 June 1958, initially with eight aircraft. Intensive work-up training, conducted during the following two months, was inter-spersed by the squadron's participation in the 1958 Farnborough Air Show. On 25 September the squadron departed Yeovilton for HMS Victorious, becoming the first Scimitar squadron to join an operational carrier. Exercises were conducted in the Mediterranean, including detachments to Hal Far and Hyères, before the squadron returned briefly to Lossiemouth on 13 January 1959. Much of the following year was spent aboard Victorious, flying exercises in the Mediterranean, North Sea, Baltic Sea and off the east coast of the USA. The latter included visits to Norfolk, Boston and New York and cross-operations with the USS Saratoga. Later in the year, the Scimitars participated in Exercise Bar Frost off the coast of Norway and the joint Exercise Longhaul with the USS Saratoga, involving defence against mock attacks flown by RAF Canberras. On 14 December 1959 the squadron returned to Lossiemouth and spent the next 10 months ashore, albeit with detachments to Victorious in February for Dart Target pick-up trials and to Hermes and Ark Royal in the late summer for training exercises. From 19 October 1960 to 8 December 1961, the squadron spent much of its time on Victorious conducting operations in the Mediterranean and the Middle and Far East. No. 803 re-embarked on Victorious for the last time on 5 February 1962 for operations in the Mediterranean, returning to Lossiemouth on 30 March. During its time on Victorious the Scimitars carried out 2,604 sorties with 2,038 deck landings, with the loss of eight aircraft and two pilots. On 25 May 1962 the squadron began a two-year association with HMS Hermes. With a complement of 9-11 aircraft, the squadron operated initially in the Mediterranean, before a cruise to the Far East between November 1962 and October 1963 incorporating exercises with US and Commonwealth naval forces and utilising Mk 20 air-to-air refuelling pods for the first time. On 16 January 1964 the squadron embarked on Hermes for the last time for Exercise Phoenix before returning to Lossiemouth on 23 February. Shortly after the squadron absorbed the remaining aircraft from the disbanding No. 800 Sqn taking its complement to 16 aircraft. The spring and summer of 1964 involved routine train-ing from Lossiemouth and air display appearances, before commencing work-up for deploy-ment aboard HMS Ark Royal. After initial operations in the English Channel and the northern waters, the squadron embarked on 17 June 1965 on its first and only Far East cruise on the carrier. Exercises were conducted in the Philippine Sea and the Indian Ocean before the carrier was called on to relieve HMS Eagle on Beira Patrol duties. After almost exactly a year away from its shore base, No. 803 returned to Lossiemouth on 12 June 1966, the cruise having claimed nine aircraft but luckily no pilots. A final short deployment aboard Ark Royal, for Exercise Straight Laced off the coast of Norway, began on 2 August 1966 before the squadron disembarked to Lossiemouth on 1 October, disbanding the same day. Codes 143-159 (June 1958 to July 1965), 015-034 (July 1965 to October 1966).

Above/right: Between February 1958 and March 1962 No. 803 Sqn was allocated to HMS Victorious. Initially a smaller white 'V' was carried on the tail, with the aircraft codes on the nose (above). This was later changed to a larger 'V' on the tail and large white codes on the engine cowlings (right).

Above left/left: During the squadron's time on Hermes (May 1962 to February 1964) the aircraft carried a large white 'H' on the tail as illustrated by XD213 aboard Hermes in July 1962. This was replaced in the final year by the squadron markings of black and yellow checks on the tail fin, with a small white 'H' on the bottom black check, as shown on XD333 as it repositions on Hermes's deck in the spring of 1963.

Above/below: For its final deployments aboard HMS Ark Royal, No. 803's Scimitars retained the black and yellow checks, replacing the 'H' with an 'R'. Two series of codes were used.

Bearing No. 804 Sqn's distinctive badge, consisting of a yellow and black tiger's face holding a dagger, XD325 and XD326 (nearest) formate for the camera during exercises in 1961.

No. 804 Squadron

The last of the four main front-line squadrons to be equipped with the Scimitar, No. 804 reformed at Lossiemouth on 1 March 1960 and by May of that year had a complement of six aircraft and eight pilots. Following an intensive work-up period the squadron joined HMS *Hermes* on 6 July for operations in the eastern Mediterranean. By mid-September the carrier was operating off the coast of Norway, with No. 804 flying mock nuclear strikes and combat air patrols as part of Exercise Swordthrust, before returning to Lossiemouth on 1 October. No. 804's second spell on *Hermes* commenced on 29 November 1960 which incorporated exercises in the Mediterranean, Middle East, Indian Ocean and the Philippine Sea. On the return journey dummy Red Beard bombs were dropped over the Filfla LABS range, before the squadron returned to Lossiemouth on 18 April 1961. The squadron's final carrier deployment began on 29 May with exercises in the English Channel prior to the carrier being deployed to the Persian Gulf as tensions between Iraq and Kuwait intensified. At the end of July the carrier participated in Exercise Bismarck which involved No. 804 scrambling to intercept 'attacking' Vulcan bombers (four 'kills' were claimed). On 10 September No. 804 squadron left the *Hermes* for the last time and was disbanded at Lossiemouth five days later. In its 18-month existence the unit had flown over 1,500 hours and made some 1,250 deck landings without losing a single pilot or aircraft. Codes 161-166.

Airwork FRU

In 1964 the Scimitar was chosen to replace the Hawker Sea Hawk as the type operated by the Fleet Requirements Unit based at Hurn, Bournemouth. The FRU was operated by Airwork Ltd with military aircraft and civilian pilots tasked with gunnery tracking, radio and radar calibration and strike attack training for Royal navy ships. The pilots (mostly ex-military) were trained by No. 764B Squadron and the chosen airframes underwent extensive overhaul at RNAY Fleetlands during 1965 before operations commenced in mid-1966. Some 16 Scimitars were operated at various times before the last examples were withdrawn from service in 1970. Codes 025-038 (1966-1968), 830-839 (1969-1971).

The FRU Scimitars usually carried four drop tanks to extend their endurance during operational flying. Seen carrying the original code sequence, XD236 (above) was lost in the unit's only fatal accident in June 1968, flying into high ground in bad weather following an altimeter failure. The second code sequence is seen on XD332 (below).

Other operators

A&AEE
All three prototype N.113Ds plus the first eight production Scimitars all underwent trials with the A&AEE at Boscombe Down, the majority of which were undertaken by 'C' Naval Test Squadron. A number of other subsequent Scimitars flew with the A&AEE at various times for trials purposes and with the Empire Test Pilot's School.

RAE
A large number of trials were carried using the prototypes and a number of production Scimitars at Bedford, Farnborough and West Freugh.

MTPS, Brawdy
The Maintenance Test Pilots School (MTPS), based at RNAS Brawdy, was allocated a single Scimitar F.Mk 1 which was used to familiarise pilot engineers with test flying procedures for advanced jet types.

RNAY Fleetlands
RNAY Fleetlands was selected as the main Royal Navy maintenance facility for the Scimitar. The aircraft were transferred to and from the Lee-on-Solent airfield from which test flights of the aircraft were flown prior to the aircraft returning to squadron service. A Maintenance Test Pilot was permanently assigned to the facility and almost all production aircraft passed through the workshops at one time or another.

AHU, Lossiemouth
New production, or aircraft emerging from major overhaul, were transferred to the Aircraft Holding Unit for an acceptance flight test by a maintenance test pilot prior to entering service or storage.

NASU, Brawdy
The Naval Air Support Unit took over the role of the AHU in the mid-1960s, accepting aircraft emerging from maintenance and test flying them before re-allocation.

Right: XD230 emerges from the paint shop at RNAS Lee-on-Solent in August 1963, following a systems upgrade at Fleetlands. After delivery to Lossiemouth by the Fleetlands test pilot, it was accepted for service by the resident AHU.

No. 807 Squadron

A quartet of No. 807 Sqn Scimitars approaches the top of a loop over the Moray Firth coastline.

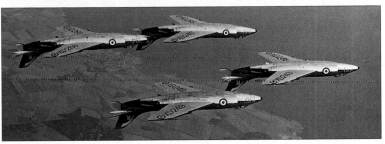

The second of the front-line units to form, No. 807 Squadron received its first Scimitars at Lossiemouth on 1 October 1958. Only 15 days later the squadron participated in the annual defence of the UK exercise Sunbeam. The majority of 1959 was spent on flying and weapons training at Lossiemouth with occasional detachments to Yeovilton and West Freugh. In September the squadron flew formation display routines at the 1959 Farnborough Air Show followed by a number of small-scale exercises conducted form their home base. After an atomic weapons course in early 1960 the squadron began work-up for deployment on HMS *Ark Royal*. No. 807's eight Scimitars embarked on *Ark Royal* on 3 March 1960 along with No. 800 Squadron, this being the first and only time two Scimitar squadrons would be deployed on an operational carrier. After exercises in the Mediterranean, the carrier went to the Arctic Ocean for extreme cold weather exercises and trials including strikes by No. 807 on targets on the north west coast of Norway and operations close to the Greenland ice shelf. After a brief spell at Lossiemouth in October, the squadron was, by early November, back aboard the *Ark Royal* in the Malta area. A visit to Grand Harbour, Malta provided an opportunity for the squadron to become the first unit to launch a jet aircraft from a carrier at anchor, two squadron pilots achieving this on 12 November. After exercises in the Malta area, followed by visits to Lisbon and New York, No. 807 disembarked the *Ark Royal* for the last time on 27 February 1961. the squadron joined its new carrier, HMS *Centaur* in April for a five-month cruise which incorporated exercises with the US 6th Fleet in the Mediterranean and operations in the Persian Gulf during the crisis in Kuwait. After spending the early autumn of 1961 at Lossiemouth the squadron was deployed aboard *Centaur* for the last time on 20 October. After guided-weapons training on the Aberporth range, *Centaur* sailed via the Mediterranean to the Far East. Exercises were conducted off the coast of Malaya and, on the return leg, in the Arabian Sea, before arriving back in UK waters on 15 May 1962 with No. 807 Squadron disbanding aboard ship on that day. Codes 190-198

This rear three-quarters view clearly shows the large underfuselage and smaller jet pipe-mounted airbrakes, and variable-incidence anhedral tailplane. This example is also fitted with a PR nose.

Above: XD219, allocated to the Maintenance Test Pilots School, departs its Brawdy base in August 1968. The aircraft was to end its days as the RAE's 'Wingless Wonder', conducting wet runway trials at RAE Farnborough.

US Spitfire operations

Part 1: Northern Europe

Many published US Air Force histories ignore the record of America's use of the Supermarine Spitfire in World War II, only presenting accounts of US-built types. Such treatment is a disservice to the pilots and mechanics who flew and serviced the large number of Spitfires which saw combat operations.

American air units first saw combat in Europe during World War I, flying, in the main, foreign-built types due to the logistical difficulties of transporting aircraft across the Atlantic Ocean, and the inferiority of US-built aircraft compared to their British and French contemporaries. In the aftermath of the conflict, US authorities vowed to ensure that this situation would not arise again, stating the intention to only supply its men based on foreign soil with the finest American aircraft, sent by whatever means necessary. This initiative was advanced in the early 1930s by the need to resuscitate America's decreased industrial productivity, following the great economic depression, using mass-production techniques and the new materials which were becoming available for industry.

When the UK entered World War II in September 1939, it was almost as unprepared to fight Germany, as the USA was to fight any country. Throughout the depression the US Army Air Corps had lobbied hard for every aircraft it could get its hands on. With very few

operational units, the service turned down thousands of applications, taking only a handful of the most qualified men for aircrew training.

At this time, Germany was beginning to threaten neighbouring countries with annexation and invasion or occupation, and although the UK began to put into place its re-arming programme, the political climate of appeasement prevented full-scale preparations. However, in late 1938, before Winston Churchill became Prime Minister, the UK had dispatched a number of purchasing commissions to the USA to explore the possibility of utilising the country's expanding aircraft mass-production facilities, situated far beyond the range of German bombers, and to determine if America could offer any combat-suitable aircraft for sale. A number of European nations, including Great Britain and France, placed initial orders, and these arms sales greatly benefited the American economy, providing a huge expansion of aircraft production and related military capability.

Production of several types of US aircraft was earmarked for the Royal Air Force,

Top: Spitfire Mk Vs from the 12th (coded 'ZM') and 109th TRS ('VX'), formate together during a publicity sortie for the 67th Reconnaissance Group in 1943. Although tasked in the tactical reconnaissance role, 67th RG Spitfires retained their armament for self defence and attacking 'soft' enemy targets of opportunity.

Above: Unlike regular RAF squadrons, the American-manned 'Eagle' squadrons adorned many of their aircraft with personal artworks. Many of them carried variations of the eagle symbol, including 'Little Joe', a No. 71 Sqn Spitfire flown by Pilot Officer Joseph Kelly.

Below: One of a famous sequence of photographs taken of Spitfire Mk VB, BM590, of No. 121 Squadron in September 1942, just days before the unit changed its identity to 335th Fighter Squadron of the 4th Fighter Group, USAAF.

Above: The aircraft in which the first 'American volunteer' squadron went to war was the Hawker Hurricane. Initially operating Mk Is from November 1940 until April 1941, No 71 Squadron replaced them with Mk IIs in the early summer of 1941. Here a pair of Mk Is returns to its base at Kirton-in-Lindsey in the spring of 1941.

Volunteer 'Eagle' ace

Spitfire Mk IIA
Flying this aircraft (P7308), Pilot Officer William R. Dunn of No. 71 Squadron, RAF, became the first American air ace of the war. He claimed his fourth and fifth victims on 27 August 1941, and remained the sole 'Eagle' ace until November of that year. According to USAAF records, Dunn only scored one 'kill', as they refused to include victories scored by its pilots in RAF service.

commencing in 1939. At this time the Curtiss P-36 and P-40 were the most capable fighter types in the US inventory and, with both Britain and France desperate for additional fighters, these aircraft entered priority production for both nations. When France fell in June 1940, the UK took the undelivered aircraft, adding them to its own orders.

To achieve a fair exchange for sales of American aircraft to the UK, an agreement, initially termed Defense Aid (later Lend-Lease), provided the organisational method by which the two English-speaking countries assisted each other in obtaining the best military equipment – including aircraft – available in either country. Supply of aircraft for, and from the UK was not always paid for in Dollars or Sterling, with much equipment being exchanged in tit for-tat agreements.

Gathering of the 'Eagles'

From the outbreak of World War II, many US pilots had expressed a wish to fight the Germans alongside the British and French. Days after Germany invaded Poland, an American in Canada named Col Charles Sweeny (who was a mercenary soldier, achieving his rank during service with the French Foreign Legion) began recruiting US personnel for service with the French air force. His plans were supplemented by his nephew in London, also named Charles Sweeny, who presented a formal suggestion to the authorities to recruit Americans in England to fight in the war. In May 1940, Col Sweeny sent his first 32 pilots to France, however, within weeks France was defeated and the surviving volunteers made their way to the UK to be absorbed into RAF squadrons.

At about the same time as the two Sweenys' efforts began, a Royal Canadian Air Force representative tasked an American named Clayton Knight, who had flown with the British Royal Flying Corps in World War I, to screen US pilots who might volunteer for military flying in Canada. Forming the Clayton Knight Committee, advertisements were placed in magazines and newspapers and some 50,000 responses poured in, of which some 6,000 pilots were selected for service with the RCAF, RAF and US Ferry Service.

Other US citizens, who eventually joined the 'Eagle' squadrons, enlisted in the RCAF and British Army, using this roundabout way to eventually receive pilot training and ultimately transfer into RAF squadrons. The motivation was certainly not pay, which was minimal, but a combination of the lure of combat flying, combined with a political desire to assist the UK and France in the struggle against Hitler's expansion plans.

On 19 September 1940, No. 71 Squadron became the first of the 'Eagle' squadrons to form, and was initially based at Church Fenton. Manned by US pilots, but commanded by an RAF officer, initial equipment comprised the obsolete Brewster Buffalo Mk I, which was used for training purposes, before the unit received the Hurricane Mk I in November, coinciding with a move to Kirton-in-Lindsey. Operational sorties commenced on 5 February 1941, consisting mainly of defensive fighter sweeps, with the squadron re-equipping with Hurricane Mk IIs in April 1941. A number of the Hurricane Mk Is were passed to No. 121 Squadron, which became the second of the trio of 'Eagle' squadrons, forming on 14 May, before it too received the Mk II and commenced combat operations. In August, No. 71 Sqn received the first examples of the aircraft with which it, and the other 'Eagle' squadrons, would be forever associated – the Supermarine Spitfire. Two months later No. 121 Squadron also converted to the type, with both units initially working up using the Mk II/IIA, before receiving the cannon-armed Mk V for offensive fighter sweep operations over northern France. At the end of September, No. 133 Squadron, which had formed as the third and final 'Eagle' squadron on 1 August, began operations, initially with Hurricane Mk IIs, before receiving Mk IIA and Mk V Spitfires in October 1941 and January 1942, respectively.

Left: It was a proud moment for the 'Eagle' pilots when they were finally integrated into the USAAF, on 29 September 1942, as the 4th Fighter Group. Here the 'Stars and Stripes' is officially raised at the home base for the first time, as a flight of resident Spitfire Mk Vs passes overhead.

Below: The 4th Fighter Group remained proud of its 'Eagle' heritage throughout the war, as evidenced by these mementoes on the crewroom wall in 1944.

Combat Colours

The 52nd Fighter Group saw little action in the skies of northern Europe before its hasty departure to the Mediterranean theatre in November 1942. Having previously operated the tricycle-landing gear P-39 Airacobra, the Spitfire Mk V, with its narrow-track tailwheel undercarriage, took some getting used to. This 4th Fighter Squadron example was one of a number that suffered training accidents in August 1942 before operations began in earnest in September.

As the USA became increasingly aware of its citizens fighting a war in foreign uniform, concerns grew regarding the effect on the country's position of neutrality. The chief of the USAAC, Major General H. H. Arnold, was determined to regain control of all US military personnel whatever uniform they wore.

In June 1941, Arnold sent a memorandum to Robert Lovett, Assistant Secretary of War for Air, outlining "Directions in which the United States can render the British the greatest assistance in air matters". The memo suggested sending "units on a volunteer basis, with the purpose of taking part in RAF guise in operations against the enemy". This measure would allow the airmen to fight as British personnel, while remaining under Arnold's control. The plan also envisaged the testing of American aircraft in combat conditions, with the ultimate intention of the units flying only US-built types. Although the scheme was never implemented, as the US entered the war months later in the wake of the attack at Pearl Harbor, it highlighted the displeasure that politicians and high-ranking officers felt at US citizens fighting beyond their control.

In complete contrast, the British were grateful to have the services of these volunteers, and a great deal of publicity was afforded to the 'Eagles'. A movie, portraying the airmen as heroes, was shown in cinemas throughout the country. As the squadrons at this time were only just getting used to combat operations, and had achieved nothing to compare to this overblown star quality treatment, it caused great embarrassment among the pilots.

A memo to Arnold, dated 31 January 1941 and bearing the comments of Brig. Gen. M. J. Scanlon, stated that he was not pleased that a British officer led the 'Eagles' and that "certain elements of the squadron (No. 71) are of the publicity seeking, promoter type" which in his mind did not compare favourably with the exploits of the Lafayette Escadrille, an American unit which served during World War I. Lovett responded, saying "there will always be a certain number of wild men and grandstanders in any such group of so-called soldiers of fortune". He wanted the the RAF to "maintain discipline" and for the US government to "deny to this outfit the right to use any emblem, symbol, or other badges or identification marks" used by the Air Corps. It was clear from this time onwards that the USAAC wanted nothing whatsoever to do with the 'Eagles'. When the USA declared war, other US Fighter Groups were selected to join the soon-to-be mighty Eighth Air Force, and the 'Eagles' were completely overlooked.

'Eagle' aces

The 'Eagles'' reputation of being unruly and cavalier is, however, a great injustice to the pilots who flew with the squadrons. No. 71 Squadron pilot, William R. Dunn, became America's first ace of World War II, claiming his fourth and fifth 'kills' on 27 August 1941. In November, two more 'Eagles' became aces and the squadrons began establishing an excellent reputation in combat. A number of the USAAF's more famous pilots gained their first victories while flying Spitfires with the 'Eagles' including triple ace Don Blakeslee (later to command the 4th FG) and the war's most famous P-51 Mustang ace, Don Gentile, who downed three enemy aircraft in his Spitfire during the disastrous Allied landings at Dieppe on 19 August 1942. On this day, the three 'Eagle' units were among the 76 squadrons assigned to cover the landings, and a number of the pilots flew four missions during the day. By this time, plans were being drawn up to transfer the three squadrons to USAAF control to became the 4th Fighter Group, Eighth Air Force. The date set for the transfer was 29 September 1942, but three days before a disastrous conclusion to the 'Eagle' squadron operations occurred.

In late August, the RAF had honoured the contribution made by the 'Eagle' volunteers by appointing No. 133 Squadron as one of the first three combat units to receive the new Spitfire Mk IX. Commanded by Carroll 'Mac' McColpin, who had claimed No. 133's first kill on 26 April 1942, the unit was tasked with escorting Eighth Air Force B-17s on a raid over France on, or after, 7 September. Weather delayed the mission day after day, and during this time the pilots were going, a few at a time, from their forward base at Great Stampford, near Debden, to London to fill in paperwork and be fitted for uniforms, prior to their acceptance into the USAAF. On 26 September the weather cleared and the order was given for the raid to proceed, however, McColpin was away in London. The mission was led instead by an RAF officer, Flt Lt E. G. Brettell. With France under a blanket of cloud, Brettell proceeded to the rendezvous point but could not locate the bombers. Unwittingly, a miscalculation of high level tailwinds had driven the squadron deep over France and, after a period of searching, the squadron began the return to base. At the time that time-aloft and fuel-expended levels suggested the formation was over southern England, Brettell spied a hole in the cloud and descended. The squadron was still, however, over northern France and found itself on top of German artillery and a Staffel of Focke-Wulf Fw 190s. Within minutes, 12 of the new Spitfire Mk IXs had been shot down with little chance of defending themselves. The RAF did not replace the Mk IXs , the squadron instead reverting back to the Mk V, after the three 'Eagle' squadrons were officially inducted into the USAAF on 29 September.

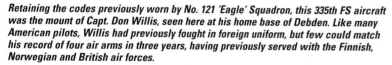

Retaining the codes previously worn by No. 121 'Eagle' Squadron, this 335th FS aircraft was the mount of Capt. Don Willis, seen here at his home base of Debden. Like many American pilots, Willis had previously fought in foreign uniform, but few could match his record of four air arms in three years, having previously served with the Finnish, Norwegian and British air forces.

Above: Learning to operate an unfamiliar type was not only a swift learning process for the pilots, but also for the mechanics. Here, a 336th FS, 4th FG Spitfire Mk VB has its engine removed for overhaul in April 1943. This example, like a number of US Spitfires, underwent major overhaul in the workshops at Audley End.

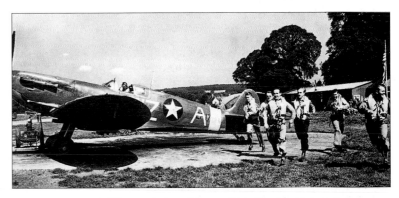

One of the USAAF's most famous Spitfire aces, Capt. Frank Hill, is seen on patrol over the English Channel in the summer of 1942. Flying with the 308th FS, Hill eventually became the 31st Group's top scoring Spitfire pilot with seven victories, most of which were accumulated in the Mediterranean theatre.

Allied plans to invade North Africa had been agreed early in 1942, and required the stripping of aircraft units from the newly-formed 8th Air Force in the UK, to enable the 12th Air Force to be established. All of the 8th Air Force fighter groups, of which there were four in mid-1942 – two Spitfire Mk V (31st and 52nd FGs) and two P-38 Lightning – were to be transferred, leaving the 8th Air Force without a single fighter group. With little enthusiasm, the USAAF requested the RAF to hand its 'Eagle' squadrons over to the USAAF. It was widely acknowledged that the USAAF 'top brass' was more proud of its own squadrons than it was, what it termed, a group of 'soldiers of fortune' who had bent neutrality laws to fight in a foreign uniform.

Formation of the 4th FG

Six weeks before the Allies launched their offensive in North Africa, Nos 71, 121, and 133 Squadrons became the 334th, 335th and 336th Fighter Squadrons of the famed 4th Fighter Group, respectively. Quickly dubbed the 'Debden Wing', the 4th FG's first C.O. was Col Edward W. Andersen, however, operational control remained in RAF hands, and an RAF

Wing Commander led the 'Debden Wing' on missions. With the Spitfire Mk V suffering from relatively short range, operations comprised mainly convoy patrols in the English Channel, fighter sweeps and coastline patrols. The aircraft themselves received USAAF insignia, but retained the same code letters allocated to their predecessors. Standard RAF Day Fighter Scheme of dark green and ocean grey upper surfaces and sky blue undersurfaces were also retained as standard.

Despite its best efforts the 4th FG did not find itself engaged with enemy aircraft frequently, and 'kills' were few and far between. One of the group's most productive days occurred on 22 January 1943, when two Luftwaffe fighters were shot down. A month later the 334th FS began the transition to the longer-range P-47 Thunderbolt, acting as a training unit for the group. On 10 March the squadron flew the P-47's first ever combat mission, led by one of

the 4th FG's Spitfire aces Lt Col Peterson. The first 'kill' by the P-47s was made by Blakeslee on 15 April, and the unit continued to operate the Thunderbolt until early 1944 when they were replaced by the P-51 Mustang.

Fighter squadrons from the US

Two months before the 'Eagle' squadrons transferred to the USAAF, two other fighter groups began Spitfire operations in the UK as part of the 8th Air Force. The decision to equip these units with British aircraft was highly contentious and involved a number of U-turns in policy during the first six months of 1942. Shortly after US entry into the war the Anglo-American agreement to conquer Germany first was formulated. The 8th Air Force would be formed to operate against the Axis from the UK, and the 12th Air Force would support the massive invasion of North Africa – planned for by the Allies for November 1942. From January

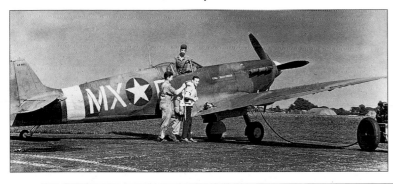

Below: The 31st Fighter Group saw the most combat action of the two USAAF groups which arrived in the summer of 1942. Involved in the disastrous raid on Dieppe, the group claimed a number of enemy aircraft during its brief period of operations. Here, the pilot of 'Lima Challenger', a 307th FS aircraft presented by a resident of the Peruvian capital, straps in to his parachute at the unit's home base at Merston. Note the small RAF serial number, EN851, at the top of the fin.

Above: One of the 31st FG's, most famous pilots was Major Harrison Thyng, who is seen here in the cockpit of his 309th FS Spitfire Mk V as his fellow squadron pilots sprint for their aircraft during a (probably staged) scramble. The aircraft were received straight from RAF Maintenance Units, and hastily had USAAF cocardes and unit codes applied, but retained the standard RAF day fighter scheme which had been introduced in August 1941.

Spitfires of the 8th Air Force

Spitfire Mk VB, 335th FS
The 4th Fighter Group only operated the Mk V version of the Spitfire, using the aircraft for fighter sweeps and coastal patrols in the English Channel region. The aircraft wore the standard RAF dark green and ocean grey colour scheme with medium sea grey undersides. Sky coloured fuselage bands and spinners were added as standard before delivery.

Spitfire Mk VB, 309th FS
The 31st Fighter Squadron received its Spitfire Mk Vs straight from RAF storage on arrival in the UK. The aircraft had the US national markings applied over the top of the RAF roundel and the appropriate unit codes added. On departing for North Africa, a number of the 31st's Spitfires were passed-on to the 15th TRS.

Below: Robert 'Fat Boy' Kraft exits his Spitfire at Membury in November 1942. A large number of the Spitfires operated by the 15th TRS were those left behind by the 31st FG on its departure to North Africa. This example was previously operated by the 309th FS.

Above: Pilots from the 12th TRS, 67th Reconnaissance Group, line-up in front of their aircraft during a visit by Brig. Gen. R. C. Candee at RAF Membury on 20 April 1943. Despite being outclassed by the Focke-Wulf Fw 190, the 8th Air Force fighter and Tac-R groups only received the Mk V, the RAF retaining the more capable Mk IXs for their own squadrons.

1942 General Arnold began to prepare the, as yet, inadequately trained USAAF pilots to fly heavy bomber and pursuit units across the Atlantic, to begin combat operations under the command of the 8th Air Force. The British had urged the US to provide fighter support for their troops in North Africa, and had asked that the units destined to arrive in the UK undergo training to acquaint them with RAF methods, before transfer to North Africa. The British were fully aware that the Bell P-39 and Lockheed P-38 fighters were unsuitable for combat in Europe, and were likely to suffer heavy losses at the hands of the German *experten*. In April 1942 Air Chief Marshall Sir Charles Portal sent a letter to Gen. Arnold suggesting "therefore why not equip US pursuit squadrons with British aircraft … and correspondingly increase US liabilities to Russia and (the) Eastern Theatre". These liabilities were part of the allied commitment to supply equipment to any country in the anti-Axis pool – resulting in the delivery of large numbers of P-39s to Russia and P-40s to the Far East and north Africa for the AVG 'Flying Tigers' and the RAF. On 20 April, Col H. A. Craig of the US War Department suggested that Arnold approve "a proposal of the British to furnish our pursuit units with Spitfires, provided we can furnish light numbers of American pursuit aircraft to the Middle East, India and Russia". He later added that he preferred the option of ferrying US aircraft to the UK, despite US production barely meeting current demands. He also found it undesirable to force US units to be "wholly dependent upon the British supply system", and the "morale factor" in Americans flying Spitfires would be adverse. In the event the opposite was true, with the pilots quickly learning to appreciate the Spitfire's abilities.

Arnold was, however, determined to stick to the US aircraft-only policy, and on 23 April named the units that were to deploy with their aircraft across the Atlantic during the summer months. These were to include the 31st PG flying the P-39 and the 1st PG with the P-38. On 14 May the 52nd PG was added to the list of units, again equipped with the P-39.

The 31st Pursuit Group (Fighter Group after May 1942) had been formed from the personnel of the 1st PG in February 1940. After its initial squadrons (39th, 40th and 41st FS) were assigned to the 35th PG for operations in the south west Pacific region following the attack

on Pearl Harbor, the 307th, 308th and 309th squadrons were formed to return the 31st PG to complete status. Bell P-39s were allocated in late 1941 and from May 1942 training for the trans-oceanic crossing began.

The second P-39 unit, the 52nd PG, was activated in January 1941 and its constituent 2nd, 4th and 5th PS received outdated Seversky P-35s, Curtiss P-36s and Republic P-43 Lancers, before re-equipping with the Airacobra in late 1941. In May, the unit moved to northeastern USA to prepare to fly its aircraft to England.

In early June 1941, following a number of training accidents and the realisation that the P-39 was not suitable for combat in northern Europe, the USAAF's plan to take its own fighters to the UK was abandoned as unworkable – the units would travel to the UK by sea under the name Operation Bolero, and on arrival be allocated Spitfire Mk Vs. On 10 June, the 31st FG embarked on a troop ship for Scotland followed by the 52nd FG on 1 July destined for Liverpool. On arrival, both units entered a period of familiarisation and training well away from the combat arena. The UK's often adverse weather conditions and non-geometrical countryside posed navigational problems not previously encountered in the USA, causing a number of forced landings away from base. Additionally the tailwheel landing gear and hand-brake lever of the Spitfire were to cause difficulties for those accustomed to the tricycle landing gear and rudder pedal brakes on the P-39. These teething problems were, however, quickly overcome and the pilots rapidly built up an affinity with the aircraft. On 26 July 1942, pilots of the 31st FG flew their first practice

sweep over the Channel alongside a Canadian squadron. Deemed ready for combat, the 31st's three squadrons moved to forward airfields in England in early August, with the 307th FS going to Biggin Hill, the 308th to Kenley and the 309th deploying to Westhampnett.

As the only USAAF group selected for participation in the raid on Dieppe, the three squadrons underwent intensive training with experienced RAF squadrons to prepare them for combat. The group's combat debut duly arrived over the beaches of Dieppe on 19 August. Lt Samuel F. Junkin, Jr, of the 309th FS, claimed a Focke-Wulf Fw 190 and Lt John White scored another victory. However, the illusion that the USAAF squadrons were invincible was shattered on that day, as four Spitfires were lost to enemy fighters.

The 52nd FG squadrons remained in Northern Ireland, completing their training in late August 1942. By early September the 2nd and 4th FS had commenced combat fighter sweeps over France from Biggin Hill and Kenley, respectively. But these operations were curtailed when the order came for both the 31st and 52nd FG to prepare for deployment to the Mediterranean theatre, for the Allied invasion of

496th Fighter Training Group

To provide the 8th Air Force Groups with air-to-air gunnery training in the UK, the 496th Fighter Training Group was established at Goxhill. A number of types were used from 1943 as gunnery target tugs, including USAAF-marked Spitfire Mk Vs, P-47 Thunderbolts and P-51 Mustangs. In February, the group moved to Halesworth and remained there for the duration of the war in Europe.

north Africa. In October, the newly created 12th Air Force took control of the 8th Air Force's fighter assets, and the 12th Fighter Command absorbed the 31st and 52nd Fighter Groups. Shortly after, the pilots of the two groups were sent by train to Greenock, Scotland to board a transport ship. Destined to see more combat than they could have imagined, the 31st and 52nd FGs deployment to the Mediterranean commenced at Gibraltar, with a briefing from Maj. Gen James Doolittle.

Tactical reconnaissance

At the outbreak of World War II observation and reconnaissance within the USAAC had changed little from World War I. Slow and obsolete high- or mid-wing aircraft equipped the few observation squadrons in existence, with a crewman holding a camera in an open cockpit shooting vertically downwards. With the USA's entry into the war in Europe, it was quickly apparent that aircraft such as these would not survive over enemy territory. The US was busy developing a photographic reconnaissance version of the P-38 Lightning, known as the F-4 (later versions F-5), but additional assets were needed to monitor German activities and provide target information in France and the low countries. The mission was defined as tactical reconnaissance (Tac-R), and the main unit assigned to the task in Europe was the 67th Reconnaissance Group. Arriving in England in September 1942, the units were initially assigned to the 8th Air Force and its constituent squadrons, comprising the 12th, 107th and 109th Reconnaissance Squadrons and the 153rd Liaison Squadron, were all-equipped in part, or wholly with, the Spitfire Mk V. A number of these aircraft had previously been used by the departing 31st and 52nd FGs. Initially based at Membury, Wiltshire, the aircraft retained their armament but did not carry cameras, the pilots instead undergoing intensive training in visual observation of enemy targets, strafing tactics and local familiarisation flying. In late 1943, the 9th Air Force relocated from the Mediterranean to the UK and the 67th Reconnaissance Group was

absorbed into 9th Fighter Command. At this time a fifth unit, the 15th TRS, joined the other Spitfire Mk V squadrons, although it was initially based at nearby Aldermaston. In 1944, camera-equipped Tac-R versions of the Mustang, designated F-6, began replacing the war-weary Spitfires, and the final example had been withdrawn by the time the 67th RG moved into France in July 1944. Although never claiming an air-to-air victory, the 67th Group's Spitfires provided valuable information during their often hazardous low-level operations over enemy territory, and also can lay claim to the destruction of many enemy targets during strafing attacks on 'targets of opportunity'.

Spitfires in blue

As the bombers of the 8th Air Force markedly increased the scope and scale of their daylight bombing offensive against targets in northern Europe in 1943, the need for accurate photo-reconnaissance of targets both before and after a strike became of paramount importance. The RAF had already established an extensive photographic reconnaissance operations centre at RAF Benson, Oxfordshire, and, on arrival in the UK in November 1942 the C.O. of the 7th PRG requested that his unit be based nearby. His wish was duly obliged, and in January 1943 the 13th PS received its first F-5A (photographic reconnaissance version of the P-38G Lightning)

Left: Seen with the upper half of the invasion stripes removed, dating the photograph as post June-1944, a 14th PS Spitfire PR.Mk XI roars in over the airfield at Mount Farm at the end of another sortie. The more rounded nose profile of the Mk XI held the additional oil needed for long endurance operations.

Below: Three views of the same aircraft (PA944) show the three colour schemes carried between June 1944 and March 1945. For the majority of its service life, the aircraft was flown by 14th PS pilot John Blyth. The first photo shows Blyth getting airborne at around the time of D-Day, with invasion stripes circling the entire fuselage. The second view shows the upper section of the stripes removed, leaving the aircraft rather untidy and with the 'P' of its serial number missing on the fuselage. The third view shows PA944 as one of the 14th PS Spitfires which had their RAF PR blue scheme replaced by bare metal, with a red cowl rectangle and green squadron rudder.

at their adopted base of Mount Farm, some five miles from Benson.

Flying the squadron's first PR mission on 28 March 1943, the 13th PS was, at the time, the only unit of the 7th Photographic Reconnaissance Group (PRG) and was assigned directly to the 8th Air Force. Over the next eight months, the three other constituent squadrons of the 7th PRG joined the 13th PS at Mount Farm, starting with the 14th and 22nd PSs in June, followed by the 27th PS in November. All four squadrons were initially equipped with versions of the F-5, although from July 1943 the 13th and 14th PS were allocated five war-weary Spitfire Mk Vs, to be used for the sole purpose of navigation training.

Initial operations with the F-5 raised a number of concerns. The aircraft suffered problems at the low temperatures encountered above 30,000 ft (9144 m), which was the preferred operating level for the majority of the missions. The freezing temperatures affected the engines and turbo-superchargers, and a lack of cockpit heating caused additional discomfort for the pilot. A less reported prob-

lem was that, in a dive, the F-5 entered compressibility at a lower Mach number than other equivalent types. The problems prompted the USAAF to impose a 300-mile (483-km) radius restriction on operations from July 1943.

From late 1943, the build up to the invasion of France called on the 8th Air Force to strike at targets deeper inside Germany, and although the F-5s performed extremely well on low-level 'dicing' missions, the USAAF Generals became increasingly concerned at the 7th PRG's inability to fulfil a growing number of operations. It fell too one man to solve the problem.

Col Homer Sanders became Group C.O. in September 1943 and, on learning on the capabilities of the Spitfire PR.Mk XI operated by the RAF from nearby Benson, began to lobby 8th Air Force Headquarters for their acquisition. At the time the 7th PRG was not subordinated to a Wing organisation, instead reporting directly to HQ 8th Air Force. It is stated that it was over a game of poker with the commander of the 8th Air Force, Maj. Gen. Ira Eaker, that Sanders persuaded Eaker that the only way that the 7th PRG could fulfil its longer range tasking was to

'Bluebirds' of the 7th PRG

Spitfire Mk IX
14th PS, 7th PRG
Mount Farm, Oxfordshire
Nov 1943-May 1945

The Spitfire PR.Mk XIs of the 7th PRG were specially requested by the USAAF to provide the unit with a long-range platform capable of avoiding interception by Luftwaffe aircraft while operating deep inside enemy airspace. Along with the larger fuel tank, other features included a heated camera bay fed with hot air from ducts running from the cabin heating system. The bay itself housed the Universal camera installation, usually comprising two 36-in (91.4-cm) focal length cameras in a 'split pair' configuration.

Seen in the colours worn by by the unit in the late summer of 1944, PL914 carries the twin serial number arrangement and underside invasion stripes of the period. The PRU blue was the same colour as worn by their RAF equivalents.

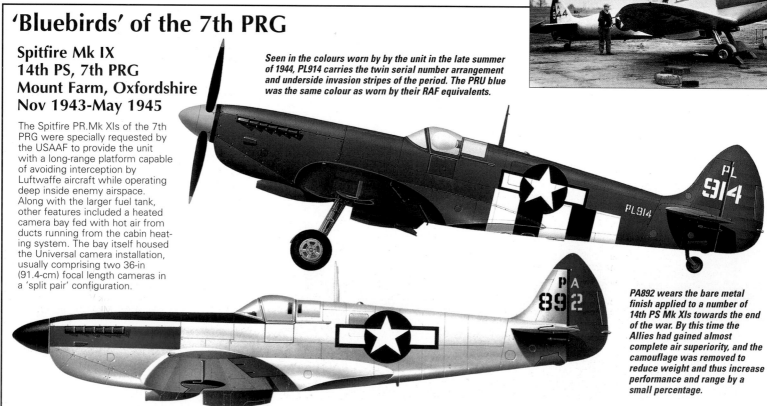

PA892 wears the bare metal finish applied to a number of 14th PS Mk XIs towards the end of the war. By this time the Allies had gained almost complete air superiority, and the camouflage was removed to reduce weight and thus increase performance and range by a small percentage.

Above: With three of the four squadrons assigned to the 7th PRG flying the F-5 Lightning, it was a matter of coincidence that the 4,000th mission happened to be flown by a 14th PS Spitfire PR.Mk XI. Col George Humbrecht, C.O. of the 7th PRG congratulates Lt Jack H. Roberts as he exits the cockpit, while in front of the aircraft Maj. Gerald M. Adams, C.O. of the 14th PS, celebrates with another 14th PS pilot, Lt Robert E. Sanford. Note the late-war bare-metal finish and the anti-glare panel forward of the cockpit.

Right: The mount of Lt Robert Kraft, Spitfire PR.Mk IX 'Dorothy' poses for the camera in the autumn of 1944. The sorties were usually flown at altitudes in excess of 40,000 ft (12192 m), and were generally invulnerable to interception by Luftwaffe fighters until the introduction of the Messerschmitt Me 262.

use the Spitfire Mk XI. Eaker duly obliged, and in November the first of the new aircraft was accepted by the 14th PS. This unit was to become the sole Spitfire operator within the Group, passing its F-5s to the other three squadrons. The aircraft itself was a far cry from its short-legged fighter brethren. To enable missions to be flown as far as Berlin, Vickers Supermarine crammed in 218 gallons (991 litres) of fuel, compared with just 85 gallons (386 litres) carried by earlier fighter versions, and a larger oil tank was fitted beneath the nose, giving the aircraft its distinctive profile. The additional fuel raised its range to 1,360 miles (2189 km), and this could be further increased by the carriage of drop tanks, for targets such as Berlin. The aircraft

could comfortably operate at heights up to 44,000 ft (13411 m) and had a maximum speed well in excess of 400 mph (644 km/h).

By early 1944, the tempo of aerial reconnaissance had increased significantly, and with plans for the invasion being formalised the 7th PRG was tasked with photographing German coastal defences from Spain to Norway. Additionally, the usual strategic targets were covered, along with the search for new menaces such as the V-1 flying bomb launch sites. On 6 March 1944, Capt. Walter Weitner made the USAAF's first photo-recce sortie to Berlin in Spitfire Mk XI *High Lady*. Two days later Lt Charles Parker repeated the mission, with both pilots having spent the majority of the mission at heights in

excess of 38,000 ft (11582 m) in an unpressurised cockpit – a remarkable tribute to their stamina and endurance. In the build-up to D-Day, the 7th PRG was absorbed into the 8th Reconnaissance Wing, which itself was re-designated the 325th Wing of the 9th Air Force in March 1944. The Spitfires continued to operated alongside the F-5-equipped squadrons throughout 1944, and by February 1945 the group had flown its 4,000th operational mission. Three months later the war in Europe was over. A number of reconnaissance pilots and aircraft were earmarked for transfer to the Pacific for the continuing war against Japan, however, US policy dictated that only US aircraft were to be used in the theatre so the 7th PRG quietly handed its Spitfires back to Britain, bringing to an end the US operations of this most famous fighter aircraft.

Paul Ludwig

VCS-7, US Navy Spitfire operations

Among the massive offensive forces to be utilised during the D-Day landings in Normandy were US Navy battleships and cruisers, which were tasked with pounding the German coastal defences. A key role during the bombardment would be that of the spotter aircraft, which were tasked with accurately directing the fire. However, the ships' resident Curtiss SOC Seagulls and Vought OS2U Kingfishers were deemed too slow and vulnerable to enemy aircraft and ground defences. In April 1944, the ship's aircraft were catapulted off and flown ashore to be placed into short-term open storage. The pilots were then temporarily assigned to a new unit designated VCS-7, to be trained by the 15th TRS to fly the Spitfire Mk V. Pilots from six ships were transported to RAF Middle Wallop and, after training, went to RNAS Lee-on-Solent to be placed under the command of the Third Naval Fighter Wing of the Fleet Air Arm. For the invasion period, two RAF and four Fleet Air Arm squadrons, plus the Spitfires of VCS-7, were tasked with the gunnery spotting role. On D-Day itself, the VCS-7 pilots flew in pairs, completing some 34 sorties. One pilot was downed but returned after the invasion. After four days of intensive flying the taskings decreased, and VCS-7 was disbanded on 26 June – its pilots returning with their aircraft to their host ships.

US Spitfire unit codes in Europe

Unit	Type	Code
Eagle Squadrons		
71 Sqn, RAF	Spitfire Mk II, IIA, V	XR-
121 Sqn, RAF	Spitfire Mk II, IIA, V	AV-
133 Sqn, RAF	Spitfire Mk IIA, V, IX	MD-
4th Fighter Group		
334th FS	Spitfire Mk V	XR-
335th FS	Spitfire Mk V	AV-
336th FS	Spitfire Mk V	MD-
31st Fighter Group		
307th FS	Spitfire Mk V	MX-
308th FS	Spitfire Mk V	HL-
309th FS	Spitfire Mk V	WZ-
52nd Fighter Group		
2nd FS	Spitfire Mk V	QP-
4th FS	Spitfire Mk V	WD-
5th FS	Spitfire Mk V	VF-
67th Reconnaissance Group		
12th TRS	Spitfire Mk V	ZM-
15th TRS	Spitfire Mk V	MX-/WZ-
107th TRS	Spitfire Mk V	AX-
109th TRS	Spitfire Mk V	VX-
153rd LS	Spitfire Mk V	mixed
7th Photo-Reconnaissance Group		
13th PS	Spitfire Mk V	none
14th PS	Spitfire Mk V, XI	none/large serial on tail
496th Fighter Training Group		
–	Spitfire Mk V	C7-
US Navy		
VCS-7	Spitfire Mk V	4?*

*4 followed by a letter (eg. 4X)

Picture acknowledgments

Front cover: Hugo Mambour/Aviascribe, Rick Llinares, Convair, Peter R. March. **4:** Boeing, EADS. **5:** Lockheed Martin, Shlomo Aloni. **6:** Northrop Grumman, DSTO via Nigel Pittaway. **7:** Daniel J. March, USAF, Bell. **8:** ADA/NFTC, Shlomo Aloni. **9:** USAF, US Navy, Nigel Pittaway (two). **10:** Nigel Pittaway, Shlomo Aloni (two). **11:** Peter R. March (two). **12:** Gert Kromhout, DoD via Tom Kaminski. **13:** Alexander Mladenov, Bob Fischer. **14:** Danut Vlad (three), USAF. **15:** US Navy, Gert Kromhout (two). **16:** Cpl Kirsty Chambers/RAAF Pearce via Nigel Pittaway, via Nigel Pittaway, Peter R. March. **17:** Nigel Pittaway (two), BAE SYSTEMS via Nigel Pittaway. **18:** via Nigel Pittaway. **19:** Iwan Bögels, Mike King/Milslides. **20:** Iwan Bögels (two). **21:** Mike King/Milslides, via Jon Lake (five). **22-23:** Dick Lohuis. **24-33:** Eurofighter. **34-43:** Mark Farmer. **44-45:** Piotr Butowski, Sergei Skrynnikov. **46:** Sergei Skryinnikov, Piotr Butowski (two). **47-50:** Piotr Butowski. **51:** Hugo Mambour, Piotr Butowski. **52:** Piotr Butowski (three). **53:** Griniuk via Piotr Butowski, Piotr Butowski (two). **54:** Piotr Butowski (two). **55:** Sergei Skrynnikov (two), Piotr Butowski (two). **56-57:** Piotr Butowski. **58:** Piotr Butowski, Sergei Popsuyevich via Piotr Butowski (two). **59:** Piotr Butowski (two). **60:** Piotr Butowski (two), Andreyev via Piotr Butowski. **61:** Sergei Skrynnikov, Piotr Butowski (two). **62:** Piotr Butowski (five). **63:** Sergei Skrynnikov, Piotr Butowski (two). **64:** Piotr Butowski (two), David Donald (two). **65:** Piotr Butowski (three). **66:** Sergei Skrynnikov. **67:** Piotr Butowski (five), Hugo Mambour. **71:** Piotr Butowski (three). **72:** Piotr Butowski (nine), David Donald. **73:** Piotr Butowski (six), David Donald. **74-77:** Senior Lieutenant Valentin Georgiev via Alexander Mladenov. **79:** Rick Llinares (four), Greg L. Davis, Ted Carlson/Fotodynamics (six). **81:** Rick Llinares (six), Ted Carlson/Fotodynamics. **83:** Ted Carlson/Fotodynamics (six), Mike Wilson, Rick Llinares (four). **85:** Ted Carlson/Fotodynamics (four), Rick Llinares (two). **87:** Ted Carlson/Fotodynamics (ten), Rick Llinares (two). **89:** Ted Carlson/Fotodynamics (seven). **91:** Ted Carlson/Fotodynamics (twelve), Rick Llinares. **93:** Chuck Lloyd, Jim Winchester, Ted Carlson/Fotodynamics (six), Rick Llinares, Mike King/Milslides (two). **95:** Ted Carlson/Fotodynamics (six), Rick Llinares. **96:** Frédéric Lert, Patrick Allen. **97:** Gert Kromhout, Roberto Yañez. **98:** MoD (two), via Patrick Laureau, Luigino Caliaro. **99:** J.L. Gayneecoetche via Paul Jackson (two), MATRA, Aerospace. **100:** Herman Potgieter, Jelle Sjoersma, Fred Willemsen. **101:** Sud Aviation (three), ECPA, Frédéric Lert. **102:** Aerospace, Westland (two), RAF Germany. **103:** MoD, Patrick Allen, Aerospace, Frédéric Lert. **104:** Peter R. Foster, Gert Kromhout, Aerospace, Aérospatiale. **105:** Roberto Yañez, Aérospatiale (two), Iván Siminic, Dick Lohuis, OGMA. **106:** GIFAS, Hugo Mambour, Frédéric Lert, Jelle Sjoersma. **107:** Danut Vlad, Nurtanio, Denel (two). **108:** MRF (three), MoD(PE) (two). **109:** RAE (four), MoD(PE). **110:** MRF (six). **111:** MRF (two), RAE. **112:** RAE, MRF (three), MoD(PE) (two). **113:** MRF (two), Daniel J. March (two), Peter J. Cooper. **114:** DERA via Daniel J. March, MRF (two). **115:** MRF (four). **116-117:** USAF, via Bill Yenne. **118:** via Bill Yenne, Convair. **119:** via Bill Yenne, USAF, Convair. **120:** Convair (two), USAF. **121:** via Bill Yenne (two), USAF. **122:** via Bill Yenne, Lockheed Martin via Terry Panopalis, AFFTC via Terry Panopalis, Petty via D. Menard via Bill Yenne. **123:** Convair (two), via Bill Yenne (two). **124:** USAF, W. Duncan via D. Menard via Bill Yenne, AFFTC via Terry Panopalis. **125:** Lockheed Martin via Terry Panopalis, AFFTC via Terry Panopalis (two), Convair. **126:** USAF (three), Larry Davis. **127:** AFFTC via Terry Panopalis (two), via Larry Davis. **128:** AFFTC via Terry Panopalis (two), Convair, USAF. **129-130:** AFFTC via Terry Panopalis. **131:** via Bill Yenne (three), USAF, D. Menard via Bill Yenne. **132:** Aerospace (two), Ken Smith via Warren Thompson. **133:** Warren Thompson, Larry Davis. **134:** AFFTC via Terry Panopalis, USAF, Ken Smith via Warren Thompson. **135:** Ken Smith via Warren Thompson, Warren Thompson (two). **136:** Ken Smith via Warren Thompson, Eric Simonsen via Bill Yenne, via Larry Davis (two). **137:** Ken Smith via Warren Thompson, Warren Thompson (two). **143:** Convair, USAF. **144:** via Bill Yenne (three), Sperry Gyroscope, USAF. **145:** USAF (two), Convair (two). **146:** Baker via D. Menard via Bill Yenne, Becker via D. Menard via Bill Yenne, Dave Menard via Bill Yenne. **147:** Convair. **148:** Larry Davis, USAF, Convair. **149:** P.B. Lewis via D. Menard via Bill Yenne, Larry Davis (two). **150-157:** via John Weal. **158:** Ray Sturtivant via Tony Buttler. **159:** MoD, Vickers Armstrong. **160:** Richard L. Ward, Vickers Armstrong (two), MoD. **161:** Michael Stroud (two), Vickers Armstrong. **162:** via Richard L. Ward, Vickers Armstrong (two). **163:** Vickers Armstrong (four). **164:** Aerospace, Richard L. Ward (two), DERA via T. Panopalis, Vickers Armstrong, Alan Carlaw. **165:** MoD, Aerospace (two). **166:** Vickers Armstrong, MoD, Michael Stroud (two). **167:** Richard L. Ward (three), Aerospace (two). **168:** MoD, Cobham via Tony Buttler. **169:** MoD, Fleet Air Arm Museum, DERA via Peter J. Cooper, via Terry Panopalis. **170:** Peter R. March (three), Richard L. Ward. **171:** Peter R. March, Vickers Armstrong, Aerospace (two), Richard L. Ward (four), Ray Sturtivant via Tony Buttler. **172:** Fleet Air Arm Museum, Ray Sturtivant via Tony Buttler, MoD (three), Eric Morgan via Tony Buttler, via Richard L. Ward, Peter R. March. **173:** Fleet Air Arm Museum, Michael Stroud, Richard L. Ward (two), Aerospace, Peter R. March. **174:** Bill Dyche Collection via Paul Ludwig, Smithsonian via Paul Ludwig, Paul Ludwig, IWM via Paul Ludwig. **175:** Smithsonian via Paul Ludwig, Paul Ludwig. **176:** Bill Dyche via Paul Ludwig, USAF via Paul Ludwig, USAF via Dr A. Price. **177:** Hill via Paul Ludwig, USAF, IWM via Paul Ludwig. **178:** Marsh via Paul Ludwig, USAF via Paul Ludwig, via Paul Ludwig. **179:** Marsh via Paul Ludwig, Bill Dyche via Paul Ludwig, Dr A. Price (two). **180:** Dr A. Price, Comanitsky via Paul Ludwig, Lombard via Paul Ludwig, Don Bilyard via Paul Ludwig. **181:** via Paul Ludwig, Bettin via Paul Ludwig, National Archives via Paul Ludwig.